Developments

D0083714

How does developmental psychology connect with the developing world? What do cultural representations tell us about the contemporary politics of childhood? What is the political economy of childhood?

This companion volume to Burman's *Deconstructing Developmental Psychology* helps us to explain why questions around children and childhood – their safety, their sexuality, their interests and abilities, their violence – have so preoccupied the late twentieth and twenty-first centuries. Reflecting on an increasingly globalised, post-colonial and multicultural world, this book identifies analytical and practical strategies for improving how we think about and work with children. Drawing in particular on feminist and postdevelopment literatures, the book illustrates how and why reconceptualising our notions of individual and human development, including those informing models of children's rights and interests, will foster more just and equitable forms of professional practice with children and their families.

The book brings together completely new, previously unpublished material alongside revised and updated papers to present a cutting-edge and integrated perspective to the field. Burman offers a key contribution to a set of urgent debates engaging theory and method, policy and practice across all the disciplines that work with, or lay claim to, children's interests.

Developments presents a coherent and persuasive set of arguments about childhood, culture and professional practice so that the sustained focus across a range of disciplinary arenas (psychology, education, cultural studies, child rights, gender studies, development policy and practice, social policy) strengthens the overall argument of each chapter. It will be invaluable to teachers and students in psychology, childhood studies and education as well as researchers in gender studies. It will also be a must-read for professionals working with children and adolescents.

Erica Burman is Professor of Psychology and Women's Studies at Manchester Metropolitan University. She is an internationally renowned researcher, teacher and activist, as well as a group analyst. Her work supports critical and reflexive professional practice with and for disadvantaged women and children.

Developments

Child, Image, Nation

Erica Burman

LONDON AND NEW YORK

First published 2008 by Routledge
27 Church Road, Hove, East Sussex BN3 2FA

Simultaneously published in the USA and Canada
by Routledge
270 Madison Avenue, New York, NY 10016

Routledge is an imprint of the Taylor & Francis Group, an Informa business

Copyright © 2008 Routledge

Typeset in Times by Garfield Morgan, Swansea, West Glamorgan
Printed and bound in Great Britain by TJ International Ltd, Padstow, Cornwall
Cover design by Sandra Heath

All rights reserved. No part of this book may be reprinted or reproduced or utilised in any form or by any electronic, mechanical, or other means, now known or hereafter invented, including photocopying and recording, or in any information storage or retrieval system, without permission in writing from the publishers.

British Library Cataloguing in Publication Data
A catalogue record for this book is available from the British Library

Library of Congress Cataloging-in-Publication Data
Burman, Erica.
Developments : child, image, nation / Erica Burman.
p. cm.
Includes bibliographical references and index.
ISBN-13: 978-0-415-37791-1 (hardcover)
ISBN-13: 978-0-415-37792-8 (pbk.)
1. Developmental psychology. I. Title.
BF713.B875 2008
155–dc22 2007031866

ISBN 978-0-415-37791-1 (hbk)
ISBN 978-0-415-37792-8 (pbk)

OLSON LIBRARY
NORTHERN MICHIGAN UNIVERSITY
MARQUETTE, MI 49855

Contents

Acknowledgements

In terms of formal acknowledgements, I should make clear that Chapter 2 originally appeared in K. Henwood, C. Griffin and A. Phoenix (eds) (1998) *Standpoints and Differences: Essays in the Practice of Feminist Psychology* (pp. 210–232), London: Sage. Chapter 3 was originally published in K. Lesnik-Oberstein (ed.) (1998) *Children in Culture: Approaches to Childhood*, London/New York: Macmillan/St Martin's Press. Chapter 4 is a modified version of a chapter that appeared in P. Reavey and S. Warner (eds) (2003) *New Feminist Stories of Child Sexual Abuse: Sexual Scripts and Dangerous Dialogues*, London/New York: Routledge, while an earlier version of the text was first drafted for presentation as an invited Keynote for OMEP (Organisation Mondiale pour l'Éducation Préscolaire) Annual Lecture on Early Childhood Care and Education, University College Cork, Ireland, April 2000. Chapter 6 was originally published in *Psychoanalytic Studies* 1, 3 (1999): 285–302 (Basingstoke: Carfax). Chapter 7 was originally published in *European Early Childhood Education Research Journal* 9, 1 (2001): 5–22 (Oxfordshire: EECRA/Amber). Chapter 8 was originally published in *Children & Society* 9, 3 (1995): 121–141 (London: National Children's Bureau). Chapter 9 was originally published in *Gender, Place and Culture* 2, 1 (1995): 21–36 (Abingdon: Carfax). Chapter 10 'Rhetorics of Psychological Development: From Complicity to Resistance', was first presented as a Keynote at the Sociedad Inter-Americàno de Psicologià (SIP)/Inter-American Psychology Congress, in Caracas, 1999 and subsequently published in *Interaçoas: Estudos Pesquisas em Psicologia* IV, 8 (1999): 11–33 (Universidade São Marcos, São Paulo). Beyond the formal acknowledgement to the publishers, I want to thank the editors and reviewers of those books and journals whose comments have undoubtedly improved my texts.

While the Introduction, Chapters 1, 5, 11 and 12 are previously unpublished, Chapter 1 is based on two papers, one entitled 'Dis/placing Developments', which was originally presented as a paper in an invited symposium that I convened entitled 'Spacing Out: Topographies of Culture, Gender and Sexuality in Psychology', to the XXVII International Congress of Psychology, Stockholm in 2000 and also builds on material drawn from a second paper, prepared for an interdisciplinary workshop, 'Rethinking

Childhoods', convened at the University of Berkeley, California, in 2005. Chapter 5 is based on a seminar paper of this title prepared for a programme on 'Contested Childhood in a Changing Global Order', convened by Pamela Reynolds at the University of Michigan in 2002, the invitation for which I want to record my gratitude. It was my struggle with this theme that – while since then updated – prompted the analysis discussed in that chapter. (A part of this chapter was translated into German and published as 'Kinder und Sexualität' in *Das Argument*, 260 (2005): 237–251.) The Introduction and Chapters 11 and 12 were written specifically for this volume.

In addition to the formal acknowledgements for the material presented here, I want also to record many personal 'thank yous'. Particular thanks go to many friends and colleagues who have supported this work:

Pam Alldred, Fernando Alvarez, Agnes Andeneas, Janet Batsleer, Liz Bondi, Jo Boyden, Jill Bradbury, Daniela Caselli, Khatidja Chantler, Lise Claiborne Bird, Jude Clark, Gerald Cradock, Mark de Kesel, Wendy Drewery, Chris Dunker, Judith Ennew, Harriet Goodman, Angel Gordo-López, Liv-Mette Gulbrandsen, Hanne Haavind, Uma Kothari, Karin Lesnik-Oberstein, Ann Levett, Eva Magnusson, Michel Marchand, Deb Marks, Patricia Miller, Richard Mitchell, John Morss, Johanna Motzkau, Olga Nieuwenhuys, Dimitris Papadopolou, Ian Parker, Vibhuti Patel, Gill Peace, Ann Phoenix, Vanessa Pupavac, Pamela Reynolds, Rex and Wendy Stainton Rogers, Irmingard Strauble, Julia Varela and Valerie Walkerdine. Sadly, Ann Levett and Rex Stainton Rogers have died in the interval between initially formulating some of this work and this book appearing, but their influences remain here in this text, as elsewhere. In particular I want to express my gratitude to Wendy Drewery, Ann Phoenix and Jaan Valsiner for their enthusiastic response to the draft of this book, a reception that helped see me through the process of revision, and to Berenice Burman and Ian Parker whose belief in the value of this work has sustained me over the long period of its production.

Erica Burman
September 2007

Introduction

This book traces different claims made for 'development', 'development' in its multiple senses – connecting children, human and international development. In doing so it aims to contribute to a critical re-envisioning of theory and practice in increasingly post-industrial, postcolonial and multicultural contexts. It takes as its key focus why debates around children and childhood – their safety, their sexuality, their interests, entitlements and abilities, and also their labour and their violence – have so preoccupied the late twentieth and early twenty-first centuries, and it identifies analytical and practical strategies for better practice. Drawing in particular on feminist and postdevelopment literatures to inform perspectives on individual and social development, the book illustrates how and why reconceptualising our notions of individual and human development, including those informing models of children's rights and interests, will foster more just and equitable forms of professional practice with children and their families.

The title and structure of the book, *Developments*, speak to its argument that claims to the term 'development' inextricably link psychological, cultural and international (social and economic) models and practices. By explicitly addressing these different 'developments' and elaborating the forms and consequences of these links, it generates new perspectives on each. Concerns that are typically treated as separable – the psychology of the individual, child development, political and religious legacies of representations of childhood within the modern Western imagination, child protection, child rights, economic aid and development policies – turn out to be integrally related to each other's conceptualisation and application.

These connections arise because the incipient social sciences of the nineteenth and early twentieth century drew upon prevailing understandings of childhood to structure and warrant their interventions. Indeed, the widespread slogan that 'children are our future' highlights the links between individual children, notions of social progress and national welfare that circulate within national and international policy debates. Thus the motif of the child, with its conventional abstraction from culture and society, obscures the ways such policies inform representations of 'race'/culture, gender and 'First'/'Third' World (or hereafter 'North'/'South') relations, whilst not overlooking the many norths and souths that lie within and across the geographical and political North and South. Indeed the fact that a recent UNICEF evaluation of the health, well-being and happiness of children in economically advantaged countries has placed Britain and the USA at the bottom is surely indicative of those disparities within as well as between countries (UNICEF 2007). The book traces how the symbolic trappings mobilised by childhood mean that educational and international development practitioners are ill-equipped by their theories, and the ways those theories are taken up, to attend to the contexts and positions of actual children the world over (that is, across so-called 'developed' and 'underdeveloped' contexts).

Here a word on terminology is needed. In general I use the terms North and South as the widely used formulation to refer to inequalities structured through colonial and imperialist legacies and actualities that, broadly speaking, map on to the historical and current relations between countries of the northern hemisphere with those of the south. Other terms in circulation include the First/Third World polarity, West/Third World, 'developed/developing countries', or 'rich/poor'. A further description gaining increasing circulation is 'majority/minority world' – which usefully draws attention to how wealth and status have been concentrated within the hands of a minority, more typically referred to as 'the West', at the expense of the rest of the world, which is in fact the majority. Useful as this formulation is, it should not be confused with other references to majority/minority status when used to refer to sociopolitical dynamics of cultural mainstreaming/marginalisation within specific national contexts. Each set of terms carries its own history, problematic and problems, not least in its totalisation and homogenisation of complex and multiple political-geographical conditions. In adopting the formulation of North/South I am aware that this opposition is not appropriate for the situation of all countries, and I do not wish to ignore the differences within countries: there are many national, regional norths and souths within the northern and southern hemispheres. With this set of caveats, however, I want to claim that this formulation retains some usefulness in characterising the agency relations of donors and recipients elaborated within aid and development policies and programmes. In part because the material presented in this book spans a considerable time period of writing, but also because none of them is entirely satisfactory, the reader will see that I move between various formulations.

Disciplining development?

One key rationale for this book is to counter how different audiences typically engage only selectively with critiques of development. As someone writing across a range of disciplines, I have become aware how these partialities of perspective give rise to some significant, and sustained, occlusions. In relation to the reception of my own work, I have seen child rights and educational researchers and practitioners either focusing on the pieces that have explicitly dealt with critiques of representations of childhood, or else they draw on my work as a critic of mainstream Anglo-US developmental psychology. It seems one cannot be both psychological theorist and commentator and critic of international child rights initiatives. Indeed it is true that very few developmental psychologists seem to address the link that forms the conceptual basis for this book, although it is fortunate that educationalists (such as Dahlberg *et al.* 1999; Moss and Petrie 2002; Dahlberg and Moss 2005; MacNaughton 2005; Penn 2005) have come increasingly to do so. The concept of development on which the discipline of developmental psychology relies, and which informs child development policies at national and international levels, has resonances with economic developmental policies whose global direction via multinational organisations and corporations (whether the International Monetary Fund and the World Bank, or Shell and Gap) are shaping and constraining the contexts for individual and national development.

It would be too easy to claim that psychologists, once again, are generally unaware of any debate happening outside their discipline, although I hope this book may function to bring disciplinary diversity in an accessible form to them too. However, as the acknowledgements to this book indicate, the papers gathered here owe much to the small international network of critical developmental psychological researchers who have supported these engagements. So rather than performing the ritual denunciation of my 'home' discipline, as a token (anti)psychologist in childhood studies arenas, the book offers a sustained critique of the uses and functions of claims to development, including psychological development, and a nuanced evaluation of the possibilities of either transcending or dispensing with, or even replacing, these.

There are also tensions in the chapters below between critique of developmental psychology and critique of the interpretations or applications of developmental psychology. While the latter might make the arguments of the book more palatable to some developmental psychologists, it is a somewhat disingenuous move that – as Riley (1983) has amply documented – underplays the active role that psychologists have taken in popularising and promoting the reception of their ideas. But, more significantly, it privileges an individualist reading of the history of psychology over an understanding of its historical and institutional constitution. Valuable critical and culturally grounded work is being undertaken within the discipline in critical and cultural psychology, for example (Shandon *et al.* 1997; Rogoff 2003), social psychology (Gjerde 2004; Jovchelovitch 2004) and psychoanalysis (Parker 1997), and cultural-historical and constructionist perspectives are becoming increasingly influential. But nevertheless this work has made headway despite rather than because of the combined pressures towards the generation of a particular kind of 'useful', policy-relevant knowledge from both inside and outside the discipline, even as its resistance also highlights the complexity and diversity of intellectual and political agendas within each too. Hence the arguments put forward in Chapter 1 about distinguishing between, and resisting, the expertise attributed to developmentalists vs. the claims to knowing we might want to assert. Nor of course am I singling out psychology or developmental psychology as sole culprit in the set of problems mobilised by 'development', but rather using this as a significant starting point for reflecting upon the wide reverberations and consequences of the 'developmental paradigm'.

At any rate, without open cross-disciplinary debate, a debate that acknowledges the specific preoccupations, legacies and problems of different disciplinary approaches (rather than imagining we dispense with such issues in some ahistorical, born-again interdisciplinary muddle), we are in danger of reinventing disciplinary orthodoxies and expertise in new forms, or rediscovering and even reifying the old ones. Such for a while was the fate of discussions of 'development' within the so-called 'new' sociology of childhood; disparaged for their 'deficit' focus but then reaffirmed with the rediscovery of the body and the material (all longstanding themes of feminist scholarship and analysis).

A further disciplinary resource drawn upon, one that marks this book as traversing the (often hidden) border between the social and human sciences, is psychoanalysis, and here I draw upon not only cultural studies renderings of psychoanalytic theory (e.g. Burgin *et al.* 1986; Penley 1989; Copjec 2004) but also a psychotherapeutic practitioner awareness of the instabilities and uncertainties of both the meanings and impacts of childhood experiences. Psychoanalytic approaches feature here as both topic and method to highlight how concepts of childhood closely connect with those of dominant cultural understandings of both emotion and memory. Psychoanalytic theory is used as an interpretive framework to understand what is at stake in the dynamics of child-viewing and child-saving: the affective positioning of the child is treated as an indicator, or symptom, of wider concerns. As Bornstein (2001) notes of child sponsorship, humanitarian interventions realised through children generate complex emotional as well as economic relationships, with ambiguous personal and political effects. These include fostering a transnational belonging at the expense of sometimes engendering local jealousies and inequalities, while the dynamic of individual empowerment they institute can, paradoxically, work to disempower parents.

A range of psychoanalytic frameworks is drawn upon – including object relations and Lacanian analysis as well as the wider range of psychoanalytic resources typically used in literary and film studies. Such symptomatic reading of the investments fulfilled by representations of childhood, connecting psychic with financial economies, can be used to generate analysis at the societal level. Indeed, the term 'investment' itself betrays semantic and practical links between children and the market that are more widely expressed by notions of 'growth' which also mobilise a discourse of nature. For this reason, at various points I draw, after Castoriadis (1994), on the notion of 'social imaginary' which applies psychoanalytic processes, alongside other discursive approaches, beyond the individual to the societal level. Closing the book, in Chapters 11 and 12 I apply psychoanalytic (specifically Lacanian) frameworks to interrogate further the motif of the (girl) child identified throughout Chapters 5 to 9 in terms of the ethical-political positions it fosters.

In an era when the United Nations Convention on the Rights of the Child (UNCRC) is becoming increasingly powerful at national levels, and with new emphasis on participatory rights, it becomes increasingly important for childhood practitioners to have access to critical conceptual resources to facilitate its implementation (see also Ansell 2005). This is a highly complex matter, since (as Mitchell 2005 concludes from his review) the Convention is ultimately a legal instrument rather than a theoretical statement about children and childhood. This means that it demands of its practitioners the continuous work of interpretation and translation into specific contexts and moments. Examples abound of 'best interest' principles being used to undermine and contradict participatory rights – and claims to expertise over determining 'competence' can trump a child's expressed wishes – whether in terms of access to contraception or healthcare (although Alderson 2002, has taken this up in a British context with some success). Particular challenges are posed by the Convention in terms of the principles of indivisibility and universality central to the 'second human rights revolution' (c.f. Gready and Ensor 2005) – whereby the generality of the Convention opens up not only spaces for cultural inflections but also, therefore, contests over how claims to equality mesh with those of difference. Here we see played out how the coercive associations between Northern-dominant Enlightenment universalism and economic globalisation generate claims to particularity and autonomy as resistance, although, as legal and political theorists are pointing out, this too is a false opposition that obscures key arenas of struggle and change (Sunder 2003).

But the claims to indivisibility that connect civil, political and economic rights should surely work to support challenges to the traditional separation of children from society. This includes moving beyond treating children as a homogeneous group, as if untainted by social divisions structured around axes of class, gender, 'race', culture, (dis)ability and heteronormativity. So instead of reiterating the exclusions and presumptions of the call to 'save the children', or the usually conservative measures generated by the reproach: 'but what about the children?', we can take forward the more socially attuned question of '*which* children?'.

Moreover – perhaps indicating something of the general marginalisation of feminist and gender studies, but also reiterating the work of abstraction performed by those who rhetorically appeal to childhood – this book both refers to and interrogates how gender criticism and child-focused research are usually treated as competing alternatives. This intervention works symmetrically to comment on both feminist and childhood debates. So I have been surprised to find childhood studies relatively impervious, and sometimes even hostile, to feminist perspectives, while as Thorne (1987) pointed out some time ago, feminist critics have not always sufficiently recognised the significance and relevance of children's rights and childhood studies (with Riley 1987, attributing this to women's positions in relation to childcare in particular). This is understandable given the ways in which women's and children's interests have typically either been equated or collapsed into each other, in ways that historically have usually worked to oppress women further (Sylvester 1998; Burman in press, a). Nevertheless some feminist psychologists have applied and elaborated broader critiques of development to question the eurocentricity, instrumentalisation and cultural masculinity of currently available psychological models of development and change (e.g. Kofsky Scholnick 2000).

Hence a further cross-disciplinary address this book seeks to bring about is to open up further the tense and contested child–woman relationship. It is widely accepted that claims over the 'end of history' and the postmodern condition highlight how the failure to deliver on the promises of modernity, that is, of social 'progress' as a national project, has compromised the credibility of the rational, scientific, industrial economy. These criticisms connect with sustained criticism and resistance from the South. Similarly the asocial masculinity of the rational autonomous model of dominant models of psychology has been exposed as a reflection of the laissez-faire liberal economic subject. Beyond the lived connections between women and children and gender and childhood, intensified via the discourses of 'nation' (discussed below), there are also various cultural sets of associations whose recent gendered shifts merit attention. The neoliberal world disorder has destabilised the traditional, culturally masculine, model of the rational unitary subject, to instead valorise flexibility, mobility and even relationship (Hultqvist and Dahlberg 2001). It is no accident that 'emotional literacy' programmes are being elaborated across the 'developed world' to resocialise angry disenfranchised working-class young men (alongside the marketing in Africa, and beyond, of self-help books on 'ubuntu' – the promotion of traditional community networks, that is, usually male extended family solidarity – as a business resource), while public concern in the North is now focused on how (some middle-class) girls are massively outperforming boys in school examinations. Such 'developments' indicate the mutability of apparently inviolable structures of subjectivity and their proximal relation to shifts in forms of capital. In particular they highlight how the cultural shifts towards positive promotion of interpersonal qualities and emotions traditionally associated with both feminisation and childhood can be appropriated by the market (and the military, see Burman 2004a) for far from feminist ends (see also Gordo López and Burman 2004; Burman 2005a, 2006a, in press, b).

The analyses elaborated in this book have coincided with, and in part benefited from, the emerging discussion of 'intersectionality theory' (see Phoenix and Pattynama 2006; Yuval-Davis 2006). While this has –

significantly – emerged from women's studies and through feminist debates about how to adequately weight the experiential and structural significance of 'race', class, sexuality and disability within understandings of women's positionings and relationships, such arguments have also key relevance for analyses of the role of children and childhoods and the evaluation of the differential distributions of development (see Chapter 8). Although a feminist commitment seems to provoke marginalisation in both psychology and childhood studies, I argue that such views from the margins are what are needed to generate the critical crossings of theory and practice necessary to challenge the hegemony of dominant formulations of development (see also Chapter 3). As with women's studies, the study of children and childhoods offers both a distinct field and a lens by which to view other disciplines, and practical and theoretical disputes. For, like gender-sensitive perspectives, it is hard to identify any social issue that is not touched upon by, or relevant to, the study of childhood. Rather it is its ghettoisation, its separation from those wider debates, that needs to be contested. Thus (alongside the cross-disciplinary awareness called for earlier) a resolutely *inter*disciplinary stance is necessary for an adequate treatment of the complex issues posed by 'development'.

Why 'developments'?

The title of this book expresses its two key claims: first, that each disciplinary address to development cannot, ultimately, be adequately understood without engaging with its others; second, that any account which takes 'development' as singular not only dangerously simplifies the diversity of possible and available forms but thereby contributes to their marginalisation, devaluation and even exploitation or oppression. The first claim is probably relatively uncontroversial, although it has far-reaching implications. As is argued throughout this book, discussions of development share common historical and cultural-political origins which underlie their political effects (Shandon *et al.* 1997). The second claim is not only epistemological or political but, as illustrated by the analytical applications to specific arenas presented in this book, has key methodological and practical consequences in terms of envisaging possibilities for change. Katz's (2004: x) geographical and anthropological analysis is based on a similar precept:

> Childhood and its material social practices are shot through with the effects of social, political and environmental change, while making it clear that children are social actors in the process. Their work and play not only intersect with and are altered by these processes, but they have the capacity to further or frustrate them as well.
>
> (Katz 2004: x)

It is important to note here that treating 'development' as multiple does not necessarily imply a relativist position – one of simply adding an 's' to ward off accusations of hegemonic privilege or implying the harmonious coexistence of the various developmental accounts. Relativism has been seen as a consequence of deconstructionist destablisings of received 'truths'. But the strategy of mobilising alternative readings, or indicating alternative possibilities, need not – contrary to some 'weak' forms of social construction (Danziger 1997; Edley 2001) – lead to a pluralist celebration of individual agency that at next blink turns round to blame the 'victim' for – what are now rendered as individual – failings. Such readings are misinterpretations of the political-ethical engagement that prompt poststructuralist and postcolonial critique (e.g. Harasym 1990; Derrida 1994), even wilfully so, in robbing them of their political bite; still less how such resources have been generative of decolonising methodologies (e.g. Tuwihai Smith 1999) identified by Canella and Viruru (2004) as specifically relevant to practitioners working around children and childhoods. They also betray a superficial grasp of their arguments. In the same way as Butler's (1990) championing of the notion of performativity was misunderstood to mean a neglect of the body and a facile underestimation of societal limits (prompting her to write a sequel, *Bodies That Matter*, Butler 1993), so attending to the ways that multiple possibilities are constrained by the specificities of power relations operating within particular conditions goes a long way to explain why and how these many ambiguities come to be realised as singular outcomes. This is something that geographers, anthropologists, even some psychologists, and especially feminists (including myself, Burman 1990a, 1993) have been saying for a while (Parker 2002). Here Mookherjee's (2006) distinction between different varieties of relativism within human rights discourse may be useful, positing a 'reconciliatory' feminism that can mobilise a 'subtle relativism of mediation' between universalist and cultural rights. Various chapters in this book take further the interrogation of what is at stake in claims to development, while Chapter 12 explicitly explores what it might do to 'imagine there's no development' as an application of Copjec's (2004) exploration of the consequences of Lacan's claim that 'the woman does not exist'.

Thus, drawing on my own disciplinary background, the key rationale for and intervention made by this book is to link discussions of models of human development and specifically child development (though interrogating how these have come to be treated as equivalent) with economic development. And by 'link' I lay claim less to a project of specifying exactly how they are, let alone should, be connected, than to assert that we cannot adequately (including ethically as well as analytically) deal with one domain without the other. Each has profound consequences for the other while, as the pages below highlight, the contemporary resonances between the terms of each set of frameworks are often unfortunate if not oppressive. As Katz (2004: x) also comments: 'In pairing development and development – children's coming of age and the structured transformation of their local environment . . . [n]either form of development can be understood fully without the other.'

Hence, a second aspect of the plural designation 'developments' is to emphasise the multiple and contested character of each of its axes or levels (individual, child, economic, national and international). Just as per capita income is not the same as either gross domestic product (GDP), nor the latter as gross national product (GNP), so – notwithstanding the shift in psychological models noted by Kessen (1993) towards the 'hardwired child', arriving ready-equipped for any eventuality, and policies promoting the 'smart child' (Cradock 2006) and preschool provision aiming to shape future worker-citizens – the promotion of children's autonomy (Lister 2005, 2006) is not the same as the creation or prefiguration of a free market economy. It is by attending to these instabilities and tensions that the crude reductionisms threatened by the uniformity of terms of developmental discourse can perhaps be thwarted. At the very least, reflection on such resonances can be useful in fostering other terminologies and, hopefully, the emergence of new strategies: reading each 'take' on development 'awry' (Žižek 1991a) to generate new critical commentary and perspectives on each.

Of course such resonances have not emerged by accident. They speak to the conditions giving rise to developmental discourse; its origins within European industrialisation and colonialism. It was this fateful conjoining of the birth of capitalism with imperialism that gave rise to a discourse on development concerned with maximisation; development as profit, surplus value, economised into units of production. Indeed, as Sohn-Rethel's (1977) analysis established three decades ago, the very move towards abstraction in number, time and space coincides with processes of reification and commodification central to capital accumulation. And here too it is worth noting that, while evolutionary theory was used to warrant the linearity of development (with women, children, 'primitives' and the 'insane' positioned on inferior rungs of its ladder, so responsible for fostering divisive relations between their liberation struggles), this was not a necessary or inevitable reading. In one of the earliest of the current wave of critical developmental accounts, Morss (1990) discusses how selection came to be privileged over variation within the reception of Darwin's work. Hence the tainted association of evolution with notions of 'survival of the fittest' reflects a history of appropriation, including a 'history of the present' (a history mobilised for present-day purposes). The contemporary vogue for sociobiology and evolutionary psychology, which thrives via the appeal to discourses of nature and the natural, necessarily founders when survival value is weighted equally with variation (as Hrdy 2003, among others, has pointed out from within comparative anthropology).

It is, of course, as problematic to attempt to read social processes back on to the development of the individual as it is to treat individual development as the prototype and site of manipulation for social development. For significant reasons, the latter has more typically dominated the academic and policy discourses since – and perhaps as a significant indicator of – modernity. Once Galton formulated the quasi-evolutionary claim that 'phylogeny recapitulates ontogeny', the project of social engineering via mapping and then intervening in children's development took shape – although we should note how civilisations the world over have probably always engaged in some such socialisation practices and indeed theorising. At any rate, as is explicated further in this book and widely acknowledged (e.g. Sachs 1992; Mehmet 1995), concerns with and practices of individual and social development, at national and international levels, share some key terms under modernity: growth, change, progress.

These applications do not even or only apply to individuals. So conceptions of stages of development, and especially the description or prescription of developmental endpoints, have been especially problematic; the former working to confirm the inferior status conferred by the disavowedly partial renderings of the latter. Once technologies of administration for the measurement and application to groups and populations had been created, this gave rise to a common conceptual and methodological framework that connected individual and social (Rose 1985). Thus there is an implicit influence of psychology within (international) development studies, in the form of approaches to the study of and intervention in community development, in particular via the application of techniques from organisation studies (Cooke 2001). This is most evident in models of groupwork and community development which subscribe to the idea that there are stages or cycles to interpersonal processes that not only institute culturally specific norms as if they were universally applicable but also open up strategies for manipulation and intervention. In particular participatory approaches were hailed to redress the problem of imposing Northern, industrialised norms and understandings upon Southern peoples by generating locally defined norms. As Chambers (2005: 72) recalls:

> It is difficult to express the amazement and exhilaration of those days when we discovered that 'they can do it', that poor people, without education, women, children and men, had capacities to map, diagram and analyse of which we had not dreamt.

But although this maybe addressed the problem of cultural imposition of developmental goals, it still leaves intact the prevailing structure of intra-community and structural power relations constituting the research and its agenda. Hence such approaches have been criticised as merely exposing local knowledges to make social structures more legible and therefore amenable to regulation (Parpart 1995; Cooke and Kothari 2001).

Thus there are ambiguities structured within the project of development in development studies of whether it is 'about' or 'for' development:

> There are those who feel that the study of development is most closely connected to ideas about social, economic and political change, while others are informed by a more instrumental goal of shaping policy and a

> practical concern with the implementation and devaluation of development interventions. Thus, there is disagreement as to where development studies should be located along a continuum from intellectual analyses and interpretations of processes of change to 'doing development' utilising the practical skills and techniques associated with transformations on the ground.
>
> (Kothari 2005a: 5–6)

These ambiguities are paralleled in developmental psychology. Moreover, there is of course an explicit link to psychology both within children's programming and via the relations between models of child and nation, as we shall see below.

Child

The key focus of this book is the interrogation of the work done by dominant social imaginaries of childhood as these impact on policies and practices around families, communities, national and economic development and, not least, on children themselves. Perhaps the most explicit preoccupation explored here is how developmental theories and practices – from psychology to economics and beyond – do not often really, or adequately, address the position of particular children in specific cultural and historical contexts (see also Ansell 2005 on this point). That is, dominant imaginaries – the sets of cultural associations and affective relations mobilised around 'the child' – oppressively occlude the real conditions of children's lives, with the complexity and diversity of children's lives typically reduced and abstracted (especially from class and national identifiers) into some notional, highly symbolised and usually singular (and often young and/or female) 'child'. This means that children whose life circumstances and practices of daily living fail to confirm to those idealised norms suffer further marginalisation, or even pathologisation. As discussed below (Chapters 4 to 8 and Burman 2006b, as well as Lavalette 2000; Nieuwenhuys 2001; Burr 2006), discussions around child labour, or working children, are a case in point – but so also are children whose lives do not conform in other ways to the dominant model of childhood as a period of irresponsibility, indulgence and play. The globalisation of childhood (Boyden 1990; Burman 1996a; Ansell 2005) remains a challenge as a key site for the reiteration of prevailing inequalities between rich and poor. (Chapter 4 addresses the particular challenges posed by policies and practices for children who have been abused, while Chapter 5 engages with the complex dilemmas around children's sexuality.)

Moreover, it is not only children who are affected by these paternalist conventions. As many commentators have noted (e.g. Coulter 1989; Holland 1992; Meyer 2007) the convention of portraying needy children abstracted from context, as the indicator of a more generalised deprivation, has consequences for the maturity, responsibility and autonomy associated with the classes, families, countries and even regions those children are associated with, with the recent vogue for white US celebrities to adopt 'orphaned' African children exemplifying the enduring character and status of this trend. The fact that (as emerged when the singer/performer Madonna adopted an Malawian child in 2006) some children in orphanages may have one or more living parent clearly illustrates how poverty and the cultural value accorded children (especially girl children), as well familial transitions, can make the economic demands posed by bringing up children intolerable (a point also elaborated by Burr (2006) in relation to South East Asia).

Indeed the colonial resonances between adult and child, and donor and recipient, along with themes of dependency that are recapitulated within child aid imagery have long been a focus of critique (Reeves 1988; Hart 1989; Gronemeyer 1992; Mehmet 1995). But notwithstanding widespread acknowledgement of this problem, there remain practical tensions for aid organisations between mobilising funding through claims about children (as in child sponsorship schemes, for example) and the increasing drift of international government organisations (IGOs) and non-government organisations (NGOs) to see aid for children as necessarily linked to broader development investment at local and national levels. In terms of contemporary challenges it is worth noting that, within this moral-affective economy, the child is more easily associated with the 'needs-based' approaches that characterised earlier approaches to development studies, while child programming actually presents a strong case for (evaluation of the) application of current rights-based models. Here too we can note how the abstraction marked by the recourse to childhood allows the segmentation of aid interventions to be played out in exclusionary ways. So, for example, in her critique of the limits of 'gender mainstreaming' as working paradoxically to reduce awareness and intervention around gender-based inequities, and as 'reducing their [NGOs] capacity to advocate, organize and intervene in terms of gender and class-based disadvantages' (p. 173), Pearson (2005) takes as a key and indicative example how Save the Children (UK) has recently abolished the post of 'gender advisor'.

Various chapters below (especially Chapters 3 to 5) refer to the history of this dominant affective relationship that has come to be associated with 'the child', as generated by the particular confluence of the new biological and social sciences, from the eighteenth century onwards in Europe, including the transformations that would come to be marked by the emergence of psychoanalysis. As Foucault (1981) among others has described, the transformations of subjectivity created by the rise of modernity were marked by the emergence of a sense of interiority, of having a sense of self that was not only continuous and stable, but also grounded by the connection between childhood and memory (Hacking 1996). While Rousseau, Froebel, Pestalozzi and others wrestled with the problem of how best to educate children – each according to the philosophical commitments informing their models of childhood (Singer 2005) – their project was a reflection of wider cultural shifts in European sensibilities that came to equate the child with the true or inner self (cf. Steedman 1995).

This remains a dominant motif of the culture and sensibility surrounding children and childhood in the North, despite its multiple proliferations within cultural, popular, professional and policy fora. So just as doctrines of original sin and essential innocence are still with us, we have jostling alongside each other calls for greater child protection in the form of segregation of children's lives (Moss and Petrie 2002) as well as castigation of child assertion, aggression and disorder (Franklin 2002a), as where 'bad' behaviour in increasingly regulated spaces is seen as amenable to management via diagnosis and medication as in the recent but escalating 'discovery' of attention deficit hyperactive disorder (ADHD) (Newnes and Radcliffe 2005; Timimi 2005). Similarly, the child as signifier of either the 'true' self, or even the (biographically prior, or never experienced but longed for) 'lost' self, has coincided with a historical sensibility of ever greater personal alienation and dislocation. New age therapies mobilise notions of the 'inner child', with idealised and romantic expressive qualities, while national and international social policies increasingly focus on modelling flexible, independent, entrepreneurial selves through their pedagogical practices (Hultqvist and Dahlberg 2001). Hence childhood becomes a site of multiple emotional as well as political investments: a repository of hope yet a site of instrumentalisation for the future, but with an equal and opposite nostalgia for the past.

It seems as if the ever greater political and existential insecurities of the twenty-first century bolster an intensification of identification with the child that can be read as an index of other key cultural-political dynamics. Pupavac (1998) discusses how the progressive undermining of parental authority under neoliberalisation has been accompanied by the increasing reliance on experts to advise on and intervene in family functioning. They are not only empowered to intervene; rather, our knowledge of this power and possibility works, like Bentham's panopticon, not only to regulate but to promote *self*-regulation. What elsewhere she calls 'the international child rights regime' (Pupavac 2002a) produces a 'misanthropy without borders' (Pupavac 2001), a transnational condition of subjectivity that is 'diminished' of its political efficacy as an effect of the extended powers of state and interstate apparatuses to intervene in our lives. Such conditions create children and childhood as risky zones; as sites for major social unease and ambivalence. For they generate a profound identification that is tempered by an equivalent resentment at the potential for intervention they embody – either wielded personally or on their behalf (see Chapters 4 and 5 and Burman and MacLure 2005; Burman 2008). There are paradoxical effects of these concerns. So, for example, in the UK the Father's Rights movements have arisen alongside British government efforts to encourage fathers to take more (economic) responsibility for their children, as part of the retraction of welfare state which correspondingly positions families ever more centrally as the sole unit of social reproduction. Correspondingly, some men are increasingly asserting claims to child contact and custody. Probably because of this political agenda, imaginaries of abuse and abusive fathers are not well conceptualised within contemporary British social policy agenda. As well as the quid pro quo or retribution for having to pay for children, Scourfield (2006) puts forward the interesting proposal that for some men such claims may be their only remaining recourse to an imaginary of family life in contexts of (marital) relationship breakdown, job uncertainties and wider social fragmentation.

Image

While mention has already been made of imaginaries of childhood, some explanation is required of the significance of, and claims made around, notions of 'image' in this book. Image (as cultural product) and imaginary (as social fantasy and subjectivity) are interrelated. Awareness of the productivity of forms of 'image' in relation to 'developments' fulfils five functions here. First, their juxtaposition mobilises a different set of semantics around 'development' that also thereby draws attention to the specific cultural technologies they rely upon. Vision is regarded as the key physical sense privileged by modernism and modernity (Jay 1993; Levin 1993). In the 'society of the spectacle' we are transfixed by, and equally transfix, others. Indeed vision is perhaps vital in the ordering of difference, and the specular is regarded as a privileged way of knowing and constructing knowledge that combines discourses of nature ('seeing is believing') and possession (what can be 'captured' in a glance) central to empiricism (and, arguably, as in Irigaray's 1985 account, patriarchy). The rise of visual technologies also therefore indicates the fateful combination of two key features of modern power characterising the industrialised North: the claims to omniscience (the 'god's eye' view from nowhere) that belies the cultural and political partialities of appeals to universal knowledge; and the commitment to an ethics of revelation, of discovery (as where the very term 'fieldwork' betrays a suspect legacy of naturalism that presumes the privileged interpretive position of the researcher, and the passivity of the 'field' of study, Burman and MacLure 2005).

Second, development work (of the many kinds addressed in this book) illustrates how apparently merely methodological issues have profound consequences, giving rise to a failure to understand how the problem under investigation may be constructed via the very practice of its investigation. Not only do such claims to knowledge work to recapitulate colonial relations, as where the act of 'giving voice' runs the risk of simultaneous exposure and surveillance. This critique is as relevant to the project of giving voice to children as it is to empowering marginalised communities, in terms of making legible practices of resistance and survival that thereby become more amenable to disempowerment and manipulation (see e.g. Parpart 1995; Marks 1996; J. Scott 1997; Cooke and Kothari 2001 on communities;

Alldred and Gillies 2002 on children; Alldred and Burman 2005). But such practices have also been criticised as failing to understand and engage with power struggles within communities, as well as the political, cultural and spatial complexity of the processes of translation and interpretation that stakeholders negotiate within any development intervention (Crewe and Harrison 1998; Larner and Craig 2005). To take what is (for me) a recent local example, the current British policy discourse of promoting 'community cohesion' nicely indicates the tensions and conflations of the liberal precepts of individual privacy and order to the level of the group, while thereby – under neoliberalism – disowning responsibility for both its oppressions and exploitations (seen now as occurring within a separate and inviolable sphere). It is for this reason that legal critics such as Sunder (2003) have refuted the perceived opposition between religion and law, seen as the contest between the domain of rationality and culture, that structures so much of the discourse around (child and social) development. She argues instead not only for recognition of the complicities of past colonial interventions and current global manipulations, but also for a better understanding of how international law should now be actively mobilised to support local struggles over the interpretation of cultural rights, interventions that are so often focused on women and children.

Third, it is no accident that the seemingly academic questions around image move us into urgent contests between claims to local autonomy vs. neocolonial intervention. For practices of representation invoke the domain of law as well as culture. In both cases, what is highlighted is that we cannot know about children and childhoods except through representational practices (in their political as well as textual varieties). The challenge we are posed with is to understand and redress how these have usually involved Northern models and agendas. Hence a key analytical question posed by this book asks *whose image* are we faced with? This highlights the importance of reflexive methodologies. For once we acknowledge the specificity and prescription of the implied position of the viewer within the viewed, we find that our object of study turns out only to tell us about ourselves (Burman 1995a). Clearly a position that merely recentres the position of the privileged Northern author/viewer (as is the danger of some current 'whiteness' studies, Ahmed 2004a) is inadequate, even if it marks an important starting point for reconsideration of dominant models and practices. Similarly, I am equally unconvinced by the adequacy of the move towards 'pedagogies of the powerful' advocated by Chambers (2005), despite its rather satisfying reversal of the usual knower–known relations to position the more powerful as in need of 'immersion' and coming to know about the peoples and contexts that they legislate upon. At any rate, there are major political and methodological challenges ahead in elaborating, implementing and evaluating practices of self-representation. Indeed, the case of research making claims to child self-representation demonstrates how this is inevitably framed by other textual and institutional representational practices

(Marks 1996; Marshall and Woollett 2000; Alldred and Burman 2005; Burman 2007b; Komulainen 2007). Representation is always a practice of power.

Fourth, it should therefore be clear that the philosophical claims I am making about 'image' go beyond specifically visual material to also include textual (written) representation. Hence the analytic focus in this book includes representations in the form of policy documents, research literature, media reports, and popular cultural examples. I recognise that the juxtapositions made here of philosophy with filmic and literary examples, alongside imagery and marketing text, may offend the cultural studies purist since they, doubtless, pay insufficient attention to questions of genre and audience. But my arguments concern what these – admittedly diverse texts – exemplify about general dynamics of viewing and relating to children. That is, I am not elaborating any particular claim about such images beyond drawing attention to their particularly privileged, and indicative, status as modern technological forms.

Nevertheless it is relevant to note the particular role played by images of children historically in print media and in art (Jordanova 1989) – even now appearing as spectacle; non-speaking, and therefore amenable to abstraction and commodification. The passivity and asymmetry of visual dynamics have played their part in securing the sentimentalised affective status accorded children; abstracted from social context as a representational cliché of timeless and culture-free innocence, their neediness warrantable only at the cost of social abjection. It is no accident therefore that agencies such as Save the Children and Oxfam have formulated policies on the representation of children. Hence in Chapter 6 I apply Winnicott's discussion of the sadism that is covertly present in sentimentality to analyse child aid and development imagery, alongside discussing the relevance of other psychoanalytic accounts (see also Burman 1994a, 1994b). The recent vogue for research with marginalised groups – especially children and young people – to involve participants in the generation of material for analysis by, for example, giving them disposable cameras to take pictures exemplifies some of the political ambiguities recapitulated within methodological practices that were identified above. Control of the research technology is no guarantee of democratic research relationships; nor does it secure participants' control over the interpretation and reporting of the work. Indeed, the latter may be neither necessarily desirable nor perhaps ever achievable. Rather my point here is that we should bring to, and into, our discussions an attention to how technological developments (with mobile phones and new information technologies prime examples) inflect as well as reproduce representational, including research, processes and service delivery.

Fifth, and finally, I invoke the discourse of 'image' in relation to 'developments' to import a discursive intervention that takes further the analysis of the cultural-technological origins of its methodologies. So, to play with its ambiguities, we can take 'developments' literally in its film processing sense, as the process of producing new images from photographic negatives – as technological artefacts or blueprints for intervention. Indeed, far from this digital age dispensing with its relevance, the potential obsolescence of this particular technological metaphor (amid its grossly unequal distributions) is surely indicative. Attention to the disjunctions between the 'negative' and its particular realisation, its 'development', prompts a dialectical reconsideration of the normative, opening up asymmetries that can pave the way for alternative perspectives.

Nation

In these times of economic and political globalisation, it may seem somewhat anachronistic to identify 'nation' as the third term of the subtitle of this book. In his review of development studies trends across a 30-year period, Cameron (2005) characterises the period up to the early 1980s as positioning the state as the prime development agency before, as he puts it, the 'intellectual iceberg of neo-liberalism' (p. 144) came to 'freeze all meaningful debate on poverty and inequality'. Contemporary globalisation 'resituates the nation state', as Gready and Ensor (2005: 5) euphemistically put it, displacing some of its traditional authority to IGOs, multinational corporations and NGOs. Discourses of 'governance' now replace those of 'government', and increasing attention is being paid to the political ambiguities attending the greater political and economic roles played by the non-governmental sector (including how this relates both to changing structures of transnational regulation and to the militarisation of both humanitarian intervention and funding, Duffield 2001; Lewis 2005). These are important discussions that reflect in significant ways upon the para- or neocolonial effects of international aid and development initiatives formulated in relation to children (and beyond children, to other recipients of aid; Pupavac 2002b, 2004).

Yet the state remains a key arena for the interpretation and application of even international policies, notably the UNCRC, and the key context in which children's developmental and life chances are played out. Nor is its political significance waning in uniform ways for all groups: for notwithstanding these days of regionally based superpowers (such as the European Union in 'Fortress Europe') and massive labour migration as a necessary feature of the movements of global capital (including women's caring/domestic labour involving children, where immigrant women do the domestic labour to enable their middle-class employers to take advantage of the call for women citizens to enter the national labour market; Hochschild 2000; Morokvasic 2004) discourses of nationality still govern access to legitimate residency and service provision through their links to citizenship entitlements and, at least at the level of popular rhetoric, structure political agendas at the level of the resource vigilant (especially right-wing politicians). Similarly highlighting national differences in historical models of and interventions for children, even across a geographically close context such as Europe, can be very instructive, in revealing how the state produces and limits particular forms of children and childhoods (as highlighted by the comparative studies discussed by Moss and Petrie 2002 and Dahlberg and Moss 2005).

For these reasons alone, the nation state merits retaining as an analytical category (see also Kabeer 2005), notwithstanding the multiple ways it is superseded or traversed by the transnational familial, as well as business relations of the global state. But more than this, the national context also remains a key site for the reworking of international policies, with multiple political valences: undoing or limiting the progressive impetus implied by international human rights legislation (as in the efforts to ward off the application of European human rights legislation in the UK, for example), or potentially providing some kind of institutional buffer to mediate international demands (as in the national variations in extradition or child custody agreements, for example). Similarly, Bornstein's (2001) analysis illustrates how cultural and national contexts of familial ties as well as escalating levels of HIV infection interact with transnational relations to structure the possibilities for, and limits of, child sponsorship. Whether as a site of application of, or resistance to, international agencies, the nation state remains a key arena for, and of, both discussion and intervention – not least in terms of broadly indicating the range of relevant linguistic and cultural practices involved.

Moreover, as a key exemplification of these challenges and contests, I draw on discourses of nation as an intertextual axis to interpellate a key inspirational literature for the analysis offered here. Yuval-Davis (1997) persuasively highlighted how the control and regulation of women's sexuality has long been central to notions of national and cultural belonging (whereby women's behaviour and dress signify cultural integrity and 'honour' across religions and cultures). This is intensified in contexts of struggle and equally of transition, as Clark's (2006) analysis of the burden of representation carried by South African women shows. It also has vital relevance for understandings of children and childhoods. If women's positions have typically been circumscribed according to traditional discourses that elide biological with cultural reproduction, then this precept also produces particular positions for children, as the future products and expressions of these cultural or national identity projects. While the arguments of Yuval-Davis and Anthias (e.g. Yuval-Davis and Anthias 1989; Anthias and Yuval-Davis 1993) have been particularly applicable to understanding the practices and positions of minoritised groups within Northern, historically Christian, national contexts (see e.g. Burman 2005b), McClintock's (1995) historical analysis has highlighted the centrality of interventions around women and children to the colonial project. She discusses how the naturalised model of the patriarchal family was formulated to warrant the equivalent inequalities instigated by colonial occupation. Themes of the safeguarding of women's sexual purity (also discussed by Ware 1992) that were central to the elaboration and consolidation of colonialism are not dissimilar to those concerning contemporary child protection (in particular, around contests over children's 'innocence', etc.).

Hence this literature works also to exemplify a key theme of this book: highlighting the interwoven character of women's and children's positions as perhaps one of the most compelling examples of the so-called interdependence and indivisibility that characterises current understandings of rights. Three key features are worth noting about this. First, it demonstrates the impossibility of dealing with one party, or set of rights holders, without addressing others – and their social, economic, civil and political rights. Indeed, while discourses of citizenship have found favour among both child rights and feminist theorists, we might note how this privileging of national belonging always threatens a corresponding marginalisation and exclusion of those who do not qualify (as in the case of detained asylum seekers, including children whose UNCRC entitlements are often dispensed with because of their precarious residency status).

Second, it also shows the limitations of taking only a synchronic or cross-sectional reading of positions: for the positions of children and women cannot be absolutely separated. This is evident where women and children are treated as politically synonymous (as historically excluded from decision-making rights, for example) or when their economic and welfare interests have been presumed to be equivalent, giving rise to the sometimes mistaken (cf. Peace and Hulme 1993) strategy of giving aid to women on the assumption that it will 'trickle down' to children.

Third, as Beinart's (1992) analysis of historical shifts in the production and content of images of African children highlights, interventions for women and children, especially in relation to childbirth and early child health, can operate as a vital site for performing the 'benevolence' of colonial rule and the shaping of docile subjects. Thus attention to gender issues inflects, and so unifies, but also destabilises the opposition between women and children. Girls are, potentially, incipient mothers; indeed they are often addressed as such within international development policy (think of the slogan: 'Educate a girl and you educate a nation'; or even more worryingly: 'Education is the best form of contraception'). As Chapters 9 and 10 argue, in such contexts it is clearly important to resist collapsing the two categories of girl and woman, even as it is equally important to be analytically sensitive to their complex interrelations. As examples of such complexity we might note Katz's (2004) description of how children's labour enabled the women in the rural Sudanese village she studied to maintain their observance of purdah; while Bravo's (2005) study showed how, in Northern industrialised contexts, culturally specific understandings of childrearing practices in relation to discipline and access to such welfare services as therapeutic support can become the arena in which professional–client conflicts are played out within women's refuges. Equally, given reactionary policy pressures that too often address the position of girl-children in terms of reproductive issues (not least with how 'sex education' becomes tied to a policy agenda of reducing teenage pregnancy, so erasing the role of boys and men, Stronach *et al.* 2007), it becomes important to attend to how the rhetorical position of 'child' (while rarely, if at all, lived 'outside' gendered meanings and relationships) may offer some release or protection from the 'dangers' or limited positions available to girls.

Contents and discontents

To contextualise and position the critical perspectives outlined in this book, it is perhaps worth indicating here something of my own trajectory: how I came to be concerned with these questions, as well as how this book came to be composed. As if to underscore the fiction of individual, biographical progress and intellectual teleologies, the chapters that comprise this book reflect how my work has not been linear in its own development. (As is addressed in more detailed in Chapter 1), I started as a classic, modernist post-Piagetian researcher, studying developmental psychology not because I was interested in children but, like Piaget (1926, 1929, 1932, 1971, 1972), through an interest in the epistemological questions *fostered by* the study of children. In that sense I was already (as it were) a paid-up subscriber to the modernist developmental fallacy (in its broadest claim of answering general questions through the study of children, or rather 'the child', as well as the specific version that the earlier you see something the more 'natural' it is; Lieven 1981; Burman 1994c). I took up Piaget's clinical method – outlined in Piaget (1929), the neglect of which has further compounded the reception and representation of Piagetian ideas in Anglo-US contexts (Burman 1996b), focusing on his earlier work (Piaget 1919, 1921, 1926, 1951, 1953) – to investigate a more 'social' aspect of children's developing understandings: that of age as a subset of understandings of time (Piaget 1969; see Burman 1990b). But my encounters with children soon forced me to realise that the methodological challenges of researching with, and making claims about, children pose all the key issues about power/knowledge relations that psychologists only inadequately, but quite typically, framed in methodological terms as the 'performance-competence' problem (Burman 1992a), while the sentiment surrounding childhood in modern contexts bolsters the logical elisions typically made from individual, to child, to nation state, that blind us to more useful ways of thinking (Rotman 1978; Broughton 1981a, 1981b).

Developments is thus composed of two different sets of material, each spanning approximately a 12-year period: the first, previously published single-authored papers that have appeared in a wide range of outlets (spanning early education, geography, women's studies, psychotherapy, literary theory, development studies, childhood studies). These papers originally appeared across a range of discipline-based outlets – and in some cases are now out of print and so unavailable. They are presented here in their original form, each prefaced by a commentary that offers specific contextualisation and reflection on the particular contribution made by the piece to the argument formulated throughout this book.

These published pieces are juxtaposed with a second set of material. These are previously unpublished papers, several written specifically for this volume, that attempt to take its arguments further. Together they address a coherent set of preoccupations surrounding the role of rhetorics and metaphorics of childhood across a range of theoretical and professional practices that also reflect upon their changes over the historical period spanned by this work. All of this material has been selected from a broader corpus of conceptual and methodological writing with the aim of constituting the most succinct and indicative statement that the themes posed by 'developments' demand.

I should clarify that, although I had originally intended to revise and update the previously published papers (to reflect shifting foci of political and intellectual debate), I realised that to do so would erase the very traces of specificity and historical location that this book argues are necessary in addressing childhood. (So instead I have attempted to contextualise each piece in its introduction, plus added notes indicating updated references or perspectives. Thus, with the exception of Chapter 3, all notes to previously published material are new, and aside from harmonising references across the book as a whole, this text remains as previously published.) The shift of focus and perspective within these papers therefore not only reflects my own personal developmental trajectory but also intimates changing debates about the nature and conditions of childhood and international development over the period. These include notably increasing awareness around environmental degradation and planetary precariousness alongside – at least in the North – more explicit expression of ambivalence about children and childhood – that moves from the cult of infantilisation of the 1980s and 1990s to the pinning of social order and economic self-sufficiency agendas on to the young, as the neoliberal agenda makes increasing inroads.

It is important to clarify that – while very much aiming to *inform* practice – this book does so primarily through an evaluation and formulation of *theoretical* resources. So the selection of papers for this volume draws on, but does not include, my more practical engagements with child rights (Burman 1996a), child fund raising (Burman 1994a, 1994b) or child labour (Burman 2006b). Rather, the focus here is on the broader, cross-disciplinary resources called for to address the complex and urgent problems posed by children and development. Together these papers present a broad and now more integrated and updated perspective on a set of urgent debates; engaging theory and method, policy and practice across all the disciplines that work with, or lay claim to, children's interests. So although composed of separate papers (which can of course be engaged with independently), the book presents a persuasive set of arguments about childhood, culture and professional practice that is designed to address and engage a wide audience. The sustained focus across a range of disciplinary arenas (psychology, education, cultural studies, child rights, development policy and practice, social policy) strengthens the overall arguments of each chapter, as well as the book as a whole.

While functioning independently, this collection is also a companion book to the second edition of *Deconstructing Developmental Psychology* (Burman 2008). *Deconstructing Developmental Psychology* is obviously much more of a specifically psychological text, critiquing the assumptions and paradigms of developmental psychology in its asocial and abstracted, and so universalised, models of infancy, language development, cognitive development and even communicative development. It directly engages with the methodological, practical and ethical-political problems to which developmental psychological models of 'the child' give rise. As a complementary and companion text, *Developments* offers both a wider disciplinary frame (engaging with literature, cultural studies, childhood studies, psychotherapy, economic development policy) and deeper conceptualisation. For after drafting the first edition of *Deconstructing Developmental Psychology* in the early 1990s I became increasingly concerned with the far-reaching role and functions of developmental psychological theorising outside its Euro-US contexts of initial elaboration (and the new second edition now engages with this much more, but with a more specific focus on educational, health and psychological practices than is the focus here). Moreover, if *Deconstructing Developmental Psychology* may have frustrated some of its (more perceptive) readers by offering little in the way of a *theory* of deconstruction (although in discussing its application it certainly declares and outlines its position), its guiding assumptions and resources, conceptual and methodological rationale – and corresponding dilemmas and debates – are amply discussed below.

I present the material here in this book, *Developments*, in the belief that its arguments are relevant to a range of practitioners as well as policymakers and theorists, including child rights activists and researchers, development practitioners, educationalists, social workers, psychotherapists and psychologists. While I doubt that my treatment of development economics is informed or critical enough to be of particular benefit to economists, anthropologists, lawyers and geographers – though I have certainly drawn upon such perspectives – I would hope that these could also gain from seeing their application to a broader set of debates. This might include, for example, helping to explain the contextual dependence or even irrelevance of chronological age within definitions of childhood – both historically and cross-culturally, and notwithstanding legal definitions enshrined in international instruments such as the UNCRC. Indeed, contexts of economic recession seem to impact on understandings of children in richer and poorer countries in polarised ways, such that in Europe and North America childhood appears now, in terms of financial dependency and delays to living independently, to extend to late twenties; while poorer children and young people 'grow up' earlier in terms of assuming adult-like responsibilities. The current (2007) debate in Canada over parental obligations to pay for their children's higher education, which has hinged on legal contests concerning non-custodial, divorced parents and even the particular topic of study, invites an understanding of childhood as dependency that is not limited by any chronological age parameter (CLE 2007; Cradock, personal communication, 23/05/07). The set of concerns constellated around children, childhoods and development can surely be regarded as posing some of the key conceptual, political and methodological problems of our time.

Concepts of process, participation, capacity building and sustainability are at the vanguard of international development policy, and the second human rights revolution champions notions of entitlement, alongside claiming the so-called interdependence and indivisibility of rights. Yet notwithstanding this, there remain fateful ambiguities surrounding children's positions in these lofty discourses that demand particular scrutiny. Moreover, as well as the need to engage seriously with these conceptual and practical dilemmas, they also offer an indicative arena and persuasive rationale for the need to link analysis and critique of the multiple levels of development together for their mutual strengthening. Hence current calls for the repoliticisation of international development policy and increasing engagement with international political economy have an equivalent resonance for all practitioners concerned with human development.

Part I

Children and development

What is at stake?

The first part of this book establishes theoretical and methodological parameters for the debates that follow.

Chapter 1, 'Dis/placing Development', opens up questions about the ambiguity and elusiveness of claims to development, highlighting the specific problems and dilemmas this gives rise to for intervention at individual and social levels.

Chapter 2, 'The Child, the Woman and the Cyborg: (Im)Possibilities of Feminist Developmental Psychology', applies these to evaluate how these dilemmas enter into the theory and practice of developmental psychology.

Chapter 3, 'Pedagogics of Post/Modernity: The Address to the Child as Political Object and Subject', builds on some of the ideas introduced there to interrogate explicit and implicit models of childhood that are mobilised in some key discussions of political theory.

OLSON LIBRARY
NORTHERN MICHIGAN UNIVERSITY
MARQUETTE, MI 49855

1 Dis/placing development

This chapter engages interdisciplinary and cross-disciplinary perspectives to offer critical perspectives on psychological assumptions underlying child development. It plays on multiple readings of notions of 'placement' and 'displacement' (connecting geography and psychoanalysis) to resituate a range of claims that underlie and justify the project of developmental psychology. I argue that psychological narratives of development have tended to presume a spurious universality and generality that is increasingly recognised as untenable. Recent critical work in psychology highlights the particular cultural-historical resources that inform contemporary psychological models. Hence this chapter explores what it means to 'place' development in terms of: (a) situating the emergence of 'development' as equivalent to 'progress'; and (b) identifying the positions elaborated for the subjects and objects of such 'development'. Examples are given from development policy and therapeutic practice, both of which draw upon idealised models of childhood and claims to empirical developmental psychological research to justify their models. The chapter moves on to motivate for a 'displacing' of 'development', drawing on postdevelopment critiques that highlight how multiple agencies and interests mobilised within any development intervention inevitably disrupt and transform its original aims. Finally, the question of whether 'development' can be replaced (or re-placed) is posed: both in terms of what such arguments mean for our understandings of development, and what remains for us to see as 'developing', or to help 'develop' (with the problem of 'helping' subjected to critical scrutiny in later chapters, especially Chapter 6).

While there is an address to the discipline of psychology, the question of what motivates *which* developmental stories get told (and which are thereby occluded) applies more generally. These cross-disciplinary bridges therefore both connect and question the nature of the relationships between models of macro-economic development and those concerned with individual and intra-psychic change. In particular, this chapter draws parallels with debates about memory as constructed or recovered within therapeutic relationships as both a disciplinary conjunction and as a methodological tactic to highlight possible tensions and resolutions of the problem of developmental teleology vs. reconstruction. This chapter highlights the importance of reflexive contextualisation as a critical resource, while acknowledging the value of addressing children and childhoods from a distance – exploring both the displacements from children performed by disciplinary approaches to development, and the displacements which the recourse to the theme of children and childhood fulfils for others. This chapter therefore interrogates what is at stake in claims to development by clarifying the diverse disciplinary claims on children and childhoods, and by outlining the rationale for the cross-disciplinary borrowings and juxtapositions taken up by the rest of this book. In this sense this chapter is both theoretical and methodological, in identifying intellectual resources to support the critical analyses which follow.

In this chapter I draw upon recent critical work from developmental and social psychology, as well as social theory, to reframe claims to and about development. I will argue for the need to move from generalised, universalised accounts of development towards more situated, nuanced developmental narratives. Although seeming more limited, I suggest that developmental work can in fact be more engaged and useful because of this. The moral-political note I am sounding here may sit uncomfortably with both positivist and postmodernist-inclined perspectives that are often brought to bear, in particular, on developmental psychology. But it is precisely this moral-political engagement that is required to make sense of the effects of the developmental discourses with which we are all saturated, but that some of us are considered to be experts upon. The British psychoanalytic writer Adam Phillips (1995: 15) noted: 'Belief, as Freud shows, domesticates desire. Experts keep us on their best behaviour.' While Phillips was referring to the transferential authority structured within psychotherapeutic relations, the self-regulatory force with which 'experts of the mind' are invested goes much further. So we have to ask, what knowledge and which experts? Who owns (or holds the power to wield) the expertise, by whose authority, and how can such claims to expertise be evaluated?

Questioning child development

A striking feature of the questions mobilised by researchers interested in children is the absence of explicit disciplinary labels or reference points. These are typically such questions as:[1]

- What do we know about children's cognitive, emotional, moral and social development?
- Is it useful to speak in universal terms of children's physiological and emotional development – e.g. developing emotional attachments, learning language, acquiring reasoning skills?

- Does child development vary in different social, familial and cultural contexts, and can we observe these differences without attaching negative evaluations to these differences?
- What is the role of interpersonal interaction in the development of cognition, language, affect, morality and self-awareness? How do the cultural beliefs, expectations, and practices of caregivers and the institutional arrangements of particular social groups influence children's development?
- What do we mean when we speak of children as active participants in their own socialisation and development? How does an emphasis on children as actors and negotiators alter our understanding of child development?

These are important questions which invoke 'child development' as the arena in which they should be addressed. Yet significantly no academic discipline, or specific practical or professional expertise, is marked by these questions. There are lessons here for the study of children and childhoods. Psychology is a key disciplinary resource that is usually implicitly or explicitly mobilised in discussions of child development. Indeed, many developmental psychology textbooks are entitled 'child development', while the domain of child development – because of the firm convictions it generates – is a particularly strong candidate for the elaboration of naturalised and normalised pseudo-truths.

The above questions gather together core issues that social and cultural preoccupations about childhood attempt to deal with, but usually only by avoiding the issues of poverty and inequality, around which the questions cohere: how these structure different conceptions of development across richer and poorer countries, as well as for working-class and minoritised peoples within richer countries. A key question is about whether it is possible to 'observe differences in child development without attaching negative answers to those differences'. At the moment, the prevailing answer seems to be no, although this of course depends on who is doing the observing, how they are doing it, and why.

I will indicate something of what might be involved in the inquiry to 'place' and 'displace' development, including some biographical and disciplinary detours, finishing with some thoughts on where this leaves claims to or about development.

What do I mean by this call to 'place' development? Placing development means here taking seriously the contexts of production of developmental theorising in terms of historical moment and cultural context. This goes beyond attending to the biographical conditions and preoccupations of those figures whose names are associated with developmental research as either its authors or its topic (although it also includes this). For only doing this would be to retain an under-interrogated focus on individuals, rather than looking at the broader reasons why that focus on individuals arises.

Placing one's own development: reflexivity and situated knowledge

A first key way of 'placing development' is to acknowledge that the analyst of development also occupies a (geographical and ethical-political) position herself (or himself). Feminist critiques of Northern, patriarchal knowledge-generating practices have called for researchers and practitioners to become more aware of how their own personal, institutional and disciplinary positions enter into their work (Wilkinson 1988; Stanley and Wise 1983). Topic and process, theory and method all turn out to be much more connected than 'scientific' claims to objectivity of the kind that underscore psychology and other social sciences typically admit. This means that particular embodied and intellectual histories must have wider reverberations with the development of the discipline. Thus (despite its renderings within an increasingly therapeutic culture, Burman 2006a), the call to reflexivity is not necessarily or specifically confessional – in the sense of demanding disclosure on the basis of which complicity is absolved. Rather, individual trajectories can be understood as resonating with, and so also exemplifying, key sociopolitical and disciplinary assumptions and dilemmas via attention to their negotiation of them (see also Lather 1991; Davies and Gannon 2005).

So, to 'place' myself. I am aware it may seem presumptuous or self-preoccupied to reflect upon my own disciplinary history. Yet this inevitably frames the pages that follow, and I do believe that, while necessarily specific and unique in some respects, such trajectories are certainly shaped by common cultural patterns as to be far from original. My structural locations as a white European heterosexual woman working in higher educational and therapeutic contexts specify me in terms of certain relations of privilege structured around class, racialisation and sexuality, and around which gender intersects in ways that do not guarantee any particular feminist identification (or feminist standpoint, Harding 1993) – for the discourses of individualism that psychology expresses go far beyond this discipline. Similarly, rather than seeing these specificities as constraints or filters to be overcome en route to matters of more general and therefore objective, valid, reliable (or whatever other words of positive evaluation psychology supplies) applicability, such perhaps mundane, perhaps embarrassing details cannot be presumed to be insignificant. Rather what Frances Cherry (1995), in her review and rewriting of the history of social psychology, calls its 'stubborn particulars' deeply structure the interpretive and interventive frame according to which developmental work is conceptualised.

The developmental trajectory of my work has moved from the general to the specific, attending to my own cultural, historical and geographical locations as a way of making sense of the impacts and meanings of my activity. This has marked my own biographical shift from a developmental psychology informed by Piagetian genetic epistemology (Piaget 1972; Burman 1991, 1992a, 1994c) into debates about methodology and qualitative and discursive research (Burman 1998a, 2000, 2003a, 2003b), and from thence to development studies (of the global economic rather than only psychological variety, Burman 1993, 1996a), to therapeutic work (Burman 2001a, 2002a) and to women's studies (Burman 2001b, 2005b). Significantly, these are all arenas concerned with constructing as much as contesting developmental projects, albeit alternative ones.

It was the sense that what psychologists know about children and childhood is more incomplete and contestable than is often portrayed (especially by psychologists) that propelled me into other disciplines and debates. Inspired by debates from postcolonial studies and critiques of models of international economic development, I became convinced of the urgency of moving from critiquing the limits and oppressions meted out by developmental psychological models and their associated professional practices in Northern contexts, to explore their resonances and reiterations within economic development policies. Alongside critiquing the hegemony of Northern models of development – structured within models of child development and then globalised in the name of international child rights (Burman 1996a) – my 'insider' knowledge of developmental psychology and experimental paradigms helped me to critically interrogate the claims from psychological research that have figured within the false/recovered memory debates (Burman 1996/7, 1997a, 1998b; Brown and Burman 1997). A common feature upon which both these areas of analysis relied was the shifting but powerful *structures of feeling* mobilised by children, their cultural, historical and political conditions, *and material consequences for* work with, and around, children. This also includes the 'inner child' invoked in therapeutic practices of many diverse kinds (i.e. not all of which are 'new age'). More recently, being able to claim the position of psychotherapist or group analyst has facilitated research partnerships that enable the documentation or dissemination of innovative and transformative therapeutic and social support practices (Burman *et al.* 1998; Aitken and Burman 1999; Spandler *et al.* 2000; Burman *et al.* 2002; Walker *et al.* 2002). Child rights organisations and child labour researchers have involved me as some kind of 'gender advisor' (e.g. Burman 2006b) – which betrays something of the contours and contests surrounding discourses of child activism – with children's rights too often pitted against women's rights (Burman 2008).[2]

I offer this account, not to lay claim to particular (or even multiple) disciplinary expertise but rather – by such juxtapositions – to highlight the relational and mutually constitutive character of such claims that became especially noticeable through my own encounters across these arenas. These different places, or positions, have not only provided specific speaking positions (and circumscribed others) but the fact of the embodied experience of moving between them occasions some reflection: different places produce different perspectives or vantage points; the associated 'speaking rights' attached to the different locations, and their variations, prompt some serious as well frivolous questions about what precisely has changed in moving between these.

As developmental textbooks tell us, concerns with development and change are closely linked with notions of causality, and it was with the aim of disrupting the linear chaining of cause and effect, alongside their restrictions and exclusions (notwithstanding so-called multifactorial models), that the call to move from temporal to spatial approaches emerged (Massey 1992; Pratt 1992; Chernaik 1996). This was hailed as a way of widening the focus from the abstracted, pointed and, often in its evaluative effects, damaging 'arrow of time' (Kofsky Scholnick 2000) to analyse instead spaces, places and contexts that did not already overdetermine or delineate consequential actors and processes.

In terms of my trajectories, too, such moves around diverse disciplinary arenas and issues have come to suggest to me some methodological principles for thinking about children and childhoods: the strategy of *displacement*, of working from a distance, of seeing how the problem at issue becomes reconfigured according to the particular presenting position. This is a particular version of going spatial, moving from time to space (so useful in countering developmentalist teleologies), but one which highlights axes of power relations, rather than flattens them into merely spatialised differences.

Placing developmental *psychology*

Second, 'placing development' means placing developmental psychology alongside other disciplines which also address developmental preoccupations. This requires us to do some reflective analysis on what we mean by development, and how broadly and specifically we interpret it within psychology. Whatever the answers (and doubtless there will be many), concerns with how people, organisms, societies, individuals and children come to be and act as they do are shared across biology and sociology, as well as those disciplines overtly concerned with time and space, i.e. history and geography. This is even before we 'go international' to wider arenas for identifying developmental patterns, which are also the profiles and privilege of global economic development. And it is still before we have come to specify developmental psychological concerns as qualifying individuals, let alone children in particular – and even here there is much common ground with childhood studies (an emerging subdisciplinary hybrid of sociology and anthropology) (e.g. James *et al.* 1998).

Concerns with explaining what happens, when it happens, who it happens to, and why, are shared across a range of disciplines. Alongside these, there is also the two-headed question of *direction* of development and developmental point (or moment) of *intervention*. In terms of direction, it is a moot question within historiography whether what we can know from historical records is any more than the story of the winners or the archaeology of the exercise of privilege (Benjamin 1970a), and moreover that a reconstruction of the past can only ever be from the point of view of current circumstances (Foucault 1980a). Thus we arrive at a circular – and inevitably motivated and partial – history of the present, rather than a linear, objective, chronological trajectory from past to present.

Therapy is a crucial arena within Western culture that combines concerns of intervention with direction, for while usually conducted *with* adults it typically focuses upon their recollections *of* childhood. Therapies of all persuasions therefore operate with powerful conceptions of development that draw upon both developmental psychological as well as psychoanalytic tropes – such as the role of early experience in determining later characterological, behavioural and relationship patterns.

The influential psychoanalyst and psychologist Daniel Stern has suggested that 'psychoanalysts are developmental psychologists working backwards in time' (1985: 19). But he distinguishes differences of project as well as temporality, arguing that developmental psychology is normative and prospective, while psychoanalysis is pathomorphic (focused on identifying the origins of pathology) and retrospective (p. 20). Yet even this differentiation between the two arenas – helpful though it may be – is belied by the common cultural and historical origins of psychology and psychoanalysis. For, as indicated by Hacking (1996), insofar as they developed separately the two disciplines were nevertheless structured by their contest with each other. Such a relationship of mutual – if sometimes hostile – reference between the two literatures makes somewhat suspect current claims to the other as impartially 'external', and thereby legitimising, as evidenced within the recent false/recovered memory debates (Burman 1998b). Hence there remain tensions concerning the interpretive relationship between clinical work with adults and observational work with children. Stephen Mitchell (1988) similarly indicates dangers of fixing together the 'clinical' and 'observed' infant, via the scrutiny of real children and parents, when the here and now is treated as isomorphic to what went before.

Placing 'truth' claims

We can draw on those other disciplines to resituate the claims to knowledge being made. Just as past debates are being re-created anew within developmental psychology, or reorganised according to current concerns, so it is useful to recall how discussions of construction of the past have a long history in psychoanalysis. Freud often subscribed to archaeological images of uncovering or releasing the past, and his later reflections on psychoanalytic process go to some lengths to acknowledge (what we would now call) the intersubjective and interactive character of memorial accounts produced within therapy. In his 1937 paper 'Constructions in Analysis', Freud uses the terms reconstruction and construction synonymously, regarding the analyst's process of construction as an ongoing and necessary part of the thinking process, only some of which might be communicated to the analysand in the form of interpretation. He thus acknowledged the interplay between transference and suggestion, and regarded the general process of interpretation as more properly termed construction.

However, the notion of reconstruction in psychoanalysis has recently received more sustained attention, and has been regarded as a major and inevitable interpretive resource within the analytic process that not only intersects with the transference but also makes it possible. Thus building a picture of the analysand's early life history is now regarded as a key part of the therapeutic process, even if that picture is constantly being revised, undergoing transformation 'from debris to meaningful presence' (Bollas 1995: 114). While Bollas described memorial accounts as unstable, oscillating between being generated and dismantled, by contrast the terms of the 'false memory' debate set up an invidious choice between believing the whole account offered (usually) by women (since this issue arose over women's claims of recovering memories of abuse during therapy) versus regarding it as either a meaningless (according to Brandon *et al.* 1998) or, alternatively, a metaphorically meaningful, potential fabrication (British Psychological Society 1995; United Kingdom Council for Psychotherapy 1997). One of the key strategies mobilised by psychotherapists in attempting to protect their knowledge claims has been to distinguish between historical truth and narrative truth (Spence 1982). So, therapists work with the *meanings being conveyed by* what is said, rather than being motivated by a concern with the verification of facts or details (Blum 1994). However, while this has been helpful in arguing for the different status of accounts in legal and therapeutic arenas, maintaining this distinction belies how historical accounts are far from literal representations of what happened; thereby conceding too much on claims to truth and reality (see Motzkau 2007).

Placing the emergence of *'development'*

We need to attend to historical and cultural contexts to account for how such widespread developmental preoccupations emerged. This is where development connects up with the wider modern project of social improvement and its subscription to the notion of 'progress'. The nineteenth-century nation state built its national identity not only on its secular reforming programmes of development, but also on its colonial-imperial acquisitions and occupations. Thus the project to 'place' development invites a focus upon the colonial legacies structured within its assumptions and practices; the normalised presumption of 'home' (i.e. Euro-US) alongside the exoticised 'abroad' (and all the marginalised/exoticised others within home too, including – as well as children – women, Jews, Romanies and 'homosexuals').

Hence, notwithstanding their differences, psychological research and therapeutic practice both employ less frequently articulated, but nevertheless still operative, normative conceptions of what development is; in terms of what is understood to be developed (Shandon *et al.* 1997). These conceptions are typically less articulated within therapeutic contexts, since our conceptions of being well, happy or fulfilled are usually only negatively defined – in terms of the absence of illness, distress or disease. But irrespective of whether we might agree with those psychologists who are calling for the development of models of 'positive well-being', the point here is that such models do already exist. The problem is that they currently function in implicit, and therefore uncontestable, forms that – through practices of normalisation and naturalisation – usually celebrate the mores of the class and culturally dominant (cf. Rose 1985). They correspondingly pathologise black and minoritised peoples, gay men and lesbians and poor and disabled people the world over whose failure to exhibit or even fit such privileged lifestyles renders them inadequate, deficient or pathological.

Thus there is something irreducibly moral-political at the core of developmental theorising; an inevitably ideological (in the sense of being formed subject to the horizonal limits of available structures of conceptualisation) kernel or trace within an otherwise seemlessly general, disinterested scheme. And the ideological traces within our current developmental schemes are heir to nineteenth-century colonial assumptions that imply the cultural superiority of Northern heteropatriarchal culture. Thus, as with any teleology, including political utopias of all persuasions, current developmental research paradigms document what they find in relation to descriptive structures that are already shot through with assumptions about what development looks like, and who is more or less developed – whether qualifying children (or subgroups of children) in relation to adults, or one society in relation to another (see Chapter 9). That this feature arises as a general effect of the methodological frameworks used in developmental psychology (both qualitative and quantitative) is itself indicative of the political interests structuring the emergence of the discipline and the role of 'method' as an implicit disciplinary fetish that also works to curtail as well as construct the domain of inquiry (Valsiner 2004, 2006; Burman 2007b).

Placing developmental *subjects and objects*

Placing development also means identifying its various subjects and objects – and the complex relations between these. Here discussion concerns who the subject of development is. While typically developmental psychology has focused upon 'the child', such singular formulation has worked to occlude culture, gender and history and indeed all matters of relationship. To summarise a well-known critique, there is a general cultural tendency for the child to function as the ideal-typical subject which is reflected in the role accorded developmental psychology within the discipline of psychology, as well as beyond it. Indeed, developmental psychology as a field of study is structured around the elaboration of normative frameworks that warrant a shift from the study of the specific child to the formulation of more general models (Rose 1985). The child occupies the position of naturalised subject that somehow exists prior to the social (and so thereby reiterates the suppression of cultural, historical, class, sexual and gendered locations) (Broughton 1981a, 1981b, 1987; Henriques *et al.* 1984). As methodological trope, recourse to research with children is almost always subject to the developmental fallacy that the earlier something is found the more enduring or 'basic' it must be (Lieven 1981; Burman 1994c).

Moreover, the very distinction between child and adult was elaborated alongside the separation made by modernity between public and private, work and play. These spaces and statuses are gender, class and age-related. Irrespective of the actual activities and abilities of women and children in building the societies we inhabit, the great paternalistic gesture of 'women and children first' is indicative of a general cultural and legal infantilisation of women, and a corresponding feminisation of childhood, that also unhelpfully blurs the boundaries between them (Sylvester 1998; this volume Chapter 9).

It is significant that it was in this dual context of shifting roles and positions of women and children that the debates in the 1990s around the recovery of women's memories of childhood abuse in therapy arose (Brown and Burman 1997). Moreover amid such flux and challenge there was a further set of cultural overdeterminations that invited slippage between 'child' and 'woman'. For within the Western cultural imaginary the child has come to signify the self, the innermost, precious core of subjectivity, within us all. Carolyn Steedman's (1995) historical analysis traces the emergence of the child as quintessential modern Western subject:

> The idea of the child was the figure that provided the largest number of people living in the recent past of Western societies with the means for thinking about and creating a self: something grasped and understood: a shape, moving in the body . . . something inside: an interiority.
>
> (Steedman 1995: 20)

Thus 'the child' seems to function within the contemporary Western cultural imaginary – and beyond, through practices of globalisation – as signifier of the authentic self. This self – whether lost or regained – circulates as a significant cultural trope. The widely circulating and popular notion of the 'inner child' – if read too simply as a literal return to an earlier biographical position – conflates psychoanalytic notions of fixation, regresssion, deferred action and transference. But rather than taking this literally, it might be better understood as a culturally available metaphor for unmet needs and desires. The challenge posed by denaturing the attractive and seemingly obvious notion of the 'child within' is therefore twofold. First, to distinguish authenticity from possibility, plausibility and credibility (Foress Bennett 1997). Thus therapeutic work is now understood as encouraging clients to create and reject alternative versions of their lives, and to explore how these are invested with different degrees of reality at different therapeutic moments (Gardner 1996). The second challenge is for us (and all the different 'us's) to recognise the status of the child as a dominant icon of authenticity, and from thence to elaborate other more inclusive (including more enabling of children) cultural representations of possibility (see also Burman 2002a, in press c).

As well as highlighting how this ideal-typical (or mythological) child is a fiction (in the sense that much of the models are based on faulty individualist premises), there is the further inquiry about who developmental subjects are, and how they are positioned by its discourses and practices. So, once we acknowledge that the scope of developmental concern lies beyond 'the child', it becomes clear that certain children and their mothers, family organisation and class or cultural background form more of a focus than others. For while white, middle-class Anglo-US women, children and – sometimes – fathers form the ideal-typical subjects of developmental theorising, black and working-class women, men and children, gay men and lesbians are its stigmatised others, topicalised only when deemed problematic. This produces the dynamic of normalised absence/pathologised presence around the selective visibility of black and minoritised families that Ann Phoenix (1987) has described.

Displacing development

Given such difficulties, what does it mean to displace development? Is this possible, and, if so, how? Without rehearsing all the critical developmental and social psychology of the past 20 years, its project might perhaps be imperfectly characterised as going spatial, or turning discursive, by textualising the truth claims of psychology (Henriques *et al.* 1984; Parker 1989, 1998, 2002; Parker and Shotter 1990; Burman and Parker 1993; Parker *et al.* 1995). That is, deconstructionist work highlights psychology's textually mediated and therefore culturally and historically located character. The project to destabilise it therefore renders it open to interrogation on moral-political as well as logical/intellectual grounds, since moral-political agendas are shown to structure it from its inception.

Displacing children

In fact, we might ask the question of whether it is helpful to think about children at all. The very term 'child' seems to occlude constitutive axes of class, culture, gender and even age in a meaningful way (let alone sexuality). 'Children' and 'childhood' as blanket categories often seem to get in the way of genuine intellectual inquiry and sensitive intervention. But their complexity becomes obvious when we consider, for example, women as mothers, especially that problematic category of 'teenage mothers' (David *et al.* nd; Stronach *et al.* 2007). Or, if we acknowledge and start to explore the contests that (women) service providers have with women in shelters, about how they discipline children or whether the children should have therapy (Bravo 2005). Or, how child abduction not only figures in coercing women back into violent relationships but also highlights state collusion in the inequalities of international relations via vagaries of custody law and extradition arrangements (Radford *et al.* 1999). Or, when we evaluate the model of aid that presumes that giving mothers resources will inevitably 'trickle down' to children (Peace and Hulme 1993). These specific and seemingly exceptional circumstances offer crucial glimpses of the structurally ambiguous and unstable parameters of relationships posed by and around children. Above all, the question that has reverberated around women's studies of 'which women?' seems to apply to childhood studies and child development: *which* children? And what 'others' do each of these kinds of children imply?

Displacing claims to children's development

This is not to say that we can suspend the power of those big questions to mesmerise and paralyse thinking. So, what exactly is known about children's development? It seems that, rather than arriving at any clear consensus on this, instead we know a lot more about why and how we have come to acquire the knowledge we have, and what its limits are. William Kessen's (1979) famous discussion of 'the American child and other inventions' illustrated the ideological underpinnings of the greater capacities that new technologies have enabled psychologists to document in children. His subsequent (1993) analysis of this 'full child' was in terms of how this helps in 'avoiding the emptiness'; a model of the subject has arisen that is less dependent on (parental or state) support in an era of lack of confidence in not only both parental authority and state welfare, but also in the security and viability of the world we live in.

So while we probably have some very broad understandings about economic, cultural and interpersonal conditions that prevent or hinder children's well-being and development, as soon as we get more specific it all becomes much more uncertain and contestable. Or perhaps we can only get specific, and so only talk about relationships. So perhaps, along with children and childhood, talk of 'development' installs altogether the wrong metaphorics (abstract, isolated, biologised). John Morss (1996: 157) proposes that 'babies do not develop: they demand'. He argues that we have to challenge the 'forgetting' of parental and other forms of caregiving – whereby their actions merely become developmental 'resources' – to address instead how we advocate for and create babies and children.

Displacing claims?

This could seem to lead us to the impasse of relativist solipsism. Indeed, there appears to be an inevitably recursive character to the chain of questions: how do we know what we know? What counts as knowledge? What are the criteria for evaluation? And who are 'we'?

Is all that is left, then, a project of damage limitation rather than radical prefiguration? The lessons of attempts to formulate a Marxist psychology (Parker 2007) or a feminist psychology (Burman 1998c) are sobering. No psychology (in itself or alone) can be emancipatory. All attempts end up being recruited into a regulatory, and implicitly coercive or colonising, discipline. Perhaps this is the same for other disciplines, under the oppressive conditions that produce and sustain them all. At any rate, we cannot positively formulate good models of child development under conditions of inequality and injustice, in the same way as one cannot really hope to be (able to be) sane in an insane world. It is not that questions of time and change are uninteresting or unimportant, but rather it is unclear why we should use children to address such concerns. Indeed it could be argued that there are more urgent issues to be working on with and about children.

Displacing disciplines #1: shifting scene/jumping ship

One familiar methodological route has been to shift disciplines to avoid the impasse in one's own. Historical and anthropological work, as well as literature and political theory, have been vital resources informing critical psychological interventions around models of childhood. They help psychologists to see how the discipline is skewed by the failure to see its own historical and structural blinkers. They also help us to resist the allure of being accorded special expert status by the current specular-techno-knowledge-society imperatives, with their overdetermined commitments to an emotionally spontaneous, creative, economically autonomous (and so welfare-lite) subject (Gordo López and Burman 2004; Lister 2005). They help us to think about the broader social agendas mobilised by structures of child concern – how themes of child security and dependence reflect wider adult-centred preoccupations about living in an uncertain, insecure world whose geographical, political and affective boundaries are imploding in a period of international state and anti-state terrorism.

But, as in intercultural relations structured by histories of colonialism and imperialism, dangers of exoticisation and romanticisation always accompany interdisciplinary dialogue. And a murkier underside: contempt. In the post-UNCRC era, Britain over the past 20 years or so has witnessed the emergence of childhood studies, a vibrant multidisciplinary and interdisciplinary scene that combines sociological insights and anthropological methods with a human rights and participatory agenda (see e.g. Prout 2000; Franklin 2002a). When I attended some of the early meetings I found myself viewed with wary curiosity: a developmental psychologist (i.e. subscriber to the wicked child-as-deficit/inferiority approach). But then there came a moment when they came up against some claim of limits to developmental competence, and the residual scientism of the social and human scientists reared its unreconstructed head, their critical suspicions all dissolved over some purportedly real developmental matter. Perhaps this is where critical developmental psychologists can play some role in resolutely refusing the mystificatory attributions of expertise, and staying true to the 'epistemological shudder' that MacNaughton (2005) aptly characterises as the conceptual-methodological stance necessary not to foreclose what we can and cannot know about children.

As with genuine coalition politics (e.g. Reagon 1983), there is no safe place in cross-disciplinary discourse; and advanced capitalism (or what some people call postmodernity) offers no place of innocence except (as is elaborated in later chapters) within the ideology of childhood. Hence its attraction, perhaps, but – as the increasingly regular media panics of 'childhood in crisis' suggest – even this is unravelling.

So, to anticipate the arguments of Chapter 7, rather than throwing the critical baby out with the critical bathwater, we might be better off giving the proverbial baby a gentle push to one side. On the other hand she might get rather cold, wet and mucky if the water is not changed; or we might all want to swim somewhere else. (Of course we should be wary of the hygienist hue here, but then such motifs have also to be acknowledged as a key feature of psychology's history, Rose 1985; Richards 2002.) Now this analogy goes a bit wild with historical and cross-cultural examples of collective bathing, and then to political economy – in terms of how most of the world's population washes in rivers increasingly contaminated by the multinational oil and pharmaceutical barons, or where global warming has either dried up the river or threatens to wash the entire village away. Or else we could plot how the tin bath came to be designed and manufactured as a reflection of the nuclearisation of the family under industrialisation, alongside the move of the toilet from outhouse to en suite as a reflection of broader cultural-historical axes of development as interiorisation that can be interpretable according to Vygotskyan (1978) or Eliasian (2000) perspectives. All this may seem a long way from child development, but perhaps not so.

Displacing disciplines #2: un/marking specificities

I started this chapter by noting how key questions frequently posed (in research and policy arenas) appear to transcend disciplinary specificity. Yet disciplinary knowledges continue to inform, and even structure, debates. Teaching women's studies helped to clarify for me how this happens in three ways: interpersonally, institutionally and nationally (at least). At interpersonal levels a dynamic of mutual deference can arise, that paradoxically recapitulates the most stereotyped disciplinary claims to expertise (as where a literature-specialist colleague said in class where we were team teaching together: 'Analysing interviews? That's Erica's area', as well as the same about 'Discourse', which – interestingly – I regarded as 'her area'. Perhaps there is a particular dynamic of ambivalence around to claims to knowledge being played out here between women's studies teachers, see Burman 2001a, 2001b). At institutional levels, there is a particular political history in academic knowledge production and its auditing within national research assessments that has allied British women's studies with the social sciences. This in turn is overdetermined by the ways concerns with gender are seen as to do with the social, and specifically sociology, as something external to the subject.

Notwithstanding – or perhaps precisely by virtue of – its seeming accessibility or democracy of address, failing to specify disciplinary approaches may mask more problems than it resolves. The very terms of the usual questions posed about children concern their emotional, social, cognitive, affective, moral development. These compartmentalisations speak to a complex history of models of subjectivity that have been reproduced and reiterated within psychological models. There is an allocation of qualities also reiterating deals over turf, or domains of expertise, between disciplines – as in the relationship between psychology and psychoanalysis, for example (with the division of labour positioning psychology as the domain of the cognitive, psychoanalysis of the affective – with similar allocations marking the psychology–sociology relation over the individual–social binary). Here methodological disputes serve as disciplinary markers – with psychology identified with as the discipline of rigorous methods par excellence; a discipline that is, arguably, merely a technology of administration (i.e. testing) masquerading as a body of theory (Rose 1985). But this masquerade has real effects. So challenging the oppressions meted out in the name of normative or typical development is perhaps more urgent than arriving at the most complete or coherent psychological theory.

Displacing expertise

In anticipation of some responses these ideas might provoke, far from deskilling or undermining professionals working with or around children, or parents, or children themselves, it is my experience that they can be empowered by the kind of critiques arising from critical approaches to developmental questions, emerging from various disciplines. This is because they lend weight to practitioners' (in the widest sense of 'practice') suspicions and objections to the dominant theories, offer positions of partnership between practitioners and those whom they work with, support their tactics of resistance, and inspire others. Examples here span education (Billington 2000, 2006; Billington and Pomerantz 2003), social work (McLaughlin 2005, 2006) and psychiatric system survivor groups (the Hearing Voices Network; *Asylum Magazine*, see www.asylumonline.net). Clearly I am invoking here some kind of lived experience to offset or challenge disciplinary power. This is because, notwithstanding the tie-up between supposed psychological expertise and bourgeois-liberal ideology naturalised into commonsense or 'second nature', it is important to acknowledge and leave space for other kinds of knowledge (however arrived at) as critical resources for resistance. Particular ideas only become influential under specific sociopolitical conditions (Jovchelovitch 2004). This should provide some solace (as well as concern), in the sense that people – even children perhaps – have some inkling of this, and their place in these conditions. This is not a romantic or voluntarist understanding of agency, then, but one that describes people's actions and reactions in conditions not of their choosing. Even, or perhaps especially, in these neoliberal times which so seem to limit spaces for critical intervention, it is important to note how claims to expertise can be mobilised in counterhegemonic directions, both in illuminating the continuities between colonial rule and supposedly disinterested scientific development consultancy (Kothari 2005b), and in opening up possibilities of claims to knowledge for diverse and historically subjugated groups in ways that show how even neoliberalism is not so watertight as to preclude oppositional practice and contest (Katz 2005).

Three strategies

Hence from this review, three specific strategies for displacing development have emerged.

First, limiting claims to universalism: under spatial-discursive scrutiny, claims to generality often emerge to be more specific in orientation and application than they appear. Rather than bolstering the fiction of global knowledge – or what feminists have called the 'god trick' (cf. Haraway 1991a) – instead there are calls to situate the speaker/theoriser and thereby make visible – instead of obscuring or erasing – the structures of privilege and power that such authority relations elaborate.

Second, identifying multiple actors and interpretors: once we depart from a narrow chronological or causally focused framework it becomes possible to document the variety of participants and their differing agencies within any developmental intervention. Thus practitioners of development – whether of the individual, national or global varieties, and especially those of us who concern ourselves with both or all of these – should instead attend to the diversity of use, interpretation and incorporation into different discourses of development, and identify changing notions of intervention. Moreover we could usefully attend to how these different notions of development are indeed connected, as well as arising as the outcome of insidiously ideological reductionisms. We need to look at the interface between different groups of actors (parents, professionals, children, psychologists, psychotherapists, lawyers, etc.), and work to document the varying and contested accounts of what particular interventions mean and what they achieve. Whether evaluating the success of sustainable agriculture, educational, or health-promoting community practices, social or environmental developments, the same project of documenting diversities of perspective and interpretation of any intervention apply.

Third, we should be highlighting the social structuring of individually accorded qualities and activities. Here once again those working with or around children, and equivalently with representations of children and childhood, have much to learn from the constructive and critical debates around the broader practices of world economic development. For these debates have come to produce the available discourses within which we think about *individual* developmental trajectories. Specifically, the distinction elaborated by Crewe and Harrison (1998) in their discussion of the tensions between reforming development and deconstructing development is useful. Their evaluation of attempts to introduce sustainable technologies to poorer majority countries, distinguished between 'development anthropology' and 'anthropology of development'. Development anthropologists are reformers 'who from the inside and through better processes of translation and communication, try to make development better' (p. 16) while 'anthropologists of development hope to stand outside and to comment . . . usually as analysts rather than developers'.

There may be useful parallels with the distinction made between 'development anthropology' and 'anthropology of development' and between the projects of developmental psychology and childhood studies, with the latter implying a shift from a depth focus on individuals to broader (and multiple) analyses of the scenes in which developments are performed, and the various actors, interest groups and audiences this involves – including genealogical accounts of how these settings came to take the forms they have. Such parallels illustrate the methodological and conceptual potential of juxtaposing arguments arising from different disciplinary engagements with development that are taken up in a later chapter of this book.

And finally . . . replacing development?

Lest the burden of this account of development's complicities seems overwhelming, let me end by warding off worries this may generate about apparently jettisoning the possibility of prefigurative or interventionist approaches. Indeed, my argument so far has not been to dispense with development, but rather to highlight how our thinking is so saturated with its ideas that we in fact cannot do so. Instead I suggest that what is needed is a vigilance about its forms and applications, and an attention to its agencies and power relations; what it affords and disallows, and for whom. This does not mean getting into the business of reconstructing another (improved) version of development – for as Foucault (1977: 230) notes, 'to imagine another system is to extend our participation in the present system'.

Rather, the project is to draw attention to the partiality and limitations of all available developmental accounts, and to resist accounts of developmental completion, including that of ourselves as (perhaps) antidevelopmental accounters. Any general model tends to obscure the complexity of practices and contexts of development, and the structurally diverse character of the economic, cultural and interpersonal relationships that produce these varied developments.

Equally, there are no innocent positions within these discussions. As Crewe and Harrison (1998) also noted, even the 'deconstructors'' position and its associated 'anthropology of development' position still retains a tendency to overstate the agency and importance of Northern development and developers, thus de-emphasising other circumstances, agencies and motivations. Currently we are equipped by our theories to do little more than plot patternings that themselves reflect broader power relationships around what is deemed significant and what is not. Attending to questions of compatibility vs. divergence of actors' interests is an important one, since in psychology we tend to be too ready either to assume the passivity of those rendered as objects of the psychological gaze, or else to identify their agency only as either pathology or deficit. This is because we often overstate the extension and remit of the discourse of development we subscribe to.

Finally, in calling for the displacement of development I am not suggesting we should try to replace a temporal with a spatialised conception of development – for this too would introduce limitations. Rather the concern here has been to spatialise time (development) in parallel with those analysts of space who have called for the need to temporalise or historicise space (Massey 1992; Chernaik 1996), and those psychoanalysts who have begun to attend to the narrative character of historical truths (e.g. Spence 1982; Blum 1994). Drawing on its psychoanalytic nuances, displacing development might sound like a proposal to shift its investments to another place or space (rather as global capital does in seeking out new markets and new sources of cheap labour). Rather, dis/placing development signals a double interrogation or analysis of positioning: simultaneously highlighting its *covert* placing *and* problematising this: not to put it elsewhere (as another kind of toxic waste dumped on the so-called Third World), nor to dispense with it (and thereby both deny its hold on our minds and deny our prefigurative ambition), but to resist its easy settlement (or re-placement) anywhere.

2 The child, the woman and the cyborg

(Im)possibilities of feminist developmental psychology

This chapter extends the methodological and theoretical debates put forward so far, with a specific focus on developmental psychology, connecting pedagogical and policy concerns with theoretical models. While bringing in key theoretical resources, it was formulated to provide an accessible account that draws on autobiographical examples to illustrate the complex positions and dilemmas produced through current models of development. It is structured around a set of questions that highlight the ways modern culture, including psychology, has carved up gender, childhood and technology:

1. Women or children first? (how this omits or renders impossible the position of girls, and infantilises women).
2. Essentialism or expertise? (political ambiguities of the authority accorded women as mothers in knowing or determining children's best interests, and which women benefit or lose out from this).
3. Relativism or realisms – demystifying what the consequences of taking a constructionist approach means in terms of acknowledging material realities and specificities.
4. Reflexivity or rationalisation? Here the reconstruction of (reconfigured) forms of authority amid poststructuralist frameworks proclaiming the 'death of the author' is critically evaluated and defended.
5. Child centred or women centred? How we can avoid a concern with child-saving as importing mother- (or even by extension culture-) blaming.
6. The child as postmodern subject? This evaluates the celebration of playfulness and spontaneity that characterises advocates of the post-modern as a model of subjectivity – and that is shown to reconstruct a very modern model of childhood.
7. The child, the woman or the cyborg? Given the legacies of the divisions between women and children, the question of whether new metaphors of political subjectivities – such as the cyborg (made famous by Haraway) offer useful ways forward is discussed.

This chapter therefore applies the methodological resources identified in Chapter 1, to redirect its conclusions in two ways. First, it takes up both the biographical and narrative features addressed there to explore seven key debates about children and development that are typically encountered as dilemmas, or even dichotomies. In presenting these different texts – some autobiographical, others analytical – the aim (as also discussed in Burman and MacLure 2005) is to exemplify a reflexive practice that fosters critical interrogation of the claims to knowledge that each genre relies upon, as well as to indicate thereby how multiple and diverse personal, interpersonal, disciplinary and institutional positionings are inevitably mobilised when focusing on children and childhoods. Second, the disciplinary border crossings made in this chapter in particular feature discussions in social theory – which in their literary form are pursued further in Chapter 3. Where Chapter 1 argued for a destabilisation of the problems with development by spatialisation, i.e. the combined strategies of placing and displacing it, here the concern is to evaluate ideal possible futures prefigured by three celebrated utopian models of subjectivity that circulate in culture.

This chapter explores intersections between feminist readings of poststructuralist theory and psychological practices through reflections on my positions as a feminist teacher of developmental psychology and the contested domain this imports between women and children, and between women (as well as between women and men). While theoretical work has explored the consequences of connecting with the epistemological destabilisations of poststructuralist perspectives for both feminism (now feminisms) and psychology, I want here to situate my engagement with these ideas from my own embodied working history. I do this by way of illustrating how both a feminist standpoint and a commitment to a postmodern-style multiplicity and diversity can be exercised (and perhaps energised) by their juxtaposition with (developmental) psychology. While feminist and poststructuralist ideas offer useful critical vantage points from which to expose the oppressive commitments and practices of psychology, I will try to indicate in this chapter something of why their hold in developmental psychology is so tenuous. In particular, I will argue that this 'resistance' makes developmental psychology not only a key arena for feminist deconstructionist work but, like any symptom, also affords a diagnostic reading of the broader complex of contemporary cultural and intellectual investments it expresses.

I direct this chapter towards the specific problematic of developmental psychology by telling some stories. Some of these are 'mine' in the sense that they draw on the narrative genre of autobiography – indeed I would claim that they are 'true' in the sense that they form part of the fabric of the historical narrative of my experience. Others of the stories are more general, perhaps shared as cultural narratives, or even myths. Hence, while 'my stories' conjoin 'experience' and analysis, I tell them in the conviction that, owing to the cultural meanings exercised by concepts of childhood, these are more than 'mine'; that they have more general resonance for the politics of psychology, for the politics of feminist practice and for accounts of the so-called postmodern. Further, in doing this I should make clear that the autobiographical material presented here is as much a crafted account as is the (apparently) 'more theoretical' argument. That such oppositions (between theory and experience) are themselves collapsing under the weight of postmodernist critiques is made evident by this book and others. Hence even the writing 'I' as articulated here can itself be regarded as an, albeit useful, fiction that is lived as 'true'.

I will leave further theoretical concerns to unfold with the rest of the chapter. What follows is an elaboration of seven key dilemmas or (sometime) oppositions that structure the engagement between feminism(s), poststructuralism(s) and developmental psychology.

So why focus on developmental psychology? Surely using such subdisciplinary categories implies an acceptance of the existing structure of psychology? First, I want to 'play' up the importance of taking developmental psychology seriously as an object of feminist critique and intervention, as a branch of psychology that has material effects on women's lives. Second, I want to ward off the dominant reading of discourse, deconstructionist and poststructuralist ideas as relevant only to specific branches of psychology that are recognised to deal with gender and the social – in particular 'the psychology of women', or 'feminist psychology', and 'social psychology'. Third, I want to propose that developmental psychology is a key stronghold of positivist and modernist thinking in psychology that makes it a particularly important arena for feminist and poststructuralist critique – but perhaps not of practice.[1]

Developmental psychology and modernity

In what follows I make general critiques of developmental psychology in order to demonstrate how this is one of the last bastions of modernism in psychology. My account is presented in general terms because it is invidious to single out specific individuals as responsible for an entire problematic (but see Burman (2008) and this volume Chapter 7 for more specific analyses). Developmentalism, the conviction that explanation or greater understanding lies in situating a phenomenon within its species as well as individual history, is one of the hallmarks of nineteenth-century European thinking (Morss 1990, 1996). We are now only too familiar with the limits of such models, of the partialities that structured apparently natural and value-free models. The child, the 'primitive', women and the mentally ill were treated as immature versions of the adult, male, rational mind, as expressions of the binary oppositions between human and animal, European and non-European, male and female (e.g. Haraway 1989). The popularity of the evolutionary notion that the individual in 'its' lifetime repeats the development of the species ('ontogeny recapitulates phylogeny') was one of the primary precipitators of what we would now recognise as developmental psychology (although it could also be seen as the founding moment of personality theory and 'individual differences' – since our current subdisciplinary divisions belie common sources; Rose 1985).

Invested and performed within the study of the child, then, were all the key preoccupations of modernity. In particular, the faith in progress – that individuals and societies develop towards some 'better', more adaptive, more beneficial form of organisation – is one vital conceptual connection that ties developmental psychology in with the colonial and imperialist themes of (equally current) models of economic development. Just as important and related to its imperialist themes are the commitments to science, truth and reason, to the objective impartiality of technologies of research and evaluation and the ways they structure positivism and empiricism so deeply within developmental psychology. If the child is the basic unit of study, the raw material for the work of social, physical and political development, then the means by which 'it' is studied are depicted as equally free from sociopolitical influence.

Two points follow from these connections between feminism and poststructuralism. First, while postmodernism and deconstruction have profoundly redefined the agenda for social psychological and methodological debates, theory and method in developmental psychology have remained relatively untouched by paradigm twists and turns elsewhere in psychology. As a teacher and researcher in developmental psychology, I have become accustomed to hearing from students, conference commentators and journal reviewers that my concerns relate to the domain of philosophy or politics, but not to developmental psychology. Second, critiques of developmentalist assumptions in psychology (e.g. Kessen 1979; Morss 1996) have remained largely disconnected from similar critiques directed towards economics (Crush 1995; Mehmet 1995; Cowen and Shenton 1996) and psychoanalysis (Mitchell 1988). Developmental psychology seems to maintain its conceptual and political integrity in the face of the broader discrediting of developmental ideas throughout social theory and practice. Why is this? In what ways is this process similar to or different from other disciplines or subdisciplines of psychology? And what are the consequences of this resistance/endurance for the project of feminist intervention?

It would appear we have to look further. There is something about the rhetorical power of 'the child', of children, that renders claims and promises of developmental psychology seemingly incontestable. Even the most confirmed relativist would hesitate to deny that 'we' (children, adults, everyone?) have basic needs (but see Woodhead 1990, 1996; Burman 1995b, 1996a), that children differ from adults in some crucial 'developmental' sense which is not mere social attribution, and that those who study, or pronounce upon or about, children do not indicate something about potent mysteries of nature and life. Age, the marking of time on bodies, seems to lie outside culture, within biology. Like gender, 'race', class and sexuality, age plays a key part in the organisation of social relations, and, like these, differential treatment is typically justified by the appeal to 'nature'. But while assumptions about gender, 'race', class and sexuality are now being increasingly understood as social constructions that are historically and culturally contingent, age, and in particular 'the child', seems particularly intransigent to this contextual analysis.

One way of trying to shake off the power of the-child-as-exemplar is to recall that, like developmental theorising, it too has a history. Carolyn Steedman (1995) points out that the power of the child not only arises from its nodal point in the modern narratives of mastery and improvement, it also personifies for the modern Western imaginary the sense of loss – of inner life forever separated from outer, of the irretrievability of the past, the transience of life and the inevitability of death – to which these narratives simultaneously gave rise as their necessary corollaries. If the child is the overdetermined trace of all these complexes of the modern condition, of what relevance is it to feminist and postmodernist work?

First dilemma: women or children first?

If developmental psychology is a prime site for anti-feminist psychological practice, then this may offer some clue as to its continuity of themes. Feminist psychologists go elsewhere – to feminist psychology or women's studies, for example – to develop and voice their critiques. Thus the child-centred focus of developmental psychology remains Western liberal individualism writ large and also (as with liberal individualism) reinscribes women's subordinate positions within the private domain (Pateman 1989). With the emergence of liberal democracy, the potential authoritarianism of the state was limited by measures assuring the privacy of the home except where family 'failed' (see Middleton 1971). This meant that the prototypical 'reasonable man' as the subject of rational law was indeed male, with women gaining little protection from such arrangements. The setting up of exceptions to the limits of privacy meant that the state could make an exceptionally visible entry into the home through its supposedly benign gaze upon the child. Modern industrialised states are characterised by a panoply of child-watching, child-saving, child-developing and educating professionals, with multinational varieties springing up to spread the good news worldwide. If, within the optimistic model of modernity, children are 'our future' (citizens and workers) then it is worthwhile to the state to ensure that they are appropriately prepared for such positions.

It is therefore no surprise that feminists have responded with some suspicion and hostility to child-focused interventions, drawing on Foucauldian accounts to characterise such practices as regulation, evaluation and control.

Further, not only do they give rise to the abuse of women by childcare professionals (O'Hagan and Dillenberger 1995), but also these regimes of truth are subjectively inhabited and experienced: we worry about whether our child is 'doing well enough', is developing at the right pace, is 'going through her milestones correctly', etc. As Urwin (1985) and Marshall *et al.* (1998) point out, this conceptual frame not only isolates each mother, and treats her as the originator or responsible agent for any 'problem', but it also thereby sets her in competition with other women.

As feminists have also pointed out, part of the power of developmental explanation lies in the slippage from the specific and singular to the general: from the child to children; from the way it is to the way it has to, or is supposed to, be (Lieven 1981). The move from normal, in the sense of statistical, description to rhetorical prescription is the ideological bugbear beleaguering the truth claims of the modern social and human sciences, but it rears its ugly head in psychology most acutely because of psychology's pretensions to scientific status. Further, if the normal becomes presumed, then it is the abnormal that excites attention or scrutiny. We thus have a double system of regulation of women: as invisible norms, or as oddities or problems. The norms (e.g. of heterosexuality, motherhood, marriage, whiteness) elude further analysis; they form the standard backcloth for the pathologisation of all those who by virtue of their sexuality, their racialised or minoritised status, their economic need, do not 'fit' prevailing norms – giving rise to what Ann Phoenix calls their 'normalised absence/pathologised presence' (1987).

Developmental psychology makes specific contributions to this tendency to pathologise differences from supposed norms because of its desire to plot the regular, general course of development. Specific aberrations from that course are then treated, in a circular argument of self-confirmation, as offering useful clues about the general, rather than, say, showing its limits. Such a commitment to the general as instantiated in the particular has been vital in producing an account of development abstracted from social-political conditions. It individualises and privatises the manifold ways in which the care and containment of the young are profoundly structured according to culturally and historically specific models of 'what people are/should be like'. Not least among these is the way general notions of the 'environment' of the child have elided the social and the biological through such key terms as 'the natural'. This has allowed the structure of normalised absence/pathologised presence to exert its full weight of scrutiny upon mothers as the designated primary carers of children.

In addition, developmental psychological knowledge is not confined to academic tracts but insinuates itself into every crevice of policy and practice around children – with consequences for women as mothers. Even psychoanalysis, with its longstanding quarrel with empirical psychology (over the demonstrability of unconscious processes), turns with respect to the tradition of child observation. So, the Tavistock Clinic text *Closely Observed*

Infants (Miller *et al.* 1989), offering eight case studies as resources for social workers, therapists and doctors unable to conduct observations for themselves, might just as well have been entitled 'Closely Observed Mothers', since its records of early infant life, of everyday tasks of feeding, nappy changes, weaning and potty training comment as much on the mothers (and the culture of mothering) as on the babies.[2] The inadmissability of the social in development returns, like the repressed, in covert form. In returning indirectly it performs a double misattribution: the interactive character of development gets located within the child, while the less facilitating or desirable features are reallocated to the mother.

Second dilemma: essentialism or expertise?

An issue related to the regulation of women as mothers by developmental psychology is, of course, the matter of those women who are not mothers. The positioning of mother versus non-mother in the credibility and authority stakes between women has also played itself out within my own trajectory through developmental psychology (and into women's studies). It also illustrates another dimension that underlies the 'theory–practice' polarity structuring popular discourse on child development (and may also offer a resource for popular resistance to 'the experts', Alldred 1996). Perhaps in a vain effort to shake off the feminine hue connoted by its gendered subject matter, or perhaps because of its implication within dominant social agendas, developmental psychologists have always been at pains to demonstrate their methodological rigour and commitment to 'high theory'. Thus I graduated from the heady heights of genetic epistemology to delivering lectures on what the baby does, and does next, to trainee health visitors, community psychiatric nurses, youth and community workers, as well as psychology students.

As I pronounced on (and often denounced) the theories, I found myself quizzed, particularly by the – usually much more mature – professionals in the groups about my own motherhood status. As (mainly) women together, we stood on opposed territory for the warranting of our (often similar) political positions. I had initially chosen to 'do' psychology because I had not wanted to specialise in any subject I had previously studied; and then took a degree in developmental psychology since it seemed to offer a way of studying all topics and issues within one discipline. I was a ripe subject for developmental modernism, and at a moment when cognitive science was going developmental, developmental theorising knew no bounds – virtual or real. As a white, middle-class young woman, accustomed to academic success as the route to mastery (Walkerdine 1985), it was the theoretical concerns that gripped me. It was also through the theory that I came to realise the limits of the models both conceptually and politically, and through a critical reading of the theory that I tried to counter the perniciousness of commonsense applications of developmental psychology.

By contrast, the professionals I taught – often older, working class in origin – were steeped in the discourses of 'practice' and 'experience' that both served them well as a resource for suspicion of abstract and inappropriate psychological theory and were a means of dealing with the relatively disempowering position of returning to the classroom. So were we, a group of – largely women-centred – women, divided by discourses of 'expertise' and 'experience' that mapped precisely on to different strategies of feminists in relation to motherhood and professionalism (see also Downick and Grundberg 1980; Oakley 1981; Gordon 1990; Ribbens 1994). In my (experience-limited) biography, theory had (in the end) offered insight and critique, while for these (experience-enriched) students theory threatened them and they challenged my rights to comment on what they knew and did on the grounds of insufficiency of my claims to know as a non-mother.

Authenticity and experience are current topics of discussion in feminist theory and research (Maynard and Purvis 1994; Wilkinson and Kitzinger 1996). Here I want to note how these different pedagogical and student positions between women are not simply complementary but mutual constructions based on historical conjunctions and contradictions of gender, 'race' and class. My position as professional expert did not simply work to offset my lesser claim to experience as younger, childless (or child free); my youth and child-free/less status could be read by these more mature women, largely with children, as indices of the privilege (or the price?) of gaining and wielding such 'illegitimate' power. By such means and for these reasons, the political critique of developmental theory I offered could be obscured, ignored or even discounted.

Doubtless these stories are not unlike those of any beginning teacher, and I do not want to imply that I had an unusually difficult time, nor that I was a particularly unsuccessful teacher to these students. What I want to highlight is the contradictory positions mobilised for (feminist) teachers and students around claims to different kinds of knowledge, contradictions that mirror the tensions within the project of women's studies between women studying and the study of women's work (Coulson and Bhavnani 1990). These express structural tensions and power relations involved in being a feminist teacher, as representing both what the students want, and what they want to resist. For women's studies this is often particularly difficult; we both challenge the academy and exemplify it. One lesson of post-structuralist ideas is that acknowledging these multiple positions can teach us better to negotiate these political dilemmas.

I present this tale because it highlights the complexities and investments set in play by the call to surrender special claims to voice or experience within the context of teaching critical psychology. Clearly it must be possible to be a non-mother/child free and be considered qualified to teach or practice developmental psychology. To do otherwise would be to essentialise the experience of motherhood (and also gender) in ways that not only abstract and reify motherhood, but also render it open to even greater individual pathologisation. While such an approach clearly runs counter to the contemporary climate of gender bending and anti-essentialism, we also know when and why we want to maintain a strategic claim on the category 'woman' (Evans 1990); we might need to reconsider speaking positions and rights in the feminist classroom in a similar light (see McNeil 1992). Claims to specificity, diversity and historical positions of disadvantage are presented and contradicted when feminists teach developmental psychology. Even if 'deconstruction' is considered too 'difficult' or esoteric to teach, perhaps it offers some useful ideas for our teaching practice.

Third dilemma: relativism or the real?

My concerns about how developmental psychology peddles historically and culturally specific notions as universal truths, alongside its warrants for coercive scrutiny of disadvantaged and minoritised groups, led me to question how relevant Foucauldian critiques are to applications of developmental psychology outside its Anglo-US context of origin. My relativist leanings brought me into discussion with international child rights activists and child welfare agencies, yet it was my expertise in the 'realities' of child development that appeared to engage them most. I have struggled to avoid being positioned as 'knowing' what children 'need', and have pondered on the necessity and desirability of developing universal indicators of child development for use in monitoring the international legal instruments for child promotion and child protection such as the 1990 UN Convention on the Rights of the Child (e.g. Boyden 1993). While measures to extend children's welfare, cultural and political rights are to be welcomed, procedures for their evaluation and implementation threaten to install highly normative and culturally specific notions of idealised child subjects and family forms (Freeman and Veerman 1992; Burman 1996a). If poststructuralism proclaims the death of the (Western Enlightenment) subject, should we not resist its reconstruction?

There are certainly residues of the child of the liberal Western imaginary structured within international child rights policies and legislation. The common slogans of 'stolen childhood', or the implicit opposition elaborated between children who 'develop' and those who (merely) 'survive' (Vittachi 1989), privilege the model of childhood associated with the Western world. The active, spontaneous, playing, problem-solving, culturally male child of Western developmental psychology sits as uneasily with the working boy or girl, with the street child, the child soldier or sex worker of the South, as it does within the various Souths within the North. As records of the drafting process of the UN Convention indicate, notions of parental care structured into international legislation border perilously close to Western-defined notions of family and mothercare (Johnson 1992). Similarly, programmes for the promotion of child development place ever greater emphasis on the role of home visits and parental training without much reflection on the cultural relevance of the theoretical resources informing their models.

However, the limits of relativism become apparent when we see respect for cultural diversity and traditions displace concerns about female circumcision within the UN Convention. Without a political framework that explicitly allows one position to be privileged, other agendas can be mobilised to win the day, and along with this 'culture' and 'tradition' become treated as essential, ahistorical categories:

> Without questioning the political uses of culture, without asking whose culture this is and who its primary beneficiaries are, without placing the very notion of culture in historical context and investigating the position of the interpreter, we cannot fully understand the ease with which women become instrumentalised in larger battles of political, economic, military and discursive competition in the international arena.
>
> (Rao 1995: 174)

Nevertheless, professionals drawing on dominant discourses of childhood are not necessarily uncritical subscribers to it. Child rights and agency workers may well make use of the sentimentalising feel-good factors of donor–recipient relations exemplified in charitable fund-raising for children (see Black 1992). However, in other contexts their funding practices may depart dramatically from the exclusively child-centred orientation their publicity implies (e.g. giving money to community projects rather than specifically or solely for child-saving), and in their practice may challenge the historical and cultural abstraction of childhood by supporting community and community-defined development (although this can run the risk of simply replacing one romanticisation – of the child – with another – the community – that itself is just as redolent of paternalistic legacies, Cowen and Shenton 1996). Moreover, the profoundly ideological discourse of child innocence, of the prior claim that children have in times of political conflict, can be deployed in surprising ways. Strategic essentialism of the child has been used (for the benefit of not only children) to negotiate temporary ceasefires for the delivery of immunisation and essential food and medical supplies explicitly on the basis that children are 'peace zones' (Boyden, personal communication).

Fourth dilemma: reflexivity or rationalisation?

Poststructuralist engagements with psychology – particularly as connected with feminist debates about research – have tended to highlight the importance of being reflexive. As a process of making clear the interpretive resources guiding one's questions and analysis, often in relation to audiences designated with particular powers of evaluation, reflexivity has been put forward as a key feature of accountability (e.g. Wilkinson 1988). Yet notwithstanding its overt recognition of contradiction and complexity (e.g. Hollway 1989), the model of subjectivity that underlies these proposals is one that resembles the rational unitary subject that poststructuralism claimed to have dispersed: Not only does a feminist reflexivity run the risk of departing from the tenets of poststructuralism (which may not be so heinous a sin), but it also fuels the charge that accounts of research are not so much an honest sharing of motives and experience, but are (conscious or unconscious) manipulations.

Posed so baldly, this tension is revealed as a false opposition: if we accept that all accounts are textually mediated or crafted, then we cannot demarcate an absolute distinction between 'confession' and 'motivated justification'. Indeed, recalling Foucault's (1981) description of psychoanalysis as the secular confessional, we might see these practices as related. Our everyday understanding of confession (outside contexts of police interrogations) is the practice of making public one's innermost, private thoughts, but this tends to underestimate the structural importance to the account of the context in which it is made (see also Burman 1992a). Inner revelation shades into (self-regulated) extortion, or at best selective recasting, to make it acceptable either to oneself or another. Talk of confession seems particularly appropriate in the context of discussions about children, where theories of original innocence, or sin, are so prevalent – as respectively drawn upon within contemporary discussions about children who are abused, or are violent.

There are two other applications of this slippage between reflexivity and rationalisation relevant to the concerns of this chapter. First, feminist (and other, e.g. discourse analytic) researchers who draw on the notion of reflexivity are clearly on shaky territory if they subscribe to claims of authentic, unmediated exhibitions of inner subjectivities (whether others' or their own). The claim that the author is dead was put forward precisely to undermine the readers' deference to authorial intentionality. This does not necessarily warrant an invitation to default on researcher or authorial responsibilities; rather, it implies the acknowledgement of the limits of what we can claim to know, and the different knowledges we bring to bear in different contexts. Similarly, the interpretation of reflexivity as an incitement to confess all, evident within some (especially novice student) readings (see Burman 1998a, 2006a, in press, b), should be recognised as a backdoor return to humanism and even positivism. Rather than aspiring for some 'total' account, autobiographical or otherwise, we should be looking for sufficient and convincing analyses of the structural relations involved in the research.

Second, the selective, and possibly distorted, character of recollection arises in an acute form in any dealings with children and childhood. Here again we encounter the vexed question of the textual structuring of 'experience', since one of the structural characteristics of childhood work is that it is almost always carried out by those who do not inhabit that social category

(Mayall 1996), but all of whom have been children. This arises for feminists as much as for any other commentators on, or researchers or workers with, children. How are we to make sense of the (dis)connections between our own memories and the (apparent) actualities of children's lives? How are we to, or even can we, distinguish what we believe are our recollections of our early lives from their continuous reconstruction in the narratives we tell ourselves (and others) about our lives? It is hard to mention these issues without invoking the spectre of 'false memory syndrome' and its associated discourse of disbelief of survivors of sexual abuse and sexual assault (S. Scott 1997). Yet the problem with this train of associations lies precisely in the ways in which dominant notions of childhood conflate our memories of the children we were with the children we study: our concepts of selfhood are so intertwined with those of childhood that it becomes hard to distinguish the longing for what we no longer have (and perhaps never had) from our convictions about (and desires for) what children are and should be now (Burman 1996b, 1996c). The task for us, as feminist psychologists, is to do the work of analytical reflection, of reflexivity – or rationalisation – to help ward off the conflation of these different projects: the repair of one's own past and the study of children's present. A more informed knowledge of the socially structured irrationality of our life narratives may help feminist struggles against injustice.

Fifth dilemma: child centred or woman centred?

It would seem that feminists are well shot of developmental psychology, and much feminist effort has been devoted to disentangling the equation between women's interests and children's interests (New and David 1985; Thorne 1987). In economic development policy, women have long been addressed as sources of reproductive labour – whether as vessels for future labour or, in current formulations, in the relationship presumed between (higher) educational levels and (reduced) fertility. Women are also now recognised as a resource for production. Either way, it is important to challenge the presumed equivalence between measures introduced on behalf of children and those for women – in both directions. Women have not particularly benefited from childcare interventions, risking not only scrutiny, but also possible removal of their children, or semi-enforced sterilisation. Women have also been targeted in developmental policy as the more effective means (than through male heads of household) of getting more aid to children: the assumption that financial aid to women 'trickles down' to children has been shown to be as erroneous (Peace and Hulme 1993) as is the notion that raising the gross national product per capita will benefit disadvantaged members of a society (Mehmet 1995).

It has been an important feminist strategy to identify women's entitlements separately and not in relation to children, and while the UN Commission on the Elimination of Discrimination Against Women was conducted alongside the Commission drafting the UN Convention on the Rights of the Child, it is significant that a major recent text, *Women's Rights, Human Rights* (Peters and Wolper 1995), makes almost no mention of children, and fails to discuss any relationship between women's rights and children's rights.[3]

It may be that child-saving always threatens to import the full structure of mother-blaming, and that child rights enthusiasts have often been anti-feminist. While the child of developmental psychology is prototypically male, the interplay of gender between child and parent in child-saving discourse works to tie responsibility firmly on to women. If the child is male, then the discourse of saving boys from bad mothers is mobilised, but more often the child in need of saving is portrayed as a girl (thus confirming the conflation of feminine gender and passivity with infantilisation and victim status). Nevertheless, it is a major conceptual and political mistake to treat women and children as absolutely separate categories. Girls (usually) grow up to be women, and we might interpret the awkward formulation circulating within contemporary (economic and psychological) development policy of 'the girl child' as (among other matters) indicating the anomaly of this position across and between these two categories (gender and age) and which are both key axes of social discrimination (Burman 1995b, 1995c).

Further, we mistake strategy for principle if we accept the liberal rights discourse that treats rights as individual and competing. Women's and children's rights may well be in need of separation, given social pressures for women to subordinate their interests to those of their children, as where the sensitive mother is enjoined by the child-centred pedagogy to disguise her household labour as play (e.g. Walkerdine and Lucey 1989). Similarly, increasingly health education campaigns are inviting pregnant women to subordinate their rights (e.g. to drink alcohol and smoke) to those of their 'unborn children'. Where this is extended to 'pre-pregnant' women we begin to see how the categories of woman, mother and child are in danger of imploding. But nevertheless, this does not mean that these categories are absolutely separable. This would be to accept the discourse of the Western patriarchal legal system as truth.

Perhaps there is something more uneasy at work here in the separation between women and children marked by the adoption of a liberal rights discourse, something that goes beyond even warding off the infantilisation of women and the feminisation of children (see also Chapter 9). Perhaps if we treat women and children as separate categories, we do not then have to attend to the ways in which feminists have been, and are, divided over discussions about children and childcare (see for example, Attar 1988, 1992; as opposed to Wallsgrove 1985). Mary Daly's (1981) description of mothers who initiate girls into oppressive practices of femininity as 'token torturers' is scarcely mother-friendly. Even within first-wave British feminism, disputes emerged over the roles of mothers, and of the relative responsibilities of mothers and the state for childcare – between empowering women through giving them the vote and improving public facilities for mothers and children (Riley 1987). Twenty-four-hour crèche provision may have been a longstanding demand of second-wave feminism, but the current revival of celebratory motherhood (in an era of economic and social decline) restates more positively the old refrain: why have children if you don't want to look after or be with them?

Here we encounter the full force of critiques of feminism as played out through differences in women's relationships to children and families. Black feminists have argued against the representation of the family as only functioning as a site of oppression for women, since it is also a source of support against a racist society (Amos and Parmar 1984; Glenn *et al.* 1995). Heterosexual privilege has long been equated with motherhood – although the increasing numbers of lesbian mothers by donor insemination (DI) perhaps shows this as the partial fiction it always has been. Nevertheless 'fitness to mother' in the sense of bearing, caring for and, crucially, access to services for assisted mothering and child custody, are all heavily influenced by norms about what makes an appropriate family environment in which children can grow up (Alldred 1995). These (examples of) structural divisions between women replay themselves anew (across divisions of class and able-bodiedness) in the mutual suspicions, jealousies and antagonisms between feminist mothers and non-mothers.

Without subscribing to romantic notions of relatedness or 'different voices' (e.g. Gilligan 1982; Fulani 1998), we can still recognise the limits of a 'rights' model – be it reproductive rights, children's rights or women's rights – for the useful but flawed legal instrument it is, and try to move on beyond the unhelpful polarities it reinscribes; on this, in their attention to diversity, undecidability and structural ambivalence, feminist poststructuralisms may be helpful.

But even the apparatus of deconstruction, including deconstructing developmental psychology, presumes the structure it sets out to dismantle. It is thus covertly dependent on, or even maintaining of, it. Further, the idea of deconstructing developmental psychology may provoke specific and contradictory reactions, particularly for women: of horror or sadism. That this is so is intimated by the images of dismemberment associated with deconstruction. Treating deconstruction as equivalent to ejection or explosion of the child subject constitutes a perniciously individualist and reductionist reading of what should be the rejection or reformulation of an entire body of theory: talk of throwing the baby out with the bathwater suffers from similar limitations. While children, like women, are considered both appealing and appalling (Burman 1994a; Chapter 6 this volume), their status as quintessential humanist subjects does not necessarily favour either. Similarly, it is probably both unhelpful and impossible simply to replace an exclusive focus on the child with one on the woman as subject. This is where developmental psychology in its lifespan varieties meets the psychology of women (e.g. Josselson 1987). The problem is not simply the gendered character of the implicit subject and trajectory of developmental psychology (though this is also a problem). Feminising the child, or taking the woman as central to the developmental account is useful, but not enough, since the unitary subject still remains (see also Burman 1998c).

Sixth dilemma: the child as postmodern subject?

If poststructuralism and postmodernism have deconstructed the liberal humanist subject, reproduced in the rational, unitary subject of modern psychology (Henriques *et al.* 1984), what kind of subjects inhabit post-modernity? Notwithstanding the proclamations of the death of the subject, a new model of subjectivity has been engendered that emphasises sponteneity, play, plurality and fragmentation. Such subjectivities explicitly challenge dominant conceptualisations of political organisation deemed inappropriate to these 'new times' of rapid political change, of epistemological, ecological and economic uncertainty, and new social movements. But far from dispensing with the Enlightenment subject, residues of the old remain to haunt us within the new. As a reversal of the serious, integrated, single-minded adult, the romantic subject of postmodernism is the child. While Frederick Jameson's (1984) influential account of postmodernity celebrates play, bricolage, timelessness and schizophrenia (or internal disintegration) as tokens of postmodern subjectivities, I will focus here on Jean-François Lyotard's portrayal (but see also Burman 1992b). As the author of one of the key works heralding postmodernity (Lyotard 1984), Lyotard's writings on childhood are particularly worthy of attention.

Lyotard's *The Postmodern Explained to Children* (1992) is undoubtedly a playful and polyvalent text, not only in its title, which beguilingly appears to promise clarity and simplicity, nor in the pedagogical position of master/teacher he covertly assumes to complement that of the child-reader. The book is introduced by its editor/translators as exemplifying Lyotard's conception of the postmodern in its fragmentary, non-linear, incomplete form. In some senses it does indeed convey some of the central preoccupations of Lyotard's ideas; and in that respect the trope of the child works in the typical modern manner of indicating an inner core of truth, stripped of trappings and defences.

Where Lyotard writes explicitly about childhood, he is treating this not as a life stage of immaturity or inferiority, but as the moment of creative chaos that precedes thought. (Here he alludes both to Nietzsche and Benjamin.) In his discussion of the teaching and practice of philosophy, he designates childhood as a state of mind, as 'the possibility of risk of being adrift' (1992: 116). Thus:

> Philosophical writing is ahead of where it is supposed to be. Like a child, it is premature and insubstantial. We recommence, but cannot rely on it getting to thought itself, there, at the end. For the thought is

> here, muddled up in the unthought, trying to sort out the impertinent babble of childhood.
>
> (Lyotard 1992: 119)

The openness and unbounded state of the exploring philosopher cannot be entered into 'without renewing ties with the season of childhood, the season of the mind's possibilities' (1992: 116). Childhood is like postmodernism: that which is ineffable, intangible, unarticulable, unrepresentable (see Lyotard 1983) – but what a modern-style mystery of childhood this is:

> The postmodern would be that which in the modern invokes the unpresentable in presentation itself, which refuses the consolation of correct forms, refuses the consensus of taste permitting a common experience for the impossible, and inquires into new presentations – not to take pleasure in them but to better produce the feeling that there is something unpresentable.
>
> (Lyotard 1992: 24)

Although cast as a mode of writing, as intimating the inchoate character of innovation and creativity, this romance of the child ultimately appeals to an embodied form, and presumed collective memory, with all its attendant normalisations and cultural assumptions. There is no equivocation about the child as subject, as an interpellated, putatively general, historical memory:

> We must extend the line of the body in the line of writing . . . Following this line . . . means that we use these forms in an attempt to bear witness to what really matters: the childhood of an encounter, the welcome extended to the marvel that (something) is happening, the respect for the event. Don't forget, you were and are this yourself: the welcomed marvel, the respected event, the childhood shared by your parents.
>
> (Lyotard 1992: 112)

Once again the minds and bodies of children have become homogenised into the child, every child, that dimly remembered part of ourselves 'we' were and are: the postmodern has mutated into the worst excesses of the modern by reinstalling the familiar subject of Western everyman in a post-Enlightenment form (see also Chapter 3 this volume).

Seventh dilemma: the child, the woman or the cyborg?

If the child irretrievably harks back to modernism, then perhaps there are other metaphors for less oppressive psychological and political subjectivities. Developmental psychology is complicit with the problems of modernity, and anti-developmental theories – though vital – stop at critique rather than creative formulation of new models. Yet if, ultimately, even non-foundationalist postmodernism retains a commitment to a humanist subject, is it possible, or desirable, to try to dispense with a model of the subject? Given the political ambiguities of postmodernism, feminists are debating forms of available conceptions of subjectivity and (individual and collective) change (Bondi 1993; Nicholson and Seidman 1995). In this chapter I have discussed the limits of child-centred models of development, and how women or even women-centred varieties fall prey to some of the same difficulties of essentialism and reification. Perhaps Donna Haraway's (1991a) cyborg manifesto, with its speculative political possibilities, offers an alternative set of metaphors on which to base a (feminist) developmental psychology?

The cyborg is ostensibly antithetical to any conventional developmental narrative: it is an entity without history, or a history of embodiment; it is neither human nor machine; it transgresses categories of gender; it is of uncertain or unallocated sexual orientation; and of no known 'race' or culture (Hables Gray *et al.* 1995). As such, the cyborg usefully highlights the typical investments and applications of developmental psychology, and in particular resists the resort to 'nature', since by definition it is an artefactual construction, a hybrid without precedent and origins. As such the metaphor of the cyborg has gained an enthusiastic reception in feminist and postmodernist circles (Stallabrass 1995; Lykke and Braidotti 1996). Still, once again, we find the monster cyborg suffers from the legacies of monstrous women and children, as indicated by the bad press it has received in popular culture (Creed 1987).

There are other reservations or limits to its radical potential. Just as the dominant cultural representation of the cyborg as invulnerable superman threatens to eclipse the figurative possibilities of this new life form, so too it reminds us of how developmental psychology has been powerfully informed by, as well as contributing to, the project of 'artificial intelligence' (see Rutkowska 1993). Haraway is very clear that she invokes the cyborg as mythical possibility, as a reminder of possibilities that technophilic and antiscientific feminists might fail to notice. But, as she acknowledges, this vision is one that we will have to struggle hard to recast in feminist-friendly ways, given the cyborg's origins in advanced war technology and (productive and reproductive) labour replacement (Macaulay and Gordo López 1995).

While the cyborg may lack its own history, it functions within historical circumstances. Haraway's challenge is for us to recognise that it can be (re)formulated to promote feminist ends. (We might note how the original subtitle of her piece, 'Science, Technology and Socialist Feminism in the 1980s', is often forgotten.) If theories of subjectivity are inevitable and indispensible tools to envisage changed social arrangements, then perhaps the cyborg offers a different set of models and images that are less caught up in the trappings of tradition and modernity. While no image is innocent or without history (cyborgs abound in all mythologies – ancient and new), what the cyborg offers the critic of developmental psychology is an alternative vantage point on its terms of reference – as neither parent nor child, and with neither absolute standpoint nor immutable difference.

At the risk of reiterating the modern story of the child as intimating more general lessons and strategies, I want to end by asserting the relevance of debates about development, change and political subjectivities for feminist politics (modern or postmodern). In this chapter I have commented on some current models in circulation, and in particular highlighted the varied and enduring character of the resort to the child – exemplified by, but not confined to, the child of developmental psychology. If turning from the child to the woman or even the cyborg fails to resolve some of the difficulties, then there are two possible conclusions we might draw: first, that no metaphor can guarantee a progressive outcome: rather, what matters is what we do with it; second, that common to all three tropes – the child, the woman and the cyborg – is that they remain singular, isolated and thus recuperable into the individualist narrative of liberal bourgeois development.

Perhaps rather than (only) leaping into new figurative utopias, there is still much mundane work of feminist (psychological) critique to be done. Along with elaborating new inspirational images, one very material and grounding critical practice of developmental psychology is to challenge the elision of the general into the singular, with all its attendant homogenisation of the diversity of gendered, cultural and historical practices. This is more modest than the grand project of reconstructing a developmental psychology that can prefigure better days, but that always runs the risk of reproducing the same oppressive structures it set out to counter. Yet it can draw on imaginary alternatives and deconstructionist destabilisations to engage in a more informed way with the complexities and poignancies of the intersections between women and children, and between women, as well as between women and men, that are brought to the fore by the feminist critique of developmental psychology. At the very least we can start to document the diversities of what we, as children, women or cyborgs, are and do: we might even find that there is already more resistance for, and will to, change than we thought.

3 Pedagogics of post/modernity

The address to the child as political object and subject

This chapter moves on from the reflexive and disciplinary-specific concerns of Chapter 2 to critically explicate a specific theme: the relationship between models of childhood and modernity as mobilised, parodied and – it is argued – ultimately reconstructed within postmodern accounts. Lyotard's (1992) *The Postmodern Explained to Children* is juxtaposed with a reading of Benjamin's ideas (drawn together from a variety of his writings – since this piece was first written before the publication in 2006 of the English translation of Benjamin's *Berlin Childhood Around 1900*). It is argued that Benjamin's conceptualisation of children and childhood anticipates postmodern discussions but avoids some of their pitfalls. However, the 'romance' surrounding the child remains discernible both in Benjamin's own writing and in the ways his commentators take this up. It seems that recourse to the child as a utopian or dystopian figure is irresistible, even to theorists whose accounts speak to the significant disenchantment with the project of societal development and revolutionary change.

This chapter grounds the discussion of history, change and development taken up in this book within contemporary social theory, with connections to literary theory perspectives on children's representation figuring as a methodological resource. It offers an analysis of the challenges posed by metaphors of childhood from within contemporary philosophy. Where elsewhere I have taken up Benjamin's writings on history to inform discussions of therapy (Burman 1996/7) and even of social science research practice (Burman 2003a, 2003b), here the focus is on a close reading of the political consequences of contrasting conceptualisations of, and claims for, childhood. This paves the way for subsequent chapters in Part II that analyse societal investments in canonical models of childhood, and how these structure the representation of non-normative childhoods. For while 'images' of childhood may reverberate powerfully within contemporary media and communication practices, the 'word children' (Stainton Rogers and Stainton Rogers 1998) of written texts have long wielded their influence on policy and practice. As Rose's (1984) classic study makes clear, there is an interactive and constructive relationship – via ideologically informed pedagogies – between supposedly fictive ideal-typical children in literature and their (child and adult) readers. The close reading of these key texts of childhood, which are explicitly concerned with metaphors for the possibility of political change, also works to inform the explicit discussions of the possibilities for 'developments' discussed in Part IV, especially Chapters 11 and 12 where Benjamin's ideas are revisited.

This chapter explores questions of the subjectivities elaborated within accounts of postmodernity by juxtaposing readings of two theorists of contemporary politics and philosophy, Lyotard and Benjamin, who explicitly invoke and address childhood in their analyses. While Benjamin analyses the cultural and political strategies of modernity in his (1929–1933) radio broadcasts for children (Mehlman 1993), Lyotard (1992) claims to explain the postmodern condition to children. I will explore areas of convergence as well as difference that give rise to correspondingly different politics, and politics of childhood. While both accounts threaten to indulge in a romanticisation which reinstitutes a model of the subject as abstracted from cultural-political contexts, this abstraction is also used to invoke the possibility of a subversive political imaginary. These familiar rhetorical devices therefore maintain a theme of the child as quintessential or idealised subject within postmodern as much as modern accounts – albeit for contrasting analytical purposes.

The texts that form my focus for this chapter were originally French and German which I have come to know only in English versions. They stretch across world wars, historical and geographical and political transitions, and new world orders, but speak to and of Fortress Europe. Their concern with childhood reflects a modern European preoccupation about themes of innocence and culpability of the past (Antze and Lambek 1996) and the possibilities for fashioning a different or better world. This mediated, textual character exemplifies one central feature of the postmodern: the non-transparency of language. The gaps of meaning, the incompleteness of understanding, the proliferation of interpretations that such transformations effect, are all part of the experience of late, or post, modernity. The two theorists, Walter Benjamin and Jean-François Lyotard, whose ideas form my focus, have also coined the terms by which we frame such debates, Benjamin in his essay 'The Task of the Translator' (1970b) and Lyotard in *The Postmodern Condition* (1984). In this chapter I explore readings of their writings about, and to, children, and consider what these offer us for a critical theory of childhood, and for the possibilities for transformed and transformative subjectivities within the problematic of modernity and postmodernity that childhood so frequently betokens.

Textual dis/locations

In terms of engaging with Benjamin, we are already involved in a postmodern style project of evocation and interpretation. *Aufklärung für Kinder* is a collection of radio broadcasts made by Benjamin, around 30 in two series called *Jugenstunde* and *Stunde der Jugend* broadcast from Berlin and Frankfurt between 1929 and 1933, before Nazi persecution led him to flee to Paris. They correspond to the period of time after Benjamin had been disallowed the possibility of an academic career (and therefore secure income) by the rejection of his thesis presented to the University of Frankfurt.[1] Although initially published as *Aufklärung für Kinder* in 1985, and included in Benjamin's *Gesammelte Schriften* of 1989, English translations are not yet available.[2] My reading of them is drawn from, and therefore constructed in relation to, that provided from Mehlman in his (1993) book, *Walter Benjamin for Children: An Essay on his Radio Years*, which, as its title suggests, is a commentary and set of interpretations in relation to Benjamin's life and work, rather than translation and exegesis. We might recall here how Lyotard (1992: 24) names the essay as a postmodern form – as 'about' rather than 'on', as striving to attest to what it cannot present: 'it is not up to us to provide reality but to invent allusions to what is conceivable but not presentable.' Similarly Benjamin (1970b: 75) writes that 'translation catches fire on the eternal life of the works and the perpetual renewal of language'. Thus we should also note how – in postmodern self-referential style – Mehlman frames his essay on Benjamin's radio broadcasts to children within the parameters of 'parquetry' or inlaid work, the term used by Benjamin 'to evoke the visual effect he trusts his discourse will have on his listeners' (Mehlman 1993: 12–13).

So already two transformations have taken place: from Benjamin to Mehlman, and from radio broadcasts, spoken narrations for a children's audience on Children's Hour, to a collection prefaced by the title 'Enlightenment', *Aufklärung*. Mehlman comments in a note on Benjamin's concerns about the Enlightenment, and his text develops a possible alternative reading in terms of the specifically Jewish Enlightenment tradition (*Haskalah*). My account here is inevitably as much an engagement with Mehlman's interpretations and representations of childhood as of Benjamin's, albeit informed by other interpretations now emerging of Benjamin's enduring concern with children, childhood and his passionate involvement in student political movements (Doderer 1996; Fischer 1996; Lehmann 1996). Rather than claiming to exhaust or extend the burgeoning scholarship on Benjamin and Lyotard, my concern is with the political rhetorics of childhood their work mobilises. In this sense, whether this is done in their own words or as rearticulated by commentators, while certainly not irrelevant, is also not essential to my claims, and further reiterates the very topic at issue between them. Taking due account of both the constructive character, and indeterminacy, of representation, I return later to

Mehlman's reframing of Benjamin's (notions of) childhood, and its diverging rhetorical ends.

Modern and postmodern contexts

Let me draw attention to a second set of estrangements and sideways connections. The texts that form my topic span a period from the 1930s to the mid-1980s; they speak, respectively, of the crisis in modernity and the character of postmodernity; they precede one another, but are intertextually interwoven: as with my own reading of them here, aspects of the first inform the second. Nevertheless, in awry and surprising ways, I will suggest that the first is in some respects the more 'postmodern' in the sense of being freer of the assumptions of modernity, and is certainly more useful for those who want to retain some place for political engagement. Walter Benjamin and Jean-François Lyotard are both important theorists of the cultural conditions for forms of thought and political intervention: Benjamin as cultural critic and apocalyptic visionary of the crisis in modern capitalism, Lyotard as paradigm commentator on its later forms of organisation; Benjamin writing on the brink of the abyss of Nazi totalitarianism, Lyotard reflecting on its aftermath, the vacuous, hyperreality of the order of technoscience, where science and reason have parted company to create a world on the brink of self-destruction, and where political agency is so alienated and fragmented that to mention this is, for many people, to comment on the banal.

An important area of convergence between Benjamin and Lyotard is their critique of modernity, of the project of Enlightenment. This is despite major differences in political orientation: Benjamin was a Marxist – albeit of libertarian and anarchist inclinations (Löwy 1985), a revolutionary; while Lyotard sees emancipatory narratives, including Marxism, as wedded to regimes of symbolic or actual violence. Both writers are preoccupied with the transformative potential of writing, whether creative or philosophical, and with the place of cultural criticism in political intervention. Both elaborate a firm critique of the notion of progress that is so central to the project of modernity – Lyotard through his analysis of the totalising character of narrative, of the impossibility of claims to universality without resorting to potentially totalitarian prescriptions, of which he regards Nazi mythologising as the exemplar, but to which he claims emancipatory narratives (such as liberalism, socialism) are also vulnerable through their formulation as political projects.

Benjamin's critique of progress is famously elaborated by the image – inspired by his meditations on Paul Klee's 1920 painting *Angelus Novus* (one of two Klee paintings that he owned; see Muchawsky-Schnapper 1989; Brodersen 1996) – of the angel of history who is helplessly blown backwards into the future towards the mounting piles of wreckage that comprise humanity's achievements:

> His eyes are staring, his mouth is open, his wings are spread. His face is turned towards the past. Where we perceive a chain of events, he sees one single catastrophe which keeps piling wreckage upon wreckage and hurls it in front of his feet. The angel would like to stay, awaken the dead, and make whole that which has been smashed. But a storm is blowing from Paradise; it has got caught in his wings with such violence that the angel can no longer close them. This storm irresistibly propels him into the future to which his back is turned, while the pile of debris before him grows skyward. This storm is what we call progress.
>
> (Benjamin 1970a: 269)

Written after the Nazi–Soviet pact of 1939 (following Benjamin's release from internment in pro-Nazi Paris), and among the last of his writings, Benjamin's 'Theses on the Philosophy of History' are regarded as 'pos[ing] serious difficulties for a Marxist understanding' (Roberts 1991: 49). In part such comments reflect discomfort at how Benjamin harnessed the power of religious imagery to fuel his political critique. The messianic imagery of the angel in the storm has prompted speculation about the influence of Kabbalah as well as the new German romanticism on Benjamin's thinking (Rabinbach 1985). [Benjamin's well-documented interest in Kabbalah is what prompts Mehlman's reading of his life and work as a working (or acting) out of the Sabbatian precept 'to defeat evil from within'.] Löwy (1985: 47) prefers to see this romanticism as a political strategy that blends anarchism with Jewish messianism in a relation of 'elective affinity' that draws on each without assimilating one to the other. As he comments: 'the two cultural outlooks have in common a utopian-restitutionist structure, a revolutionary-catastrophist perspective on history, and a libertarian image of the edenic future' (Löwy 1985: 47).

That Benjamin was torn between the call to Jewish scholarship, drama as political intervention, and intellectual critique of capitalism was reflected in his friendships with Gershom Scholem, Bertolt Brecht and Theodor Adorno, respectively. Benjamin's 'revolutionary nostalgia' (Eagleton 1985) or 'creationist materialism' (Žižek 1989) for a pre-capitalist era exacted criticism from Adorno on the grounds of mysticism and the positing of a mythical archaic Edenic bliss. While Scholem and Adorno were able to suspend their mutual suspicion and dislike to edit a collection of Benjamin's correspondence together only after his death, they were, it seems, united in their disapproval of his friendship with, and enthusiasm for the work of, Brecht. The friendship with Brecht, according to Löwy, is also what marks the temporary suspension of what is otherwise perhaps the key enduring theme of Benjamin's work: the criticism of 'progress' which 'receives in his work a peculiarly revolutionary and subversive quality' (1985: 53).

Perhaps it is the apparent pessimism and apocalyptic imagery that affords the continuities between Benjamin and Lyotard, and invites his designation as a prophet of postmodernity (or even descriptor of psychoanalysis; Žižek 1989) as much as critic of modernity. The image of the angel caught in the storm of progress provides in graphic form a representation of dialectical development (Löwy 1985). Moreover, the critique of simple, modern chronology, through this assertion of the inevitably retrospective movement of being impelled into the future looking backwards, is also helpful to ward off attempts to mark modernity and postmodernity as successive historical periods, rather than a description of form and possibilities. Thus according to Lyotard (1992: 22) postmodernism precedes, rather than succeeds, modernism:

> A work can become modern only if it is first postmodern. Thus understood, postmodernism is not modernism at its end, but in a nascent state, and this state is recurrent.

Recast within postmodernist rhetoric the sense of ineffability, of being condemned to miss, of the tragic grandeur of Benjamin's writing acquires a new positive valence:

> The artist and the writer therefore work without rules, and in order to establish the rules for what *will have been made*. This is why the work and the text can take on the properties of an event; it is also why they would arrive too late for their author or, in what amounts to the same thing, why their creation would always begin too soon. Postmodern would be understanding according to the paradox of the future *(post)* anterior *(modo)*.
>
> (Lyotard 1992: 24, original emphasis)

For all their diversity, Lyotard's writings stand as transitional between phenomenology and psychoanalysis; and between the Marxism of the eurocommunist French left, disillusioned in the face of Stalinism, and the flight into democracy through consumption. His book *The Postmodern Explained to Children* indicates his movement to re-engage with moral-political issues after the nihilism of his (1974) book, *Economic Libidinale*. The notion of the 'event' drawn upon above is closely linked to the conception of childhood through the Nietzschean sense of rupture (see Descombes 1979; Lyotard 1983; Dews 1987). It is this which, albeit in an implicit way, takes us into the idiom of birth, growth and cycles; postmodernism as antecedent possibility, modernism as its arid remains. Such residual organicist imagery sits uncomfortably with the technophilic anti-developmental terms in which accounts of the postmodern are usually cast. Or are they?

The child, as an always utopian – or dystopian – figure becomes a topic; whether as political resource or liability. We must always be wary of its selectivity, and here I draw on the discourse of selection advisedly, deliberately, for Lyotard explicitly takes Auschwitz 'as a paradigmatic name for the tragic "incompletion" of modernity' (Lyotard 1992: 30), its rational technological project of genocide as 'the crime opening post-modernity' (1992: 31). Similarly, Benjamin's (1970a: 247) warning that '*even the dead* will not be safe from the enemy if he wins' stands as a sinister prophecy of Holocaust revisionism and false memory debates (see Burman 1996/7).

Children, Enlightenment and postmodernism

Given Benjamin's and Lyotard's status as critics of development and progress, then, it is surely of significance that both produced material addressed to children, or at least cast within the rhetoric of talking to children. Benjamin's *Aufklärung für Kinder* and Lyotard's *The Postmodern Explained to Children* take different material form and 'speak' to or 'of' children in contrasting ways. Nevertheless I want to suggest that a juxtaposition of these works repays the work of interpretation and speculation. I will argue that reading (a reading of) Benjamin's works *for* children alongside Lyotard's pronouncements *about* children prompts new vantage points upon the political possibilities of the postmodern. I will also comment on the politics and pedagogics of childhood involved in readings of these texts.

While both texts (about Benjamin and by Lyotard) mobilise familiar representations of childhood, like Frisby (1996) and Doderer (1996), I will suggest that, paradoxically, despite Benjamin's own autobiographical and others' psychobiographical treatments of his works, and despite its earlier formulation, his work is both more politically useful and in some respects more in tune with postmodernist thinking. (While I recognise that such evaluative formulations run counter to the discourse of the postmodern, it is precisely the moral-relativist tendencies of postmodernist discourse that I am most concerned to ward off.) Benjamin offers an account of childhood that treats this not as some prior, integral life stage, but as the encounter with the cultural-political, as the engagement with artefacts, in the pleasures and constraints of their consumption. Childhood is thus not outside culture, but is its production; although children are nevertheless addressed as potentially transcending or comprehending such positions.

The status of child in the postmodern parallels questions about the end of the subject and the end of history. The 'discovery' of the child as the implicit residual subject could be read as seriously undermining postmodern claims to its deconstruction (Burman 1992b). It seems that, as an alternative to the split, alienated and depressive position of the modern condition, all the postmodern offers by way of a model is either chronological regression (from adult to child) or psychotic disintegration (into schizophrenia; Deleuze and Guattari 1977; Jameson 1984). However, Walter Benjamin made a place for the present to redeem the past through struggle, that is, he retained the possibility of a revolutionary future. His evocations of a mythical past were less a call to return to an archaic golden age, than a utopian strategy to strive to recover what should have been: the claim to 'weak messianic power' that 'cannot be settled cheaply. Historical materialists are aware of that' (Benjamin 1970a: 257). In their different (cultural, political, geographical) milieux, Lyotard and Benjamin espouse a different politics, yet these arise from a similar recognition of the problems (with modernity).

Thematic a/symmetries

I now offer some context for juxtaposing these texts. First, the differences. Clearly it is foolish and ahistorical to try to evaluate the work of Lyotard and Benjamin in relation to the same criteria since they worked within different cultural-historical moments. Benjamin was informed by modern Jewish messianism and new German romanticism which predated but still coloured his anarchist and then (arguably) Marxist politics (Löwy 1985; Rabinbach 1985); Lyotard retains a Nietzschean suspicion of all systems and political projects as inciting totalitarianism, and struggles to ward off the seductions of psychoanalysis. While both theorists write from some sense of historical crisis and state violence, Benjamin faces the descent into fascism while Lyotard addresses the aftermath of Stalinism. Benjamin maintained an apocalyptic redemptive-restorative messianism while Lyotard oscillates between espousing political nihilism and liberal democracy. Not least of the asymmetries is that Lyotard draws on Benjamin, significantly specifically in relation to his representation of childhood.

Yet notwithstanding these differences, we can note a continuity of interests between these two authors: in the permeability between the psyche and the city; in the distribution of subjectivity; in pleasure and consumption. Thus we see the sensual, playing, uninhibited child as the model for both modern and postmodern subject. Similarly, Mehlman (1993), writing of Benjamin's unfinished study of French capitalism and consumption, the *Arcades Project*, links the 'kitsch' of childhood gaudy pleasures with the project of reawakening old – political? – desires. The child, like the collector, emerges as a new transgressive subject who disrupts the regime of use value in fetish relationships to objects, and subordinates the ethics of tradition to the sign of genuineness. In particular, there are four areas of convergence between Benjamin and Lyotard which feed into this common image of the child: first, the disruption of the realist notion of truth as singular or transparent; second, the role of narrative forms for strategies of legitimacy; third, abandoning the orderly march of history in favour of a more contingent, spatial and arbitrary notion of knowledge as collection or bricolage; and fourth, a representation of subjectivity as partial and fragmentary.

Elaborating these in turn, first, both theorists share a preoccupation with disrupting transparency theories of language and truth. Lyotard's rationale for 'The Postmodern Condition' relies upon his claims that the grand narratives of legitimation – even those espousing claims of emancipation – including reason, science and (benign) state sovereignty – have lost all credibility within conditions of capitalist technoscience. He argued against the totalising character of claims towards the general or universal (including the general good – such as is put forward by Marxism), as tending towards totalitarianism or at best a coercive normativity. Thus 'legitimacy is secured by the narrative mechanism . . . it secures mastery over time and therefore over life and death. Narrative is authority itself. It authorizes an infrangible *we*, outside of which there is only they' (1984: 44, original emphasis).

The very project of the pursuit of truth becomes suspect, and such claims to do so become topics of scrutiny as motivating narratives that patently depart from that which they proclaim. Similarly in his essay on 'The Task of the Translator', Benjamin highlights the radical non-unitary character of the relation between languages, and between language and meaning:

> Just as a tangent touches a circle lightly and at but one point, with this touch rather than with the point settling the law according to which it is to continue on its straight path to infinity, a translation touches the original lightly and only at the infinitely small point of the sense, thereupon pursuing its own course according to the laws of fidelity in the freedom of linguistic flux.
>
> (Benjamin 1970b: 80–81)

A second major area of convergence concerns a sense of the break in tradition of contemporary consciousness and the significance of narrative modes for strategies of legitimacy. Benjamin (in 'The Storyteller') talks of the demise of storytelling with the rule of information, linking this with new modes of warfare, and the modern disconnection from the role of death in our lives. There is a shared concern with the power of naming and the structuring effects of narrative (with corresponding comments on the significance of names in the enculturation of children, and storytelling as a mode associated with, but not exclusive to, children). In addition to this there is an acute analysis of the possibilities of quotations. Benjamin's ideal work of art consisted entirely of quotations exemplifying what he called a method of 'drilling rather than excavating' (Benjamin, quoted in Hannah Arendt's Introduction to his *Illuminations*, p. 42). Indeed, 'naming through quoting became for him the only possible and appropriate way of dealing with the past without the aid of tradition' (p. 53).

Third, common to both Benjamin and Lyotard is the image of bricolage or collecting rather than orderly systems of knowledge, history or aesthetic criteria. The collector – of which Benjamin says the child is the prototype – inhabits a different world 'in which things are liberated from the drudgery of usefulness' (ibid. p. 47). Tradition separates the positive and negative, whereas collecting levels out all differences and puts forward the criterion of genuineness. Thus the 'passion' of collecting is 'always anarchistic, destructive. For this is its dialectics: to combine with loyalty to an object, to individual items, to things sheltered in his case, a stubborn subversive protest against the typical, the classifiable and idiosyncratic' (ibid. p. 49).

Finally, fourth, both theorists focus on partiality and fragmentation of subjectivity. While he asserted the non-transparency of language, however, Benjamin was concerned with language as cultural artefact and constructor of reality. But beyond this – more 'realist' – endeavour, Benjamin was willing to invoke a different starting point, an alternative tradition in place of the dominant one he critiqued. Just as the paradisic past of Benjamin's 'Theses on the Philosophy of History' allows no easy interpretation as either retroactively rhetorical-inspirational or metaphysical-theological, so the 'good-old-days' of storytelling, the perfect presence of the original (untranslated) work or the fetishised authenticity (instead of literary merit) of the collected work all disrupt the sanctity and harmony of the past even as they allow its invocation. In other words, unlike Lyotard who treats all references to tradition or futurity as harbouring totalitarian totalisings, Benjamin engages in a play of construction and deconstruction that mobilises what it disallows. He thereby reinstitutes the desire for, if not the possibility of, a different set of social arrangements.

Enlightenment for children

In his account of Benjamin's *Aufklärung für Kinder*, Mehlman discusses some 22 of the 30 radio broadcasts Benjamin made (the final one of which he reports is lost). They largely take the form of historical and contemporary cautionary tales. Some focus on stories of deception, where the deceit turns on the broader crime of dissimulation (as in the trickery of the bootleggers who, adopting the disguises for alcohol warranted by prohibition, are able to sell tea at inflated prices to travellers precisely because they believe they are purchasing *more* than tea). Such stories provide perfect vignettes on to the crisis in capitalism, as in Benjamin's broadcast of 'Die Briefmarkenschwindel', the stamp scandals where in order to prevent forgeries genuine stamps are required to be postmarked, but the act of postmarking allows for stamps to pass as forgeries more easily because their surface is obscured. Drawing links between this text and Benjamin's 'The Work of Art in the Age of Mechanical Reproduction', Mehlman (1993: 17) describes this story as 'a primer of deconstruction' according to which the postmark functions with an inherent ambiguity of the sign:

> that essential swindle affecting stamps not from without, but from within: in the post-marks of which we can never be quite sure whether they are signs of validation or disqualification, and which seem to be supplanting the postage stamp *per se* as an institution.
>
> (Mehlman 1993: 19)

Mehlman classifies these broadcasts as concerned with the theme of fraud, and later discusses other stories, about more celebrated figures known for their trickery or sorcery (Cagliostro, Dr Faust, Rauberbanden, Hexenprocesse, Die Zieguner).

The second theme that Mehlman identifies is one of catastrophe, or (natural or man-made) disasters, based on relatively current events of the time: the railbridge disaster of the Firth of Tay, the earthquake at Lisbon, the flooding of the Mississippi in 1927, together with one musing on the relationship between Herculaneum and Pompeii. Mehlman reads these stories as together demonstrating the mutual translation of fraud into catastrophe that underlies Benjamin's critique of progress. The third key theme he identifies – that he surmises was somewhat imposed on Benjamin – is concerned with Berlin. This takes the form of recollected walks, commentaries on areas of the city, discussions about dialects, and shopping. Mehlman goes on to treat these commentaries on Berlin and the pleasures and decays of the city as metonymic referents to Paris, and from thence he weaves his own narrative about Benjamin's life and death.

Explaining the postmodern

Turning now to *The Postmodern Explained to Children*, this is a text of Lyotard's writings, first published (as *Le Postmoderne Expliqué aux Enfants*) in 1986, with the English translation published (in Sydney) in 1992. With its subtitle of *Correspondence 1982–1985* we learn that, unlike Benjamin's scripts, this is not text specifically addressed to children. It comprises short pieces, letters addressed to specific individuals, which the editors of the original French edition see as:

> help[ing] to clear him of certain accusations: irrationalism, neo-conservatism, intellectual terrorism, simple-minded liberalism, nihilism, and cynicism, among others. That is, they are texts that may edify, or clarify points of contention about Lyotard's ideas.
>
> (Editorial Foreword)

Although edited, their status as texts addressed to specific other readers is retained by naming the original addressees and dates on which they were written. Lyotard is reported as having been reluctant to agree to publication on the grounds of the naivety of these texts addressed to children; that, if they were published, their deceptive pedagogical clarity would do nothing to lift the quality of a controversy which was already confused enough. But the editors report convincing him by arguing 'that it would not be a bad thing for even a vague sentiment . . . to appear unaffectedly and in all its indeterminacy'. In sanctioning this edition, Lyotard is therefore invited to exemplify his arguments about incompletion and lack of artifice/defensiveness which forms his topic – the will to mastery and totality as central to all authoritarianisms – in outlining postmodern writing as a form of political intervention (for him this is all the political is). In this sense this book reinscribes its argument about the rhetorics of childhood (as repudiating inhibition, as a celebration of partiality against simplifying totalisations) that forms its topic. Lyotard's preoccupations in these letters range from: definitions of the postmodern, how to conceptualise power – with Nazism as the exemplar of rational, technoscientific power – to the relationships between narrative and strategies of legitimacy. He also discusses modes of writing that allow for resistance, and deals most explicitly with matters of pedagogy and childhood in the final chapter on the possibility of philosophy.

A/symmetries of address

The two texts are clearly differentiated by their contrasting modalities of performance: Benjamin's by voice, Lyotard's by letters. Nevertheless, both assume surprisingly modern confessional forms: both promise to reveal new intimacies or insights about their authors, precisely by virtue of their apparent inconsequentiality. Once again we encounter a modern conventional ideology of childhood, which accords the non-serious, or the playful, privileged status in informing us about the truth, including the truth of the inner self.

Benjamin: 'to' rather than 'for' children

One of the key asymmetries in the two works is the relative visibility of children in their texts. While Mehlman (1993: 2) comments that 'Benjamin, in some of his most striking texts, pretended to write in intimate contact with a dimension of childhood', Benjamin's broadcasts to children are almost devoid of representations of them. This is despite the fact that Benjamin was very interested in children and childhood as a site of commodification. He was an avid collector of children's books and toys, wrote about the origin of toys (as artisanal imitations rather than objects for diversion) and with Asja Lacis, his lover through whom he came into contact with both Brecht and Bolshevism, wrote the 'Programm eines proletarischen Kinderstheaters' in 1928 in which they argued for the impossibility of moral education. Elsewhere he designated as colonial pedagogy any deliberate efforts (whether by National Socialists or Communists) to instil particular norms or values upon children, and was himself actively engaged in student politics. Mehlman (1993: 37) notes that the only radio broadcast that explicitly rewrites a text for adults as one for children ('Neapel') is one he jointly wrote with Asja Lacis, and regards the preoccupation with toys as indicative of Benjamin's interest in the structuring and interpermeability of subjectivity through and with cultural artefacts, since 'the toy is above all that wherein the child negotiates the imposition of an adult agenda' (p. 4).

Thus we can gain some clues about Benjamin's views on children and childhood. Doderer (1996), quoting from a radio broadcast Benjamin made about children's literature (18 August 1928), sees in his theory of children as independent readers a representation of childhood as 'a sort of philosophical place in which knowledge is absorbed and assimilated' (p. 174). Similarly the focus on children's theatre arose from a conception of it as offering a carnival of performance rather than the repetition of formal pedagogy:

> The child does not express itself through things, but things through itself. In the child, creativity and subjectivity have not yet celebrated their bold meeting.
>
> (Lehmann 1996: 189)

It is not that children are accorded special insight, but that they afford a *'suspension of all knowledge'* (Benjamin, quoted in Lehmann 1996: 185, original emphasis). (Chapters 11 and 12 take up the metaphor of 'suspension' in terms of the relations between knowledge, memory and childhood.) This interruption of the positing of knowledge is what links Benjamin's representation of the child with his notion of the signal, or the gesture:

> Truely revolutionary is the effect of the *secret signal* of the future that speaks out of the gesture of the child.
>
> (Benjamin, quoted in Lehmann 1996: 187, original emphasis)

His discussion of the child's gesture imbues this with a quality of 'presence of mind [which] means letting oneself go in the moment of danger' (ibid.). Benjamin is thus subscribing to a variety of spontaneism that portrays planning and even intention as constraining and spoiling, since the key feature is the *interruption* of rationality. Lehmann (1996: 189) notes, but limits, the political ambiguities of such a model as follows:

> It is tempting to speak of irrationalism here, but in contrast to the vitalistic and 'philosophy of life' ideologemes of programmatic irrationalism, Benjamin is concerned with localizing non-conscious impulses and structures in the realm of practical expressive behaviours, not with their ideological hypostatization. They have a concrete place, such as the theatre, the text, and the child's gesture. Benjamin attempts to give this de-subjectivization a political name when he describes the child itself, and not merely the community of children, as the 'child's collective'.
>
> (II, 766)

Returning to the broadcasts, the only one in which a child figures (as topic rather than addressee) is 'Berlin Spielzeugwanderung', which retells the then well-known story of a little girl, Tinchen, whose wanderings into temptation are prompted by her mission to save her brothers from the evil magician. The girl as suffering and tested subject places the story within familiar genres of modern folk tales: she is, Benjamin comments, Faust as a little girl. It is the pleasure and temptation of gifts and toys that prompt the kidnapping of the boys, and the story concerns the various ways Tinchen is (almost) tempted to depart from her plans to rescue them. But Benjamin transforms the tale so that Tinchen's arenas of temptation become the galleries of toys in Berlin shops, and dwells upon their pleasures (at the expense of resolving the tale with the rescue of the brothers).

Mehlman analyses this tale as an early version of a piece to appear in the *Arcades Project* expressing Benjamin's enduring fascination with the forms and processes of commodity fetishism. Benjamin's treatment of the Tinchen tale is also used by Mehlman as the link to Benjamin's own desires for the 'procuring street' expressed in his autobiographical piece 'A Sexual Awakening', where Benjamin describes the occasion of becoming separated from a relative who was taking him to a synagogue service at New Year, and experiencing a rush of excitement: 'the violation of the holiday united with the procuring street, which made me anticipate for the first time the services with which it was to supply adult desires' (Benjamin, quoted in Mehlman 1993: 70).

The pleasures of Berlin, which Mehlman treats as equivalent to those of the Paris where Benjamin lived during the 1930s, become for Mehlman a metaphor for his lingering there. In Mehlman's text the explicit reference to the child rapidly metonymises into Benjamin himself, and more than this, the tale becomes an allegory for his own end ('the ultimately tragic decision to remain in Paris as war approached', Mehlman 1993: 71). This is portrayed by Mehlman within the framework of a Jewish secular messianic tradition which treats capitalist consumption and fascism as the twin evils that Benjamin struggled to 'defeat from within'.

Yet in Benjamin's own text (as far as is discernible from available translations), children are addressed as fully participating social subjects – albeit in the process of (self) discovery. Taking 'The Stamp Scam' as an example (as one of the few complete texts available in translation, reproduced in *London Review of Books*, 3 August 1995: 5), while this broadcast in general is driven onwards through third person statements (such as 'This is the moment to evoke' or 'It should be said in passing'), the child audience is enlisted into generalised personhood as ambiguous participants through statements prefaced by 'Few collectors know', or 'Contrary to popular belief', and in more covert ways through the occasional 'of courses' which both recognise the audience's presence and accord them knowledge of the practices under discussion. Further, Benjamin's occasional second person address to his hearers positions children as knowing subjects engaged in practices of – not only consumption – but active (even subversive) exchange. The formulations below convey something of both his style and argument, with the formulation of 'you all know' treating children as versed in this particular practice (of stamp collecting) – while not necessarily as experts, but as practising participants, as in: 'You all know, thanks to your catalogue . . .; If you happen to subscribe to a stamp collecting journal you will know . . .; You are aware that as soon as there are stamp collections there are forgeries . . .; Those of you who remain stamp collectors . . . with practice, you will find ways to fend off forgeries . . .; You all know that mass mailings, already today, are sent out not with stamps but with postmarks . . .; Those of you who would not like to be caught short would perhaps do well to envisage a collection of postmarks.'

There is nothing mysterious about the address to children in this text; it is a clear act of edification, education, a synthesis of Benjamin's ideas about the scandalous indistinguishability of authenticity and fraudulence, and about how technological developments challenge notions of originality and reverse values (such that the postmark supplants the stamp as the collector's item). Not for nothing were these texts named under the rubric of Enlightenment. Further, the third term of the real, the world outside the home is one of transgression, the thrilling invitation to consume its pleasures. The practices of development – happenings in Benjamin's sense – are therefore initiations thoroughly tied to cultural-political contexts rather than abstract mental attributes of the child. The child *as child* is not addressed as some pre-given subject outside culture, but as initiatory consumer.

Lyotard: 'about' rather than 'to' children

By contrast, Lyotard appears to invoke the figure of the child much more readily. This occurs most explicitly in the final chapter, 'Address on the Subject of the Course of Philosophy', but there are references scattered throughout the text: on the pedagogical and normalising roles of narrative, so the child, 'like immigrants', 'enter[s] culture through an apprenticeship in proper names' (Lyotard 1992: 41). He muses on the evils of technological progress as '[a] final blow to humanity's narcissism: it is at the service of complexification. At this moment the stage is being set in the unconscious of the young. In your own' (1992: 100). This last comment makes a typical shift of topic from children as future citizens to the damage done to that part of ourselves that corresponds to it. In the 'Gloss on Resistance', alongside a critique of economic 'development', Lyotard advocates as a strategy of resistance a mode of writing that 'follows the line of the body' to:

> use these forms in an attempt to bear witness to what really matters: the childhood of an encounter, the welcome extended to the marvel that (something) is happening, the respect for the events. Don't forget, you were and are this yourself: the welcomed marvel, the respected event, the childhood shared by your parents.
>
> (1992: 112)

Here we see connections with Benjamin's notion of the event: for Lyotard the child is the event – the possibility of 'happening'. But unlike the violent rupture of the call to, or of, the past in Benjamin's apocalyptic exhortation to 'sieze hold of a memory as it flashes up at a moment of danger' (Benjamin 1970a: 259), Lyotard's representation invites a more contained and domesticated reading; one which is normalised through the generalised appeal to the child 'we each were' (and supposedly still are at heart), eclipsing such questions as 'were we really?' and 'who are "we"?', and installing a normative originary story within the patriarchal family.

The final chapter of *The Postmodern Explained to Children* considers whether the course of philosophy follows a philosophical course. This text was written in response to an inquiry about a course from a father to Lyotard, who then replies to his son. We are treated to an explicitly didactic interlude framed as 'the prospectus for the "Education and Philosophy" seminars sent to me by your father . . . A few words to the son' (p. 115). This developmental question about the course of philosophy prompts a set of comments about the nature of childhood in relation to philosophy:

> The assumption is that the mind is not given to men as it should be and has to be re-formed. Childhood is the monster of philosophers. It is also their accomplice. Childhood tells them that the mind is not given. But that it is possible.
>
> (p. 115)

> Secondly, we know that commencing does not mean proceeding genealogically (as if genealogy, and especially the diachrony of historians, was not in question). The monster child is not the father of the man; it is what, in the midst of man, throws him off course *[son décours];* it is the possibility or risk of being adrift. We always begin in the middle.
>
> (p. 116)

Lyotard draws out the implications for philosophy, philosophy education and education per se of this understanding of the 'monster childhood' as intrinsic to the creative philosophical process. Didactically and pedagogically, he proclaims that there can be no pedagogy and links this not only to the project of writing, but also to some fairly conventional comments about the state of schools today and the crisis in childhood, according to which children may be less childlike than adults:

> Maybe there is more childhood available to thought at thirty-five than at eighteen, and more outside a degree course than in one. A new task for didactic thought: to search out its childhood anywhere and everywhere, even outside childhood.
>
> (Lyotard 1992: 123)

More than this, he identifies the domain of childhood with the insubstantial and unformulated (or even unformulatable). Premature and impertinent, the act of writing strives to be before it is. Here, then, the condition of childhood is a state of impatient striving, of impudent claims that cannot yet be delivered:

> I think writing a philosophical text, alone at one's table (or taking a walk . . .) implies exactly the same paradox. We write before knowing what to say and how to say it, and in order to find out, if possible. Philosophical writing is ahead of where it is supposed to be. Like a child, it is premature and insubstantial. We recommence, but we cannot rely on it getting to thought itself, there, at the end. For the thought is here, muddled up in the unthought, trying to sort out the impertinent babble of childhood.
>
> (Lyotard 1992: 119)

The psychobiographical child

In the remainder of this chapter I move from the contrasting rhetorics of childhood motivated by Benjamin and Lyotard to consider the frames that constrain or warrant such readings. Specifically, my concern shifts to focus on Mehlman's rhetorics of childhood mobilised through Benjamin, as informed also by Lyotard's treatments of 'the child'. I have already discusssed how my access to Benjamin's broadcasts is structured through Mehlman's account. Here we encounter a psychobiographical child, since Mehlman's essay on Benjamin's broadcasts is explicitly premised on a reading of the radio broadcasts as equivalent to a psychoanalytic encounter with Benjamin:

> For we are dealing here with a record of a contractual mandate assumed by Benjamin: to speak non-stop for 20 minutes, on schedule, before an invisible audience, from the perspective of 'childhood', on any subject of his choosing.
>
> (Mehlman 1993: 3)

Mehlman argues that the case for this psychoanalytical treatment is bolstered, rather than undermined, by Benjamin's own dismissiveness of the material's worth. Benjamin is quoted as having written:

> As far as whatever I do for merely economic reasons is concerned, in magazines or for the radio, I no longer write out almost anything, and simply expedite such affairs through dictation.
>
> (Benjamin, quoted in Mehlman 1993)

The broadcasts are interpreted by Mehlman as 'in important ways . . . lacking in "composition", bereft of that "secondary elaboration", which is the ego's prime instrument of defense' (Mehlman 1993: 3–4). These considerations are used by Mehlman as warranting the status of the '*Aufklärung für Kinder*, an adult's on-schedule, nonstop, virtually unedited discourse of and for childhood, as the closest we can hope to come to the transcript of a psychoanalysis of Benjamin' (p. 5). Mehlman proceeds to use Benjamin's broadcasts as a rendering of Benjamin's own life and preoccupations.[3] He does this in two ways: first, as a prefiguring of events in Benjamin's life and death – specifically in his interpretation of how Benjamin's account of 'Die Mississippi-Uberschwemmung 1927', the Mississippi flood of 1927, foreshadows his own end, with its central character throwing himself in desperation into the water just before rescue arrives. He treats this as equivalent to the circumstances of Benjamin's own death (although both Eagleton 1981 and Löwy 1985 offer different interpretations of these final events): '"Die Mississippi-Uberschwemmung 1927" thus manages to anticipate in its second half the end of Benjamin's life even as it rewrites as a tale of the Mississippi the underlying configuration of the 1923 essay "The Task of the Translator"' (Mehlman 1993: 3–4).

Second, he treats the radio broadcasts as prefiguring the themes of Benjamin's later work, with the broadcasts functioning as the arena or playground for the development of his ideas. He thus draws connections between them and Benjamin's 'Theses on the Philosophy of History', his unfinished *Arcades Project* and his pieces on 'A Berlin Childhood'. The theme of fraud and catastrophe he links to Benjamin's theory of the 'interception' of the symbol by allegory, the 'weak messianism' of the theses via the kabbalistic apocalypse: 'Thus "kabbalism", (false) messianism, and biblical apocalypse invest our twin series of fraud and catastrophe, even as they may facilitate their apparent mutual translatability' (Mehlman 1993: 27).

From content to pragmatic form

If Mehlman resorts to psychobiographical representations of the development of Benjamin, Lyotard presents childhood as form rather than content. So in the 'Memorandum on Legitimacy', Chapter 4 of *The Postmodern Explained to Children*, Lyotard comments: 'The important thing for our question seems to me to be the pragmatics of narration itself rather than the analysis of narrative contents' (Lyotard 1992: 55). What are the narrative pragmatics of this reading of Benjamin? Mehlman's developmental/psychoanalytic project to unravel the truths of Benjamin's inner self and development is itself replete with imagery of childhood. His primary claim is that the text is the child, in the sense that the radio broadcasts are treated as Benjamin's playground, the forum for the elaboration of his later ideas: 'This capacity to shift from translating the work to prefiguring the life is an indication of just how nodal and hybrid a formation within Benjamin's oeuvre the radio scripts of *Aufklärung für Kinder* may be' (Mehlman 1993: 34). But other varieties of positionings can be identified. First, 'we' are the children, as those who want to learn and struggle with such writing. 'We' as child-learners, who struggle with 'difficult' writing, would look to such a title as offering a simple 'child's version' as a 'beginners guide': 'The circumstance [of Benjamin's radio broadcasts] is, at first blush, as implausible as an anthology of fairy tales by Hegel, a child's garden of deconstruction by Derrida. And yet it is precisely that latter case, a hybrid of the French philosopher with Robert Louis Stephenson' (Mehlman 1993: 2).

Is the address to the child different when we are concerned with postmodernism rather than Enlightenment? Mehlman's account contrasts with Lyotard's titular address *to* children, which speaks to adults *about* children, or tries to evoke the child within the adult. While children figure in Lyotard's text, unlike Benjamin's broadcasts they could scarcely be considered for children. Nor are they introductory, although they may be informative. As the translators to the English edition comment:

> So the promise of the title to 'explain to children' what adults find obscure is surely ironic and not to be taken literally. It will not have explained the postmodern. Rather, it will have shown why it is necessary to approach the philosophical questions raised by postmodernity both with patience and with the mind of the child. For childhood is the season of the mind's possibilities and of the possibility of philosophy.

(In this spirit they go on to acknowledge 'the other "kids" who have helped us along the way with the translation'.)

We might summarise this difference by saying that Benjamin assumes a didactic *address to* children, whereas Lyotard (didactically) invites us to *be* children. In both cases authorial (adult) claims to make such recommendations are assumed. Yet Benjamin in Enlightenment style portrays children as in need of (political) edification; Lyotard too adopts such a pedagogical position (albeit that we are the indirect audience for these pieces) only with the added prescription that we should be children. In both cases a thoroughly modern notion of childhood is invoked as a state of potentiality, of possibility.

As with the Mehlman text, then, we can explore the role childhood plays in the narrative form of Lyotard's text. First, the appeal to the child is used to warrant the publication of these short texts to disarm criticisms and critics of Lyotard. Second, as indicated earlier, the writing is qualified as childlike in its naive (and deceptive) pedagogical clarity. However, third, these pieces are offered as a record of thought in its moment of becoming; incompleteness as a condition of genuine development (as opposed to oppressive constraints performed in the name of 'progress'): 'to appear unaffectedly and in all its indeterminacy' (Editorial Foreword to Lyotard 1992). Nevertheless, fourth, he wards off a reading of childhood as outside reason; rather, incompletion is a condition for change and genuine reflection:

> 'What would happen if thought no longer had a childhood?'. In these pages Lyotard approaches the postmodern as a way of maintaining the possibility of thought 'happening' – in philosophy, art literature and politics; of thought proceeding when it has lost faith in its capacity to repair the crimes of the past by guiding the present towards the end of the realisation of ideas. If it is no longer possible, or credible, to assume the authority to speak for the future, what escape is there from an endless repetition of the already said? But thought has to proceed.
>
> (Editorial Foreword to Lyotard 1992)

In true modern style, the child is appealed to as a symbol of our ideal/better selves – or at the very least Lyotard's formulations are vulnerable to recuperation within that modernist rhetoric. While Benjamin's broadcasts are to children as specified, real entities situated within concrete practices, Lyotard's address is to the metaphorical child. Whether as life stage, writing style or metaphysical quality, these are decidedly modern conceptions.

Intertextualities

The two texts stand not only in a relation of historical, but also intellectual, succession to each other. Lyotard writes after, and through a reading of, Benjamin's work. He refers to Benjamin three times in this book, once specifically in relation to Benjamin's writings on childhood. This is precisely to justify the links he (Lyotard) makes between childhood, the event and resistance to totalitarianism. His point here is to warrant his reading of childhood and celebration of childishness not as that which is ineffable and inadmissible, but as the style of production of such incursions. It is worth quoting the passage in full:

> Let us recall – in opposition to this murder of the instant and singularity [that characterises totalitarian bureaucracy] – those short pieces in Walter Benjamin's 'One Way Street' and 'Berlin Childhood', pieces Theodor Adorno would call 'micrologies'. *They do not describe events and inscribe childhood but capture the childhood of the event and inscribe what is uncapturable about it*. And what makes the encounter with a word, smell, place, book or face into an event is not its newness compared to other 'events'. It is its very value as an initiation. You only learn this later. It cut open a wound in the sensibility. You know this because it has reopened since and will reopen again, marking out the rhythm of a secret and perhaps unnoticed temporality. This wound ushered you into an unknown world, but without ever making it known to you. Such initiation initiates nothing. It just begins.

> You fight against the cicatrisation [mark left by scar in the process of healing] of the event, against its categorisation of 'childishness', to preserve initiation. This is the fight fought by writing against bureaucratic Newspeak. Newspeak has to tarnish the wonder that (something) is happening. The same thing is at stake for the guerilla of love against the code of feelings: to save the instant from what is customary or understood.
>
> (Lyotard 1992, emphasis added)

Thus Lyotard's reading of Benjamin takes the child as guardian of the event, drawing on Benjamin's designation of the event as the index of a history that is not dead (or, for Lyotard, does not kill us – by terror or totalitarianism). The child therefore becomes the icon – not of that which is not captured by, or doomed to repeat, a symbol of presentations and possibilities (Lyotard 1983), the mistakes of the past, nor as overwhelmed by the enormity of its legacies – but of its conditions of production. But this distinction is hard to maintain. The child returns as that which is daring, open, fresh, as being prepared to take risks, as living with the uncertainty of outcome, being non-goal directed (and subscribes to the modern liberal ideology of play):

> [Thought] has to relinquish its presumption, set out without knowing its destination or its destiny, leave itself open to the unfamiliarity of whatever may occur to it, and make rules in the absence of rules.
>
> (English Foreword to Lyotard 1992)

> Childhood is the season of the mind's possibilities and of the possibility of philosophy.
>
> (Lyotard 1992: 116)

> One had to – one has to – endure the childhood of thought.
>
> (Lyotard 1992: 118)

There is thus a further irony that lies behind the initial irony of the title of Lyotard's text – the apology for its obscurity becomes a restatement of its rationale. The issue is not how to explain the postmodern, but rather how we should, and could, approach these questions. So it becomes explanatory, even didactic, in specifying the attitude of what we must have been in order to understand the questions through the invocation to recover the child within.

The child as synonym for creativity is treated by the editors as exemplified in Lyotard's own text. It is incomplete, composed of fragments of correspondence that are not bound together in any coherent whole – except through the trope of the child. It contradicts some of his earlier writings (he explicitly retracts the 'exaggerated' importance he accorded narrative). It is partial (both in the sense of being addressed to specific individuals, and as following particular – didactic – agendas). And it is intertextual, making mutual reference between the different parts with such comments portrayed as exemplifying the style its arguments advocate.

In the end Lyotard's celebration of childhood arises through its counter-position to modern mastery – the mastery of technoscience which disallows the genuinely innovatory. Since both Benjamin and Lyotard are hostile to the project of the Enlightenment, the child that is invoked is not the child of developmental psychology, of normative regularities and natural rhythms (Morss 1996; Burman 1997b, 2007a). Nevertheless, through the link with the body/sensual, this conception is tied to nature and thus recuperable to bourgeois/romantic progressivist notions. This becomes explicit precisely where Lyotard becomes most programmatic about how to make intervention (in his conception, through writing):

> We must extend the line of the body in the line of writing. The labour of writing is allied to the work of love; but it inscribes the trace of the initiatory event in language and thus offers to share it, if not as a sharing of knowledge, at least as a sharing of a sensibility which it can and should take as communal.
>
> (Lyotard 1992: 112)

The charge of organicism is precisely the one that commentators (after Adorno) have worked hard to defend Benjamin from (see e.g. Löwy 1985). But it is less easy to see how Lyotard can avoid this. While there is nothing new about according divine powers to children, the 'weak messianism' that Benjamin endows to all people in marking our redemptive claims to happiness is formulated as a call to action, to settle those claims justly (not 'cheaply'). Lyotard has no such depth to the surface of his call to style. This is all there is: the child as the contour of the writing of the body cannot be defended from such charges.

At issue is not the project to connect with the body – for this, as so much current theory claims, is the way to retrieve theory's links with specificity and materiality. Rather, the problem is the generalised and thereby naturalised, model of the child that he invokes. This is a variety of child that totalises, idealises and excludes in the very ways that Lyotard resorted to it to escape.

In terms of our theme of intertextualities, if Lyotard traces his claim to the child through Benjamin, it is significant that Eagleton (1985) develops his vituperative critique of postmodernism, and specifically of Lyotard's account of *The Postmodern Condition*, through juxtaposition with Benjamin. Eagleton would therefore strongly argue against the enlistment of Benjamin into Lyotard's account of postmodernity. The first incompatibility is Benjamin's 'revolutionary nostalgia' ('the power of active remembrance as a ritual summoning and invocation of the traditions of the oppressed in violent constellation with the political present', Eagleton 1985: 64), vs. the Nietzschean 'active forgetting' of history ('the healthy spontaneous anamnesis of the animal who has wilfully repressed its own sordid determinations and so is free') espoused by poststructuralists. At issue here is the critique of metanarratives, and, as such, claims to have ended history. Eagleton refuses the viability of the distinction between modernity and postmodernity by reference to Benjamin. His charge of ahistoricism and Nietzschean forgetting is not without resonance in *The Postmodern Explained to Children*. For here Lyotard explicitly refuses a periodising definition of postmodernism and states:

> You can see that when it is understood in this way, the 'post' of 'postmodern' does not signify a movement of repetition but a procedure in 'ana-': a procedure of analysis, anamnesis, anagogy and anamorphosis which elaborates an 'initial forgetting'.
>
> (Lyotard 1992: 93)

Eagleton claims that (unlike the privileged jetsetters who perhaps really do inhabit a postmodern condition) most of us live in a largely modern world, or straddle the contradictions of postmodern calls to pleasure and consumption along with modern commitments to work and relationships: 'We are still, perhaps, poised as precariously as Benjamin's Baudelairian *flâneur* between the rapidly fading aura of the old humanist subject and the ambivalently energizing and repellent shapes of a city landscape' (Eagleton 1985: 72). It is amid an equivalent ambivalence that the rhetorical trope of the child is caught: as inevitably modern even as, and precisely through which, it is hailed as postmodern. At issue is not a call to dispense with metaphorics of childhood – for this – whether we inhabit a modern or a postmodern world – would seem to be impossible. Powerful and apparently unavoidable, the issue is to know what it is we are doing with the address to childhood.

Towards endings: forwards into the past

In this chapter I have analysed the problematic of the appeal to the child in contemporary cultural theory through a reading of the writings of Lyotard and Benjamin on this topic. I have argued that the play with imagery of childhood is a dangerous game for political progressives engaging with postmodern discourse. Its problems arise because of the maintenance of precisely the modern relations of oppression that advocates of the postmodern claim to transcend, through the idealisation and naturalisation of the implicit subject of the child. Moreover, the fashionable claims to ineffability or inarticulacy threaten to allow bourgeois-humanist assumptions (of nature and development) to return with all their corresponding (racial, class and gender) exclusions and hierarchies, and to render them even more incontestable. Combined with an implicit mysticism, the return to the natural, through the generalised and abstracted character of the child invoked, is particularly worrying. However, given the mediated character of the textual explorations of childhood in this chapter it is perhaps fitting to close by highlighting a further diverging narrative, also warding off significant assimilation of the commented upon text to its commentaries. Benjamin's angel is impelled backwards into the future – progress is thus inevitable and lamentable, but can be disrupted by inspirational 'memories' of different social arrangements. Mehlman's essay on Benjamin, however, inverts this dynamic to step backwards into the past facing forwards. This reversal of Benjamin's design serves to pin down precisely those elements of significant indeterminacy that are all that remains of historical contingency and turn them into fact – a strange reading indeed of the possibility of 'the event'.

As part of his 'psychobiography' Mehlman positions us, with him, as contemporary readers of Benjamin, in an appropriative move reading the history and theories that form the problematic of Mehlman's (and our?) own childhood as the Central Park of New York that Benjamin wrote about and aspired to reach (Adorno had arranged a visa for the USA) but was never to see:

> Walter Benjamin, that is, was not merely the absence in whose shadow, in Central Park, we played. He was a *raconteur*, an entertainer of children with words we never heard, but which, after the fact, may be read, such is my intent, as an unsuspected matrix out of which much of what is most forceful in contemporary criticism may be derived.
>
> (Mehlman 1993: 7)

This general contemporary position then becomes specified as referring to Mehlman himself. We move from child to adult: Benjamin's texts are 'a child's garden: one whose own blooms, transplanted, much of an entire critical generation, my own, might be construed, after the fact, as having passed its maturity cultivating' (Mehlman 1993: 2). But there is also a more historical-epistemological differentiation in Mehlman's text, according to which Benjamin figures as the child, with us as adults. In this, Primo Levi is presented as the quintessential post-Holocaust (adult) subject – the survivor who has lost his childhood innocence – characterised explicitly by Mehlman as the ability to love:

> There is a sense, of course, in which to have died before the genocide is tantamount, in this last half of the twentieth century, to having retained a certain innocence, even childhood. For this reason we will conclude these pages on Benjamin's scripts for children by examining a

> text that takes up elements that have surfaced in our reading, but with a devastating hindsight – if not maturity – that were denied to Benjamin himself.
>
> (Mehlman 1993: 91)

Mehlman traces connections through Freud, as well as his reading of Benjamin's broadcasts, on the play between catastrophe and trauma, and thus paves the way for the larger, but largely implicit, preoccupation he brings to the book; with why Benjamin did not avoid and avert the repetition of trauma that was his death, and the death of millions of others. He therefore makes the classic psychohistorical move (glossed as postmodern intertextuality) to read history back on to biography. Cast within the rhetoric of poststructuralist-informed literary criticism, this becomes: this is what Benjamin could have known, or: these are intimations of events we might wonder whether he knew when writing at this earlier point, had he written this later. That is, it is in a mood of wondering: our wonder at what it could have been like to be him. Thus, as the unknown, Benjamin is addressed within the same discursive complex as that in which we place children within post/modern educational and philosophical practices. What is it like to be you? What do you know? What do you know now that you will come to know you knew later? What do you know now that you will lose later? (i.e. what access to hidden truths can you reveal to us?)

Ultimately, for Mehlman, the connection between catastrophe and repetition revolves around why Benjamin remained in France when he could have escaped to North America: what trauma did he set out to repeat by thereby bringing about his own death? This is the key question US (and to a lesser extent British) post-war Jewry asks of (mainland) European Jews: how could you not have known? In what ways did you know, but chose not to know? But aside from the question of responsibility and collusion here (and the dependence of the argument on a psychoanalytic account of unconscious knowledge), there is the question of the foreclosure of history. 'Looking back now', the analytic project of reading converges with the psychoanalytic project of understanding. But both operate within a framework of overdetermination that threatens to flatten out historical accident and opportunity into a smooth linear pathway to the present as we know it now to be. Such a narrative move would function precisely to disallow the kinds of historical ruptures and possibilities that Benjamin so vividly portrayed in his *Theses*.

Thus Mehlman offers a dystopian progressivist account of Benjamin in his psychoanalysis of Benjamin's texts for children; dystopian, because the world we live in has scarcely 'progressed' from the one that Benjamin inhabited. The events that informed and ended (or made him end) his life, that is European fascism and the Nazi genocide of Jews, are (indicators of) what makes this world a dystopia. Mehlman explicitly marks this in his text in two ways: the bulk of his 'essay on [Benjamin's] radio years' (the subtitle of his book) is framed within a chapter that is called 'Childhood', while the second and final, much shorter, chapter he calls 'Maturity'. In this he juxtaposes Benjamin's intimations of the future 'Nazi beast' (through a reading of a final set of Benjamin's radio broadcasts for children entitled 'True Stories about Dogs' which retell some 'traditional dog stories', interpreted by Mehlman as exemplifying the master–slave dialectic) with Primo Levi's treatment – of both the same stories and other works. The theme now shifts from trauma and catastrophe to collaboration and complicity; Levi's explicit ruminations on these, Mehlman's speculations on Benjamin's collusion in his own death (that it was not clear that he would not have been allowed over the border, the scenario of his death that Mehlman interprets as foretold/retrospectively reflected in Benjamin's story of the survivor of the Mississippi flood disaster of 1927 who killed himself in desperation just before rescue and salvation arrived, but see Eagleton, Löwy, Broderson and Žižek for alternative interpretations). However, the theme of childhood as innocence returns metaphorised as the poetic reality of biography, marking the developmental connection between Benjamin and Levi:

> Thus do we encounter, at the heart of Levi's memoir, the twin motifs of fraudulence and catastrophe (the flood), whose meshing provided us with the subtext of Benjamin's radio scripts. As though the adult Levi, in the wake of his personal catastrophe, were seeking to piece his life together again on the basis of a structure that might have been absorbed on German radio during his childhood.
>
> (Mehlman 1993: 94)

By such rhetorical moves, and in his misguided misrenderings of a Benjaminesque theme of restoration, Mehlman succeeds in warranting the imposition of a unitary childhood upon those not (wanting to be) wracked by survivor guilt. The invocation of a lost past takes the form not of a return to a mythical past that is fictive but inspirationally real, but rather the desire to figure a subjectivity that has escaped the trauma of existence in late modernity. This kind of childhood is thus absolutely metaphysical and runs counter to both Benjamin's and Lyotard's conceptions. Moreover, the attitude of mourning that drives it, while perhaps a comprehensible response to the events that have accompanied or preceded our lives, leaves us fixed upon that past tragedy and renders us incapable of attending to current and future projects, including children's own.

Part II

Developing images

This part of the book builds on the theoretical critiques of Part I to move into policy discussions. The focus is on representations of childhood, as a way of illustrating the textually mediated character of models of children and childhood, with a particular attention to contemporary images of children.

Chapter 4, 'Childhood, Sexual Abuse and Contemporary Political Subjectivities', addresses questions of representation in terms of campaigns around child abuse.

Chapter 5, 'Sexuality: Contested Relationships Around the Control of Desire and Action' explores in relation to two filmic texts how the gendering of childhood not only inflects discussions of childhood sexuality but also indicates the emergence of a new political subject.

Drawing on psychoanalytic theory, Chapter 6, 'Appealing and Appalling Children', addresses the complex emotional dynamics mobilised by representations of children that are invoked especially by charity appeals.

These chapters combine to underscore the more implicit and sometimes less comfortable responses to representations of children and childhood that need to be understood in order to bring about change. They pose questions about the conceptual and methodological underpinnings of models of reflexivity, and how these can perhaps help support more accountable – if not transparent – practices of representation.

4 Childhood, sexual abuse and contemporary political subjectivities

Taking child sexual abuse as its key frame, this chapter explores a range of textual representations that elucidate ambiguities surrounding the special status accorded childhood within the UN Convention on the Rights of the Child (1989). These ambiguities include apparent contradictions around the significance accorded gender, the ways childhood functions culturally as an icon of the true self (and even the lost self), and with the 'natural' qualities associated with childhood giving rise to some key tensions in practice. The analysis is used to help explain claims for the contemporary crisis around childhood, and with this it becomes possible to move beyond both the unhelpful status of childhood as originary state demanding restoration and overgeneralised developmental claims, to instead focus on what particular children in particular contexts need now.

While explicit links are made between individual and economic development, and between normative childhoods lived in the North and South, this chapter takes policy and popular cultural texts from my local context (Manchester, UK) as the primary arena for analysis. There is an attention to how practices of 'de-' or 'under'-development are actively pursued at home as well as away, so disrupting the simplistic mapping of north and south as geographical regions, to address racialised and class stratifications. In doing so, it departs from the previously published version of this text (Burman (2003c) in the Reavey and Warner 2003, collection), being based on a longer and earlier version, which is now updated here to take account of later developments, in particular in relation to the children's charity fund-raising campaigns discussed. Hence alongside some attention (through the cultural examples) to the affective responses to and the consumer characteristics addressed to and associated with children and childhood, we see as an emerging feature how poverty and economic factors are rendered invisible and so undebatable, even (or especially?) as discussions of child abuse (and especially child sexual abuse) gain greater attention.

This chapter situates discussions of child sexual abuse by first highlighting childhood as a conceptual-political construct accessible only as mediated by practices of textualisation. Second, it explores some political consequences of the particular texts of childhood we are currently heir to, and in particular the need to ward off some of the current political and textual imperatives attending these. Five narratives of childhood, in which child sexual abuse is crucially implicated, are critically interrogated. These are: the special status of childhood; the gendering of the child; the child as true or lost self; the naturalness of the child; and claims of the 'crisis in childhood'. In this regard six specific current textual varieties are discussed: childhood as originary state; the rights or privileges of childhood; giving children back their future; children as prefiguring our future; the general (Western) culture of infantilisation; and the child as superegoic injunction. Third, and finally, I identify as an avenue for subverting the seemingly incontestable and monolithic character of development the strategy of using the homologies between the different 'developments' to indicate alternatives.

The chapter addresses three main areas. First, it highlights the textualisation of childhood, within whose broader forms representations of child sexual abuse occur. Second, it explores some political consequences of some currently circulating texts of childhood to ward off the current political imperatives (towards action and intervention) attending these. Finally, the chapter ends by attempting to identify strategies for the subversion of the models of development that discourses of child sexual abuse fracture, but equally by which they suffer.

Framing childhood texts

It is fitting that I start by clarifying the purpose of my own text here. Even though I am as subject as anyone else to the discourses of childhood I want to topicalise, I nevertheless want to offset the reproduction of their effects by commenting upon them. Of course I cannot prescribe how any reader of this text will interpret the arguments I present: whatever my intentions, my account will be understood differently according to readers' specific positions, histories and preoccupations. This reflects how, under late capitalism, authorial intention is rendered increasingly irrelevant in relation to audience receptivities (see discussion in Parker 2002). But contrary to a relativist position, I want to assume some responsibility for interpretation that my speaking position here endows.

In relation both to child sexual abuse and the broader discourses or narratives of childhood that this gives rise to, my focus is on moral qualities that surround texts of childhood. So, since part of what I want to talk about is the emotionality surrounding children and childhood, let me make clear at the outset that my aim here is to not to instil states of guilt, sentimentality, titillation, pity, horror or outrage. As explored further in

Chapter 6, these are, however, well-rehearsed, culturally sanctioned responses to children – whether the specific individual children of our homes, schools, streets and shopping precincts, the children of our families – or more abstract, distant or even rhetorical categories of children. Notice how I am now speaking of the spaces of childhood, mapping the geography of childhood living, and the ways this intersects with other institutional arenas of production and consumption (Boyden with Holden 1991; Moss and Petrie 2002). But outside the allocated spaces of childhood within Western industrialised life, children inhabit shadier places where they are regarded as not belonging. Here they appear as matters of management and policy – children in care, children in need, children subject to child protection legislation, children on behalf of whom we intervene to 'restore' the conditions for the kind of childhoods we approve. Moreover, beyond these, there are other children who are seemingly active agents in warranting these somehow 'abnormal' interventions; with such interventions formulated as 'in the best interests of' or 'on behalf of' children who work, children who have sex, children whose work is having sex; children who steal, bully or even murder (see Burman 1995c). Where, then, do children who have been sexually abused fit into this broader landscape? Are they damaged but innocent (but where does this leave those who might be 'culpable')? Are they tainted with the crime and offence that they themselves have been subject to? Let us pause for just a moment to take stock.

A first point to note is that I have hardly begun and yet we are already in the domain of normative prescription: the 'shoulds' and 'oughts' of what children are like, with correspondingly negative evaluation of children who don't 'fit' our notions. Second, the much vaunted pleasure children bring seems to subsist within two sets of relations: for 'what children are' is constituted within sets of institutional relationships that are currently the site of much political focus – the family, schools, healthcare, etc. The uneasy relationship between children who have been sexually abused with the overall category of childhood is precisely what is at play here; for the above throw into question the viability of precisely those safe, comfortable spaces for children – family, schools, care – they are said to protect. Moreover, I would also suggest that the 'right' kinds of childhood also exist because in some sense they repudiate, but at the same time require for their existence, the very stigmatised forms of childhood that they thereby display they are not (see Chapter 8).

So – to return to my initial comments about emotions and standpoint – even before we move to take account of the more metaphorical or rhetorical appeals to childhood, we are into affective domains that are highly politicised and highly emotionally charged (see also this volume, Chapter 6). Even before we start to link children and development with broader social themes and trajectories it is clear that (what counts as) a desirable or undesirable childhood stands in a relation of mutual constitution: each in some sense relies upon the other.

I should perhaps make clear that I am not a child rights, child policy, or child services specialist. Nor am I even a specialist in development studies in the broader sense of international economic development – although I like to explore how the different notions of development are related to each other (and I will say more about this soon; see also Chapter 9). My interest lies in the claims made for and about children; and, beyond individually embodied children, in the notions of childhood these presuppose, and their corresponding associations and reverberations. I want to discuss the political subjectivities mobilised by such notions, hopefully the better to determine which political subjectivities we should assume and of which we should divest ourselves (and our children).

There are two additional points to note here. First, I am using the terms 'subject' and 'subjectivities' (as in my title 'political subjectivities') in the double senses highlighted by Foucauldian analyses, i.e. as subject *to* as well as subject *of* (Foucault 1980b). Hence I am speaking of forms of subjectivity or experience *as produced through* discourses or institutional frameworks of meaning, but also as functioning as – albeit circumscribed – agents within these (see also Fraser 1989; Hekman 1990; McNay 1992; Bell 1993a, 1993b). Such approaches have been taken up by feminists as helpful to analyse both processes of subjugation, and also how subjugated knowledges subsist whose expression and expertise can be mobilised. Hence although I will be concerned more in this chapter with the political subjectivities mobilised *around* children (including children who have been sexually abused), rather than by them, there are implications of this kind of analysis for highlighting and situating children's agency, of which I can only offer some indications here.

Second, it might be argued that such work is a luxury, the privilege of the academic who does not (have to) work with, or legislate about, the actions of, or care for, 'real children'. Even if this were true I would want to suggest that distance perhaps offers space for reflection that can be of value – for these analyses do offer a range of ways of thinking about the political and affective imperatives that surround children. In particular we can more easily ask questions about how things came to be this way, and thus come better equipped to policy and management development discussions to ask whether these are the only, or best, ways of thinking *about* children, and our dealings *with* children.

Texts of childhood

Notions of childhood evoke concepts and practices such as nature, biology, stages, bodies, growth, (im)maturity, rights, vulnerability, and innocence. These combine moral-political evaluation with apparently 'natural' terminology (of growth and maturity), but slip easily into consumer discourse (of value increase, as in the Laura Ashley children's clothes slogan of the mid-1990s: 'fashion for the upwardly mobile'). Additional associations might include childhood as: social category, original sin, otherness – as well as other age-related categories such as baby, infant, newborn, neonate (the technical term) or toddler, of the kind that appear in developmental psychology textbooks. (Indeed there is still – to my knowledge – an as yet unconducted study of developmental psychology textbook covers and contents that would document and analyse the ways such popular cultural images reinstate themselves within the domain of the technical study of childhood.)

All this is even before we import the rhetorics of development associated with children and childhood. Here notions of progress, improvement, skill and adaptation emerge, words that migrate or even flow easily between the specific and the general, or from individual to social allocation. This happens whether we are talking about a single child or children, or about descriptors of species as well as states or conditions; or, further, from discussion of states of individual minds or bodies to evaluations of the relative status of nation states. Here we begin to see the political load carried by the discourse of development, and by children who are so often positioned as its bearers. Children thus provide the conceptual and emotional means by which contested social hierarchy can be perpetuated by being mapped onto an apparently natural asocial category (Burman 2007a).

This is what I mean by the textualisation of childhood. For – irrespective of whatever children are 'really' like – we cannot know them or about them except through particular cultural and historical frames, or discourses, that structure that 'reality'. Moreover, what really makes this matter is that these cultural and historical frames have varied and do vary quite considerably, with significantly different positions elaborated – not only for children and those subject to the injunction to develop. All those others – girls and women, working children, black and working-class people, people with physical or learning disabilities, gay men and lesbians – are rendered invisible by their normalised (inferior) developmental status. Yet their positions and livelihoods are nevertheless constituted by (or perhaps it would be more accurate to say constellated around) our topic/subject. So there is a contest over *whose definitions* of development hold sway. It is part of the argument of this chapter that the dominant naturalised discourse of ('normal' or 'typical') development has obscured this contest, and so has helped to produce the position of the abused child as different, abnormal and outside prevailing discourses (including policy discourses) of childhood.

Hence hierarchy is explicitly structured within the lexicon of age and life stages (of baby–child–adolescent–adult, for example). But there are equivalent, if less naturalised, social and spatial distributions of 'differences' structured around gender, sexuality and 'race'. Such hierarchies clearly have important histories in colonialism and imperialism as well as current allocations (between the 'First' and 'Third' World, see Sachs 1999). But somehow the blending of history with hierarchy has been easier to recognise in talking about age. So we could conceivably consider the textualisation of the child as a paradigm case of other such ideological constructions. At any rate let us consider five points: the special status of childhood; the gendering of the child; the child as true/lost self; contestations around the naturalness of childhood; the need to situate the contemporary 'crisis' of childhood.

The special status of childhood

The UN Convention on the Rights of the Child as a piece of legislation was passed in record time (see my discussion of this in Burman 1996a). Yet this was at a price. In some senses it can be argued that children – as the starting point or supposedly raw material for social development – are the victims of the asocial model of the bourgeois individual of modernity. For as the prototypical subjects of modernity, of the modern project of social improvement, it has been the fate of children to be talked of as though gender, culture and sexuality are additional qualities to be grafted on to some apparently prior or pre-given 'child'.

Thus the 'special'-ness of children seems to be at the expense of being apart from the very social structures concerned with protecting or promoting them. The costs of this for the adequate analysis of, and engagement with, children who have been sexually abused are serious. For, once so identified, they seem neither to belong to the category of childhood (since this has been constituted as safe and innocent), nor to the social structures that both constitute the domain of childhood and accord them such anomalous status within it. Moreover, the singular status of 'the child' confirms her or his position outside communities: that is, outside not only cultural communities, but also communities of other children – including siblings who form significant, if not primary, caregivers for many of the world's children, and in particular *political* communities of other children. Here we might recall analyses of how 'the child' of developmental psychology and educational practices emerged at a political moment within industrialising societies when children and young people were becoming economically active and increasingly organised (Hoyles 1989; Hendrick 1990). These indicate that the claims to the special protection with which contemporary childhood has been invested paradoxically correspond with the denial of children's agency.

So, to offer some crude but illustrative examples, currently in the UK the legal system does not regard young people as capable of political participation (via casting votes) until the age of 18, of consenting sexual activity until 16, nor of earning a sustainable wage comparable to the minimum pay level, while the question of whether children and young people should be held legally responsible for their actions has been hugely exercised by the Bulger case (Burman 1995c). Elsewhere in the world (and more probably in the UK than most people would like to realise) children bear arms (Park 2006), bear children, and work long hours for little pay (Schlemmer 2000). Notwithstanding children's physical and emotional vulnerability, it seems that there are broad cultural-political investments in maintaining children and young people as docile and dependent through educational, legal and welfare practices that portray them as deficient and therefore in need of training and/or protection. There may be practical political demands to be made that correspond to the claims made for the movement for Democratic Psychiatry (Parker *et al.* 1995), of calling for legal responsibility as a means of warding off their status as asocial and disenfranchised (see also Waites 2005).

Gendering the child

Children are generally treated as a unitary category unless marked explicitly by gender. Thus the new development category, 'the girlchild', produces girls and young women as both not quite child and not only woman, for as a new hybrid the 'girlchild' somehow represents a doubled position of vulnerability to abuse and oppression – whether in terms of labour or sexual services. Despite this, the qualities accorded children typically remain allocated according to conventional gender stereotypes. Thus the child of development, the developmental subject who is active, playing, problem-solving and singular – is culturally masculine and often is portrayed as a little boy (as in Piaget's mini scientist, Piaget 1957). Here it is also worth remembering that across the world it is boys who manage to access the efforts towards universal primary education better than girls. Correlatively, the *state* from which development takes place is typically a feminised/infantilised arena. Thus girls represent childhood as a state of neediness or difference, including desirability, or sometimes inherent maternity; while boys represent a forward-looking potential (with the recent shift in aid imagery from girls to boys occupying an ambivalent place here).

However, we should note that contexts of abuse fracture the dominant conception of childhood as devoid of gender, as much as of sexuality. For in understanding how sexual abuse comes about, we have to address the different (sexed and gendered) positions of boys and girls as subject to actual or potential abuse, and so begin to acknowledge the complex and constitutive intersections between these (Warner 1995, 2000). Policy discourses of sexual abuse are themselves gender stratified, with boys and girls being understood as being abused under different conditions (but with the abusers in both cases largely being men). But we should pause to note the potential conflation between vulnerability and feminisation that itself speaks of a culturally dominant discourse which transcends both the gendered and sexed positions of actual children. Further, this not only implicitly pathologises their autonomy but also disallows (attention to) their resilience and resistance.

The child as lost/true self

In the effort to repair the gap, to restore a subjectivity (and correspondingly a gender, culture and sexuality) denied to the child by virtue of the limitations of these prevailing models, many fictions and fantasies have been born. These fantasies indicate how children – especially little girls – signify not only the inner, fragile self, but also have come to express longing and loss within the modern Western imaginary. Carolyn Steedman (1995) suggests:

> The child within was always both immanent – ready to be drawn on in various ways – and, at the same time, always representative of a lost realm, lost in the individual past, and in the past of the culture . . . The idea of the child was used both to recall and to express the past that each individual life contained: what was turned inside in the course of individual development was that which was also latent: the child *was* the story waiting to be told.
>
> (pp. 10–11)

Hence the romance of the other is rendered docile and diminutive in the form of the little girl, who is positioned as in need of protection, or even of seduction (see also Stainton Rogers and Stainton Rogers 1992). This romance is written into models of psychological development as an origin story, with development marking distance from a thereby inferior, devalued but also fascinating, place:

> The child was the figure that provided the largest number of people living in the recent past of Western societies with the means for thinking about and creating a self: something grasped and understood: a shape, moving in the body . . . something *inside*, an interiority.
>
> (Steedman 1995: 20)

It is a significant challenge to take seriously how deeply such gendered imagery informs not only concepts of childhood, but also Western subjectivity more generally. The figure of the little girl has come to figure as both prototypical subject and object in ways that have got in the way of attending to the needs and capabilities of specifically gendered and embodied children and young people.

Contesting the naturalness of childhood

Thus the figure of the child – with its appeal to the natural, the divine and the taken for granted – has flourished precisely to the extent that it obscures its cultural and ideological origins. Herein lies the key to the current concern around children. The docile vulnerability that prompted protection and warrants education is thrown into confusion when some categories of children (notably working-class and minoritised children, as well as those who have been abused) demonstrate themselves to be not so innocent; and the perplexity this generates is illuminating in two ways. First, not only is the price of that protection the injunction to be innocent but, second, this clarifies how the very category of childhood presupposes the absence of all those ('knowing'/'knowledgeable') qualities of adulthood.

One political and psychological project of investigation that follows is this: if children are, after all, more like adults in matters of desires and complicities than had been supposed (or attributed), then what, if anything, develops? While much developmental psychology preoccupies itself with this matter, I think the more important, because more easily avoided, topic to consider is just *how and why we came to accord* such different qualities and proclivities to adults and children (respectively). What investments lie within such distinctions? And what social-political questions are obscured by a contest for entitlements based on presumed constant and natural age or gender categories?

Situating the contemporary crisis of childhood

It seems that the contemporary crisis of childhood arises at a confluence of three key debates. First, there is unprecedented attention to the prevalence of the sexual abuse of children. While current reports of abuse both in private homes and residential care abound, there is a corresponding focus on those who abuse. But the emotional response unleashed towards those deemed at fault tends to resolve itself upon marginal individuals rather than institutional structures. This was graphically indicated by the disturbances in Portsmouth and other British towns in the summer of 2000 in which Far Right groups mobilised supposedly to support communities in the protection of their children, culminating in indiscriminate attacks on individuals rather than campaigning to improve services (Bell 2003).

A second context is the increasing publicity (and litigation) concerning people (mainly women) in therapy claiming to have recovered memories of abuse. This has thrown societal investments in constructing nostalgically happy childhoods and happy families into disarray (Burman 1996/7; Brown and Burman 1997; Haaken 2003). Third, there are further ramifications surrounding the crisis of development and the project of modernity – both in terms of its manifest failure and in the sense of the rampant de-development being perpetrated in the name of the benefits of globalisation and the free market. While most of the world still lives in acute poverty, notwithstanding the supposed cancellation of the world debt, the goals of sustainable, ecologically sound and equitable subsistence look more and more remote (see Sachs 1999).

All of these factors give rise to an ever-increasing scrutiny of the supposed local index or representative of development: the child. For children form a key focus of intervention for all these disparate concerns. Moreover, these debates in turn relate to two other key contexts. First, there is an increasing professionalisation of talking and helping relationships within the condition of alienation in late modernity. Increasing social isolation and erosion of community/communal arenas for talk and support have fuelled the need to seek out professional spaces for talk and support (Parker 1997; Nicholson 1999). Alongside this there is a correspondingly burgeoning bureaucracy around 'development' in the political sphere. (Think of how much supposed international 'aid' is spent on 'home' government consultants and agencies.) Second, in the contexts of increasing cuts in state welfare provision, there is a rampant proliferation of the privatised service sector, servicing both therapeutic and development studies needs (Cooke and Kothari 2001).

Traversing current texts

My arguments so far about the obscuring of culture within the discourse of nature may be familiar. They highlight how the naturalisation of childhood gives rise to corresponding pressures to homogenise all children and developing subjects. But it is also worth noting their political significance in a number of ways. Hence Valerie Walkerdine (1990a) indicated how such naturalisation of gender also includes condoning gendered aggression. Moreover, as I will now discuss, the abstraction of the child affords a slippage from individual to society, from the child to the nation, from the lost to the true, authentic self; and – most significant in relation to child sexual abuse – from the feminised subject in need of protection to the patriarchal superego urging action (or restraint from action). In short, ambivalent political agencies are constructed by, and in relation to, these texts of childhood. I turn now to discuss five illustrative examples.

Originary state

There is an emptiness at the heart of the originary state of childhood. Like many significant political spaces of occupation, it is deemed to be without content or habitation. Similarly, the blank slate of childhood – within developmentalist accounts – is waiting to be inscribed by the social. The dependent, vulnerable condition of childhood calls forth all our practices of education, training and welfare intervention (including the policing of families and stigmatisation of culturally minoritised practices, e.g. Phoenix 1987; Burman *et al.* 2004). Here it is worth recalling that the political affiliations of environmentalists (as opposed to maturationists) in relation to child development have historically been directed towards public health rather than moral degeneracy positions. This social reforming, philanthropic position within the English medical and mental hygiene movements of the early twentieth century marked out the medics from the budding psychologists. For it was the psychologists who were more inclined towards genetic determinist (and eugenic) positions – with all their attendant practices of classification, segregation and containment (see Rose 1985).

Yet this apparently benign position itself belies practices of colonisation and (at best) ignorance in failing to acknowledge or draw upon what lies there already. The injunction to facilitate development can oppress, can break up communities, can work to pressurise peoples who are not – as they say within 'progressive education'-speak – 'ready'. Given the many possible connections one could make here, let me offer a local one; that is, local to me. In Moss Side in Manchester, the government response to protests in the early 1980s over police brutality and interference within the African-Caribbean community was to widen the main road running through its centre, and thus demolish one of the main organising centres of that community. In the name of development, the main shopping centre with its local market stalls was closed and a big supermarket and business parks constructed. The local housing of big 'terraces' of high rise housing was demolished. Or rather, as was heralded on the barbed wire that kept people out, this was 'land reclamation' – a nice resort to the discourse of nature in the name of political appropriation.

So this area was forcibly emptied and advertised as in need of 'development', a 'development site' opportunity. It is worth noting here that the existing nursery, where mothers left their children secure in the knowledge that, as a black-led service, they were getting culturally supportive care (in terms of forms of relationships as well as food) was also closed. While its replacement had new premises, it was long regarded as lacking the cultural sensitivity and community credibility of the old nursery. To cap it all there was a self-conscious irony in the official signs and adverts: the pseudo-graffitti sign announcing the current building programme for a new shopping precinct reads: 'there's a renovation going on'. Indeed, once the revolution has been quelled, capitalist development (i.e. market-led 'renovation') could begin. Wiping that slate of development clean, producing that originary state, was not an obvious, innocent, or only rhetorical, activity.

Similarly we might pause to consider what racialised as well as gendered and sexualised positions are erased in keeping childhood safe, and what work of inscription belies its designated originary state of empty readiness. For it is this work that is highlighted by the position of children who have been sexually abused. Children who have been sexually abused perhaps 'hold' or represent the most stigmatised childhood knowledge that needs to be repudiated in order to safeguard prevailing power relations. As with black, working-class and all other subaltern knowledges, this illustrates the discretionary character of our apparently boundless and unconditional indulgence to children.

Privileges/rights of childhood

Second, once childhood has been constituted as an original state, certain rights or privileges attend it. The UN Convention on the Rights of the Child is as ambivalent a political document as any in the sense that what counts as rights, and why, still has to be interpreted within each context and as such is amenable to considerable mediation and manipulation. But it is still a vital starting point for further mobilisation (Freeman 2000, 2002; Mitchell 2005). Significantly if predictably, though, protection rather than promotion figures most highly on the institutional agenda. This is seen worldwide in the difficulty of securing investment in promoting children's psychological and educational development, rather than only trying to reduce infant mortality – giving rise to rather bizarrely titled books such as Myers' (1992) *The Twelve Who Survive* – to drive home how those children who are likely to live to adulthood are also in need of support.

Once again, coming closer to my home, let me consider the little leaflet Manchester City Council delivered door to door entitled: 'The Ten Things Children Need Most'. On the inside first page there is a list of children's 'needs':

> to feel safe and secure; health and happiness; cuddles and good touching; lots of smiles; praise and encouragement; talking; listening; new experiences; respect for their feelings; rewards and treats.
>
> (Manchester City Council/Area Child Protection Committee/ Manchester Social Services leaflet 1999).

Who can fault these? It seems a comprehensive list – except that it fails to mention issues of power, consultation or authority. Moreover, the rest of the leaflet is concerned with issues of safety and protection, and in particular is addressed to parents who might be experiencing difficulties, or want to intervene to help others in difficulty. Indeed the final page has a list of agencies for 'Getting Help'. Interestingly, the 2007 version is explicitly addressed to parents, and the ten 'needs' have become 'top ten tips'.

No wonder babies evoke such strong feelings, since they command such institutional support and intervention. But it is as if these babies exist either outside relationships, or within an adversarially constituted context (which is of course the primary way the individualist discourse of rights conceives of relationships, Pateman 1989). Thus people rush to save children and babies, and children (apparently) love to have babies as toys or dolls (especially ones that cry and wet themselves and generally make work and require attention, thus driving home the socialisation feature of 'play' as a rehearsal for childcare and household labour). The late 1990s craze for 'alien eggs' and 'embryos' was perhaps one of the more bizarre examples. This even gave rise to a dramatic ambulance dash to a hospital when a children's toy – found discarded within its slimy jelly in a litter bin – was mistaken for a foetus, and apparently a number of such 'security scares' were documented in Britain alone (*Guardian* 4 November 1999: 16).

'Giving children back their future'

Why do we rush to save children? Why should we pause to think about this, when the imperative to do so seems so strong, and indeed it has been called 'natural', or 'instinctive'? Yet the fact that this is not so, since certain cultural and especially economic conditions need to prevail before such 'natural' qualities are elicited or displayed, is precisely what is at issue (cf. Scheper-Hughes 1989). Let us pause a moment to consider Rahnema's (1997) advice:

> Before intervening in people's lives, one should first intervene in one's own: 'polishing' oneself to ensure that all precautions have been taken to avoid harming the objects of intervention. Many questions should be explored first. What prompts me to intervene? Is it friendship, compassion, the 'mask of love', or an unconscious attempt to increase my powers of seduction? Have I done everything I could to assess the usefulness of my intervention? And if things do not proceed as I expect them, am I ready to face the full consequences of my intervention?
>
> (Rahnema 1997: 387)

There is a lot of talk of lost childhoods and restoring childhoods. What is less often reflected upon is *whose* childhood we are referring to, or rather imposing, here. In the context of child (sexual) abuse, neglect or deprivation it is easy for these broader questions to feel like liberal agonisings, or inappropriate hesitations. Yet aid organisations have themselves become much more careful about, and critical of, the political positions mobilised for donor and recipient when images of children are used, especially in the context of international development causes (Black 1992; Save the Children 1992; see also Burman 1994b, 1996c).

Moreover, once we are outside the determinist discourse of original sin, what seems attractive about the modern developmental discourse of childhood is the indulgence or reforming 'understanding' it accords children. Recently in England the charity Barnardos was at the centre of controversy because of its media campaigns. The first of these tried to ward off the discourse of blame attending various 'social misfits' through invoking the childhood history carried within, or alternatively conceived as producing, the adult. As a journalist commentator put it:

> It's an advert based on the sort of solid truth that flashes through your mind every time you hand over 50p to a beggar – that everyone is born an innocent baby, and what is it that goes so wrong as to put that little ball of trust and love out on The Strand at midnight?
>
> (Stephen Armstrong, *Guardian* 24 January 2000: 4)

The images at issue substituted a child for a young adult in a succession of contexts that included being in prison, homeless, on the streets, on drugs or alcohol, about to jump off a skyscraper to a sure death. Thus they offered a dramatic invitation to see the inner needy or suffering child within the adult. These images of damaged children were invoked to account for socially useless, often morally degraded people. It is perhaps significant that the only girl/female image was also the only one specifically mentioning 'abuse'.

The small text beside the image in each case opened with a statement of original damage/trauma: 'neglected as a child', 'written off as a child', 'battered as a child', 'abused aged 5', 'made to feel worthless as a child'. This was followed by an appeal for understanding and assertion of a 'possible' link between a childhood situation and the current situation of marginalisation/self-harm/destitution: 'it was always possible', 'there was always a chance of', and finally 'it was hardly surprising' ('that Carl would turn to alcohol'; 'Martin could see no other way out', etc.). The Barnardos director of marketing and communications behind the campaign, Andrew Neb, was reported as saying: 'Whenever you see a homeless person and sniff that it's all their own fault, it's worth remembering that it was probably something in their childhood that pushed them into it' (ibid: 5).

So in terms of mitigating the discourse of blame or social responsibility, 'giving people back their future' is about attributing them with a traumatised past. This might in some circumstances be helpful, and perhaps is so if it prompts less stigmatising approaches to working with homeless people, people with mental health problems or drug users. However, there are two obvious problems. First, there is the familiar problem that once the past is seen as the traumatogenic place of origin it is all too easy to conveniently 'forget' present day sequelae/causative circumstances. In particular, individualised, family-oriented explanations frequently function to exonerate state-neglect or deprivations.

Second, the 'shock value' of this campaign relies upon a denial of what is actually the case: we are supposed to be shocked at these images precisely because their estrangement relies upon seeing children (rather than adults) depicted as doing such things as taking drugs and sleeping on the streets. That is, the assumption is that the people involved *were* the children these adults now *are*. What all the public debate and criticism generated by this campaign failed to note was an obvious fact. This fact is that children, real chronological children, not metaphorically fixated or developmentally arrested adults functioning *as* children, *are* in these states on streets the world over.

It seems, paradoxically, that we are more willing to be sensitive to the damaged children *reconstructed* through contemporary adult damage/failure than failing/deprived children in the present. Opportunities were presented by this campaign to make even more explicit political analogies. The British visual satirist Steve Bell's 'take' on these ads (*Guardian* 28 January 2000: 22) portrayed the then British opposition leader, the Conservative William Hague, as a baby feeding on the drugged bottle of Clause 28 (the clause of a local government act passed in the late 1980s to prohibit progressive local authorities from instituting anti-discriminatory practices around gay men and lesbians, and in particular to challenge the supposed promotion of homosexuality and representation of 'pretended families'), and using the 'enema of extreme euroscepticism' (another key feature of Tory policy). Here Bell subverted the discourse of damaged childhood as accounting for current adult condition to comment instead on current Tory leadership policy. He represented the conditions of a privileged indulgence in childhood to insinuate this as 'causing' Hague's (thereby problematised) adult hobbies and policies. The text reads: 'William Hague: age 38. . . . Fêted as a child, it was always possible that William would turn to martial arts and self-defence'. (At this time press coverage had focused on how former Olympic champion, turned Tory politician, Sebastian Coe, was in training in ju-jitsu with William Hague.) By contravening the norm, Bell highlights how such childhood explanations are typically invoked only to account for where development went wrong. That is, the discourse of pathologisation, through focusing on the designated 'bad/limit' cases, can work to disguise how some people remain advantaged through this. Bell parodies the versatility of the formulation of 'as a child it was always possible that [s/he] would turn to', exposing the partiality of the political character of the attributed conditions, and the supposed causalities that warrant attention and intervention. Instead we are invited to ask: *which* childhood?

Irrespective of all the sentiment around babies and small children, they somehow fail to attract identification in the ways that adults, as more integrated, perhaps conventionally more morally accountable social subjects, do. Or perhaps if Winnicott (1958) is right about the hate that lies within sentimentality, it is precisely because of this lack of identification that such sentiment occurs (see Chapter 6 this volume). As I have already indicated, there may be political lessons here for ways of making children matter more – by being explicitly offered greater political involvement as actors rather than objects. In terms of child sexual abuse, we need to move beyond the portrayal of children and young people who have been sexually abused as 'victims', and instead acknowledge the more complicated but active strategies that enable them to survive, cope and even perhaps displace their abuse as a primary (historical or current) identity.

As an aside it is perhaps worth noting the two successive campaigns mobilised by the same organisation. A year later, Barnardo's (2001–2) launched a campaign specifically addressing the sexual abuse of children. Here instead of invoking the innocent inner child of the damaged adult, they mobilised the trope of premature ageing via the elision of age and (in this case inappropriate) experience. The same device of temporal transposition is used to signify trauma and appealing for exoneration, but now the bodies of young children have the aged and lined faces of old men and women superimposed upon them. Significantly, the image of the 'girl' is located within a private setting, sitting on a bed; while the 'boy' is shown near a latrine in what is understood to be a public men's toilet. In both cases, the shadowy abuser (portrayed by his size and clothing) is an adult male. These images also shock in their grainy, black and white explicitness; they have less of the 'puzzle' element than the earlier images, since the discourse of premature ageing is perhaps more readily culturally available but is rarely graphically depicted. The byline, 'child prostitution steals children's lives', offers little in the way of a narrative of recovery or survival, just as the 'experience' of abuse is portrayed as premature ageing that brings on vulnerability, infirmity and proximity to death. Indeed, Cunningham (2002) has noted how this motif is a classical nineteenth-century portrayal of the child, but now it is rendered devoid of its developmentalist claims: 'No trope is more pervasive and powerful in the nineteenth century than that of the chid with an adult face, old before its time, precocious, and in need of returning to the lost world of adulthood' (p. 2).

Before we leave this topic, it is worth noting that the most controversial of the Barnardos campaigns was not, in fact, the focus on sexual or even societal abuse, but the subsequent (2003) campaign on child poverty. Here a series of images was fronted by an initial one showing a newborn baby with a cockroach in its mouth, accompanied by the headline 'No silver spoon'. This was a dramatic evocation of developmental differentiations rendered by class inequalities. It seems significant that this, of all their daring campaigns, is the only one which was actually banned (generating 'a record 466 complaints to the ASA [Advertising Standards Authority]', *Guardian* 20 November 2003: 11). Poverty, therefore, is even more shocking to mention than explicit or organised child sexual abuse. Indeed, later Barnardos campaigns have shied away from such controversial imagery instead to take up the frisson accorded scans and neuro-imaging, and invoke foetal imagery to depict the new start and 'new life' they provide for their beneficiaries.

General culture of infantilisation

As I have already noted, children usually appear as talked about, rather than talked to, or indeed as the speakers. Within popular culture, where *we* are addressed as children it is often within the discourse of moral indulgence/desire for (escape from) responsibility. In the contemporary culture of infantilisation there is a representation of a pleasure-seeking child inside the reluctantly responsible (and productive) adult. Indeed many current advertising campaigns (especially for computers and cars) rely on just such an appeal to the inner child (in such contexts usually portrayed as a boy).

Entertainment itself can signify warding off an impending ageing/maturing process. The 1999 Virgin advertisement displayed on hoardings all over Britain, 'delay becoming your parents', advertised website listings of shopping, cinema and shows explicitly to market consumption as the route to slow down the inevitable (now naturalised) process of becoming the responsible adults 'your parents' presumably are. It is naturalised by virtue of being a process that can only be 'delayed' rather than prevented or avoided, and also through both the use of the family kinship term 'your parents' and the generality of pronominal reference 'your' (since we all have, or have had, parents of some kind). The paradox here, as with all capitalist injunctions to 'enjoy' (cf. Žižek 1991b), is that 'you' need to do that supposedly very unchildlike (and therefore parent-like) activity, i.e. work/sell your labour, in order to generate the money to escape from the parental condition. We might further note here how an ideological rendering of history is presented, with 'our parents' portrayed as the boring, exploited classes, not the militant, class-conscious, struggling organisers they might well have been, or indeed be. But beyond this we could also acknowledge how children too are subject to such injunctions to demonstrate their (childhood or adult) social participation through consumption and leisure activities that require money (see also Burman and MacLure 2005). Hence, as Mizen and Pole (2000) succinctly put it, working children in Britain 'work to play'.

Similarly, at around the same time the publicity campaign for the caffeine-stimulant drink Red Bull portrayed a row of young men and women poised on the edge of a bridge, figuratively or symbolically pushing themselves to the limit, with the slogan 'sleep when you're dead'. This was an address to young people to live to the full, because anything less is to be boring/dead. Alternatively the late 1990s advertising campaign slogan for the soft drink Tango, 'you need it because you're weak', offered a discourse of childlike exoneration to justify the moral failure/limits of self-restraint (so incited, but at the same time regulated by, overdeveloped societies; see discussion of this in Parker 2005).

Hence the culture of infantilisation carries mixed messages as an image of adult subjectivity. Alongside indulgence there is dependence. Or rather an attribution of being incapable, and therefore untrustworthy, of managing matters – with Britain becoming a massively surveillant society, with not only more CCT cameras than any other country but also exceeding other countries in the collection of biodata. While Bywater (2006) bemoans this state of affairs and impotence and therefore lack of autonomy, Pupavac (2002a) takes up this characterisation in terms of the broader consequences of a diminished model of political subjectivity

Child as superegoic injunction

The final, fifth set of discourses I will discuss marks a shift from the cloyingly coy attribution of 'voice' to the child, although it is in fact only a particular variant of it. This is the moral injunction to action when spoken using the voice of the child, as in the widely available picture postcard of the 1990s: 'the planet is unique; it has to be protected', which draws on a double notion of futurity. This is mobilised both by the explicit concern with planetary/environmental future and by the commonly circulating discourse that '*children* are our future'. This device of being addressed *by* 'our future', and also advocating for our future, beats a powerful tune. The coy appeal here usually mingles with a faintly fascist air suggested by the image of a pale-eyed white (boy) child's direct gaze. Could this hint at a discourse of the authoritarian personality revisited upon the now terrorising child?

This seems to indicate a more general theme of the child as moral guarantor – the well-worn 'out of the mouths of babes' narrative, 'The Emperor's New Clothes', alongside the shlock film chestnut of the child's capacity to shame others into 'doing the right thing' (see also Edelman 2005). Yet there is a danger in overplaying this discourse of moral reproach.

It could generate further resistance (rather than compliance) to its powerful combination of resources. For it invokes the forces of the past (as in the children we once were, or – especially in the context of the abused childhoods so many of us seem to have had – *wished* we were) with the moral responsibility for constructing the future we would like to secure/enjoy. This resistance is what (after Winnicott 1958) fuels some of the sadism within the sentimentality surrounding children, which is perhaps what makes such campaigns that allow for multiple readings via humour more successful (see Chapter 6).

Subverting developmental totalisations

I have been moving between texts of child development and economic and world development – arguably performing precisely the kind of reduction, or assertion of homology, that I would want to problematise within prevailing developmental discourse. However, I want to finish by moving from these 'little' texts of child development to the broader discussions of economic development by way of indicating something of how such juxtapositions – although sadly too commonplace via their common political agendas – can be used subversively. For these debates have come to produce the available discourses within which we think about *individual* developmental trajectories (whether normalised, or – as in contexts of abuse – thereby problematised).

Connections include how the general models obscure the complexity of practices and contexts in which children survive, live and indeed develop, and the structurally diverse character of the economic, cultural and interpersonal relationships that produce these varied developments (see Crewe and Harrison 1998). Our theories do not currently equip us well to do more than plot patterns that themselves reflect broader power relationships around what is deemed significant and what is not. Instead, we need to attend to the question of compatibility vs. divergence of interests, since within psychology and social welfare practice we are perhaps too quick either to assume the passivity of those rendered as objects of the psychological gaze, or else to identify their agency as pathology or deficit (cf. Phoenix 1987). This is because we overstate the extension and remit of the discourse of development we subscribe to. Equally, like the children who form the topic of this chapter (and this book) there are no 'innocent' positions within these discussions. All of us are implicated in the discourses I have identified. There is no 'outside' to development discourse. Rather in conclusion, I suggest, following critics of international development policy (e.g. Rahnema 1997; Crewe and Harrison 1998; Sachs 1999) that – since we cannot entirely reject it – we practitioners of development should instead attend to the diversities of use, interpretation and incorporation of different discourses of development, as well as identify changing notions of intervention. We can do this whether we are practitioners of the individual, national or global varieties of development – whether of its 'normal' or 'atypical' forms. Indeed this approach applies especially to those of us who concern ourselves with both, or all, of these. Moreover, in terms of child sexual abuse, we need to analyse the interface between different groups of actors that surround caring as well as abusive relationships, and work to document the varying and contested accounts of what particular professional interventions can mean, and what they achieve. (This point is elaborated in a range of professional and development contexts in Laurie and Bondi's 2005 collection.) Whether evaluating the success of an economic development intervention, such as the introduction of a particular resource or technology, or educational, care or health-promoting practices, the same project of documenting diversities of perspective and interpretation of any intervention applies. This is one vital way, in my view, that we can begin to map what Katz (1996: 498) termed 'renegade cartographies, rooted in experience and wrought of involvement [which] struggle to name a different spatiality and chart the politics to produce it'. By such means we may be better equipped to explore the range of political subjectivities mobilised and motivated by children and notions of childhood.

5 Sexuality

Contested relationships around the control of desire and action

Chapter 5 builds on the analysis provided in Chapter 4, attempting to comment on and rectify the framing of children's sexualities in terms of abuse (discussed in the latter) by setting this theme within a wider context. Discussions of children's sexuality are fraught and traversed by discourses of danger and prohibition; whether in terms of children's needs for protection or societal protection from other children and young people. In this, policies on children and young people exemplify the moves to individualise 'risk' and map it on to particular, vulnerable bodies. Yet the desires of children and for children arise in relation to each other, and so both need to be understood. This chapter deals with the public, media and parliamentary response to a satirical television programme screened on British television on 'paedophilia', by analysing its counterdiscursive relationships with other more normative texts. In particular, juxtapositions are explored with the film *Amélie*, where the seductive qualities of the representation of youth functioned to generate only acclaim. These examples are taken as the arena for wider discussion of the ways gender and childhood produce particular discourses of sexuality. Moreover, it is suggested that the vulnerable, feminised subject has now emerged as a new prototypical Euro-US subject, whose seductive feminine character obscures the paternalist colonialism and self-serving character of 'her' interventions.

This chapter anchors many of the themes of this book, starting out by exploring how discourses of abuse frame all discussions of children's sexualities. It spans five distinct areas: first, reviewing historical and current accounts of children's sexuality; second, offering a sustained discussion of the ways gender structures discourses of both children and sexuality; third, the focus on the filmic text *Amélie* highlights the multiple identificatory and political functions fulfilled by the gamine figure of the girl-woman, as indicative of a wider cultural-economic shift in models from covert cultural masculinity to femininity to meet the demands of advanced capitalism. (These features are further discussed in relation to contemporary debates over girls' school 'overachievement' in Burman 2005a.) Other links between feminisation and neoliberalism are elaborated in Burman (2004a), and specifically in relation to emotions and representations of childhood in Gordo López and Burman (2004), but its arguments were first formulated in this longer text. The fourth part of the chapter is the primary place in this book where a sustained account of Steedman's (1995) influential analysis is offered, and this is used to place the arguments formulated about *Amélie* in context. Building on this, the fifth section considers the intervention made by a spoof British television documentary on the topic of paedophilia, screened in 2001. The chapter ends by returning to the psychoanalytic theme of the structure of jokes, as indicative of the anxieties and occlusions within prevailing representations of children's sexualities. Methodologically, then, this chapter draws on a range of conceptual and analytical frameworks to address the complex question of children's sexualities. It resists policy prescriptions, although such do follow from the analysis presented – across a range of disciplinary and geographical applications. The focus on texts – historical, current, fictional, popular, satirical – works to emphasise the impossibility of engaging with the question of children and sexuality outside cultural-historical practices of textual mediation. What this opens up, then, is the possibility of generating more emancipatory texts surrounding children.

> It seems that the large majority of authors, both men and women, who have written about the sexual enlightenment of youth, have concluded in favour of it. But the clumsiness of most of their proposals as to when and how this enlightenment is to take place tempts one to think they have not found it easy to arrive at this conclusion.
>
> (Freud 1907: 179)

This chapter is more about *how* than *what* to do, for the topic of childhood sexuality is so contested and foreclosed an arena that it is hard to do more than begin to explicate our current difficulties. Moreover, when I say 'our' difficulties, I do not simply mean some generalised, globalised Northern or Euro-US commentator. For it seems, perhaps through the globalisation of children's rights discourse (Ennew and Milne 1989; Burman 1996a), and albeit in different ways, policymakers and practitioners alike the world over are approaching their own limit points in thinking about children's and young people's sexualities. This does not, of course, mean that we are all equivalently ill-equipped to address this question. For while those outside Northern cultural centres are clearly not immune from its effects, they may well be in contexts that more easily expose the limits of its perspectives. The question, therefore, is really why conceptualising children's sexualities is so difficult, and what is needed to be able to move on to think more helpfully about this key topic.

Anticipating some practical links

In this light, my focus here will be more analytical than programmatic. Insofar as what I have to say relates directly to social policy and national or international legislation, clearly discussions of childhood sexualities connect with laws concerning the age of consent. That is, at what age children or young people are considered capable of making informed choices, in this case in relation to having sexual relationships. This also implies analysis of how this 'benchmark' relates to others we make for children's other 'rights' or 'freedoms' *to do* things – the right to political involvement, the right to self-expression, for example; as well as rights or freedoms *from* exploitation, abuse, etc. In general, and notwithstanding the contemporary emphasis on participation within current discussions of the UNCRC, and claims of the generative character of rights-based approaches (Gready and Ensor 2005), legislation around children is generally regarded as far better at protection than promotion; at welfare rather than self-determinative rights; and in this we can see liberalism's historical structural connections with late capitalism (Lukes 1973) through its upholding of the public–private dichotomy that precisely creates the conditions for women's and children's exploitation and oppression. For while it is not difficult to generate consensus about the wrongs of coercing children (to have sex or to work, for example) – though why this is the case will form one of my key foci – it is much more difficult to elaborate what they should be free to do, how, and (the crucial 'developmental' question) when. I can only note here how the policy tendency to reduce the political ambiguities of 'what' (children's work or sexuality should be) to 'when' itself speaks of, or makes recourse to, the role of developmental psychology, as the current arbiter of children's developmental needs, in naturalising a whole host of contested normative and highly political, culturally and historically variable judgements. But see Morss (1990, 1996), Singer (1992), Stainton Rogers and Stainton Rogers (1992, 1998) and Walkerdine (1988) as well as my version in Burman (2008).

Notwithstanding (or perhaps because of) my own disciplinary position, it is precisely because developmental psychology has little to offer to such discussions that I will be looking elsewhere – to history, sociology, cultural studies, and critical social theory in general, for interpretive resources. In relation to the topic of this chapter, key political and intellectual resources to be named are feminist, lesbian and gay studies,[1] for these draw attention to the second key tension underlying debates on childhood sexuality. For if the dominant agenda is protection from abuse – with an abusive relationship defined as under-aged sex – what remains crucially unanalysed is what acceptable (adult) sexuality is.

Childhood as the projected landscape for societal anxieties

Alongside the familiar trope of statistics around teenage pregnancies and sexually transmitted diseases, the other key strand of analysis must be an awareness of anxieties around homosexuality. Or – if we can manage to make it shed its individualist, psychological connotations – perhaps we could say that structural, institutionalised homophobia drives policy. Same-sex sexual practices are, in many parts of the world, subject to different ages of consent than heterosexual sex; even if they are acknowledged or permitted at all.[2] Hence the uninterrogated norm that remains unlegislated over (unless involving other claims of violence or exploitation) is heterosexuality. One key recognition within recent feminist discussion is that so much attention has gone into defending against the dominant problematisation of lesbian and gay relationships that there is little work exploring what heterosexuality is (Kitzinger and Wilkinson 1992; Richardson 1996). Foucault's analyses highlight how norms are produced through the definition of their infraction/pathological deviation. Rather than silencing discourse on homosexuality, he showed that the early sexologists and psychologists displayed a prurient fascination in producing, classifying and documenting representations of what they considered sexual aberrations or deviations (Foucault 1981).

Just as the dynamic of normalised absence/pathologised presence (Phoenix 1987; Burman *et al.* 2004) characterises the representation of subordinated (and especially minoritised) groups within any society, so the forms, contents and relations of children's and young people's sexualities are occluded by the massive weight of contemporary social anxiety this provokes. Childhood sexuality is only really known about insofar as it is a social problem, to be legislated over, therapeutically explained, or otherwise sanitised away. Alongside the massive edifice of child protection legislation, disclosure and investigation protocols, there is little we can say about children's sexuality outside of the frame of pathologisation. Indeed this applies also (or especially to) adults looking back on their childhood experiences who cannot but absorb, if not actually be tutored in, discourses of damage or victimhood, as currently the main available method of warding off guilt or legal responsibility. The discourse of survival only mitigates, rather than avoids, the same complex of problems (O'Dell 1998).

Sexuality and nature: knowledge as sin, knowledge as power?

As a key binary opposition structuring modern modes of subjectivity, knowledge is largely counterposed to innocence. This is given particular weight within legal practice, significantly also mapping on to adult and child relations, and thus contrasts with the newly emergent political discourse that would associate knowledge with power. Such binaries are not only historical products of very culturally specific contexts (James and Prout 1990; Holland 1992; Archard 1993; Jenks 1996), but they also structure the very domain of sexuality. Jacqueline Rose's (1984) influential analysis of 'the impossibility of children's fiction' rested upon the claim that since Locke and Rousseau 'the child' has been seen as 'a pure point of origin in relation to language, sexuality and the state' (p. 7). In particular Jordanova (1989) highlighted how, within European culture from the mid-eighteenth century, notions of 'nature' came to replace custom within criteria for judging the sexual activities of the young. Moreover, it was not so much the regulation of sexuality as 'the formation of new households and new lives' (Jordanova 1989: 18) that formed their focus. She highlights the paradoxical character of this new association of children with 'nature' within Western culture (in art and literature as well as medicine, for example):

> This naturalism produced a logical trap. . . . Separating nature from society allowed the naturalness of children – pure, innocent, asexual – to be contrasted with the uncleanness of the corrupt adult world. But an inclusive approach validated sexuality as part of nature, hence how could it be depraved? These views coexisted uneasily. It is indeed hard to reconcile the belief that children are natural and asexual with the view that sexuality is integral to nature.
>
> (Jordanova 1989: 18)

Hence within Euro-US culture, in its big developmental story of mastery over nature, knowledge as sin and knowledge as power are intertwined. Knowing 'in the biblical sense' (as itself a nice reflexive comment on an increasingly secularised – but still culturally Christian-dominated – world) is sexual knowledge; that is precisely what – within the modern Western imaginary – children are deemed to lack (or be free from). Indeed, as Stainton Rogers and Stainton Rogers (1998) note, 'adult' connotes sexual or erotic, as in 'adult movies'. Yet carnal knowledge – in the sense of knowledge of the body and its appetites – is also precisely that which is associated with childhood, as spontaneous and close to nature. Hence the consternation caused by the photographs of Sally Mann and more recently Tierney Gearson, working within the apparently new genre of 'mother-photographers'. The pictures they took of their children exercised definitions of whether or not meaning lies in the eye of the beholder, to the extent that Gearson's photos, when exhibited in the Saatchi gallery in London in early 2001, were raided under child protection legislation by the British Metropolitan Police who referred them to the Crown Prosecution Service.[3] A seemingly less controversial but equally contemporary take on these themes is expressed within the idiom of child rescue: not only, therefore, should we interrogate what we are 'saving' children *from*, but also what *for*.[4]

Here we see intimated a key area of tension between some child protectionists and feminists. For the protection of children can seem to normalise the sexual exploitation or oppression of adults – so that since the most frequent 'victims' of each are female – we see a potential 'stand-off' developing between those who champion children's and women's rights. But this political and disciplinary tension also does not preclude that other significant body of work that connects girls' and women's abuse, but does so in an individualising move to link childhood abuse with the likelihood of making abusive relationships in adulthood (e.g. De Zulueta 2006). Here we see the increased influence of a more biologically based psychoanalysis, with a focus on attachment histories (see Burman 2008, Chapter 7). Its assumptions about 'cycles of abuse' have been roundly criticised, especially by feminists (Reavey and Warner 2003; Chantler 2006).

This is the problematic that Freud's theory of childhood sexuality both emerged from and addressed (cf. Ellenberger 1970). Not that he invented such notions (for they are part and parcel of the rise of modernity), but clearly his work has done much to sediment them within contemporary Euro-US culture (Parker 1997). However, as is widely noted, Freud's account of infantile sexuality offers only ambiguous resources for debates about children's sexuality (not least due to the vicissitudes of his own opinions on the matter, cf. Masson 1984; Rush 1984). In the first place, the (polymorphously perverse) sexuality attributed by Freud to children is precisely not that which adults experience or enact. Rather his very point was to show the flexibility, mobility and malleability of (all) sexuality; that is, to show sexuality as a gradual, multiple and unstable construction – with the elaboration of aims and objects shifting according to context and experience and over the lifespan, so that they precisely cannot be read from adults back on to children (although the retroactive reconstruction of events lies at the heart of the case study method of clinical psychoanalysis). So while feminists and other sex radicals have drawn on Freud to destabilise prevailing gendered and sexed binaries (e.g. Mitchell 1974; Burgin *et al.* 1986; Weekes 1996), other accounts (Archard 1993) highlight how the 'latency period' subsumes most discussions of children's sexuality – although such periodisations of the organisation of sexual interests and structures into age-related, developmental stages is itself a creation of the post-Freudians (Leader 2000).

All of this is not to say that children do not have sexual knowledge or sexuality.[5] Nor does this diminish how children are subjected to sexual abuse – whether by being willingly, as well as unwillingly, involved in sexual practices of whose meanings and consequences they may not fully aware. But even if they are aware, it is largely agreed that it is the violation of the relationship of trust and dependence in the context of the structurally unequal relationship between adult and child that constitutes it as abuse, and (especially in relation to incest) that compromises notions of informed consent (Archard 1993; Warner 2000). As Warner notes:

> All instances of child sexual abuse involve sex. Without sex, or more accurately the sexual gratification of the abuser, it would not be child *sexual* abuse. All instances of child sexual abuse involve the abuse of power. Without the abuse of power it would not be child sexual *abuse*.
>
> (Warner 2000: 29)

So when adults, discussing their childhood experiences of abuse, report (e.g. on radio or television talk shows) that they came to understand (through their therapy, for example) that they were victims of abuse, rather than collusive or responsible, this indicates the nature of their (and others') anxieties. I will not go into the debates about 'false memory syndrome' here, except to note that this is another, but particularly key, arena in which the same social anxieties around gender, childhood sexuality and the contest around private/public responsibilities at issue here are being played out (see Burman 1996/7, 1997a, 1998b, 2002a), and in which discourses of the 'inner child' have come to figure in confusing as well as indicative ways (see also Haaken 1998).

A further key resource that informs contemporary representations of sexuality, both gay and heterosex, is HIV/AIDS. This is a further frame bolstering the dominant discourses connecting children and sexuality, confirming its dangerousness. It remains a critical project (in multiple senses) to promote policy discourses, including health promotion campaigns, that enable more affirmative formulations of sexual desire, and in particular for young women to assert their negotiating power rather than – as with prevailing approaches to sex education and teenage pregnancy prevention campaigns, treating women as responsible (see e.g. Stronach *et al.* 2007 on British policy; Macleod 2002a, 2002b, 2006 on South African policies). Shefer and Potgeiter (2006) offer a useful account of both the impact of, and strategies promoted by, HIV/AIDS from the South African context.

There is no domain of knowledge that can be accessed to correct or counterpose the dominant discourse of sexuality as something only imposed *upon* children, rather than a property *of* children (and to imagine there were should surely only indicate yet another romanticism visited upon children). Rather than either mourn this absence, or constitute some artificial anthropological 'other' (of which 'the child' is surely our most 'local' variety), I suggest that we should instead attend closely to the forms and functioning of this lacuna. For, as Foucault would suggest, the explicit prohibition disguises a set of attributions that themselves reveal indicative discursive structures of child concern, including the eroticisation of children. To echo Rex and Wendy Stainton Rogers (1998) in their discussion of what they call 'word children':

> The aim is not to answer questions (such as what motivates paedophilia?) but to question questions. Indeed, as it should by now be fairly obvious, we are not convinced that the sexuality of children is a scientific question at all. What we think we can study (and ultimately *all* that we can study) is discourse on children's sexuality.
>
> (p. 194)

To sum up my argument so far. First, I am suggesting that there is a need to reconceptualise access to sexual knowledge, to move away from notions of complicity to focus on power, including crucially the power relations that construct the ways we view children.[6] This does not necessarily translate directly into implications towards 'sex education' as a form of 'child protection' (for this subordinates discourses of desire to abuse once again, or else its converse: culpability), although it clearly nods in this direction. The key issue here is to avoid pathologising children for 'knowing', and in particular to consider *which* children/cultures/families get stigmatised by exhibiting such 'knowledge' (e.g. working class, and black women and families in the heartlands of the North, though mapping through neo-colonialism also on to global majority/minority relations).

There is a second point that I will move to discuss next. The general cultural silence about, in particular women's, sexual desires renders women's active engagement in sexual relationships – in positions other than victims – incomprehensible (Haaken 2002). Moreover, we should not forget that it is the sexuality of men – both heterosexual and homosexual – that is implicated within almost all discussions of child sexual abuse.

There is a third related point. We need to attend to the occlusion of incest within discussions of abuse, with abuse often being figured within the genre of 'stranger danger' so critiqued within the representation of rape. In fact child sexual abuse, like the rape of women, happens in supposedly normal, happy, not necessarily deprived families; so we must ward off the temptation to place the abuse outside, and so maintain intact, the safety of 'our' homes. In particular we need to attend to the role of gender in the conceptualisation of abuse.

Women and children: gender and childhood

The domain of childhood sexuality is overshadowed by images of abuse. It is overdetermined by the relations between gender and childhood in a number of complex ways. Girls, women and children are semiotically linked through mutually implicating discourses of feminisation and infantilisation. Both women and children have been (at least historically) legally positioned as minor political actors, who generally were formerly (if are not actually) regarded as the property of their husbands/fathers. Moreover, the grounds on which women have been denied political power were because of their supposed childlikeness in being closer to 'nature', including notions of immaturity and inferiority or deficit in relation to the male-defined norm of maturity (Birke 1992). Developmental hierarchies, echoing the great (patriarchal and colonial) evolutionary chain of being (positing the adult male as the pinnacle of maturity) portrayed women as closer to children (Haraway 1989; Morss 1996; Burman 2008). But if children and women share positions of non-responsibility for their actions, then the position of girls – who are, in the usual course of events, destined to become women – is doubly troublesome. For they seem to embody a double dose of vulnerability and corresponding need for protection on the grounds of both youth and gender. Let us look at five issues: the elision of the girl-woman within cultural reproduction; the gendering of the childhood; the girl as prototypical woman; reversing the sex/gender polarity; unholy alliances.

The elision of girl-woman within cultural reproduction

Girls' and women's sexuality has been a longstanding site of particular regulation owing to women's accorded positions as representatives of cultural purity and reproduction. This position extends beyond the physical bearing and caring for children to being responsible for (including morally guarding and modelling) the next generation of citizens. We should note here links with constructions of national identities. This is what differentiates discussions of childhood sexuality; for the sexuality of girls and boys is subject to rather different, if equivalent, discursive complexes. Thus every contemporary religion and dominant culture more or less explicitly holds these values because of the links between culture and nation, and the patriarchal character of the public–private division (Pateman 1989), such that patriarchal relations bolster the nation-state (Yuval-Davis 1997). It is important that not only minoritised cultural and religious practices, specifically Islamic notions of honour and shame, should get talked about in relation to this. The debate that gripped the British media in October 2006, prompted by Cabinet Minister Jack Straw's comments about his supposed communication difficulties with veiled women, merely illustrated the latest reiteration of a well-worn theme. While this debate functioned as a pretext for the outpouring of white (liberal and reactionary) anxieties about cultural differences, cast within a frame of the purported oppositions between multiculturalism, assimilation and integration (or even feminism vs. multiculturalism, see Phillips 2007), what it really highlighted (apart from the fear that underlies racism) was how the regulation of girls' and women's conduct – including their dress and appearance – is at issue precisely because it is treated as a transcultural universal indicator of culture. It was this feature – presumably because of the naturalised character of the elision between culture and the surveillance and control of women's dress and appearance – that failed to be problematised in the whole furore.

Girls' sexualities therefore become a site of regulation and problematisation at the outset. This is literally often from the outset of their lives, since the position of the girl is infused with the *potential* for dishonour/moral reprehensibility, even if she never behaves as such. A form of original sin, rather than innocence, therefore structures dominant approaches to the treatment of girls, of which current concern over teenage pregnancy (in minority countries or overpopulation in majority contexts) is perhaps only a secular form. The persistence of such discourses is seen in the lesser outrage generated by the sexual abuse of girls than boys (although the dishonouring of women is of course a key longstanding theme within familial and national disputes), and in recent years we have seen how rape has emerged as a *political* tool of national subjugation, although it is likely that it always has been a feature of war and occupation (Bourke 2004). Significantly, also reiterating the gendered public/private opposition, this association between rape and politics-with-a-big-'P' is what has brought sexual violence into discussions of torture and persecution, that enable it in some contexts to 'count' in asylum and immigration claims (Palmary 2006a, 2006b). In general, the greater prevalence of 'asking for it' discourses work to transpose the sexual evaluation of women back on to girls, treating them as 'becoming women' rather than children (Burman 1995c; this volume Chapters 8 and 9).

Highlighting the gendering of childhood

One by-product of this unsatisfactory state of affairs is that it at least does bifurcate the notionally gender-free category of the child. For dominant discourses of sexuality (especially as informed by psychoanalytic ideas circulating in culture) attribute sexuality as much more 'natural' to boys (cf. Walkerdine 1990a). Indeed, in terms of the regulation of young sexualities it was the masturbation of boys that preoccupied the modern European imagination, rather than the attribution of any such desires to girls (cf. Jordanova 1989). Moreover, the difficulty of envisaging active female sexuality outside conditions of abuse has been identified by Jan Haaken (1998) as central to what is occluded by the 'memory wars' over false/recovered memories of abuse in therapy. As her account lucidly demonstrates, feminists have also been guilty of emphasising the position of women as victims so that it is hard to envisage ways for women to perceive or engage in sexual fantasies or relationships outside contexts of abuse. In broader terms, insofar as there may have been a shift in the gendering of the ideal-typical child from cultural masculinity to femininity to accord with the changing demands of neoliberalism for flexible, emotionally literate workers (Burman 2006a), it is significant that this also connotes the constitution of a docile, conscientious but dispensable workforce – individualised and un-unionised. (Though it is important to emphasise here that this image does not recognise girls' and women's active organisation and resistance to such conditions, see e.g. Sudbury 1998; Wilson 2006.)

The girl as prototypical woman

There is a third consequence of the elision between childlikeness and womanliness that – if they appeared to have travelled away from them – brings discussions home to Northern market centres. For the ever-increasing demands for women to be thinner and younger looking have intensified the erotic gaze upon young women. In addition to the ever-decreasing body weight of fashion models (Wolf 1990) (and notwithstanding some protests over 'size zero' designs emerging in 2006 from within the fashion industry) and the escalating rates of eating distress across the world (Littlewood 1995), within many conventional narratives the young (inexperienced, supposedly asexual) girl is the prototypical male object of sexual desire. As Archard notes:

> Most worryingly, innocence itself can be a sexualized notion as applied to children. It connotes a purity, virginity, freshness and immaculateness which excites by the possibilities of possession and defilement. The child as innocent is in danger of being the idealized woman of a certain male sexual desire – hairless, vulnerable, weak, dependent and uncorrupted.
>
> (Archard 1993: 40)

(On the theme of hair/lessness, as connected with gendered sexualities, see Lesnik-Oberstein 2007. Indeed Rose (1991) discusses John Ruskin's refusal to consummate his marriage with Effie Gray because he had not anticipated a woman's – hairy – body, and that he later fell in love with a ten-year-old girl.)

Therefore not only does this innocence attract abuse rather than protection, but it also highlights the complex intersections between representations of femininity and childhood. Moreover, these discourses show a propensity to flip into reverse, so that the equally current debate over childhood obesity (with the British emerging from a recent 2006 survey as the most overweight nation in Europe) rapidly reveals its gendered and classed features and associated anxieties of social disorder and unruly desires. The announcement in July 2006 that more people in the world are overweight than underweight obscures the complex intersections of poverty and weight and their variations across the world. Overwhelmingly in Euro-US contexts, overweight is associated with being poor, while 'healthy eating' in such overdeveloped contexts is expensive, as the fast food outlets who target the poor know only too well (Schlosser 2001). As well as passive, unhealthy television addict 'couch potatoes' or asocial computer nerds (still conventionally culturally gendered as masculine), the 'weighty' young women of Britain invoke images of binge-drinking ladettes out on the town, whose violence as well as alcohol (and other drug) consumption now matches or surpasses that of their male counterparts ('Girls "more likely to drink and smoke"', *Evening Standard* 18 May 2006).

Reversing the sex/gender polarity

Beyond this there is a further conceptual link between discourses of gender and performativity. Once we acknowledge that the eroticisation of girls/children is inscribed within the conditions of gender and childhood, then sexuality – whether attributed or experienced – becomes central to the formation and definition of gender, rather than being merely grafted on to it. Judith Butler's (1990, 1993) work has done much to unsettle the binary sex/gender framework underlying much second wave feminist theory, positing (hetero)sexuality as constitutive of, rather than arising from, gendered positions. There are significant implications of such analyses for the conceptualisation (and practice around) child sexual abuse (Warner 1995, 2000). Thus, that the sexual abuse of girls is primarily heterosexual and of boys homosexual (since in both cases the abuse is mainly carried out by men), indicates the centrality of the gendered as well as sexed character of their abuse. Indeed, such gendered associations may well contribute to the difficulty boys and men who have been abused may experience in disclosing this, because of its feminised/unmasculine connotations. So while we may wonder how useful it is to retain the general category of children's sexuality (or child sexual abuse for that matter), we might equally step back from the presumption of the priority of gendered identifications to consider other axes of convergence and divergence produced through specific sexual orientations or experiences. As Levett notes:

> While a recent and growing literature suggests that boys are often sexually abused in contemporary Western society, it is not always clearly argued that the implications for boys and girls are different because of the association between gender and power. Boys grow into men and therefore into subjectivities in which coercive sexual relating and the active perpetration of sexual assault, on children and women, become a possibility (even if only in thought and fantasy).
>
> (Levett 1994: 243)

Unholy alliances?

The traditional binary structuring the double standards of sexual evaluation for women in the post-'sexual revolution' topography of the North (i.e. virgin vs. whore; or slag vs. lesbian for young women, Cowie and Lees 1981) has fed into a collusion between feminists and the moral majority, as in the 'unholy marriage' over some feminists' demands for anti-pornography measures and censorship, for example. Alternatively, libertarian approaches to women's and children's sexualities also tread a dangerous path that attracts other undesirable allies. Thus paedophile organisations have traditionally been among the few who have supported efforts to elaborate an agentic analysis of young people's sexualities (Stainton Rogers and Stainton Rogers 1992).[7]

This means that it is hard to prefiguratively envisage, rather than proscribe, available possibilities. While it may currently be impossible to go beyond prevailing dichotomies – of victims vs. perpetrators, for example – nevertheless failure to so implicates us both in clear injustice and defensive avoidance, so that exploring what lies behind the avoidance becomes an urgent and necessary task.

Childhood sexualities therefore trouble our notions of both adult sexuality and gender relations, implicating questions of power both through and beyond discourses of abuse. My focus hereon will be on some recent texts that have in particular caught the British and European imagination. Thus one key question is how much further they resonate beyond this location and temporal horizon, including in relation to the US, the origin point (and addressee) of so much of popular culture, yet also a site of contrast with European art forms and genres.[8] While clearly such an approach could be viewed as reproducing current norms of cultural parochialism (if also dominance), I justify this, first, on the grounds of the need to interrogate that which is usually overlooked (the normalised absence, so avoiding reproducing voyeuristic structures of pathologisation of the 'other'); and, second, in so doing to highlight other culturally sedimented power relations at work to promote, and perhaps constrain, the discourses of universalisation and naturalisation that so imbue representations of childhood.

Amélie: or the work of the gendering of childhood in the social imaginary

In the following discussion I now move from analysis to explication of what is accomplished by the cultural subscription to the motif of the (abused, girl) child. I want to argue that current representations of the little girl as quintessential moral, feeling subject function according to a dynamic equivalent to Freud's jokes (Freud 1905a). For, seduced by her charm, she warrants the setting in circulation of assumptions that, if they were expressed by a boy or man, would provoke critical scrutiny. Yet they escape this because they emanate from a young, gamine woman. Such are the hallmarks of the early twenty-first century hit film, *Le fabuleux destin d'Amélie Poulain* [The fabulous fate/destiny of Amélie Poulain] (dir: J.P. Jeanet, France, 2001), which in English goes under the shortened title of *Amélie*. (Indeed, even this shift can be seen as doing the work of generalisation and universalisation, in contrast to the specified – first and last named – identification of the French title.) Significantly hailed as both 'the quintessential French film' and as 'the key contributor to French cinema's recapture of its national box office' (programme notes), themes of national cultural identification are mobilised.

This chapter could have been based entirely on an analysis of the backdrop to the opening credits, which show the young Amélie engage in (or perform/display) quintessential 'childlike' activities. The posters advertising the film show a grotesque close-up of the 'naïve gamine' (sic, programme notes) white, French, adult Amélie (Tautou), with a second showing her younger self from the credits, with raspberries stuck at the end of her fingers that she is about to eat with great gusto one by one. In a third shot she is seen (as a young adult) sitting in the stalls of a cinema, gazing up at an invisible film screen (which we later realise also expresses her efforts to project into reality her own life's desires).

It is important to pause to ask that question which is somehow so normalised within cultural narratives as to escape attention. What is the function of the presence of the earlier little Amélie in the film? Through this, the film provides an explanatory narrative as to why Amélie should adopt as her mission in life the project to 'fix' things for people, to solve puzzles and right wrongs. The young Amélie of the opening credits functions as the narrative/chronological 'baseline'; the origin point of a normal, playful, engaging and communicative child, confirmed by her antics as demonstrably normal so that this can become retroactively animated as a site of loss and mourning. In this, we see the familiar conflation of logic with chronology that is so central to the recourse to developmentalist explanations (cf. Stainton Rogers and Stainton Rogers 1998); in this case it anchors the reading of Amélie as 'basically' a normal, happy, well-adjusted, inquiring child, to whom life has dealt some difficult experiences. For, I want to claim, Amélie is the everyman and everywoman of modern Euro-US subjectivity, carefully crafted as the alienated, disconnected and thwarted young person who has lacked crucial conditions in her life to enable her to engage with people, with the world. As viewers of this film, 'we' are invited to position ourselves as like her, fundamentally good, loving and life-loving; but we have encountered obstacles which have prevented us from realising all we wanted to be. We somehow (for Amélie seems as mystified by this as we are – both about her and ourselves) lack the right skills, the right experiences to 'get it right' (and to find 'Mr Right'). Life, the world, has stopped us from becoming what we should have been, and blocked our access to being the adult that the child we feel we were was promised to become.[9]

The child as therapeutic subject

There are connections between the popular discourse of the 'inner child' and its retroactive (and now also prospective) mapping on to children; either the children we were, or the children and childhoods we should have had. (Indeed the British playwright Dennis Potter made a feature of getting adults to play children in his *Blue Remembered Hills* and so recreate a particular world of childhood.) This shift to portraying adult needs through the device of children's vulnerabilities is a tactic wittingly used by national and international child aid organizations (cf. Save the Children's 'Our job is to bring out the child in him', advertisement in *Guardian* 26 February 2001, portraying the then British Chancellor of the Exchequer, Gordon Brown). As discussed in Chapter 4, it was also explicitly used by the British children and young people's charity Barnardos in its advertising campaign of 2000, where in poster images a child substitutes for a young adult in a succession of contexts that dramatically invited the viewer to see the inner, needy or suffering, child within the adult. As already noted, the only girl/female image was also the only one specifically mentioning 'abuse'.

As discussed in Chapter 4, the cost of mitigating the discourse of blame or social censure (in terms of exoneration from the moral discourse of being undeserving of support or as responsible for their current circumstances and, perhaps, unhelpful habits) is the attribution of a traumatised past. Positing the past as the traumatogenic place of origin occludes present day sequelae/causative circumstances, privileging individualised, family-oriented explanations over state-neglect or deprivations. Another key assumption underlying these images is that the people involved *were* the children these adults now *are*, overlooking how real chronological children, rather than metaphorically fixated or developmentally arrested adults functioning *as* children, experience these issues everywhere.

Such discursive connections inform analysis of the film's narrative. It is significant that Amélie's traumatic childhood experiences concern emotional neglect and loss rather than abuse,[10] for this is of course a much safer site for audience identification. This forestalls a narrative of irreparable damage (of the kind invoked by the Barnardos' images). It also highlights her potential to be able to make the transition into ordinary connection. This traditional psychoanalytic model, which normalises her story via a therapeutic narrative, is secured by the portrayal of her 'normal/naturalness', the spontaneity and creative prankishness of the little girl. Moreover, there is other work performed by such devices. I want to note two themes here.

Racial purity in evocations of the past

Amélie's world evokes a timelessness that, as commentators have noted, connotes post-World War II Paris rather than that of 2001. Indeed (perhaps even biographically determined, for the lead actor's name is indeed Audrey), she is the contemporary Audrey Hepburn figure. Her Paris is saturated in golden light and populated by individuals possessing idiosyncratic 'likes' and 'dislikes' whose quirks are all equally weighted together in this vibrant, teeming, prototypical city. This is bolstered and naturalised by the images of nature that the film opens with (the butterfly and the arbitrary but far-reaching effects of its wing movements, and paradoxical images of individualist agency – as with the suicidal fish). But this is a cleaned up city, with no rubbish or greyness; no drugs, violence and homelessness; and the only black/non-white character is a learning disabled young man of (unspecified) Arabic background who functions as one of the prompts for Amélie's actions of compassion/pity/revenge. Indeed, this can be read as a fantasised reversal of current Middle East/Europe relations – with the 'foreign' man thereby kept safely away from the paternalistically inclined woman, and outside the conventional structure of white woman/black man relations (e.g. McClintock 1995).

It is as if we are being invited to think: remember, this is what, underneath it all (but underneath all what?[11] Exactly *what* are we being invited to shed?), 'our' Paris is really like. Released at a historical moment of intense xenophobic anxiety around numbers of black refugees and asylum seekers within Europe (even before the 'war against terrorism' of autumn 2001 demonised the Taliban, and by implication all people of Asian/Arabic backgrounds), is this the subjectivity of 'Fortress Europe', a racist fantasy of an all-white Europe?[12] Significantly, at another key moment of the film, Amélie speculates on what might prevent her designated beau from making it to the rendezvous she has set up. Here we are party to a remarkable representation of a fantasy chain of events that include him being abducted and caught up in political plots and intrigues that end with him in a tent on what possibly (mobilising a set of associations that are affective rather than logical but culturally potent) 'could be' (cf. Ahmed 2004b) the Afghan border. (That of course he has no conscious part in, since he too is an innocent casualty of an arbitrary and uncaring world.) At which point Amélie decides that she couldn't get involved with a man wearing a woolly hat, who eats borscht. This is a fascinating depiction of a swift chain of ideologically structured associations, dramatically illustrating the racialised structure of the attributed cultural-political imaginary that – once formulated – hovers tantalisingly between reflexive critique and disarming indulgence. At this moment, perhaps, the film almost unravels itself and exposes its preoccupations.[13]

Here we might recall the precipitant to, or constitutive moment of, the elaboration of Amélie's 'mission'. For her discovery that launches it occurs as she is watching the news of the British Princess Diana's death. Indeed the television reporting of the circumstances of Diana's car crash continues as the camera follows Amélie pulling out the box of childhood treasures (signifying the unrealised desires of childhood hopes?) stowed years before within the skirting board of her apartment wall. What is the significance of the elaboration of this context for the moment of definition of Amélie's 'destiny'? Is it perhaps a cautionary tale of a fairytale princess whose life choices or (thwarted?) sexual appetites led her astray to tragic conclusions?[14]

Feminising the liberal human subject

Below the surface of this *cinema patisserie* (as one widely quoted but anonymous commentator has dubbed the film) is unalloyed liberal humanism, complete with its dynamic of philanthropy, discretionary magnanimity and implicit, if not explicit, injunction for those helped to be like their helper in their wants, desires and actions (cf. Gronemeyer 1992). True, Amélie does not seek explicit recognition for her deeds; but the film narrative ensures she gains her identificatory satisfaction. There is no space in the film for people (whether viewers or her 'beneficiaries') to dispute or be appalled by her interventions; no possibility for Amélie's 'good deeds' to backfire by 'rectifying' the key misfortunes that turn out to hold together a fragile identity and grasp on reality, without which the character she aims to 'help' disintegrates. Perhaps even more significant is how there is no possibility envisaged that gaining a little bit of what they deserve could simply emphasise the scale of her beneficiaries' more general deprivation, and so enrage them more. To take one memorable example, Amélie does not ask the blind man for permission to whisk him across the road and babble about all the objects, activities and people she can see (thus driving home all that his disability makes him miss). As if further emphasising how this act fulfils her needs rather than his, she does not even enquire where it is he wants to go, before she just as peremptorily leaves him at the metro station and moves on to her next mission. Rather, the viewer is invited to be caught up in her warm glow of evangelical conviction that she is good, confirmed by the portrayal of the blind man's wonder, and his disorientation portrayed as welcome and uplifting. Further, the film displays an implicit hierarchy of who deserves more. Amélie's colleague in the café gets set up to have a sexual clinch with the jealous twitchy customer in the café toilet; whereas Amélie's own (hetero)sexual conquest is long, tender and private, as the culmination of the film narrative.

Not only is it as if the objects of her charity have no unconscious (by which they would in some sense enjoy, or gain gratification from, their symptoms, Žižek 1991b) but, further, it offers reassurance that things can be made better by bestowing a little care and attention, and goodwill. This is a psychoanalytic narrative of pure ego psychology; of adaptation to prevailing conditions, not an analysis of the psychic struggle to resist this. For we should note that the 'good deeds' that Amélie performs intervene only at the level of the personal and idiosyncratic. Her rescuing of the underdog or marginal person lies outside the domain of any political programme or commitment, and her tactics are equivalently opportunistic. She is portrayed as driven by identification, by the desire to overcome her isolation and inhibitions, and ultimately to make an intimate relationship.

If this detailed analysis of a single film narrative seems overblown, its significance lies in the response it appeared to generate. The film attracted widespread critical acclaim; has been frequently called a 'feelgood fairytale' which 'will leave audiences glowing even after the film has finished' (programme notes, Cornerhouse, Manchester, October 2001). I too 'felt good' when I saw it. But it is striking how any attempts to discuss the film seem to be met with a 'Don't!', as if to indicate some guilt about the enjoyment it provides. So what is wrong with a cathartic experience of this kind?

> The very idea of childhood itself is crucially implicated in the structures of feeling that define the bourgeois nuclear family and which prioritize emotion as a structuring and motivating force both for public and private life in contemporary capitalism.
>
> (Lesnik-Oberstein 1998: 7)

Before Hollywood schmaltz there was Victorian Gothic melodrama. *Amélie* stands not only in the longstanding tradition of the sentimentalisation of children, especially little girls (cf. the Maurice Chevalier song: 'Thank Heaven for Little Girls'). She is also heir to the structure of subjectivity that invests the young girl/woman as the human prototype, or rather, in a way that seems designed to foreclose such critical reflection. Lesnik-Oberstein notes of the function of children within literature:

> The 'child', in rescuing particular historians and children's literary critics from language and textuality, is made to preserve for them a safe world of an emotion which is spontaneous, caring and unified, and only in aberration abusive, violent, or divided against itself.
>
> (Lesnik-Oberstein 1998: 26)

Indeed, in addition to the underlying gender stereotypical, heteronormative narrative of a young woman's search for love, the film totally relies upon her gender (and her youth) for the plot to 'work'. The success of the film suggests that women and girls have now become normalised as identificatory sites across gender (as other recent films such as *Tideland* and *Pan's Labyrinth*, with young girls as primary protagonists, also indicate). A feminisation of the liberal human subject is performed that sits alongside the feminisation of labour and a proliferating psychological culture that promotes emotional literacy as the route for social progress, rather than investment in public services, for example (Squire 2001; Burman 2006a). Surely the meddling undertaken by Amélie, if conducted by a man (especially a white man), would elicit suspicion, hostility and resistance? Whereas, precisely mobilising the discourse of powerlessness and inconsequentiality signified by the combination of her gender and youth, done by a beautiful young woman it acquires a charming, rather than insulting, patronising or imperialist character. For as a girl/woman her very vulnerability and femininity exonerate her from such charges.

'Amélie' as the contemporary 'Mignon'

My analysis of *Amélie* has been informed by Carolyn Steedman's (1995) analysis of how the figure of the little girl emerged as the exemplar of modern Euro-US subjectivity. Steedman (1995) traces the story of Mignon across its many forms, but as centrally concerned with the figure of a little girl/young woman of uncertain origins and transient involvements, who became an object of fascination and identification for European audiences throughout the nineteenth and early twentieth century. While originally scripted by Goethe in the eighteenth century (although this fact only became widely known in the mid-nineteenth century), the story underwent mass circulation and was performed widely across Europe (and across genres and classes) throughout the nineteenth and early twentieth centuries.

Steedman's account of the prevalence and varieties of the story of Mignon from the highest cultural forms (e.g. arrangement of her theme song by Schubert) to the lowest (doggerel verse performances in East End London theatres) throughout this period of European modernisation and industrialisation highlights the consolidation of a structure of subjectivity, the formation of an interiority, an inner self, that was personified by the trope of the little girl. She concludes the book with the sentence: 'since the end of eighteenth century the lost object has come to assume the shape and form of a child' (p. 174). I suggest that, along with the markers of atemporality within *Amélie*, this structure of identification is central to its success.

Steedman's analysis links the mythic figure of Mignon, and her capacity to move audiences, with the nineteenth-century emergence in Europe of concern over child labour and sexual exploitation. She draws connections with the beneficent, if eroticised, gaze of the London-based philanthropic journalist Mayhew, whose interviews with young working girls such as the 'Watercress seller' helped to pave the way for British parliamentary debates on the employment and protection of children (also discussed in Steedman 1983). The figure of the feminine/feminised child acrobat populates many European stories of this period, from which Steedman concludes: 'The acrobat is always an expression of regret for one's lost native land' (p. 111). Thus the voyeurism attending children brought with it an awareness of their suffering and exploitation within a context of cultural-political transitions that was visually represented by the 'strange dislocations' of the child acrobat.

So by such moves, Amélie's struggles, like Mignon's, are thematised as 'our' own, 'our' stumbling efforts for connection and belongingness. Her antics make others act out what she needs to do herself, rehearsing and vicariously resolving her own existential dilemmas. We watch her knowing that this is her struggle for redemption from a world of narcissistic isolation (melodramatised by the black and white film reels of her life we see her watching at home). She experiments in manipulating others to take risks with their lives as if to learn from them how to do it herself; but at a safe distance (just as we do by watching her).

A further resonance arises between the film star and the acrobat as the object of our gaze. Steedman (1995) highlights the fascination which the acrobat attracts; we watch her spectacle breathless and amazed; and in the case of the child acrobat, the inexperience signified by youth compounds the sense of their physical vulnerability to instil a sense of anxious thrill. The dynamic of watching with a fascination that is also horrifying and horrified is central to the uses of images of children in charity advertising (as Save the Children 1992 acknowledged in issuing guidelines on the representation of children). Here, classically, it is the ambiguously gendered, but usually female, child who is used to elicit money (see Chapter 6). Steedman considers why it was that (girl) child acrobats caught the popular imagination of Victorian audiences, in terms of generating anxieties around abusive working conditions, rather than (the usually male) sweeps. She proposes that it was precisely because they were more attractive to look at (and despite their far fewer numbers).

> Conceptualisation of cruelty to children was a development of these years [the 1880s], but the means of seeing and writing about the physical abuse and distortion of children's bodies had been available from the 1830s onwards. The chimney sweep and the acrobat bore the marks of adult intervention in a strikingly visual manner. The little acrobat had the aesthetic advantage over the sweep of being pleasing in appearance, and bearing witness to a more elaborate form of adult intervention.
>
> (Steedman 1995: 110)

The overdetermination between the feminisation of childhood and the infantilisation of women is confirmed in the figure of Mignon, and recapitulated in *Amélie* where the camera, as (perhaps) our phallic speculum (cf. Kaplan 1983), caresses and pursues Amélie's anxious and tentative forays into the world of relationships. We are witness to the crafted painful story of Amélie's entry into the designated adult social world of meaningful heterosexual relationship. However, her very intensity, as recapitulated by the intense visual focus on her throughout the film (again noted by many critics) betrays her own social ineptitudes in a manner reminiscent of the fascinated gaze of nineteenth-century audiences on the steps and slips of the child acrobat.[15]

Like Amélie, Mignon is alone and unused to relationships. Her familial and 'personal' links are disconnected and disrupted. Steedman discusses the motif of Mignon, as constituted not only as the recurring object of the male gaze that ultimately is resolved into (what would now be recognised as) a narrative of sexual, as well as physical, abuse. Beyond this, the identification with her speaks to her role as the repository of all the nostalgic longings for the losses and thwarted desires that modernity has imposed:

> The idea of the child was used both to recall and to express the past that each individual life contained: what was turned inside in the course of individual development was that which was also latent; the child *was* the story waiting to be told.
>
> (Steedman 1995: 11, original emphasis)

But the voyeurism also speaks to the erotic, but proscribed longings, mobilised *by* her:

> Throughout the nineteenth century, Mignon was also what she always had been: just a word, just a name – a word for little girls on the street

> (in the general sense, but gesturing also towards the other sense), the word for little girls you fancy.
>
> (Steedman 1995: 38)

It is this double dynamic of identification and projection (including of erotic investments), structured by the current dominant meanings accorded our embodied histories, that renders the status of childhood, including childhood sexualities, so problematic. Moreover, alongside cultural overdeterminations linking femininity and childhood, Steedman's analysis illuminates why it is so hard to separate representations of childhood from those of abuse. For childhood, as reconstructed within the modern Euro-US imagination, is precisely that period or condition which can only be remembered as spoiled, precisely by virtue of our emotional connection to and separation from it, culminating in the sense of it being over. Thus, if our very conceptions of little girls are culturally invested with the narrative of our own wounded histories, then they are already constituted as abused.

Before we leave *Amélie* to move on to another key text, some final comments on gender are needed. Steedman makes much of the androgyny of Mignon; of her ambiguous gender (and corresponding sexuality) – much of which is resolved by the later established narrative of abuse. While appearing gender-unspecified, Mignon's status as an identifiable human subject is finally resolved in favour of being female. (Here we should recall that this fable gained its wide circulation at around the same time that Foucault claims gender and sexual identities became sedimented as stable and singular, Foucault 1980c.) We might want to argue that the debates about the cyborg beloved of contemporary feminist theory as disturbing gender binaries, and refusing sexed and gender specifications, are heir to the motif of the child acrobat (cf. Haraway 1991a). But what is crucial is that, notwithstanding the lack of feminine trappings (reflected in the unfeminised name Mignon), 'it' (as Steedman often calls her) is gendered as female. Much as, in the end, Piercy genders her cyborg as male, reflecting its intended purpose as a war machine (Piercy 1992; see my discussion in Burman 1999; Chapter 2 this volume). As many feminists and others have pointed out, the youthful, boyish girl is a key sex symbol within Euro-US culture – and rapidly spreading beyond, which is reflected in the reiteration of the descriptor 'naïve gamine' accompanying commentaries on *Amélie*.

To sum up: in this part of the chapter I have been arguing that, as indicated by themes of *Amélie*, three key slippages are performed in the mobilisation of indulgence surrounding the girl/child. First, representations of childhood work retrospectively to secure a narrative of developmental causation (and the fact that identifying this dynamic has a range of political possibilities is indicated by the ways this theme is taken up in Chapter 12 in terms of the potential to draw on this theory of trauma as an 'antidevelopmental' resource). Second, there is a racist vision of a homogeneous society, divided only by 'natural' categories of age and gender relations, and overdetermined by classical colonial themes of protecting (white) girls and women from contamination by (black) men. Third, affective structures of sentimentalisation mobilised around (girl) children contribute to a depoliticisation of available explanations for the conditions of people's misery that distracts attention from structural inequalities, and then renders these as personal circumstances amenable to relatively simple correction once appropriate (i.e. feminised) human involvement is supplied. In case there is any doubt about where this leads, it is worth noting how advanced capitalism is now increasingly valorising childlike spontaneity and feminised 'people-skills' (Gordo López and Burman 2004), and 'emotional literacy' schemes gain state endorsement to sanitise the anger of the new male disenfranchised (Burman 2006a; Parker 2006).

Brass Eye: the repudiation of (the repudiation of) paedophilia

If Steedman invites us to consider to what extent our loving or surveillant gaze on children is an eroticised one, then *Amélie* perhaps could be said to ironise what else the erotically charged figure of the girlchild/woman warrants. Certainly much time and effort is invested in looking after and at children. On this point we might note also how nineteenth-century campaigners against exploitative child labour practices, probably for political rhetorical purposes, would describe 15-year-old girl factory workers as 'infants'. Engaging critically with Jim Kincaid's (1992) arguments, Steedman discusses the gaze of the nineteenth-century child welfarist as 'what is for us the irreducibly paedophiliac gaze turned upon the girl child' (Steedman 1995: 7). The thought that we who champion on behalf of children might also be implicated in the practices of those whom we vilify as abusing them is rarely admitted. Indeed, along with the 'terrorist', the paedophile represents the contemporary threat to the social order but one that, unlike the terrorist, can be nicely sustained and contained as individual (rather than systemic). The paedophile has become a key monster in the contemporary British, if not Euro-US, imagination. Whether and how this development corresponds with the widespread application and publicisation of children's rights discourse through the UN Convention can only be a matter of speculation. It does however coincide with an unprecedented level of concern over child sexual abuse, with major investigations currently underway in Britain and the Republic of Ireland into the condoning of systematic abuse within precisely those institutions – schools, residential care, church groups, youth groups, as well as families – devised to educate, look after and care for children and young people.[16]

During the summer of 2000 Britain witnessed a set of profound and disturbing events that disrupted the usual pattern of more explicitly racialised and classed seasonal disturbances (see also Bell 2003).[17] Increasing practices of surveillance of released or identified 'sex offenders' combined with greater public access to previously classified information to produce a violent outpouring of apparently grassroots community mobilisation against a few individuals whom it emerged were on such a register. Moreover, the violence spread to others – men, women and families – not only those under suspicion of having connection to any sex offender, but those who had none whatsoever. People moved out of their houses and areas in fear. Any spurious link could warrant direct, deadly action (including firebombing houses as well as physical attacks). A paediatrician in Wales was attacked because her professional title bore a resemblance to the term paedophile. Significantly all this happened alongside the first wave of forced dispersal of refugees, and within months of the government failing to repeal Section 28 (the section of local government legislation passed under Thatcher prohibiting 'the promotion of homosexuality' that was specifically directed against educational initiatives formulated to challenge homophobia in schools). At the same time the debate about reducing the age of consent for gay men to be equivalent to that of heterosexual relationships was rumbling its way through parliament (but after it had had its most widely publicised debate in the Lords).

The summer of 2001 saw a different scandalisation around paedophilia, albeit one that exemplified precisely what it aimed to incite comment upon. The *Brass Eye Special* on paedophilia,[18] screened on 26 July enraged the British press at a time when parliament was in recession, with the ethnocentrism of its news coverage at these times giving rise to its designation as 'the silly season' (i.e. when the absence of 'serious' news means that issues that would usually attract little attention can get blown up into major news items).[19] Or perhaps this was the object, coming as it did a year after the events it satirised. 'Within hours of being aired at the end of July the *Brass Eye Special* had became the most complained about show in British television history' (*Guardian* 7 September 2001). The tabloid press took up the then British government Minister for Child Protection's (Beverley Hughes) claim that the programme was 'unspeakably sick' (although it later emerged that she had not seen it, *Guardian* 7 September 2001), with the *Daily Mail* dubbing it 'the sickest TV show ever' (*Mail* editorial 30 July 2001). Its broadcaster, Channel 4, largely defended it, arguing in a statement (reported on 27 July 2001) that the programme '*Brass Eye* takes as its central subject paedophilia, challenges what Morris [the writer/director/lead] perceives as the hysterical way the media treats the issue and tackles inconsistencies in our attitudes to children and sex'. Nevertheless, broadcasting regulators censured the broadcaster and demanded that the channel apologise for the offence caused.[20]

As a spoof documentary, even the title *Brass Eye* both evoked and satirised the panoptical, roving and colonial-surveillant gaze of self-styled 'serious' exposé programmes (of which the longstanding British prototypes would be *Horizon* and *Panorama* – both invoking visual metaphors). But as its title suggests, rather than seeing or revealing, *Brass Eye* reflected back to its viewers what they are, and how they look, through an ironising (cheaper and cheekier than gold) hue. It interpellated and implicated the viewer at a number of different levels, making it disturbing viewing indeed – not least for the initially subtle but then increasingly wild exaggerations of the conventions of the genre of news reporting – that themselves promote the titillation of horror. Indeed, the primary focus on forms of representation and the subject positions thereby elaborated worked to comment specifically on the sensationalisation and exploitation of its topic.

Resembling the documentary genre, the programme moved between 'on the spot' reporting, accounts of research and interviews with 'experts', and also included 'personal' accounts.[21] It also parodied the fund-raising/health promotional marketing device of 'celebrity endorsement', using noteworthy personalities to publicise campaigns. It reported on 'Bandaid' type stunts (such as the assembling of children in stadiums to keep them safe from paedophiles), and culminating in a studio song led by the presenters with a school choir. It covered areas of social concern in relation to child sexual abuse such as the use of the internet, and claims of links between pop music and the sexualisation of little girls (including also their willing engagement in this).

Whilst (perhaps) the programme aimed to draw attention to devices of representation, the outrage it provoked reflected precisely the elision it tried to highlight. For the outraged reception treated the form as transparent and addressed only the content it presented. Problems of reading and interpreting any text are exemplified when debating issues around the representation of children and the dynamics mobilised, even in the name of commenting upon them. Moreover, tempting as it would be to recount the details of the different satirical components to this programme, this would perhaps obscure the most important issue. For to be distracted into discussing individuals or specific instances recapitulates one of the key problems; we are talking about something that lies beyond individuals, and specific actions or examples, but enters into the understanding and evaluation of truth claims.

I want to suggest that if *Amélie* entertains because the film narrative recapitulates the workings of a joke, *Brass Eye* exposes the structure of the joke-making apparatus, with the 'butt' of the joke shifting from the gullible (lynchmob-inclined) public,[22] and thoughtless celebrities, to problematise our own credulity as viewers and the very moral system that guides our evaluation. As one media critic was quick to point out:

> The celebrity vignettes are not there, as some have suggested, to show how little attention famous people pay to what they are saying. Rather, they are offered as illustrations of the way truth is produced in society by thoughtless people reading unedited versions of other people's thoughtless scripts. This point was reinforced by the three Labour ministers who condemned *Brass Eye* in terms that indicated that they hadn't watched it. . . . The thing that makes Morris' programme so

> remarkable as a piece of political satire is its utter disinterest in the small potatoes of personality. While other, smaller minds are banging on about this or that act of hypocrisy and throwing mud at political figures, Morris has been engaged in the much more difficult task of creating a critique of society that doesn't rest on calling individuals to account . . . Last Thursday's *Brass Eye* would have made much easier viewing if its target had been easy to isolate. In spite of appearances, the programme wasn't about the media . . . it made use of this familiar vernacular to say something much bigger and scarier that any mere parody ever could.
>
> (Raven 2001: 5)

The arbitrariness of our scandalisation and its equally likely response of titillation was expressed within the programme's fake commercial break, with the screening of 'ads' for two contrasting programmes bearing the same name: 'The Pedo-files'. The first was presented with the image and gruff masculine narrative voice of a Schwarzenegger-type figure 'delivering justice on the men who have sex with our children . . . I was one. I killed the paedophile in me; they don't deserve punishment they deserve gunishment' (my transcription). This was followed by a second (delivered by an unseen woman with a jolly voice-over) announcing a new series, 'The pedo-files, one hundred kids and a sex offender on an island . . . what is going to happen?' (ibid.)

Where central truths become organised into unquestionable orthodoxies, we enter a domain of fundamentalism. Any fixed certainty of the kind being so strenuously asserted as in the public outrage to the *Brass Eye* programme must in some sense defend against its opposite. That this is not a unique instance, or a specifically British phenomenon, was illustrated by how in 1998 the animation *South Park*, not usually known for proscribing any topic, made it clear that 'paedophilia' was off limits (and the fact that this was considered so noteworthy was indicated by the extraction of this discussion for a British television retrospective compilation programme themed for each year).[23]

Finally, in terms of exposing covert themes warranted by prevailing discursive arrangements, a key moment occurred in *Brass Eye* when the presenter asked the question 'Why are no paedophiles black?', which was followed by a simulation of the programme being cut or taken off air. What was the function of this? The ludicrousness of the question indicates something of the structure of the conventional representation of paedophilia. For while of course there are black paedophiles – for child sexual abuse is noted to occur equally frequently in all classes and backgrounds in majority contexts – rather the figure of the black man is perhaps so always-already sexualised as to escape specific gaze in relation to the scandalisation around paedophilia. To normalise representations of abusers in this way would be to throw into question the structure of the Euro-US racist imaginary with its attendant allocations of gender and sexuality. Or perhaps this question was posed in the voice of the white working class, who are most commonly portrayed as the perpetrators, thus giving voice to the classical ways in which white and black working-class communities are divided. The simulation of the programme being cut or censored highlights this as a critical moment of anxiety (although in a Lacanian or Benjaminian sense it might precisely offer the moment of 'interruption' that presents the greatest possibilities) – although significantly this issue did not figure in any of the complaints about the programme.[24]

Contested relationships

How do these fictional (historical and current) texts help illuminate what is at issue in addressing children's sexualities? The meanings accorded childhood as the mirror of cultural representations of nature and society invite us to consider *whose* sexuality is at issue. Following (after Foucault 1980c, 1981) the logic of analyses of power/knowledge that portray sexuality as relationship not possession, we cannot divorce ourselves from long-standing structures of child watching that both eroticise children and repudiate this desire. It seems there is currently no way to recognise a child's desires, or claims to sexuality, without becoming involved or implicated in them.

To return to more everyday practical concerns, there are of course explicit relationships at contest: between, for example, an adult male child abuser and a child. But this characterisation is, as the *Brass Eye* programme highlights, clearly insufficient since most abuse actually occurs in relationships where the adult is trusted by and well known to the child. Further, as feminists have long pointed out in relation to all forms of domestic violence, the narrative of happy, well-adjusted families is maintained by the myth of 'stranger danger' (e.g. Hanmer and Itzin 2000). Beyond this, all state structures are now implicated in the organised, systematic sexual abuse of children, quite apart from the explicit trafficking in children, and child prostitution (cf. Ennew 1986; Narveson 1989; Desai 2006). Thus key relationships at contest include those of the state and the multinational producers of culture that market children and women's sexualised bodies as commodities to buy and possess (by women and children as well as their desirers). At more mundane levels, the layers of professionals whose business it is to evaluate and legislate upon desires, including those exhibited by as well as in relation to children have little more to offer:

> There is a paradoxical conflict of interest between modern efforts to remedy injustices and eliminate the exploitation of children, including 'acting in their best interest' on the one hand, and the play of middle-class power on the other. When the capacity of families and communities to find their own remedies for problems such as child sexual abuse

> is taken away, we find that the law and welfare procedures do not offer better remedies.
>
> (Levett 1994: 258)

Moreover, while crucial in bringing issues of sexual abuse to public attention, there has been a general sidelining of feminist thinking that has occurred within the professionalisation and medicalisation of sexual abuse. As Emerson and Frosh (2001) noted in relation to the clinical and research treatment of young male abusers, such professionalisation closes down possibilities for the kind of feminist-informed constructionist approaches that can destabilise hegemonic masculinities and identify possible spaces for non-abusing identities and practices:

> These mainstream formulations represent and depend upon powerful pathologising and individualising interpretations of boys' sexually abusing behaviours, drawing on an array of professional frameworks, established theories and clinical models, which, just as they tend to marginalise and suppress contested approaches, privilege the interpretive frameworks of experts in the field over, for example, an abusing boy's own meaning-making activities. Thus it is always the expert and not the boy who qualifies as a knower.
>
> (Emerson and Frosh 2001: 85)

Alongside the medicalisation of 'sexual abuse' into 'paedophilia', which detracts from its everyday character, together with Waites (2005) we might note the silence on children having sex with each other. So although 'incest' is sometimes used to refer to sibling sexual relationships, this has largely dropped out the sphere of public concern (Bell 1993a). While the damage of sexual abuse is generally regarded as not necessarily so much concerned with sex as with the betrayal of trust and imposition of deception (cf. Warner 2000), this may be true also of sibling relations. Moreover, our current procedures can prevent, as much as they incite, disclosure. As such they run the risk of recapitulating the very dynamics of abuse that they seek to expose.

We are left weighing up the conundrum that the legacies of liberalism elaborate, with one set of interests in portraying children's desires as private matters (reflecting individualism and the public/private divide); and another betraying the state regulation always enacted in the name of attending to, and so governing, individual 'choice' (Rose 1990). Further, through close scrutiny of some widely circulating texts I have tried to highlight the implicit structure of racialisation (central to all universalised categories – and common to the representation of childhood abuse no less than supposedly 'normal' childhoods). Finally, it is relevant to recall that the general focus on child abuse obscures how abuse occurs not (only) because of 'bad' individuals or families, but because societies abuse children by the conditions they create for them, including subjecting them to war, famine, poverty (cf. Cairns 1992).

No kidding

So, in terms of control of desire and sexuality, I have been suggesting that we cannot know about desire and sexuality outside the prevailing structures of regulation and surveillance that produce them. This may seem a rather deterministic picture, offering little in the way of positive outcomes or ways forward. But at least highlighting the scale of the conceptual problems involved may indicate how efforts directed towards individual regulation can only have limited effects (e.g. intensification of surveillance of sex offenders, or restricting children's movements to keep them safe). Practically, Waites (2005) notes how in practice police interpret sex offences flexibly, rarely charging a 17-year-old young man having sex with a 15-year-old young woman, and he calls for the lowering of the age of consent to reflect this.

Even if we cannot get outside the structure of meanings surrounding Euro-US childhood as a signifier of selfhood, interiority of subjectivity, I have been suggesting that we can at least recognise some of its consequences. These include how it is organised to ignore, overlook or reject children and childhoods that do not 'fit' it. We can try to remain alert to its exclusionary character, and its exercise and function within the reproduction of prevailing structures of classed and raced – as well as gendered – inequalities, and the complex contests as well as intersections between these.

Instead, perhaps we can acknowledge and explore the mixture of emotions that comprise current configurations of sexuality: including attraction, curiosity and identification; and recognise the myriad ways power relations enter intimate, and not so intimate, relationships with children. Rather than demonising the presence and exercise of power in sexual relations, but equally not exonerating or underestimating these, we could apply such analyses to inform how these aspects also structure relations of care; to include pity and disgust, as well as nurturance and pride. Relations of dependence necessarily involve trust and intimacy, and therefore also include the potential for exploitation. There are various conceptual and methodological frameworks that could support such perspectives – ranging from the psychoanalytic (as taken up in Chapter 6) to the baroque (MacLure 2006).

Two central problems remain: first, how to move beyond current chains of signification that link, and mutually constrain, women's and children's desires (and 'rights') within prevailing discourses (and legislation) that deny or limit the expression of sexuality; second, for both women and children, how to create conditions for the articulation of desire that are not framed by discourses of risk or abuse.[25] While hegemonic, these are of course not the only available repertoires structuring representations of young people's (including girls') sexualities. While clearly *Lolita* (and other more nuanced cultural representations such as *Taxi Driver*, *Paper Moon* and *Léon* – and my discussion of *Amélie*) reflect the projection of desire directed towards young girls back to their desirers as a wish fulfilment, there may be other ways of acknowledging or attributing young people's sexualities that do not merely bolster the fantasies of the cultural subject of liberal masculinity. The ambiguities mobilised by more recent cultural texts such as *Hard Candy*, the 2006 film that shows a young girl mobilising her attractiveness/ sexuality to lure the adult man in order to exact violent revenge for his transgressive desire for her, may be a case in point.

It is likely that, if we manage to recognise (as opposed to overlook) these ways, they may indeed challenge core features of dominant understandings of both femininity and childhood. The 'wanton, ribald and feisty heroines' (Warner 1997: xv) of Angela Carter's final (1992) book *Wise Children* exhibit a wisdom that is not remotely romantic, nor are they passive enough to elicit romanticisation. Other authors have proposed turning to fantasy and science fiction to unsettle received understandings of gender, sexuality and childhood (e.g. Stainton Rogers and Stainton Rogers 1998). Notwithstanding my focus in this chapter on fiction, I remain convinced that, useful as this strategy may be, there are plenty of real-life examples for us to work with – if only we can understand (if not shed) enough of our conceptual baggage around the cultural-historical framing of childhood to recognise this. In this chapter I have attempted to turn the tables on dominant sentimental discourses of childhood by analysing what lies behind seemingly 'innocent' popular cultural texts,[26] and how these leave unquestioned key problems that more controversial treatments (such as *Brass Eye*) highlight. I have proposed moving beyond the structure of subjectivity that consumes women's and children's sexualities as entertainment (in popular culture) as well as business (the professionalisation of abuse), to take the former as seriously as the latter. By such means we might anticipate structures of emancipation around gender, age and sexuality that include not only children and young people, but us all.

6 Appealing and appalling children

Focused on a detailed analysis of a corpus of charity appeal texts, this chapter explores the positions made available for their readers and, in particular, deals with their more and less comfortable features. The chapter has an explicit address to psychotherapists, who after all (as professional carers who treat the relationships they form as the medium for change) have a responsibility to understand the dynamics of imaginary relationships surrounding children, and of the desire to help. But the relevance of the arguments made applies much more generally as well. Images of children – whether happy or distressed – abound in Northern popular media. However, as Chapter 5 elaborated, this implies less a concern for children than with other qualities associated with children, because of how the image of the child has come to personify adult inner selves. This dynamic of identification structures the commodification of children, in the sense that such associations are mobilised for the marketing of other products and issues. But perhaps a less obvious consequence is that it also gives rise to the abstraction of the child or children, since they always represent *more than* themselves.

While a particular range of popular cultural texts involving images of children is discussed here, the arguments presented in this chapter draw on a wider systematic study that is elsewhere discussed in terms of methodology precepts (Burman 1996b); in relation to the representation of gender (Burman 1995c); and as specifically applied to contexts of humanitarian disaster relief (Burman 1994a, 1994b, 1994d). These arguments are taken up in Part III of this book in relation to international development policy. The focus of this chapter is on the analytical tools that can help explicate why and how such texts exert the power that they do and, as such – notwithstanding shifts and turns in representations of children since this text was first drafted – I would claim remains as relevant as ever. Indeed, the recent trend for celebrities to adopt African/Asian 'orphans' provides a rather concrete example of the desire to bring 'home' that which our ambivalence about children has placed at a distance while, more locally, discussions of children focus on antisocial behaviour (see also Franklin 2002a). Similarly, the 2005 exhibition on the history of media coverage of famines (in London and now an ongoing online gallery and educational resource on www.imaging-famine.org) provides a dramatic visual commentary on these themes, while my analysis concurs with some of the more general conclusion drawn by Taylor (1998) in terms of the qualities of these images to 'provide moments of identification and reflection, moments of rejection and denial, and moments to be inquisitive about the dreadful fates of others. These reactions are often aroused by the mortal terrors of the flesh. They are not insignificant reflexes, nor should they be stigmatised as simply unworthy or shameful' (p. 7).

Hence the key question taken up in this chapter concerns what is at stake in the dynamic of helping, as exemplified within the project of helping, or saving, children. How can we acknowledge and respond to conditions of children's distress adequately, without smoothing away either the pain or the differences between us and those we help? How can we help in ways that do not require those whom we help to occupy a position of gratitude, or even to be or become like 'us'? The chapter reviews how the motif of the child, as the signifier of 'need' (whether in relation to children's needs or for more general populations), has generated widespread criticism. It continues to be mobilised as a key fund-raising strategy. To understand why, the chapter analyses the emotional dynamics of viewing these appeals. Drawing on a range of psychoanalytic frameworks used in contexts of both therapeutic and cultural analysis, it takes seriously the set of responses addressed by the request 'please don't look away'. Rather than reiterating the prevailing sentimentalisation of children, this is instead taken as the topic for analysis – in the course of which we come face to face with the negative responses generated both by children themselves and by attempts to coerce us into 'caring' about them. Drawing on such perspectives, the chapter concludes by identifying some possible ways out of these dilemmas, ending up by highlighting the status of child as 'boundary object' that brings together both psychoanalytic and sociology of science frames (a conceptual move developed further in Burman 2004b).

This chapter attempts to connect the private and individual world of psychotherapy with general cultural-political discourses and practices around children and childhood. Questions of the meanings and representations of childhood are as relevant to psychotherapists, including child psychotherapists, as they are to social workers and policymakers. A therapeutic encounter with any child engages with personal investments and identificatory relations that we work hard to disentangle. However, it is all too easy, in the midst of a very individual and personal relationship, to lose sight of the culturally constructed ingredients that inform the dynamics of specific adult–child relations. Equally discussions of childhood experiences with adults in psychotherapy mobilise representations of norms and ideas of childhood – if only (or perhaps especially) in their transgression. My concern here is therefore not to discuss specific histories of working with children, but rather to draw on the concepts and discussions generated by such analyses to address the broader cultural patterning of more public representations of childhood, which works to produce particular categories of children. I will be arguing that the current split and polarised character of contemporary images of childhood functions to maintain a particular defensive structure that prevents us from addressing the complexity and challenge of dealing with our own investments.

I analyse the identificatory relations elaborated by, and warded off by, representations of childhood. The material I am analysing correspondingly forms the sociocultural landscape within which particular interactions (therapeutic and otherwise) take place. While we cannot step outside such associations, acknowledging their forms and effects enables us to be better equipped to interpret and renegotiate them. My focus will correspondingly be on the kinds of texts and images that circulate across Europe and the so-called 'developed' world. The fact that I discuss both visual and verbal texts is important, since both often function together to develop a range of contradictory subjective positions and reactions. I will be addressing topics seemingly far away from the central concerns of psychotherapy, namely, sociological analyses of the contemporary cultural meanings of childhood, and the politics and tactics of child-saving and fund-raising appeals. However, I will be treating these as a crucial exemplary forum to explore the psychodynamics of the spectacle. In terms of my title, I will argue that the cultural appeal of children both suppresses and correspondingly constructs its converse: of horror and fear. This psychodynamic landscape is enacted within the discourses, politics and practices of childcare, child-watching and child-saving, in terms of gendered and culturally distributed polarisations between deserving and undeserving children.

Subjects and objects

At the outset, in motivating this culturally based analysis, I should make clear that in using 'we' and invoking a collective response to, or understanding of, these issues and texts, I am addressing you, the reader, as a participant within contemporary cultural practices. This means that I am assuming that through 'cultural competence' within everyday life and through common features of psychic histories I will touch on later, we have acquired an acquaintance or facility with these issues – in this sense they are very much group-constructed and related phenomena, even though there will be undoubted variations and idiosyncracies of response and interpretation. I will be dealing here with readily available, high exposure material, that may be both so common as to scarcely merit notice, or of such media saturation as to evoke relief if it passes without comment. While I draw on psychoanalytic concepts, unlike the project of therapy, this chapter is not an evaluation of the personal significance of individual interpretations made of the material, but is rather concerned with the use of psychoanalytic concepts to enrich our understanding of the dynamics of contemporary cultural politics. Hence my focus here is on applying psychoanalytic ideas to the structuring of cultural practices and the range of readings they afford. I am therefore appealing to a sense of the viability of the readings I propose, rather than implying that those are the only readings, or that you, as reader, will necessarily or primarily identify with them. What is important is that you recognise them as discourses, or frameworks of meaning reflecting cultural assumptions and institutional positions (cf. Parker 1992; Burman and Parker 1993). Part of that recognition (or in Lacanian terms, misrecognition) relies upon an address to forms of subjectivity constituted by psychoanalysis (Parker 1997, 2004).

In addition, my aim is to indicate connections between the apparently diverse and separate areas of aid programming/appeals and psychotherapy. I shall be exploring questions and dynamics about cultural investments in childhood that both domains share. Hence, the appeal and horror of childhood address emotive areas that touch on the project of therapy, including the investments of therapists, at the level of professional practice rather than only as cultural participants. More than this, I am aware that my analysis, and particularly the description of images, could be understood as reproducing precisely those readings that I try to challenge. While some such mobilisation may be an inevitable aspect of an analysis of this kind, I hope that embedding these dynamics within a critical framework will help to secure the texts to the narrative that I will outline.

Spectacular dynamics

It is a cliché to say that every picture tells a story. But the stories that pictures tell are narrativised by the verbal text which accompanies them, as well as the resources we bring to our readings of them (as Berman 1993 elaborates in relation to the role of photographs in therapy). Discussing pictures of children, Pat Holland (1992) points out how disjunctions between image and verbal text simultaneously both indulge and repudiate culturally prohibited readings. In this sense, the words and images function in a mutual relation of releasing and securing variability of readings. Examples of such disjunctions that I will discuss include mobilising fantasies of the sexualisation and sadistic abuse of children. I will draw on applications of psychoanalytic concepts to film theory and cultural studies to elaborate this set of psychodynamics.

But before this, since it is going to figure heavily in my narrative, I will consider a range of psychoanalytic readings of identification. This is generally considered central to the constitution of human subjectivity. It is clearly vital for notions of self, and for boundaries between self and other.

The concept of identification is linked to discussions of narcissism, and is seen as having its origins in mechanisms of oral incorporation before its later emergence within modes of object relations. It is also accorded a crucial position as an outcome of the Oedipal period. Laplanche and Pontalis (1973: 205–208) discuss the relations between everyday meanings and the range and development of Freud's uses of the term. While Freud did not systematise the varieties of forms of identification, Laplanche and Pontalis take Chapter 7 of 'Group Psychology and the Analysis of the Ego' (Freud 1921) as the closest to doing this. In this, Freud distinguishes three modes of identification: (a) based on resemblance or assimilation, which Laplanche and Pontalis treat as centripetal, that is, where the subject identifies with the other (here constructed through the emotional tie with the object); (b) as the replacement for the abandoned object choice (as in post-Oedipal identification), which is centrifugal, that is, the subject identifies the other with himself/herself; and, (c) identification with others based on a common shared trait (e.g. the wish to be loved). This is seen as a form of hysterical displacement, which Laplanche and Pontalis take as combining both centripetal and centrifugal forms, and which they see as making possible the constitution of a 'we' (of the kind I am addressing or appealing to here). I want to draw on this analysis to analyse the forms of collective identificatory relations produced and rehearsed by the imagery of children. But here we also need to attend to the object relations set up by the textuality of the performance or display of these images. This leads me to the psychodynamics of the image.

The key article that precipitated the now extensive engagement between psychoanalysis, feminism and film theory was Laura Mulvey's (1975) 'Visual Pleasure and Narrative Cinema'. In this article, Mulvey outlines how the gaze apparatus central to Lacanian theory is enacted within the process of viewing (whether a film, or by extension a picture) in terms of the distribution of identifications, and the (technical as well as psycho-) dynamics of projection and displacement. The key psychodynamic relations elaborated in relation to the objects of the gaze are voyeurism and fetishism: voyeurism, in the sense of one's own investments being depicted as belonging to or acted out by another; and fetishism, in that a particular attribute or part of an object is made the receptacle for the investments its whole elicits. Hence, the axes of metaphor (similarity, condensed identification) and metonymy (substitution) are replayed within the activity of viewing. The relations of identifying other with self, or self with other, can therefore be continuously mobilised and shifting. While this framework has been applied to discussions of the representation, and especially the question of the represent*ability* of women (e.g. Rose 1986) and the gendered identificatory positions elaborated (e.g. Kaplan 1983), I want to take up these ideas in terms of representations and practices of child-watching and child-saving.

By way of reflexive framework, I want to make two points clear: first, that what I am doing here is a form of child-watching that is also subject to equivalent dynamics; second, that taking the representational practices of child-saving and child-watching activities as a topic does not belittle the activities that lie behind them. By contrast, these are the issues that preoccupy charity and aid organisations, who themselves argue for the relevance and urgency of these questions for their work (Reeves 1988; Coulter 1989; Save the Children 1992; Burman 1994a, 1994b).

Appealing children

Turning now to the images, there can be no doubt that the dominant, culturally vaunted perception of children is that they are appealing. They elicit strong 'aah' responses which grab attention. Such is the power of this icon of the child and the practices which support it that it occludes the ambivalence of our actual relations with children and childhood. (As a key example of this, in her analysis of her women's group discussions, in which the pain and burden of bearing, and bearing responsibility for, children was a major topic, Carol McVey 1994 reports how the group was interrupted by a phone call from another friend announcing that her daughter had just had a baby: immediately, reactions of pleasure and excitement replaced those of resentment and resignation.) As any perusal of postcard stands across Europe (and perhaps the world) will reveal, images of children, especially babies, sell, and sell products. (I do not have space here to develop these arguments in relation to the actual market in selling babies, but there are clearly continuities; see e.g. Ramirez 1992.) Closer to (my) home, the gurgly, hairless image of a chubby white baby is so synonymous with commanding instant attention that it is used to sell advertising space by Manchester Metrobuses, with the slogan 'Smile!'

Identifications with these images work in multiple ways. Babies signify happiness, innocence, freedom from responsibility, of being cared for (the first, centripetal, identificatory relation in Laplanche and Pontalis' schema). They may also invoke the phantasy of uncomplicated relationships (the bald hairless baby mobilising conventional connotations of asexuality). Or we identify with being nurtured, of being able to call forth this powerful response, of omnipotence. Alternatively, this may be displaced so that, in our relations to this baby, we are positioned as competent providers, enabled to indulge our infantile pleasures through indirect identificatory interaction; that is, supplying these needs for the baby, rather than being the baby. These images are also culturally positioned within the domain of asexuality, although this presumption thereby provides a constant source of play and transgression (e.g. the slogan on a French postcard 'Look [sic] d'enfer pour mieux te plaire' ['Look of hell to please you more'] accompanying image of sexualized female baby). This allows sensuality and lack of inhibition over homoerotic and so-called perverse attractions to be indulged (sometimes at the level of unconscious phantasy, sometimes in actuality – as in infant and child sexual abuse). Moreover, we should note here the parallels and connections between the representational burden carried by babies and children, and that of women (see Burman 1994c, 1995a, Chapter 9).

Although presented as universal and enduring characteristics, this much vaunted conception of what children are like is (with corresponding reversals that I will discuss) culturally and historically specific. The disciplines of sociology and anthropology of childhood take as their starting point that the conception of childhood as a period of dependency and immaturity is modern and Western (Ariès 1962). The emergence of 'childhood' can be linked to processes of industrialisation, with the introduction of compulsory schooling working to create a dependent, malleable workforce rather than a young and active, economically autonomous population (Hendrick 1990). Hence the model of the child as innocent, unknowing and therefore in need of containing and training owes much to the legacies of romantic poets and humanist reversals of puritan doctrines of original sin. More than this, our cultural and subjective investments in this conception of 'the child' reflect much more pragmatic preoccupations with the regulating of families and maintaining social order.

Whatever their political and ideological origins, the contemporary Western conception of child–adult relations is organised around at least three bipolar dimensions. Since the unconscious does not obey the laws of symbolic logic – specifically those of non-contradiction and singularity, the identificatory relations clustered around these qualities can be read in both directions. First, there is the opposition of innocence and experience: children are innocent and lack experience. But this opposition can be reversed since, according to the Wordsworthian lyricism that still circulates within our Western cultural sediment, children are also party to knowledge and experiences that adults lack or have 'forgotten'.

Second, children are dependent while adults are autonomous; so, children are considered (legally, morally) irresponsible (exceptions to this I address this later), while adults have responsibility and power. But, in these days of alienated labour and political disenchantment, the power of adulthood can feel considerably compromised and the responsibilities onerous. This can generate envy of the freedom we see our children exercising – a freedom they may not experience or recognise, except perhaps through the weight of our projections inviting them to see these as 'the best days of your life'.

Third, we see children as being spontaneous while we are reflective. In psychoanalytic theory, spontaneity is associated with the vulnerability of frustrated need as well as pleasure, and so the development of processes of reflection and symbolic activity is understood as prompted by the capacity to tolerate absence or defer gratification. However, culturally, spontaneity is highly valued as the emotional and creative counterpart or other to the cold, logical rationality of the modern Western world. We view children's spontaneity through the misted lens of our current 'prisonhouse' (cf. Wordsworth) of regulation and self-regulation.

Thus, as an audience we are constituted as a collectivity to mourn together, that is, we are centrifugally identified with each other through a common narrative of lost love and power. Childhood becomes the projective slate on to which our phantasies of escape and thwarted desires are written. In that sense, childhood, and the wishes its imagery invites, secures the toleration of our adult dissatisfactions. The boundary between adult and child thus reflects and reinscribes that of desire and loss in multiple ways. As the cultural replaying of the Oedipal story, we are constituted as adults by our repudiation of the passions and desires of childhood (cf. Dinnerstein 1978). What we gain by this is not only common membership of the group, but also common access to the narrative of loss. We retrospectively construct the story of childhood as fulfilling those features we currently lack, as the domain of lost potency and passion, so that in it we can, in the slogan of a car advertisement, 'Remember that feeling of total control' (Peugeot 1992). But, perhaps as a defence against regressive pre-Oedipal ties, the 'total control' associated with childhood is also mocked at the very moment it is invoked. We are addressed within the terms of the triangular relation that operates between: us, the image, and the text. The text marks us as participants in the symbolic order, as having made the transition into culture. The feeling is one to 'remember', because it is lost, it is in the past. But the image invites a more direct identification of desire through substitutive association with the product (the car as symbol of potency) that the text both acknowledges but limits access to. The image is thus a mirror in the Lacanian sense of reflecting back to us a distorted representation of what we are through the installation of a narrative of what we were. The image is therefore a medium as well as a mirror, a site for the projection and construction of phantasies of the past as well as its screen.

Moreover, the reason why we accede to this symbolic imperative is because what is being warded off here is the *im*potence of childhood; because what we 'remember' is not only 'those feelings of total control'. Even when, or if, we felt powerful as children, doubtless we did not much of the time. Recast from, and through, the position of Oedipal mastery, such omnipotence can now be improved upon, so that the flaws in it as manic defence against helplessness and dependency can be better shored up. What practices of consumption offer in these texts and products is the commodification of a sanitised version of childhood, importing fragments of childhood subjectivity (or by constructing narratives of personal history) that generate enough anxiety to motivate (psychic and financial) investment in what are significantly called 'goods'. Thus television advertisements elaborate themes of the modern nostalgia for past happiness (the golden glow of bike rides up Northern English village hills in bread advertisements; or the rural idyll evoked for the sale of honey and blackcurrant drinks).

A late modern variety of the cultural investment in childhood is more oriented to the commitment to the future (James and Jenks 1994). Instead of the casting backward, the mourning of lost connections or continuities, here childhood is more explicitly mobilised as potential, as futurity. In some cases children's developmental potential is represented as taking indeterminate directions, with uncertainties that may make incalculable demands – specifically financial demands, as exploited in the baby imagery for selling bank accounts. In others, children are accorded the positions of moral evaluators on the evils of adult (especially environmental) overconsumption. We are called upon to save the planet by the children who are 'our future'. But children also represent our better, ideal selves, and even are accorded access to perspectives not seen by, or permissible to be expressed by, others (cf. the little girl's drawings used to reflect back to her father his unhealthy and undesirable image in a late 1990s British television heart health promotion advertisement).

Co-ordinating all these representations is the cultural opposition of nature vs. culture. Children are natural (but as we shall see, this also sets out some of them as unnatural). The more unnatural we feel ourselves to be as adults, the greater our investment in inscribing those qualities within this alternative domain of childhood. On the one hand we may gain some comfort from feeling that we are trying to regain something we had and have lost, rather than something we have never had at all, but on the other, the cultural attributions of childhood can be read as projections not only of what we lack, but what we have always lacked. Only now, in the act of acknowledging such loss, these investments are retrospectively desired and derogated alternately, and finally displaced on to (one of) the other(s) of modern Western adulthood (with, for example, women and the Third World subjected to similar dynamics).

Sadism vs. sentimentality

So the converse, and complement, of identification is difference. We treat children as different from us, as well as expressing the best, or worst parts of us. In its apparently benign form, this elaboration of separation and difference is marked by the sentimentality that drips off the dominant imagery of children. Sentimentality indulges children; it protects them from evaluation according to the same criteria as adults. It separates them from adults. The cost of having access to those areas of pleasure, those unconditional demands for nurturance and attention that, at least in theory, child-centred approaches require of us in our relations with children, is denial of full subjectivity and humanity. Moreover, in compensating for the loss, and marking the separation, the positions we as adults adopt, or are accorded, reinscribe existing power relations: I, the adult, can define the terms on which you, the child, relate to me, and not vice versa. So this distancing move, the repudiation of identification, also permits the expression of aggression.

Winnicott (1958) suggests that the cost (or perhaps the gain) of sentimentality is sadism (and here we take up themes from Winnicott's work introduced in Chapter 4). Sadism involves satisfaction gained from the suffering or humiliation of others. Four sets of affective investments and relations are maintained by the sadism of adult sentimentalisation of children. First, in marking the boundary between self and other, or subject and object, the subject is protected from identification with the pain. Second, thus split off, representations of childhood can function as a place to deposit unwanted feelings (and, as I discuss later, children also connote vulnerability, pain and humiliation). Third, in assuming the paternal, culturally sanctioned position of sentimentalising children, we are also acting out the rage of the surrender of our lost love(s). Finally, the aggressive relation is overdetermined by the need not only to confirm power over the feelings mobilised by the imagery of children, but is also called forth to ward off retaliation from the objects of our scorn, and to limit claims to empathy.

Thus there is aggression within pity. The withholding of empathy or identification offers lots of opportunities for acting out repetitions of, or alternatively reparations for, past insults. But both positions are enacted from the secure position of the Other to the pain. Alice Miller (1985) has elaborated the investments at work when we claim that what we are subjecting children to is 'for their own good'. At the very least, the claims of doing things in children's 'best interests' implies that children are not the best judges of their own interests, so that (as children's rights activists point out) assuming the rhetoric of acting 'in the name of the child' often works precisely to deny children's agency, autonomy and participation in decision making (Boyden and Hudson 1985).

To apply this to another vexed cultural arena, fairy stories are far from only being children's stories, although currently their primary circulation in the West is now mainly in this form. As is evident from the moral panics and attention accorded to the scrutiny of children's literature, we know that the 1960s attempts to clean up the gore and violence made for arid, unengaging reading, and, if we agree with Bruno Bettelheim (1983), proscribed these as a key arena for the working out of anxieties and conflicts (see also Rustin and Rustin 1987). Put another way, we could regard the fact that we confine the circulation of this key repository of repressed cultural knowledge and projection to the arena of childhood as an expression of our efforts to contain that work to the period of childhood. But it could also be understood as a venting of our anger upon them: either because children are allowed access to areas we are now barred from, or as a means of ensuring that they do not escape the pain of the trials of initiation that we were forced to endure (cf. the critical analyses of children's literature as producing the psychic structure on to which dominant gender and heterosexual relations will later be inscribed, Walkerdine 1987).

Appalling children

The discourse of nature associated with children arises from (the cultural investment in) their exemption or exclusion from culture. A consequence of this is that childhood is abstracted from culture and history. The meaning of being a child appears to transcend particularities of geographical context and sociopolitical conditions. In part, this assumption reflects the benign paternalism (in all its gendered and colonial meanings) of a willingness to oversee, to repress difference, and to extend our understandings of children to Others. But in addition, our definitions of children are cast in such universalised terms that it is hard to make them admit their own specificity. A key example here is the normative definition of child development from psychology which renders the current Eurocentric model of childhood into a technical form that appears as neutral and value-free. This is then globalised (Boyden 1990) as scientific and culture-free in, for example, UNICEF policies and programmes (Burman 1994a, 1996a, Part III this volume).

So saturated with projections is the image of the child, as signifier of vulnerability and need, as inviting indulgence, that it seems to transcend the child itself. The child as fetish works to secure our links with what we should have been and should be, but were not and are not. The naturalisation of childhood enables us to maintain the icon of the child as expression of our hopes, as the cultural expression of personhood (cf. the potency of images of 'the child within'), as the core of authenticity unravaged by contaminating civilisation. As a reflection of these investments, the abstraction of this category and quality of childhood is thus divorced from the actual, lived contexts that children both inhabit and which produces them as children.

This is reflected in the representational practices of picturing children, especially in aid appeals, where children are usually portrayed alone, or sometimes with their mothers. Pat Holland (1992) comments on the absence of adult men in aid imagery as confirming the connotations of passivity and helplessness conventionally conveyed by women and children. We can extend this in terms of the Oedipal relations set out between viewer and viewed, where 'we' are positioned as competent, rescuing, law-bearing fathers in judgement of, and coming to the aid of, the women and children. This is sometimes made quite explicit in the textual address which wards off apathy, resignation and passivitiy to position 'us' as omnipotent (such as 'You can help save children's lives in Somalia', UNICEF media campaign 1992; and 'Now, Mr Major what about Tuzla?', Oxfam media campaign 1994). But this genre also harks back to the earlier pairings of madonna and child. As the Other to that pair in disaster imagery, we are both God and man.

The earlier discussion of sentimentality highlights the anger and rage that lies beneath its surface. Moreover, these dynamics are mutually constitutive and maintaining: appealing children stand in relation to, and call forth, appalling children. The correlate of the cultural celebration of childhood is its vilified counterpart. As Holland puts it: 'Without the image of the unhappy child our contemporary concept of childhood would be incomplete' (Holland 1992: 148). Thus the image of the unhappy child works both to remind us of its converse of paradise lost (hell and torment), and thus works to limit the desire to restore it. The distribution of sanctified vs. penalised, or 'real' vs. 'stolen', childhood, maps on to cultural and racial privilege such that it is mainly black children who figure in newspapers and television reports as signifiers of need.

Moreover, geographical as well as chronological distance wards off the anxiety provoked by identification with distress. As critics inside charity and aid organisations are pointing out, publicising humanitarian emergencies through the depiction of children in need, especially black children, works to confirm paternalistic relations already inscribed through colonialism. 'We', the audience constituted, interpellated by such dynamics, are addressed in aid appeals as white, rich, adult, competent. 'We' have what 'they' lack; giving confirms 'our' sense of power, reassures 'us' that 'we' are not 'them'; wards off the anxiety of too much identification with the distress. (This is not to say that we should not give, but rather to say we should address what else is going on when we give or act, see Burman 1994b.) In this sense we have investments in positioning the source of the need as far away (generally in the Third World, and typically in girls). Having kept it at a distance, this absence can (so to speak) make the heart grow fonder, such that we have desires to bring such unfortunate children 'home' to us, to share the privileges that 'their' need has confirmed for 'us'. Meanwhile the children closer to home are the ones on whom we visit moral panics about violence and sexuality.

Thus the activity of child-saving poses questions about whose child is being saved: our idealised conception, or the real children whose lives and welfare are at risk? Some such blurrings and continuities may be a necessary part of any 'altruistic' gesture. But where 'our' investments clash with 'theirs' in this enterprise is in the way childhood, and the actual children whose violation of this category is used to mobilise us, or to solicit money from us, appears as outside culture. 'The child as the idiom of hunger' (Black 1992) or as the signifier of need organises three dynamic relations. First, it infantilises all those people in need, thus reproducing colonial-imperial discourses of 'they can't look after themselves' and invoking the rage as well as the care of the parent. Second, and more particularly, it positions parents, communities and cultures as neglectful or irresponsible in failing to meet the needs of their children. Third, the abstraction of distress signified by children disallows analysis of the social, geographical and political conditions that gave rise to the crisis. This naturalises the problem, so that we, as spectators and potential rescuers, avoid implication in producing the situation. Thus the victims of these disasters thereby become treated as responsible for bringing it upon themselves. The naturalisation of children is an important political and psychological component in this chain of meanings. Moreover, this victim-blaming is overdetermined by the psychic and commercial investments maintained by donor–recipient relations, according to which criticising the donor is not regarded as a good fund-raising strategy (Burnell 1991).

An important example of the (literal) political capital of the presumed transcendence of both children and childhood is the slogan 'a hungry child has no politics' used by the US to promote its belated and duplicitous response to the 1984 famine in Ethiopia (belated because it suppressed knowledge about the impending crisis for years; duplicitous because the US withheld food aid from Ethiopia, and liberally dispensed it to the Sudan as part of the programme of Cold War politics; Gill 1986). A more recent mobilisation of culturally specific, but purportedly universal, attributes of childhood is the United Nations emergency intervention strategy of designating children as peace zones to justify temporary ceasefires for the purpose of dispensing primary health care interventions like immunisation (UNICEF 1992a).

Disaster pornography and the sadism of the spectacle

It is a moot point within feminist accounts (e.g. Kaplan 1983; Kappeler 1986) whether technologies of representation necessarily involve relations of dehumanisation and subjection. But in the case of media reporting and coverage of emergencies and disasters, there can be no doubt that these generate powerful dynamics of anxiety to be warded off. The term 'disaster pornography' was coined by workers in the organisation African Rights to describe the appalling activities of news reporters in Somalia (Omaar and de Waal 1993). They describe how the press disregarded the dignity and distress of the people they scrambled over in order to find the most gory or painful scene to photograph. So the act of depicting this distress was always at a remove; through the lens, and from there stretched across a screen or newsprint on to which our identifications and subjectivities could be attached or dispersed.

However, in terms of the ways we are construed and constructed within such appeals, inducing guilt by juxtaposing what 'we' have, with what 'they' lack certainly is widely used to limit as well as mobilise identification. Sometimes this takes the form of comparative living standards (e.g. 'Do you really need £10 more than she does?', ActionAid). At other times 'we' are addressed in ways that make us personally responsible for the resolution of 'Starvation or Survival' (Ethiopiaid) or of 'Making the Difference' (Oxfam). The urgency of the situation is emphasised in images or texts highlighting youth and vulnerability. 'Her fourth birthday may well be her last, but she isn't ill. She's poor' (ActionAid); 'Hungry, lonely, scared. How you can help' (NSPCC); 'Please sponsor her today. Tomorrow may be too late' (ActionAid). For the more attentive viewer who takes a leaflet, a narrative of 'before and after' is elaborated, with a shift in image from stern, reproachful or wretched expression on the child's face, to one of relief and happiness at the back of the leaflet next to the coupon that you, hopefully, have filled in and returned with your donation.

What is significant here is the prevalence not only of images of children as indicators of more general need, but of little girls. Girls form the main image corpus of aid appeals, thus (as discussed in different terms in Chapter 5) invoking a familiar (in a double sense) elision of women and children within the more general discourse of the disempowered and incapable. I return to this later. Here I want to note the gaze; these children are portrayed as objects of our gaze, as too abject to engage with us ('Her fourth birthday'; 'Tomorrow may be too late'). The more severe the crisis, the less likely we are to exchange a direct look. Rather, we see (typically) children, and perhaps their mothers, in their own private world of suffering. It is only where the text is accompanied by a more preventative message or programme that the child is depicted as able to look back; and when she does, her gaze invites address and in some cases makes reproach. Analysing aid imagery depicting damage, horror and need, Holland again comments:

> The image operated in a dangerous area between sympathy, guilt and disgust. In abandoning the attractiveness of childhood, these pictured children may well have sacrificed the indulgence childhood commands. Without the flattery offered by the appealing image, they may arouse adult sadism without deflecting it and confirm a contempt for those many parts of the world which seem unable to help their own.
>
> (Holland 1992: 154)

Looking vs. looking away

I want to delve further into film theory as a resource for understanding the dynamics of child-watching. Barbara Creed (1987) draws on Kristeva's (1982) notion of 'abjection' to apply it to the fascination and repugnance generated by horror movies. The moment of abjection corresponds to that of differentiation, thus marking the borders and boundaries of the mother–child relationship. It wards off fusion or merging with a (mythical and archaic) mother, signified by blood, death and disease. But this produces not only the desire to return to and repeat the abject repudiation of/by the mother, but also the need to repel the corresponding threat of self-annihilation. According to this analysis, the function of horror is precisely what makes it monstrous, that is, it brings about 'an encounter between the symbolic order and that which threatens its stability' (Creed 1987: 49), or between 'the maternal authority and the law of the father' (p. 51). However, toleration of the position of abjection is culturally necessary, not only because of the (cultural and actual) links between destruction and creativity, but also because of its role in rehearsing the proper place adopted by the subject in relation to the symbolic order. The horror film thus constructs particular subject positions in the very process of disrupting conventional strategies of identification: the spectator is forced to look away to avoid images of horror. What the horror film genre does, then, is to saturate its audience with gory and painful scenes, which at the same time are inevitably 'deliberately pointing to the fragility of the symbolic order in the domain of the body which never ceases to signal the repressed world of the mother' (Creed 1987: 52).

Creed's analysis is primarily concerned with the representation of femininity as 'monstrous' within the horror film genre. As such, it is important to note that she is talking about culturally constructed narratives of separation and warding off disintegration, rather than according the 'archaic maternal monster' any necessary place in psychic development. The relevance of her analysis here arises in part through the close connections between cultural-psychological meanings of femininity, children and the South, all of whom are 'others' and 'objects' to the dominant white, Northern, culturally male subject. Moreover, her analysis of the innovations and interventions of the horror film genre in the strategies of looking and identification usefully inform that of the spectacular dynamics elaborated by images of (often black, female) child suffering.

Developing Creed's analysis, horror confronts an audience with the precariousness of mastery of the symbolic order, so that images of death, symbolised by the monstrous, threaten boundaries of the 'self'. Significantly, she comments that death images are most likely to cause the spectator to look away, to not-look:

> Strategies of identification are temporarily broken, as the spectator is constructed in the place of horror, the place where the sight/site can no longer be endured, the place where pleasure in looking is transformed into pain and the spectator is punished for his/her voyeuristic desires.
>
> (Creed 1987: 64)

The sadomasochistic dynamics of child suffering appear to participate within this cultural dynamic of fascination and repudiation. We are pushed to the limits of what we can bear to see, that is, we are challenged to stay watching by our identification with those represented until we can no longer engage without merging with them. 'To be heard above the noise, you have to push boundaries' ('Shock Tactics', *Media Guardian* 15 March 1999: 3). Like the horror film, then, images of suffering children:

> put[s] the viewing subject's sense of a unified self in crisis, specifically in those moments when the image on the screen becomes too threatening or horrific to watch, when the abject threatens to draw the viewing subject to the place 'where meaning collapses', the place of death. By not looking, the spectator is able momentarily to withdraw identification from the image on the screen in order to reconstruct the boundary between self and screen and reconstitute the 'self' which is threatened with disintegration.
>
> (Creed 1987: 65)

Interestingly, the dynamic of the desire both to look and not-look is explicitly topicalised in aid appeals. 'Please don't look away' reads the text of ActionAid ads, adopting the voice of a dishevelled (usually) little girl. 'Don't look away' was the main headline for the Oxfam Rwanda appeal in 1994. Injunctions to 'make the difference' include reference to our own psychic needs which are precisely what prompt us to make those differences, or separations, between ourselves and those depicted as abject, as well as between those depicted and their abject conditions. Such slogans acknowledge the desire to defend, but appeal to the viewer to move beyond rendering the viewed as only abject. Paradoxically, by symbolically prefiguring the defensive response, such texts allow movement away from the image, disrupting the identification with the horror and threat of disintegration or incorporation and then allowing, or perhaps creating the conditions, for it to return. That is, a three-step process is structured whereby we are enjoined to look, not-look, and then look again. The disruption of identification is necessary to produce the more 'mature' position of the adult, Northern donor, while this in turn relies upon the recollection of the infantile horrors it wards off. Like horror films, then, horrifying images of suffering children produce temporally structured dynamics of spectatorship that these appeals both highlight and engage with. (Chapter 12 takes further this discussion of the socio-temporal structuring of identification and vision.)

Interventions

Other texts employ different strategies to explicitly engage with the dynamic of sadism in aid appeals, by both acknowledging it and thwarting it at the same time. Beyond the omnipotence we are accorded to 'make the difference' between 'life and death' or the agency to withhold support that is mobilised in the ActionAid appeal 'Tomorrow may be too late', the text 'Send the money and the kid gets it' co-opts the genre of gangster movies and ransom demands (British Heart Foundation advertisement). This ad shares features of aid appeal construction: a child, here a baby, represents the need of a larger population (people with heart disease), and the baby's sideward turn of face and closed eyes (as well as neonatal status) limit personal identification or engagement and claims to full human subjectivity. But here our investment in childhood is literally held to ransom: and the simple substitution of a preposition from 'or' to 'and' (in 'and the kid gets it') turns sadism into salvation.

Moreover, in this text we are also addressed as cultural participants, who appreciate and engage with film and television entertainment rather than being solely invoked as moral guardians, or as subject to moral guardians, of humanity. Christianity forms the background for, if not the current basis of, many Northern charities (cf. Gronemeyer 1992). Rebellion against sanctimonious moral imperatives and claims to moral righteousness can function as a means of displacing resistance against the horror and need invoked by these appeals. Instead, the pressure to avoid engagement with the crisis can be acted out through the derogation and iconoclasm of a culturally privileged arena: like Philip Larkin ending his phone calls to Kingsley Amis with 'Fuck Oxfam' (*Guardian* June 1993). Perhaps the avoidance of appeals to justice and morality, but rather to the rules of the underworld in the British Heart Foundation advertisement discussed earlier ('Send the money and the kid gets it') offers possibilities of engagement without feeling coerced by the full force of legitimised moral institutions. We are not explicitly or directly addressed by the text and its 'critical parent' power, and our corresponding resistance to its indictments may thus be moderated. (It should be noted that there are changes developing within the genre of aid appeals, so that, for example, Oxfam is now fronting some appeals with the picture of a frowning young man, who is clearly a young adult; competent and challenging, demanding rather than appealing.) As a report reviewing current publicity campaigns about child sexual abuse noted (*Media Guardian* 15 March 1999: 3): 'The trick is to create something that moves people without shocking them into thinking there's nothing they can do: to stand out without alienating support.' Humour is explicitly harnessed as a way of reframing modes of engaging with horrifying images.

Natural and unnatural children

If childhood is natural then not all children partake of the category. Actual, real children often fail to live up to our phantasised investments. And the children who transgress this model most are those who most deviate from the white, middle-class, Northern children that formed the sample for the generation of the scientifically naturalised model of child development (c.f. Burman 1994a, 1994b, 1994d). This means that Southern children, minority black children, working-class children the world over, and especially girls (since the culturally privileged model of the playing child is really a boy; Walkerdine 1988; Burman 1995c), all violate the model of the happy, playing, discovering child. In particular, children who engage in paid work and children who live away from traditional cross-generational families violate this understanding of what children should do and be. While we may defend strongly against the recalled, culturally encoded or culturally encrusted powerlessness of childhood, we also have powerful reactions to children who are active and autonomous; children who are not passive and dependent; who are not innocent. Perhaps these children highlight our dependence on them to confirm our agency through their passivity; perhaps we fear their vengeance for the burden of need and suffering we have made them bear. But on top of the deprivations they already experience, these children pay a high price for their transgressions of our norms. In the case of street children in Brazil and Guatemala, we know that many are murdered by police and that children of the streets the world over are hounded and criminalised (Glauser 1990; Pheterson 1992).

So the obverse of real, natural children are these unnatural ones. And what is an unnatural child? Since childhood lies so close to, is both the human connection with, and expression of, nature, then perhaps these children are not children at all. Further, given their anomalous status as both quintessentially reflecting human qualities and aspirations and as the counterfoil to current ugly forms of human existence, then children who fall outside such descriptions not only invite expulsion from childhood, but thereby from humanity altogether.

Two examples closer to 'home' illustrate these points (and we can speculate here why child-saving should feel so much easier when displaced to 'far away' places). The first was the British Bulger case in 1993, in which once responsibility was supposedly established and especially when the child murderers could be named as Robert Thompson and Jon Venables, torrents of hate were unleashed in the British press. The bestial terms of the media descriptions (usually reserved for multiple rapists and mass murderers) betrayed intense subjective interests in warding off identification with the two ten-year-old boys and their actions. The press accounts of the boys' lives, habits and hobbies were structured by a discourse of predestination that exonerated us, as citizens, professionals, parents, onlookers who saw little 2-year-old Jamie Bulger being dragged away, from blame. The responsibility was firmly located within 'them' not 'us': that is, with the boys, their mothers and their working-class homes. Even in the 'quality' British press, the discourse of 'environmental deprivation' soon gave way to a thoroughly personalised pathologisation of these children, those families, and that place, Liverpool, icon of inner city desolation and deprivation.

Thus our responsibilities are confined, repudiated. In terms of the identificatory relations elaborated, we become not guilty perpetrators but helpless onlookers to a tragedy. The masochistic subjection to gory details of the accounts is preferable to sadistic identification with the boys, but both positions interrelate. We turn the damage into sadistic rage caused by the narcissistic assault on our sense of ourselves through our investments, in particular on our conceptions of childhood. In order to restore our sense of ourselves and the world we want, these children are no longer regarded as children. Little James Bulger, as the dead child victim, secures our model of passive innocent child, while the two boys are demons, wild beasts incarnating evil.

While boys who murder are excommunicated from childhood and humanity, the arena in which girls gain similar attention and treatment is around sexual abuse (as Chapter 4 also argued). But, again articulating gendered ideologies, while boys are perpetrators, girls are victims (and let me emphasise I am not discussing the actual gendered distribution here, but the dominant cultural representation). If an eight-year-old girl sexually assaulted by her male adult baby sitter is, in the judge's words, 'no angel', then what is she? Are children angels? The cultural icons of podgy white baby cherubs with wings, or long-haired, blue-eyed girls with halos, suggest they are. And if they are not angels, it seems they can only be devils. The doctrine of innocence thus never strays far from that of original sin. Specifically, the boundary between childhood and adulthood is heavily marked by the attribution of knowledge, and specifically conventionally recognised sexual knowledge (which is why theories of infantile sexuality are so disturbing to traditional categories, see Chapter 5). Children, girls, who are forced into positions of sexual knowledge through abuse are either pinned down into a passive career of victim that makes it difficult to become a survivor (Warner 1995) or are catapulted out of the category child to become sexual(ised) woman. Within dominant discourses of childhood, developing an understanding that accords children some agency whilst also maintaining an analysis of adult–child relations as power relations remains deeply problematic (cf. Kitzinger 1990; Stainton Rogers and Stainton Rogers 1992). That this is so is indicative of the cultural investments maintained by the adult–child boundary.

Complementaries and mutualities

In conclusion, I have been describing the intrapsychic relations mobilised within representations of adult–child relations, specifically through images of children. In multiple ways, children mark the borders of human rationality and carry the residues of desire and horror that this produces. However, I have attempted to go beyond the prevailing cultural polarities of age, gender and culture to explore the complexity and multidirectionality of the investments mobilised by the images and our viewing of them. Central to comprehending these textual dynamics is a theorising of the subjective positions set up for the reader/viewer. I have drawn on both psychoanalytic theory and its application to cultural studies and film theory, as well as discussions in the sociology of childhood, to illustrate how the positions of adult and child are defined in relation to each other, and thus maintained by each other. In this sense, the child functions as a boundary object – in the senses elaborated both within psychoanalytic theory and sociology of knowledge (Star and Greisemeyer 1989) – defining and negotiating the borders of participation in humanity (see also Burman 2004b). Contemporary images of children tend to be either sentimentalised or horrifying. I have been arguing that these are dual aspects of the same dynamic. While some appeals mobilise both the fear and the indulgence, others both acknowledge and disrupt the sadomasochistic relations that spectatorship sets up, for example, of disasters and humanitarian emergencies, but as also elaborated in more mundane popular cultural forms.

Where does this leave us as therapists and cultural analysts? Can we avoid these intrapsychic investments or the relations they determine? My purpose in writing this piece has not been to indict those who work with children, or to insist that they inexorably subscribe to all of these features. Rather, my aim in juxtaposing mass circulation representations with the individual dynamics of therapy has been to portray something of the broader cultural context in which such therapeutic encounters take place.[1] In these cultural case histories we are both patients and therapists as we maintain our daily practice. I am reminded here of how Bettelheim (1985), when writing about the mechanisms of Nazi murder, torture and humiliation informed by his experiences in Buchenwald, acknowledged that his analysis functioned as a defence against the horror at the same time as increasing understanding of how it could come about. No doubt, in analysing the intersubjective and intrapsychic relations set up by representations of children, I too am constructing a position of omnipotence to ward off the identification with the suffering and violence depicted. In this sense, analyses inevitably construct a further level of sadomasochistic identificatory relations. But by doing this, we can perhaps also come to recognise the conjoined nature of split forms of childhood, and better address our engagements in, and relations to, the themes of helplessness, fear and rage they evoke.

Part III

International development

This part of the book takes forward the connections with international 'development' by focusing specifically on policies concerned with gender and economic development, and the representation of 'child rights'. It draws on the conceptual and methodological analyses elaborated in Parts I and II to explore how these inform interlinked configurations of individual development, child development and national and international economic development. It marks a rhetorical move in the book from analysis to more focused engagement in developmental policies and practices.

Chapter 7, 'Beyond the Baby and the Bathwater: Postdualist Developmental Psychologies for Diverse Childhoods' – directed towards psychologists and educators – applies the general argument put forward so far (on the problems of current developmental psychological models that, far from fostering a genuinely universal model instead constitute a globalisation of Northern cultural and economic values) to specific examples in international development. Moreover, it moves on to identify some characteristics of these models that might not fall prey to those difficulties and so offer some helpful ways forward.

Chapter 8, 'Developing Differences: Gender, Childhood and Economic Development', addresses the uneasy relationship between measures of national and international development with child development indicators, focusing in particular not only on the distortions of psychological theory inscribed in economic development policy that resolve development back on to abstracted individuals (as discussed in relation to renderings of Bronfenbrenner's 1977, 1979 'ecological model' of human development in Burman 1996a), but also on the consequences of the polarised concepts of childhood and developmental opportunities in relation to understandings of work vs. play and North–South relations.

Chapter 9, 'The Abnormal Distribution of Development: Policies for Southern Women and Children', takes this analysis further to focus specifically on policy consequences of the conceptual ambiguities and instabilities between gender and childhood (identified in Chapter 5), specifically in relation to the relationship between policy understandings of the positions of girls and women.

7 Beyond the baby and the bathwater

Developmental psychologies for diverse childhoods

This first chapter of Part III draws together the critiques presented so far to take up the challenge of addressing how children develop within diverse class and geographical contexts, including how to avoid reproducing the problems identified within the available models. The chapter brings together the arguments made in earlier chapters, that address the exclusionary character of Euro-US models of childhood and their inscription within international child and economic development policies, to return to the consequences of such critiques for theorists and practitioners of child development. Anticipating the burgeoning of educational research that now takes this forward (e.g. Moss and Petrie 2002; Dahlberg and Moss 2005; MacNaughton 2005), it is argued that this involves moving away from the prevailing isolationist research and policy focus on young children to instead analyse how diverse contexts and environments not only support or surround children's development but also deeply inform what and how they develop.

It revisits the baby/bathwater motif introduced in Chapter 1, offering a more systematic treatment that – consistent with the approach taken in this book – draws attention to its linguistic-cultural and performative features. But here, in contrast to most critiques of deconstructionist interventions which claim they are either only negative and offer no helpful ways forward, or that they are culturally relativist, the chapter attempts to address the 'so what?' question. While it is not proposed to throw the baby (of developmental theorising) out with the bathwater (of changing conditions), it is argued that we need instead to change our cultural-political metaphors and models to see 'the bathwater' as crucial to the baby's flourishing and well-being, rather than as dispensable or replaceable. This chapter adopts a programmatic narrative voice making specific calls to engage in, and correspondingly refuse to engage with, certain ways of dealing with and conceptualising children.

Developmental psychology as a modern, Northern (minority world) discipline has been wedded to an individualist model of child development that treats the baby or child as an isolated unit of development. Heir to both romantic and functionalist traditions within its Euro-US context of formulation, within this paradigm the child develops according to regular, predictable patterns (sometimes described as stages) that are presumed to be largely universal in their structure. Yet this universality – like the modern liberal-bourgeois subject that inhabits psychology – and harboured especially within developmental psychology – is actually culturally specific: it represents the culturally Anglo-US, white, middle-class, masculine subjectivity of the mid-twentieth century. As a result cultural diversity – in terms of aims as well as content of development – is subordinated to this naturalised (in the sense of rendered as inherent, pre-given) and normalised (treated as the benchmark for evaluation of acceptable vs. deviant ranges of diversity) linear model of development.

Hence programmes of child development frequently mirror those of economic development in their assumptions by virtue of the common cultural-historical resources informing both. The challenge is, therefore, to find ways of opening up discussions of how children develop within diverse cultural, class and geographical contexts that draw on the strengths of available theories without reproducing their cultural privileges and globalisations. Drawing upon examples from a range of cultural contexts, I argue that this involves departing from the prevailing isolationist research and policy focus on young children. Instead we should analyse not only how different contexts and environments support or surround children's development but also how the cultural 'bathwater' enters into the shaping and elaboration of the baby it supports.

The baby and the bathwater

There is a well-known English saying, 'throwing the baby out with the bathwater', which invokes a metaphorical warning, as in: 'don't let's throw the baby out with the bathwater'. I want to subject this warning and its problematic to some scrutiny. I want to linger over it and ponder its forms and relations. Perhaps you will think I am labouring or over-interpreting an innocent phrase. But – as those of us involved with childcare and education are surely only too well aware – practices of labour and interpretation are always implicated within particular gender, class, historical, geographical and cultural relations, and (therefore) are never innocent. Similarly, word play is no more a frivolous activity for adults as it is for children; it is rather central to the struggle for the elaboration of more adequate tools of thought.

I want to offer two reasons for framing my discussion around what I will call 'the baby and the bathwater' paradigm. First, the fact that this is an English phrase – albeit with broad circulation – precisely expresses its difficulty. For we know that language creates and governs the horizons of what we can envisage. Language is a key expression of cultural practice, and I want to argue that the apparently general accounts which developmental psychological theories offer are not so at all. Rather they are deeply culturally embedded records of particular times and places. Or, more specifically, they are records of a dominant culture, but one which has acquired such prevalence and predominance as to have become invisible, or presumed. This is where the agenda of attending to complexity, diversity and multiplicity that brings us here has arisen: to counter the globalisation of one specific model of children's development.

Second, it is (I think) significant that this saying has been applied somewhat unreflexively to discussions of developmental psychology. Perhaps readers also recall discussions that took the form 'but rejecting Piaget wholesale is like throwing the baby out with the bathwater', or more controversially perhaps 'to say that inheritance does not play a role in intelligence is like . . .', or more recently 'legislating against waged work for children is like . . .'. As is the way with many words and phrases, there has been an erosion of meaning that obscures the guiding framework, a linguistic drift towards weaker application of the metaphor.

Indeed those of you who recognise such subscription to 'the baby/bathwater' trope as an exemplar of an argument based around a false opposition will already anticipate my discussion here. I want to resist this dynamic of abstraction (from 'babies' to 'baby') and of metaphorisation (to say that 'it's only a manner of speaking, just words'). I want to suggest that doing this, taking our incidental assumptions seriously, is relevant to the broader project of resisting the abstraction and globalisation of (Northern) models of development. Instead of the focus remaining on the terms identified ('the baby', 'the bathwater'), we should rather invite an equivalent attention to why these were identified as the key players in this relation, and indeed whether this is the appropriate way of conceiving of the action taking place. I want to propose that attending to the unacknowledged cultural connotations and legacies structured within the problematic of 'the baby and the bathwater' in fact represents – homologically rather than only metaphorically – some of the key broader challenges posed to all of us concerned with elaborating more adequate and culturally located accounts of the contexts and processes of children's development.

The baby and the bathwater as the dualist paradigm

Let me begin by reminding ourselves of what 'throwing the baby out with the bathwater' is generally understood to mean, in terms of how it functions in conversation or argument. Let us initially note something obvious (for often what is obvious is precisely what needs commenting on as exhibiting unspoken cultural assumptions that can be oppressive in their presumptions): it is typically invoked when motivating for a sense that something good or worthwhile is about to be rejected, or jettisoned, along with unwanted debris – whether literal or conceptual. There is a sense of a danger of overpurging, of over-evacuating, of expelling or getting rid of the object of your interest, concern or intervention in the act of being too vigorous or zealous. After all, as the image invites us to imagine, if we found someone emptying a bathtub with the baby still in it we'd be justifiably worried for that child's safety, wouldn't we?

Fictional fantasies of childhood

But here we see we have already entered the world of the image – for surely talk of the baby and the bathwater conjures up images – of what? Is it just me, or do other people see a Disney technicolour cosy fireside scene of a mother washing her child in a tin tub, of tender bodily care, of intimacy and play, all lit up by the nostalgia and sentiment of *times that never were*. Of course we know that the mother/child dyad is a recent post-World War II fiction of Northern societies, and that 'the mother' as full-time carer of her child was, and is, never as widespread as has been assumed to be the case – in terms of class, cultural, historical and geographical distributions. Moreover, we also know that – contrary to its typical representation within child development texts – the mother/child paradigm is woefully inaccurate. The reduction of the idealised heterosexual 'parental' couple to the 'mother/child' couple performs a number of significant ideological moves. It shifts the onus of responsibility for childcare, welfare and development on to mothers, with legal, policy and practice effects we now expend significant amounts of time and money trying to counter – especially in terms of women's mental health. Further, the prototypical male baby cradled in his mother's arms essentialises traditional gender relations (whereby women care, and men are cared for, or serviced) and, in its normalisation of the heteroerotic character of intimate physical caring between parents and their small children (which after all forms the basis of all available accounts of how we come to form adult intimate relations), it marginalises homoerotic desire.

We may know all this, yet somehow, as soon as we enter the world of developmental psychological theory, we seem to shed our knowledge that each child usually grows up in a family with other children, and indeed that the family itself may be joint, or locationally distributed – whether via joint households or children living across households (as in joint custodial or extended family contexts).[1] The innocent trope of 'the baby and the bathwater' fills our minds, despite the fact that in practice not only might there be more than one 'baby' in the bathtub, but the bathers, that is those who wash the babies, might vary too (and very likely will include some children of the same generation of the baby being bathed – older sisters in particular). Indeed (you are probably already thinking) surely the very notion of an enclosed space in which bathwater accumulates speaks of a specific set of cultural-religious practices; for many children bathe and are bathed in running water, and by this I don't mean only steamy showers in chrome-tapped and tiled bathrooms.

We could carry on touching up this rose-tinted image – of soapsuds, sponges, child-centred toys in the bathtub. After all, bathtimes are hailed by developmental psychologists and parent trainers as important times for interaction, relationship building, language development, eye–hand co-ordination and the like. But do we really know how much these recommendations are framed by the cultural assumptions arising from the material and ideological contexts of their formulation?

. . . *and their oppressions*

And so we arrive at some of the ideological residues of this formulation. We have a conceptual domain with, first, a singular subject – the baby, or the child; and, second, the bathwater portrayed as the child's context – the 'other' of the baby, what it is not. These are two presumed separate entities, with no other parties explicitly specified (although we will move on soon to consider what this might mean). Similarly, modern developmental psychological models have typically worked from individualist assumptions; of what the (presumed separate, individual) baby does, and does next. Development is typically portrayed as an isolated activity, as an epic odyssey or journey, a trajectory that seems to speak of the specific child, but is in fact a methodological abstraction, a statistical fictional 'individual' synthesised through analysis of multiple patterns of populations in the course of which she has been stripped of all that tied her to her time, place and position (Rose 1985; Burman 2008), but which retains traces of a very particular set of cultural values.

Not only does this elaborate a fictional, mythical norm – mythical because no one 'fits' it; but the quasi-scientific status of this norm – as 'fact' – facilitates a slippage from description to prescription such that the very contingent conditions – and contestable assumptions – which gave rise to this norm become rendered invisible and thus accorded 'natural' status. Whether milestones, gender types, reading ages, cognitive strategies, stages or skills (and the toys and consumer products these inspire), they become enshrined within an apparatus of collective measurement and evaluation that constructs its own world of abstract autonomous babies; of norms, deviation from which are typically only acknowledged in the form of deficit or 'problem'.

Struggling to mind the gap

The Vygotskian notion of zones of proximal development (e.g. Cole and Cole 1989; Newman and Holzman 1995, among others) and the recent emphasis on language as the site for the construction and negotiation of intersubjective meanings arise precisely to counter such individualist legacies. The British psychoanalyst Winnicott, that creator of the phrase the 'good enough mother' has sometimes (probably unfairly) been blamed along with Bowlby for the closure of the wartime daycare facilities that freed up British women to do low-paid factory work and so contribute to the war effort (see Riley 1983). But Winnicott is also credited with the saying 'there is no such thing as a baby', meaning that we can only see the complex of relationships (Phillips 1988). This is strikingly resonant of more contemporary discussions of how 'the individual' arises as a constructive effect of temporally and historically particular relationships (Newson and Shotter 1974; Parker 1998).

Yet the fact that discourses of 'maternal deprivation' (and maternal responsibility) exercise such power on our minds is not only due to one or two theorists – or even the apparatus of developmental psychology. For the model of the child as problem solver, constructing and manipulating mental logical-mathematical schemes that then mediate 'his' engagement with the world, expresses a modern Northern view of the individual that dates from the time of the seventeenth-century French mathematician and philosopher, Descartes, with his famous formulation: 'I think therefore I am.'

In privileging thought over action and interaction, and positing thinking as an individual mental act that precedes action and relationships (see Rotman 1978; Broughton 1981a, 1981b), we see effected within northern European, and in particular Anglo-US, culture the dualism that the 'baby and the bathwater' paradigm expresses: once severed, we psychologists and educators are then faced with the task of trying to heal the rifts between nature and culture, between the individual and the social that are created by our cultural-political heritage – although through globalisation this is now a much more extensively subscribed to approach (so rendering inadequate any simple polarisation between minority and majority approaches to early education and schooling). And, significantly, the gender, class and cultural relations – that privilege male over female, white over black, heterosexual over homosexual, middle over working class – are deeply implicated within the technological and colonial development of nineteenth-century Europe. Cultural analysts and philosophers have pointed out that one conceptual condition for all of this was the fixing of all these categories via the notion of 'identity' (cf. Henriques *et al.* 1984). And here maybe we have some clues about how to move forward.

Situating the struggle

So our psychological and educational interventions therefore do not enter a politically neutral space but are always already saturated with cultural assumptions. Once this subject of development is depicted as alone or singular within the task of development, then other features follow. Issues of culture and gender disappear within the generalised framework; for the singular child – once abstracted from context – comes to lack such markers, but becomes 'pure' potential, development in action (and so we have all these models, stages and phases, from Gesell to Piaget and beyond). But to use another metaphor, what is on offer becomes a standardised recipe that can never be cooked, or can never be recognised as being 'done', since the ingredients always have more qualification and specification than as defined by the instructions. Herein lies the paradox of a general framework such as that of the 1989 UN Convention on the Rights of the Child. For irrespective of its laudable aims, its principles still require translation or interpretation into specific cultural practices, and therefore offer scope for the maintenance of some of the same sets of abuses it was formulated to eradicate (Burman 1996a).

Of course culture and gender never disappear; the fact that they seem to is a classic vanishing trick of the dominant culture that normalises what is presumed; and only renders visible that which is abnormal, unusual, inadequate or deficient. Thus the child of developmental psychology is – culturally speaking – a boy; the problem solver or mini scientist (as Piaget 1957, liked to see 'him'); while the state of childhood (as dependency and incompetence) from which 'he' develops is feminised. Here we can note the classic colonial/industrialising frameworks in action – that portray women, children and so-called primitives as inferior, less developed and ranked on lower rungs of the ladder of evolutionary development. The feminisation of childhood is part and parcel of the same dynamics that feminise and infantilise majority peoples (or the so-called Third World), and produce the elision between women and children that makes it so difficult to think of their interests as separable (and so makes it difficult to engage in progressive alliances between the two movements). Thus, allocated to women and all so associated is a position of passivity, inferiority and deficit (see Chapters 8 and 9).

But let us pause to ask: Why? If we know all these problems only too well, why do these impoverished formulations and representations continue to populate our imaginations? Why are we saddled with this seemingly unshiftable apparatus? One significant answer is that it is much simpler to govern a standardised subject; simpler to formulate policy for, provide for, assess, evaluate such a subject – but this is an administrative rationale that masks deeper issues. A further reason is that we underestimate the extensive character of what drives it. For 'it', the apparatus of developmental psychology with its generalised unit of development, the child, implies and reflects an abstracted unified state that addresses and constitutes its subjects; a state that presupposes and covertly maintains national boundaries of cultural homogeneity. Herewith lies Fortress Europe and its constitution of its 'others', and the corresponding problems of elaborating a genuine multiculturalism.

Such are the ideological and politico-economic conditions that gave rise to modern developmental psychology (Burman 1994c, 1994d, 2007a). The 'baby and the bathwater' expresses in microcosm the broader narratives of modern industrialisation, at a moment of national and increasingly transnational economic development. Its privileging of abstract rationality and technological knowledge is deeply structured by all the key binary oppositions that compose Northern/minority culture; male/female, white/black, self/other, culture/nature, reason/emotion (Walkerdine 1988).

Covert subjects of late modernity

We could perhaps say that children – as the starting point or supposedly raw material for social development – are the victims of the asocial model of modernity's bourgeois individual. For as the prototypical subjects of modernity – of the modern project of social improvement – it has been the fate of children to be talked of as though gender, culture and sexuality are additional qualities to be grafted on to some apparently prior or pre-given 'child'. Thus the special status accorded children seems to be at the expense of separating them from the social structures concerned with protecting or promoting them. Moreover, as we have seen, the singular status of 'the child' confirms her or his position outside communities. Outside, that is, not only cultural communities but also communities of other children – whether siblings who form significant, if not primary, caregivers for many of the world's children, or *political* communities of other children. Here we might recall the analyses made by Hoyles (1989), Hendrick (1990) and others of how 'the child' of developmental psychology and educational practices emerged at a political moment within industrialising societies when children and young people were becoming economically active, increasingly organised and therefore challenging – as are working children across the world today (Gulrajni 2000; Liebel 2000).

A significant conceptual link here is that the only mode of relation between these enclosed, pre-given individuals turns out to be precisely the sort of exchange relation celebrated by bourgeois liberalism, flattening out power relations in favour of market 'choice', while the discourse of skills foreshadows the role of the worker in the industrialising economy (Harris 1987).

Further, children are generally treated as a unitary category unless marked explicitly by gender (giving rise to the new international development category, 'the girlchild', who emerges as both not quite child and not only woman; see Burman 1995b). But despite this, the qualities accorded children remain allocated according to conventional gender stereotypes, with practical correlates. So that, along with the cultural masculinity associated with the active, playing, problem-solving and singular developmental subject (who is also often portrayed as a little boy, Broughton 1988), it is also worth remembering that across the world it is boys who manage to access the efforts towards universal primary education better than girls (see Chapter 8).

Functionalist approaches breed the romance of the child

It is a paradox that, despite the manifest failure of the project of modernity (with its associated lexicon of progress, liberation and leisure through technological assistance and 'bigger is better' philosophy), developmental discourse seems to be the place where these hopes persist. On to the child we heap the thwarted longings of decaying societies and try to figure something better. It is a hard burden for children to carry. Surely they should be their own future, not ours.

Moreover – as with orientalism (cf. Said 1978) – there is a seductive lure around such places and peoples identified as feminised/infantilised. For if the trajectory of individual and social development is a heroic masculine story of technological progress, then the costs and struggles this involves produces nostalgic desires for individual and collective pasts and unrequited longings (as discussed in Parts I and II). Hence the trope of the child, and specifically the little girl, arose as the representation of the inner self. As the historian of childhood Carolyn Steedman notes:

> The idea of the child was used both to recall and to express the past that each individual life contained: what was turned inside in the course of individual development was that which was also latent: the child *was* the story waiting to be told.
>
> (Steedman 1995: 10–11)

So, as discussed in Chapter 5, the romance of the other is rendered docile and diminutive in the form of the little girl (Stainton Rogers and Stainton Rogers 1992). This romance is written into models of psychological development as an origin story, with development marking distance from a thereby inferior, devalued but also fascinating place.

Postdualism and contextualising developments

We have now reached the 'so what?' point: where the critique of 'what's wrong so far' stops and the question of 'so what happens next?' is asked. What indeed does it mean to 'go beyond' the baby and the bathwater – or (in the manner of performative approaches currently circulating elsewhere in social theory, Butler 1993) to 'do' postdualism? It would scarcely be in keeping with the kind of critique of total or grand theories that underlies my account so far to now wheel out my own variety (and so highlight the capitalist subtext to possessive individualism of 'now buy my new improved version'). All I can offer right now is a set of intellectual and political preoccupations that I would hope could facilitate the emergence of useful and challenging work. I will group these within the thematics of 'contextualising development' and 'decentring the developmental story'.

Contextualising development involves four related features, each of which concerns making alliances rather than maintaining prevailing oppositions that structure policy and academic debates.

Subverting developmental reductionisms

First, we can use the links between different kinds of 'developments', in particular those between economic and developmental psychological development, rather than (only) trying to shed them. It is important to ward off the traditional dynamic of reduction between social and individual that has invested 'the child' and her surrounding contexts with stakes beyond their/her own development and welfare, and it is just as important to highlight the oppressive consequences of attempts to fulfil broader economic and political agendas via child, school and family interventions. Fortunately we are not alone in these kinds of struggles, and we can find allies and helpful ideas within parallel struggles, in particular within development studies. Such a project of subverting the convergence between economic and psychological developmentalists effectively turns the tables, so that together the two disciplines of regulation and control – both wedded via a misguided ideological interplay of individual, regional and national development[2] – can brush history against the grain (see e.g. Sachs' 1992 collection which does for the category of international development what is needed for our models of individual development). Moving from critique and conceptual framework levelled at one discipline to the other facilitates not only an unravelling of each discipline but indicates areas of divergent as well as common concern that ultimately unhooks the invidious reductionisms. In their book entitled *Whose Development?* Crewe and Harrison suggest (of international development interventions):

> The 'deconstructors' of development have argued that a tendency for oversystematised and simplifying models misinterprets and misconstrues the nature of social action and, relatedly, that the diverse motivations and perspectives of different actors in the development process are overlooked. They rightly assert that more sensitive translation and interpretation will not resolve these divergences. These critics also observe that developers are predisposed to find a uniformity and predictability within the communities with which they work that does not exist in reality.
>
> (Crewe and Harrison 1998: 16)

These comments apply as much to the problems of current models of developmental psychology as they do to world economic development – in terms of how the general models obscure the complexity of practices and contexts in which children live and develop, and mask the structurally diverse character of the economic, cultural and interpersonal relationships that produce these varied developments. They go on to point out:

> There is an implied compatibility, or even confluence, of interests between different people that should be explored rather than merely

> taken for granted. These more radical theorists see development itself as a Northern-generated idea that has served to perpetuate relations of subordination in its creation of the 'Third World' and its under-developed 'other'.
>
> (Crewe and Harrison 1998: 16)

Similarly, work with or around children too easily presumes the passivity of the objects of the psychological gaze (and so reproduces it), or else it works to identify their agency as pathology or deficit. This is because it under-estimates the relevance and applicability of its discourse of development.

Transcending child vs. woman-centred accounts

Second, the opposition between the baby/bathwater or the (putatively male) individual child and the (thereby feminised) environment maps onto the historical tensions between child-centred vs. woman-centred accounts. We need to move beyond the oppositions between women's and children's interests to address the interrelationships as well as tensions between gender and childhood – both in terms of the practical gender relations of childcare and education, employment and even including architectural practices, and within our conceptualisations of gender and subjectivity as engendered within children. Historically much of women's oppression has been in relation to the presumptions around children (including bearing them, looking after them, being responsible for what they become in later life). Correlatively some child rights theorists and practitioners have tended to isolate themselves from the enormously fruitful feminist discussions of the covert and far-reaching scale of gendered assumptions within our frame-works as well as our particular practices.

While it is important to maintain the independence of the interests of women and children, it is also practically and conceptually necessary to recognise their interrelations: for boys and girls (usually) become men and women; and in general it is women who care for and teach children. Somewhere, somehow, the arguments elaborated separately about women's and children's interests/rights have to meet up (apart from having separate Conventions – see Chapters 8 and 9 this volume); and where they do – as in say Valerie Walkerdine's and others' work on the relationships between class, pedagogy and mothers and daughter's relationships to psychology and education (Walkerdine and Lucey 1989; Walkerdine 1990a, 1990b; Lucey 2001) – they offer startling insights on both. We have a lot further to go in working this out (see also Burman in press, b).

Beyond cultural chauvinism and cultural relativism

Discussions of 'going beyond' prevailing oppositions structured by modern-ist legacies often get caught into a new version that seems to paralyse further work. Clearly it has been important to point out the ethnocentrism and colonial heritage of psychological models, and how the extension and remit of Northern-based (minority world) models have been exaggerated. But the alternative to the cultural chauvinism of previous grand theory seems to be a cultural pluralism/relativism that seems to disallow judgement and ushers in a kind of moral nihilism that reflects the worst aspects of liberal tolerance: a tolerance that ultimately – in the name of cultural respect or difference – can become one of 'I don't care, you can do what you like' disinterest that ignores the actual power relations governing the liberal so-called 'free' (but not free at all) marketplace of ideas and practices.[3] But are we really caught between being paternalistic and colonialist if we think that child exploitation is wrong? Or if we feel committed to supporting a particular kind of educational intervention?

Becoming trapped in this position arises from a misunderstanding of the critiques of universalist approaches. The problem with these was not only that they proposed general schemes that transcended specific contexts, but that they eschewed acknowledgement of the specific contexts that structured their – thereby rendered covert – ideological assumptions. Surely all of us in the childcare, welfare and education professions are only too aware of the tensions between 'speaking *for*', and 'speaking *as*', specifically as they arise in relation to the representation of interests of a constituency such as children or young people who have historically been offered little opportunity to participate in decision or policymaking. As adults in positions of relative power, we have responsibilities to explicate (rather than eschew) our commitments; and we also have power to negotiate and consult with, and to provide opportunities for, those for whom we speak to make their views known.

From agents to actors/relationships

We need to draw on the critiques of dualism and take them forward in terms of envisaging forms of subjectivity and activity that do not privilege or rely upon abstracted agentic subjects. For these ways of thinking about individuals and identities are the residues of the developmental models whose persistence could inadvertently reproduce the inadequate and exclusionary premises from the old models, and so limit our future work. Instead we can engage in some (sustainable) cultural and disciplinary tourism and experiment with ideas from outside the psychology and education of the North. This is not because the geographical/cultural periphery of the South has any privileged access to authentic truth, but because sometimes surprising and interesting effects result from such border crossings. Whether we draw on actor network theory, complexity theory, macro-ecology, Gibsonian affordances, the activity theory of Leontiev, African or Asian-centred or other non-Northern European indigenous frameworks, we need tools to help us think about development in less individualistic ways, beyond culturally dominant centres, and to help us to be alert to contextual relations, connections, embeddedness, and rootedness of our social categories.[4]

In particular, this should not be read as simply calling for the jettisoning of the notion of the individual. As feminists and child rights activists have rightly pointed out (Jackson 1992), it would be ironic indeed if we dispensed with the notion of the individual as reactionary cultural baggage just at the very moment when women and children were beginning to acquire some hard-won rights thereby. Rather what I am suggesting is that we should recognise the tactical character of our engagement with the discourse of individualism via rights approaches and work alongside this towards formulating more genuinely interpersonal and intersubjective approaches to development and education.

Decentring the developmental story

I want to call for a decentring of the traditional developmental story that is enshrined in the baby/bathwater paradigm, in two directions. We need, first, to move away from the prototypical child as the developmental subject or the unit of development and talk instead of diverse children and childhoods. But the second direction is the correlate of first. For we also need to move away from the traditional abstracted story*tellers* of development (i.e. us), and as researchers, policymakers and educators – those who work with, for and around children – begin to address what our positions and locations might mean for how we interpret and engage with these issues.

Let me focus a little on what the second point might involve. For I do not want suggest this is a reflexive matter of sorting out our own personal childhood histories. Relevant though this may be to child-saving and working (see Chapter 6 this volume), this involves more than therapeutic personal reconstruction (see Chapters 2, 8 and 9 this volume). I want to suggest that we should engage in four sets of contests and refusals of dominant presumptions surrounding children, in order to move towards four aims.

Contests

First, we need to be contesting the *forms of emotionality around children*. While images of children tug at the heart strings (and sometimes open the purse strings), the indulgence surrounding children is a form of paternalism that disempowers them. As discussed in Chapter 6, sentimentality mixes pity and sadism (Winnicott 1958), as children's aid and welfare organisations are now acknowledging and working with (e.g. Save the Children 1992). Maybe we cannot avoid approaching our dealings with children through the lens of the childhoods we did and did not have or perhaps would have wanted. But this cultural baggage belongs to a First, or minority world subject. Compassion and curiosity evoke different identificatory relations. Perhaps we should be asking ourselves and others who work with children to approach them in the same ways that we want them to approach us – as a good perspective-taking or modelling exercise (see also Rahnema 1997).

Second, we need to contest *childhood as a domain of normative regulation*. We know that not only are children regulated and measured, surveyed and evaluated in relation to fictitious norms elaborated by dominant models and associated practices, but also that the judgements we (often unfairly) arrive at have consequences for the ways we see families and cultures. It may seem far-fetched to claim a link between the prototypical child of developmental psychology and the emergence of the nineteenth-century nation state, with particular roles and oppressive expectations elaborated for the carers (usually women). But contemporary feminist theory is now highlighting the role of national identities as implicated in the elaboration of cultural and gendered identities. Women's accorded positions within cultural as well as biological reproduction (Yuval-Davis 1997) highlight how children form the node or pivot around which other key structural relationships are performed.

Third, we need to contest and attend to the *metaphorics of childhood*. Here the contest or challenge is not to expunge but to interrogate the origins and consequences of these metaphors. How we see children – children as our future; children as our (individual or collective) past; children as good, innocent and sacred; or children as beastly and uncivilised – these are all key cultural resources that inform our frameworks for what development is considered to be, to be for, its starting points and its goals. This tells us about ourselves, about what we are supposed to be – in ways that normalise who 'we' are. It is worth reminding ourselves that one of the reasons why we might be either unduly indulgent or alternatively punitive towards children is because our own hold on received versions of maturity and competence is so fragile – thus expressing our own insecurities through our identification or repudiation of identification with children (issues discussed in Chapter 6). Moreover we should also address how metaphorics of childhood are used to frame putative (political) subjectivities; whether our own in being mobilised to help or rescue; or children's own in being enjoined to fulfil our, rather than their own, expectations. The motif of the child can function as a superegoic injunction telling us (and them) what to do (as in 'The planet is our future. It has to be protected', portrayed as expressed *by* a – white, boy – child *to* us). But this blends fantasies of our responsibilities for ourselves and our children with children's own wants and desires, and thus invites not only an assimilation of children's interests into national, international and ecological concerns, but perhaps also generates an irrational anger for the shame generated by failing at doing all this (see also Burman 1999, Chapter 4).

Fourth, we need to *situate the contemporary crisis of childhood* in relation to broader discussions of developments in disarray, and families in transition. The numbers of children suffering abuse, exploitation, neglect, malnutrition, abandonment and displacement are key indicators of global crises – of poverty, disaster and war. But recent moral outrage around violent, abusive and even murderous children has highlighted how children only qualify for the privileges of childhood if they play (rather than work), are asexual and without aggression (Bradley 1989; Burman 1995c). Even beyond such salutory lessons in the exclusionary and mythical character of contemporary Anglo-US/minority world models of childhood are the class and cultural evaluations that they bring in their swell. The current crises around childhood cannot be dissociated from broader global social and economic changes within gender and labour relations, and their corresponding reflection within family organisation and functioning.

Refusals

From the contest I will move now on to four refusals. By refusing I mean we should be stubborn and look for stubbornness, not to dismiss or to dispose of these features, but – by recognising them – to try to afford other vantage points on how they have configured the ways we think. Fran Cherry's (1995) book *The Stubborn Particulars of Social Psychology* offers a dramatically different reading of some of the paradigmatic studies within social psychology. By asking 'who?', 'which?', and 'where?', Cherry exposes the suppressed gender, class and cultural contexts of these key works, and thereby arrives at a convincing re-evaluation of their claims. Acknowledging the stubbornness of the particular, its inevitable persistence as an invisible trace no matter how apparently abstract or general the story or model, is a valuable strategy.

So here (rehearsing some of the arguments from Chapters 1 and 4) are four stubborn or persistent contexts for our conceptualisation of children and childhoods that demand refusal or vigilance.

First, we should refuse the *special status of childhood*. While we grant special privileges and qualities to children, we do so at the cost of abstracting children from the social relations that give rise to them and thereby perpetuating their mythological status. For as soon as children exhibit behaviours considered unchildlike they are regarded as outside the category of childhood (Kleeberg-Niepage 2005). We preserve our concept of childhood and eject particular kinds of children from it rather than adapt the original model. So we need to beware of the hold of this specialness on our minds with a view to putting into question when and where this is helpful (see Gronemeyer 1992 on relationships reinscribed within 'helping'), and whether we should be changing childhoods rather than only children. Let me make clear here that I am not advocating refusing special measures for children as strategic/tactical interventions, but rather the reification of that 'specialness'.

Second, we should refuse *the (covert) gendering of the child*. There is a tendency to talk of children as if gender does not figure or matter, and these matters are taken up in other chapters in this book. But there is no geographical, cultural or discursive space that is gender-neutral, and even the discourse of neutrality suggests the suppression of struggle rather than the transcendence and blending of distinct differences. But just as culture and class mould different childhoods, so boys and girls inhabit different developing worlds. Refusing to take at face value the apparent absence of gender-marking within discussions of childhood is important both to expose the covert gender assumptions that – within patriarchal societies inevitably – enter into the ways we think, talk and act, and to prompt attention to *which* different experiences are being marginalised or subordinated within such supposed generality.

Moving on now, third, we need to refuse to invest children with qualities of *lost or true selfhood*. If authentic selfhood is a lifetime project and possibly a fiction produced by modern therapeutics (Parker 1997), then we do (conceptual as well as moral) wrong to impute children with such developmental burdens. Such moral evaluation only invites failures of attainment and corresponding disappointments (for us about them, and thus affecting the effectiveness of our responses). Moral action and intervention with and on behalf of children are better motivated and structured according to more local concerns, with our frameworks and assumptions governing childhood displaced a little, put to one side.

Similarly, and fourth, *the naturalness of the child should be refused*. For 'natural' children can only exist alongside unnatural ones, and how we determine which is which is surely more a matter of moral-political evaluation than empirical fact. Claims to nature usually operate as warrants: either to discount or to dismiss the intentionality of action (as in 'it's only natural; boys will be boys'). Either way, discourses of nature have rightly elicited concern for their resistance to change, for their determinism, and ultimately for their victim-blaming (Lieven 1981). However seemingly benign, we need to be alert for where and how claims to naturalness are being deployed, and to what effect.

Aiming towards . . .

Finally, I want to highlight four areas that moving beyond the 'baby and the bathwater' and towards (what I have called) postdualist approaches to developmental psychology might mean. For far from critique ushering in a paralysis, there is plenty we can do.

First, as I have already suggested, it means situating ourselves within our accounts of childhood, including our investments – both economic and fantasised – within particular childhoods. Returning to Crewe and Harrison's (1998) provocative critique of progressive international development projects (also mentioned in Chapter 1), they also point out difficulties with the turn towards deconstruction (that has been so useful for promoting critical work). They note that this position still tends to overstate

the agency and importance of Northern development and developers, and ignore or devalue action that is independent of the developers. While they discuss this in terms of the tensions between what they call 'development reformers' and 'development anthropologists', I think this applies equivalently to tensions between (deconstructors of) developmental *psychology* and childhood studies:

> Developers remain at the centre of the analysis while other people's actions are read merely as responses to the fixed centre, rather than as formed and influenced by all sorts of circumstances, many of which will be unconnected to development activity.
>
> (Crewe and Harrison 1998: 18)

Paradoxically, this process of situating oneself, far from privileging it, should rather help throw into question and open up our accounts to other actors and agencies.

Second, we can try to move away from unified versions of childhoods, families and cultures to focus instead on multiple perspectives. This is not only a matter of documenting and celebrating diversity, but also involves *working with* the conflicts and power relations operating between these – whether between differently embodied and situated childhoods or between different constituencies' perspectives and constructions of these (including professional, familial, cultural and class-based differences), and the various 'stakeholders' within any developmental intervention.

Third, I think it is a real challenge for us to move away from the clear, if arduous and oppressive, certainties provided by unitary, universalised models and learn to live with the tensions. For staying situated, and so not falling prey to the dualist oppositions structuring the baby/bathwater paradigm, means surrendering claims to absolute truths and seeing such claims as always complicit within acts of verbal and sometimes physical violence. We are unaccustomed to not resolving uncertainties; but this lack of foundationalism does not mean moral torpor or inaction, but rather being clearer about the tentative strategic foundations that warrant one's interventions.

Fourth and finally, there is a move from programmes to the programmatic. I think we should not be afraid to be prescriptive, or to acknowledge the moral-political character of our interventions. Rather it is a matter of using this attention to particularity and specificity to create other plural methodologies for mapping the complexity of childhoods and relationships around those childhoods. Moreover, borrowing once again from discussions in economic development, we might also come to recognise that mapping, however benignly conceived, is a methodological act of appropriation and surveillance.[5] Notwithstanding the importance attached to participatory learning and co-operative research, I want to caution against a too uncritical subscription to this 'method', or its adoption as a technique. As Cooke and Kothari (2001) point out in their discussion of the 'new tyranny' of

participatory research within international development work, the efforts to promote participatory approaches still run the risk of insufficiently theorising the ways we produce what we intervene within, with consequent effects on what we 'discover' and what we make of these 'discoveries'. Here we might do well to recall how secrecy and inscrutability have enabled many oppressed peoples to survive, and how enlisting people (including children and families the world over) into participatory projects can make findings which are produced *in response to* Northern developmental agendas apparently originate from within indigenous communities and so grant the interventions proposed by the projects incontestable warrants (see also Parpart 1995; J. Scott 1997). So *working with* the moral-political partiality of our accounts about children and their contexts also means coming to terms with the provisional and relational character of all our claims, including the evidence on which those claims are based.

Remoralising the gaze: the baby/bathwater revisited

Having considered who does what in this encounter (and who else might be involved) we have now arrived at the moral evaluations at stake in this sorting out process of what to keep and what to throw away. Furthermore we have come to see how typically there is a viewer implied within evaluation; a third party – that we are being urged to agree with or identify with, as an invisible surveying other. This third party assumes the power of scrutiny and judgement; who says 'do throw' or 'don't throw' to us, as the implied supporter of these evaluations. Significantly, this moral evaluation comes from outside the interaction: as if the morality and knowledge lies outside the baby and the thrower (or throwers) of its bathwater.

I have been discussing the problems inherent in the erasure of this culturally and embodied structure of evaluation. Alongside the need to situate and embody child development and educational practices for the promotion of diverse and multiple childhoods, I have argued for the need to embody and render *ourselves* (especially including the diversity of who 'we' are) visible within these research, measurement and evaluation encounters. Hence, instead of being more or less reluctant, or intrusive, voyeurs on the intimate dealings of babies and bathtimes, I have suggested that we bring ourselves in as explicit actors. By such means we can come to see moral-political judgements (about development as with everything) as not only necessary and inevitable, but we can also render them into more visible forms that can be more readily contested. Hence the parameters governing inclusion or exclusion, of retention and rejection, and especially the structures of identification mobilised therein, can be opened to re-evaluation.

A final word on 'the bathwater'. Talking of the morality of exclusion and rejection ('throwing'), begs this question: how do we know that the bathwater should be disposed of? And, further, why does our phrase not tell us where to put it? The unspecified destination of the bathwater remains an

absent trace of broader and deeper difficulties that implicate the model not only within national but also colonialist/imperialist paradigms. Drawing on contemporary critiques of identity (e.g. Henriques *et al.* 1984), we can point out that (materially as well as linguistically) what is excluded becomes identified with its location; ground used for dumping becomes a dumping ground, and then a dump. Surely those of us in overconsuming societies have some responsibility to consider what we are dumping, and where. So where does our toxic bathwater go? Does it accumulate and contaminate elsewhere? And where is 'elsewhere'?

We know from environmental discussions that the richest countries of the world consume the most resources and also produce the most waste, while the poorest countries, and the poorer places within all countries, become the sites where such waste is deposited – such that the effects of exposure to this waste contribute to their poverty via ill health, as in both chronic malnutrition and sickness (see also Sachs 1999). Examples of this are too numerous to mention, but we only have to think of where it is that nuclear weapons testing and dumping takes place; where the 'world free trade zones' are; where the new markets for the tobacco industry are; on which populations drugs trials are conducted; let alone the more perhaps mundane matters of where scrap and landfill sites are in all cities; and how children's unpaid and lowest paid labour both historically and currently keeps household and industrial economies running.

Over the years I have been approached – sometimes by colleagues who have travelled overseas, sometimes even by letters from universities and childcare organisations – requesting books and materials on child development to be sent to African countries, to Latin American countries, to the Indian subcontinent. They are asking for the donations of materials for courses within educational institutions that have few or no resources. In my department (of psychology) we have held book collections to send to the 'transitional' countries of eastern Europe too. At these times I look at my collection of unwanted big tomes on child and human development that were sent to me unsolicited by publishers and that I have spent years commenting on and disparaging. They are big, glossy, attractive books with lots of coloured pictures, helpful summaries and question 'boxes' that make them accessible, but with checklists and test manuals that produce a standardised knowledge out of a set of provisional and contestable debates, and thereby covertly do the work of globalisation that we are all now trying to challenge. Should I now send this intellectual toxic waste to these countries to poison (fill with Northern debris) the minds of childcare workers? But on the other hand, could they be useful or selectively appropriated (in the ways all ideas and practices are) in ways that I, from my position, cannot (yet) envisage?

But if we take a more conservationist or environmentalist 'take' on the 'baby–bathwater' couplet, in fact we effect a reversal. For surely this bathwater is a resource, something we can analyse for clues as to what this baby

is all about, including what we think it should not contain (e.g. aggression, impurity, Bradley 1989) and the relations of activity and passivity presumed (why assume the baby is thrown, maybe she wants to jump?). As such, far from jettisoning our cultural legacies (which is an impossible and probably undesirable demand), we can perhaps instead use these to better effect to look within and beyond ourselves and our categorisation systems, and emerge better equipped to work with those who have historically been devalued and excluded in order to build others.

8 Developing differences

Gender, childhood and economic development

Taking up the analysis of popular cultural representations of children and childhoods, particular attention is paid in this chapter to key policy texts concerning both international child development and international economic development. This is done through a focus on the bifurcated character of discourses of North and South and the effects of urbanisation. Here the trends noted (of young populations in the South, especially in rapidly growing Southern cities) have only intensified since this piece was initially drafted (Ansell 2005). (This is despite the 'problem' of ageing populations in the North – due to improvements in health and welfare – as well as how, through neoliberalism, new neocolonial inequalities are being played out outside Northern contexts.) The occlusion of the conditions of these children's lives is shown to continue in the representations of childhood that inform the Human Development Index (HDI), a measure elaborated initially within the United Nations Development Policy (UNDP) document of 1989, coinciding also with the passing of the UN Convention of the Rights of the Child. Analysis here focuses on the third UNDP report of 1992 that was used to formulate World Bank Policy, including early programmes of Structural Adjustment. It therefore precedes the introduction of a Human Poverty Index (introduced from 1997) and a Gender-Related Development Index Measure and Gender Empowerment Measure added from 1995, but the latter two are still regarded as limited and inappropriately interpreted (Shuler 2006).

While the HDI claimed to champion people rather than income, it is still regarded as falling far short of providing an adequate measure of disparities in or inequalities of quality of life, either across countries or regions. Assumptions underlying this measure are critiqued, on both conceptual and methodological grounds, many of which continue to be discussed a decade later (see e.g. Foster 2004; Haque 2004; Chatterjee 2005; Despotis 2005; Ranis *et al.* 2006). The HDI is based on the combination of three measures: longevity, knowledge and income. As Kamdar (2005: 3760–3761) notes, the actual relationships between these measures as contributors to quality of life have yet to be determined, while it fails to include the range of (political, economic, creative) 'choices' and even human rights that it specifies as part of its notion of 'human development'. Further, the index does not allow for indicators of improvement in well-being. It functions as a linear measure of deprivation, which thereby omits many important features of the social and cultural context of any society. This account should be read alongside other longstanding and current critiques of development 'aid' (e.g. Hayter 1971, 2005; Hobart 1993; Pottier 1993; Middleton and O'Keefe 1998), as well as accounts which challenge the assumptions now guiding aid as a means of securing political stability and therefore new structures of world governance (Duffield 2001).

This chapter discusses how scrutiny of some of the specifically developmental psychological research drawn upon within the HDI indicates some key slippages of reading and interpretation. These bolster the move towards an abstracted and generalised model of childhood that fails to fit the populations upon whom it has been applied. Hence it is argued that the reduction of space to time in models of development elaborated within such documents transfers relations of difference into those of order. In order to counter the naturalisation and abstraction of development, which reflects and contributes to the cultural and economic domination of the Northern hemisphere over the South, the chapter ends with a call to attend to both the specificity and diversity of children's developments.

In this chapter I trace connections between representations of childhood and North–South relations through a reading of key international aid and development texts. I will illustrate some consequences of the historical and geographical mappings of gender, culture and childhood by juxtaposing psychological models that inform aid programmes for children of the South, and models of the process of development in which so-called 'developing countries' are said to be engaged.

Since this is an enterprise full of irony and paradox, I cannot claim to offer a coherent narrative in elaborating these themes. Rather, this chapter attempts to indicate how different disciplinary areas and professional practices (of economics, geography, psychology, law) are structured by a common set of assumptions that link North and South, and the children of the North and South, within structural relationships of inequality. Insofar as arguments can be drawn out from this complex set of overdeterminations between adults and children, men and women, North and South, I will be suggesting that addressing the positions of children of the South confronts Northern academics and policymakers with the contradictions and limitations of our Northern, class-based and gendered models of – both psychological and economic – development. This is a polemical text, in which I will argue that the challenge of supporting Southern children requires a reconceptualisation not only of how we see those children, but more than this to evaluate the discursive and political practices that structure their positions. If we fail to do this, the (economic and psychological) models of development currently used stand to gain a spurious credibility and longevity by their globalisation through international legislation.

I will begin by recalling the economic discourse of development and its connections to psychological varieties, before moving on to explore the resonances between the iconography of children, and women, and the South. Through these I analyse the cultural-historical assumptions that structure dominant ways of conceptualising both economic and individual development. These arise: first, as metaphors used to describe development; second, in the ways we distinguish who develops and how we interpret those differences; third, in discussions of the role of women as mothers and as workers. This chapter therefore moves from discussions of different arenas of development to the representation of urban and rural physical space. I will suggest that the distinction between innocence and experience is transposed or reversed by Southern children and Southern cities, particularly within discussions of child labour. Examination of key texts on international child development policy suggests that these assumptions are maintained within the accounts of developmental psychology that inform aid and development programmes. The final section explores similarities between the concept of human development that underlies international economic development policy and that of models of child development.

The cultural economy of development

In speculating upon its multiple meanings, it is helpful to recall that the invention of 'development' as an economic term simultaneously constituted the concept of 'underdevelopment', with both terms deriving their current forms from Harry Truman's inaugural presidential speech, on 20 January 1949. By this, development became an assumed goal, or even right, for all, yet:

> For two thirds of the people on earth, this positive meaning of the word development – profoundly rooted after two centuries of its social construction – is *a reminder of what they are not*. It is a reminder of an undesirable, undignified state. To escape from it, they need to be enslaved to others' experiences and dreams.
>
> (Esteva 1992: 10)

Central to the arguments that I will put forward is that the implicit comparison within the term development, rendered explicit within the Human Development Index (HDI) that I discuss later, is itself a construction, an abstraction. More than mere construction, as Esteva points out, it is a fiction with its own productive and reproductive force:

> The word [underdevelopment] defines a perception. This becomes, in turn, an object, a fact. No one seems to doubt that the concept does not allude to real phenomena. They do not realise that it is a comparative adjective whose base of support is the assumption, very Western but unacceptable and undemonstrable, of the oneness, homogeneity and linear evolution of the world.
>
> (Esteva 1992: 1–2)

Parallels can be drawn between descriptions of the development of richer and poorer countries, and accounts of development from children to adults. In discussions of aid and development policies, the social and economic domains are seen as distinct entities, rather like the way the developmental psychology has tended to treat the social and cognitive as separate (cf. Harris 1987, on the continuities between representations of early development as skills and the instrumentalism demanded by market forces). In both, development is assumed as an unproblematic and unexamined end, with little definition of precisely what develops, or where development leads. In both, ultimately, development elaborates a relational hierarchy, that is, with the 'more developed' exhibiting those features that the 'less developed' lack.

Accounts of *individual* development abound with naturalistic and evolutionary discourses which presume the inevitability and unidirectionality of development (Morss 1990). That development can be 'arrested' or 'delayed' merely reinforces the normative chronology that underlies such evaluation, and where development goes wrong malfunctioning agents like parents or genes can be identified. Development thus becomes a reified process, abstracted from the material and political practice of human activities. Within economic development policy the metaphors of development shift and mutate to assimilate changing calls to include participation, planning and environmental considerations (often with the double-edged discourse of self-reliance). The concept of development is now exhibiting what Esteva calls a 'conceptual inflation' so that from simple 'development' we now have sustainable development, human-centred development, integrated development. Not only does the multiplication of forms correspondingly increase the demands to live up to development, but it also obscures the unitary, if anomalous, model at its core. The banner of development marks a homogenisation, a loss of diversity as the 'Westernisation of the world'.

'Progress' is the key term that links both sets of development narratives together, and this enjoys such rhetorical power in both that failure to adopt this discourse prejudices the persuasive capacity of one's arguments. It is an instructive reflection of the coincidence of preoccupations and practices between the two sets of discourses of development that the following critique of international development policy, as failing to confront the ideological themes at its core, applies just as relevantly to developmental psychology:

> By now development has become an amoeba-like concept, shapeless but ineradicable. Its contours are so blurred that it denotes nothing – while it spreads everywhere because it connotes the best of intentions. . . . Though development has no content, it does possess one function: it allows any intervention to be sanctified in the name of a higher good. Therefore even enemies feel united under the same banner.
>
> (Sachs 1992: 4)

The space and time of development

Current discussions in geography and cultural studies form a useful resource for any project exploring the double nuances of 'development'. Drawing on postmodern and postcolonial writings, these disrupt the traditional Northern oppositions between rural romanticism and urban decay (here I am using the terms North and South to refer to hemispheres of the world, although – as I remark often in this book – there are of course many Norths and Souths within this global North and South). Thus they show how images of the South reshuffle romantic attributions of authenticity and origin to add a post-industrial twist to the polarisation between nature and culture. The city as the icon of Northern industrialised progress has become, almost in the way of a postmodern parody, superseded by the image of Southern urban decay. In a postmodern world, development and degeneration coincide and the boundaries between what is 'natural' and 'man-made' have become blurred by the global environmental consequences of local human actions and their colonial displacements. Now it is the cities of the South that reflect back to the North the empty promises of the development story, the story of progress and embetterment, while the North disowns and re-presents its systematic exploitation and impoverishment of the South to position the 'Third World' as the repository of human and environmental damage.

A similar set of significations and slippages underlies another development story, the story of *individual* growth and development. Children in modern industrialised societies, that is, in the North, symbolise what is natural and good, spontaneous and authentic. The set of privileges and positions this elaborates intersects with North–South relations so that Southern children who violate this Northern imagery appear as *unnatural* children. A consequence, then, of the globalisation of Northern sentimentalised models of the child is that it can fuel racism towards peoples who fail to fulfil what appear to be children's 'natural rights'. Moreover, as I argue elsewhere, the precise qualities of children and responsibilities towards them (as defined within policies claiming to respect children's natural rights) rest on irreducibly ambiguous foundations which may function in practice in ways that depart quite dramatically from the 'best interests' they purport to promote (Burman 1993, 1996a).

The infantilisation of the South

Organisations involved in international aid and development lament the fact that disasters and fund-raising appeals constitute a primary resource for Northern people's representations of the South (Black 1992). Development educators are finding it hard to dislodge the images used which affirm qualities of poverty, deficit, and dependence (Graham and Lynn 1989). These contribute to the racism directed towards black people in the North, as well as in the North's relations with the South. In constructing representations of need, of grateful recipients, the aid imagery predominantly depicts *children* as its beneficiaries. In part, this is a reflection of the sentimentality that surrounds children within Northern ideologies, so that children are accorded the position of innocent victims, who therefore elicit sympathy without being held responsible for their suffering (while by implication their parents and families are responsible). Where they are depicted accompanying their children, Southern women are represented as helpless, rendered into a state of childlike dependency not only through their need, but by implication through having transferred their parental responsibilities to the Northern donor (Holland 1992; see also Chapter 6).

There is now a substantial body of work which suggests that the iconography of the South within the Northern media infantilises peoples of the South as passive and powerless. It also indicates a process of feminisation, determined not only by the overt infantilisation of women as helpless victims, but also more implicitly through the gendered assumptions inscribed within definitions of development (Broughton 1988; Burman 1995b, in press, a). The positions of adult and child, like the symbolism of culture and nature they reflect, elaborate positions of superiority and inferiority, of reason and emotion, of maturity and immaturity. Each of these map on to historical definitions of men and women, and white people and black people. The binary opposition of adult and child is thus played out through colonial relationships of paternalism, so that relations of patronage, of help, of aid, secure the sense of competence and potency of Northern adults (Burman 1994a, 1994b).

Nevertheless, there are some senses in which the equation between women and children and the South does have some genuine currency. For all its problems, discussions of the feminisation of poverty do at least indicate that women-headed households suffer the most economically from the global recession of multinational capitalism, and highlight the prevalence of exploitative forms and relations of production that are associated with women's labour, such as casual short-term contracts, long and irregular hours and homeworking (Mitter 1986). Similarly, the association between children and the South holds in the sense that high birth rates combined with short life expectancy means that Southern countries have very young populations. In addition to the 15 million preventable deaths of children each year, over half the world's population is under 15 years of age and this is overwhelmingly concentrated in countries of the South (Ennew and Milne 1989). As child rights activists point out, this means that Southern issues are very much children's issues (Boyden with Holden 1991). Paradoxically, the quintessential child that underlies international policies for children is very much a Northern child.

Rural and urban myths

These spatial distributions between North and South connect with the representation of – specifically urban – space in contradictory ways. City and psyche are connected in the North with the associations between the gendered division of labour and segregation of public and private space. As an orientalist reversal of the opposition between rural and urban space wrought through industrialisation, discourses of modern Northern post-industrial alienation elaborate images of the North as urban decay, with the South as virgin and uncharted lands. Yet the South does not fulfil this rural nostalgia. While one half of the world's population lives in urban settings, it is now estimated that young people below the age of 19 now form the majority of city populations in the South (Boyden with Holden 1991). In terms of the links between economic and individual development, this means that it is children and young people who are exposed to the dangers and pressures of cities. Moreover, partly through the imposition of structural adjustment programmes, it is the poorest and least urbanised countries that are currently exhibiting the greatest increases in urban growth (Patel 1992).

Moreover, while the supposed dangers of urban life (pollution, drugs, homelessness) may appear contemporary, cities of the South have long been portrayed in the Northern colonial cultural imaginary as the mysterious, sensual, transgressive, feminine body to be fathomed. In her analysis of key Anglo-Indian texts, Ching-Liang Low (1989) documents how the 'vile native city' functions to provide the foil for the good, clean Anglo-Indian one. Despite its disgusting qualities, the 'native city' exerts so strong a fascination that white male colonialists were driven to dress up as 'natives' in order to explore its secrets. The city is explicitly feminised as a body to be possessed.

So there is nothing new about the representation of cities of the South as feminised places of carnivalesque intermingling of vitality and danger, of youth and death, of desire and disgust. These qualities reflect the dynamic of displacement (both real – as the migration and dislocation of peoples, and symbolic – as psychic projections of unwanted fears and desires) brought about by colonialism. That these sentiments continue to thrive can be seen within the popularity of films of empire which maintain this imagery. The South therefore reflects back to the North the grotesque consequences of colonialism masquerading as development. Like nuclear waste dumped in the Pacific, or the ravages of Agent Orange in the Puerto

Rican rainforest, the North, having exported its intractable problems and dangerous experiments, then treats these as indigenous properties and problems (that it can be called upon to remedy – at a price). The market of development is far from free.

Innocence and experience

If the South as a region is feminised and infantilised, what kinds of infants and children inhabit it? In modern thought the child represents the original, natural, romanticised source and core of personhood. Northern images of the child link categories of the natural with innocence (often signified by the girl child), thus setting up an opposition between innocence and experience that is supplemented by discourses of childcare and child protection, and reflected in the cultural polarisation of naivety and damage. In her analysis of popular representations of childhood, Holland (1992) argues that images of children function within discourses of a pre-industrial rural idyll (p. 14), so that the nostalgia for a harmonious childhood merges with that for a mythical harmony of society (p. 93). Talking of the genre for 'realism' in 1970s British artistic and documentary representation of inner city life and inner city children, Holland comments[1] on the residues of rural naturalism and romanticism that lurk even within images of Northern urban decay:

> The conscious realism of this urban imagery sought to reject the moralism and Romanticism which linked children within the rural and with organic nature, but in treating the town as a space for discovery it created its own urban ruralism. Children were not expected to invade the centres of modernity and power. . . . The hiding places, nooks and crannies of the inner city were for all the world like the lanes and copses of the countryside. This imagery set its face against the hardness and glitter of the new city in a nostalgia for the manipulability of the old.
>
> (Holland 1992: 95)

So, just as the South is no rural idyll, as a counterpoint to the industrialised, 'developed' North, so children of the South may exhibit little of the passive innocence characteristic of Northern idealised representations of children. The problem is that when children (in the South or the North) violate these ideals then the penalty incurred may be that they are no longer accorded the indulgences or privileges associated with the status of childhood (few though these may be). Hence (as noted in Part II) the difficulty of integrating an acknowledgement of the sexuality of children with the imperative to protect them from exploitation. So central is the desexualisation of children to their (covertly sexualised) representation that the 'knowing' child is rendered culpable (Kitzinger 1990; Stainton Rogers and Stainton Rogers 1992). Similarly, since the dominant definition of childhood is a Northern (and mythical) model rendered global, then children of the South who of necessity deal resourcefully with the conditions they live in[2] may thus invite further stigmatisation for their failure to conform to the image of the innocent, helpless child:

> The child who appeals to the viewer, humbly requesting help, has remained the mainstay of aid imagery. But children's actual response to conditions of deprivation may well refuse qualities of childhood which give them their pathos. . . . The engaging impudence of the street urchin carries overtones of both sexuality and children's contribution to the tourist economy of those states (through state prostitution and sex tourism). But it needs only a slight shift of perspective to see the child on the streets as an undesirable vagrant.
>
> (Holland 1992: 161)

All work and no play . . .

This issue becomes particularly apparent in discussions of child labour. Without denying the widespread exploitation of children, it should be acknowledged that the Northern scandalisation over children's involvement in paid work perhaps belies particular investments in its repression of how Northern industrial wealth and progress was based in part on the exploited labour of women and children. This forgetting is also in spite of the fact that nearly all children all over the world engage in some form of work, some of which is paid work (see, for example, Morrow 1994). It is relevant at this point to note that among the motives for introducing the compulsory schooling of children in Europe was the aim of making working-class children dependent, since they were a financially autonomous and potentially demanding – or even unruly – social group (Hendrick 1990). So amid this moral panic over economically active and autonomous young people, it is not surprising that research documents how (in this case Norwegian) children who take on particular domestic responsibilities, and who may receive some remuneration for this, develop a changed sense of their status and feel more adult (Solberg 1990). Yet children of the South routinely work and while many, but by no means all, work in exploitative circumstances, they usually either elicit pity or are thereby classified as deviants, outside the category of childhood. Even aid agencies such as Save the Children are unwilling to acknowledge the nefarious activities conducted by street children involved in its schemes in South America and therefore fail to engage with children whose circumstances fall outside the dominant representations of childhood (Peace, personal communication 1993). Similarly, policymakers are now discussing the ambiguities of the 'best interest' principle governing child rights legislation as an exemplar of the tensions between respecting cultural diversity and children's rights (Alston 1994).[3]

There are two important issues relevant to those researching for or around children's issues. One is that the model of schooling that is deemed to be every children's right is a practice geared to the production of a Northern model of industrialised childhood. This therefore can contribute to the marginalisation and disenfranchisement of traditional cultures and practices:

> Childhood becomes a period of preparation for the labour force, in which skill acquisition (of the limited kind needed by the labour market and for the limited numbers which can be absorbed) is only part of the process. Another function of education is a hierarchizing mechanism, which preserves the knowledge territory of elite dominant cultures and nurtures only those from the masses who can be trusted to conform. This is now further served by the problem solving, scientific, technological culture of transnational enterprises, which intensifies the process of denigration and devaluation of ancient cultures that began in the colonial period.
>
> (Ennew and Milne 1989: 66–67)

Second, so central is the role accorded to play within contemporary models of child learning that the child who works is seen as less than childlike. Valerie Walkerdine and her co-researchers' work on British teachers' accounts of girls' and boys' performance in mathematics highlights how girls, because they are good and neat and work hard, are regarded as less interesting and less clever than their more disruptive, inattentive and often less successful male counterparts (Walkerdine 1990b). Because the active, discovering, problem-solving, playing child reflects the culturally sanctioned attributes of the male child, it is debatable whether girls are regarded as developing children at all (see Burman 1994b, 1995b). This argument clearly has its parallels with the situation of children of the South. Moreover, the definition of play constitutive of Northern childhood has been so commodified that it now requires that especially purchased objects are marketed for their qualities of skill or concept development. Therefore, rather paradoxically – given the theoretical definitions of play as non-goal directed and non-evaluated activity, the toys specify their modes of use and purposes.

Clearly children who work do not need to be further stigmatised for failing to conform to Northern romantic representations. The issue in legislating upon and regulating child labour is to distinguish between 'a child's right' to do useful work under proper conditions and with fair pay, compared to the child's right to protection from exploitative labour practices which can mean lives and dreams are lost for ever (Ennew and Milne 1989: 75). The drive towards compulsory and free primary schooling worldwide rests on an assumption that involvement in schooling will decrease children's economic activity. This assumption has been found to be unmerited – and one possible explanation for this is the need to buy uniforms and equipment (Boyden 1990). Moreover, parents may have justifiable reservations about sending their child to a school which international authorities themselves admit may be of poor quality, or may provide education in a colonial language (Vittachi 1989; Colclough with Lewin 1993). These factors therefore may lead a child to fail to make good progress or may distance them from their cultural background. Boyden with Holden (1991) claim that the UN figures of increases in primary school attendance over the last 20 years are greatly inflated by the many children who repeat classes year after year, who are failing to complete either through inadequate teaching and support or because the system of delivery is too inflexible for their work commitments.[4]

Local and global childhood

If the model of childhood operating in Northern industrialised societies is an inadequate description of the children who are then found wanting when measured in relation to it, then it is even less appropriate for Southern children who differ from and transgress those Northern defined norms even more. The 1989 UN Convention on the Rights of the Child attempts to elaborate international standards for the care and welfare of children, and as a description of basic child welfare, protection and political rights it is to be welcomed. However, notwithstanding its rapid passage through the United Nations, and most widespread adoption by member states, its impact in actually changing the conditions of children's lives remains to be seen (see, for example, Freeman 1993). My purpose here is to highlight the cultural resources that underlie supposedly neutral, general models of childhood. While the tensions between universal rights and cultural-regional variation were central to the key conflicts posed by the drafting of the Convention (Johnson 1992), what is less often acknowledged is how the resources for the supposedly general models are described from highly culturally and class-specific research.

I have discussed elsewhere how the particularly cultural privileging of masculinity in developmental psychological models gives rise to differing ways of conceptualising the needs of, and interventions for, girls (Burman 1994d, 1995b, 1996a). In these, I document the surreptitious maintenance of culturally specific residues within supposedly general international policies for children. In particular, the selection of the individual child as the unit of development is characteristic of Northern developmental psychological models, and this is explicitly reinforced by UN representations of psychological research.[5] This bolsters the individualism that underlies Western Enlightenment thinking which is writ large in international rights legislation, and inscribed within modern developmental psychology. It is not only reproduced in the model of child development that underlies the Convention. Once there, the inscription of individualism within psychology functions to naturalise it (that is, treats it as natural and inevitable). (For a more extensive critique of the varieties and interpretations of the developmental psychological theories subscribed to in UNICEF policies, see Burman 1996a.)

Not only is 'the child' thus abstracted from the material and emotional conditions that shape him or her, but the child's 'development' is divorced from or set alongside that of others, especially his or her mother. This gives rise to tensions and contradictions in policy statements, where the 'girl' child is treated as both a variety of the (retrospectively specified) male child and as an incipient mother. This is especially evident in calls to increase girls' access to and duration of schooling, which are financially justified in terms of 'population policies' through the reported correlations between female education, later marriage and reduced family size (see Colclough with Lewin 1993). Locally produced but purportedly general developmental psychological models are thus globalised within international aid and development policies. Drawing on these analyses, my primary purpose here is to take further the cultural continuities between economic and psychological models of development through a close attention to some key UN documents. But before this let us stay a little longer with the naturalisation of child development, and the corresponding individualisation and privatisation of the responsibility for children.

Cultural deprivation, women's work and the marketing of obsolete theories

The history of psychological and educational practice in the North tells a story of how 'home–school relations' and parental involvement schemes have functioned as a key arena by which to regulate and evaluate working-class and minority groups, with interventions cast within a model of amelioration of cultural deficit (Sharp and Green 1975; David 1988; Walkerdine and Lucey 1989). Now, as is usually the case when the local market has become both saturated and more discerning, this story is exported to the South in the form of international aid and development programmes. We know that preschool education is not the panacea for social inequalities in the North, yet we are implicitly enjoined to presume it may be for the South. This is certainly a cheaper and less disruptive intervention than cancelling the Third World Debt or addressing unequal terms of trade. While the buzz words of international aid and development programmes are 'participation' and 'community development', the practice of these widely acclaimed sentiments is hampered (among other reasons) by the impoverished model of human development that underlies it.

Further, just as in the North, these individualising and pathologising models specifically target and regulate women. It is women as mothers who are evaluated by home visitors for their skills in keeping children fed, stimulated and educated. Breast may be 'best' (pace Stanway and Stanway 1983), but that does not mean that nurseries taking children of working mothers less than a year old should be closed down, as is the consequence of introducing measures for child health and development in Costa Rica, for example. To take a small cultural text as illustrative of more general discourses, even fund raising for the provision of adequate drinking water can become an occasion for rehearsing ideologies of motherhood. The 1992 WaterAid campaign in Britain exhorted safe drinking water as not only vital to self-reliance (part of current aid and development discourse, Burman 1994a) but also as a means of promoting attentive mothering. The text reads:

> WaterAid encourages people to take responsibility for their own lives . . . 'Now my children are clean,' says Alice. 'We have learned to protect the health of our families. They now do not have diarrhoea.'

Safe water not only saves lives but it allows mothers to spend more time with their families. In this, access to water becomes transposed from a basic human lack to a failure of knowledge and care. There is no reason to suppose that 'Alice' was unaware of the value of washing to prevent disease; she simply did not have the means to carry this out. The reference elsewhere in the text to the time spent walking many miles to fetch and carry water as now being available for women to devote to their families indicates a similar move whereby these women are retrospectively designated as neglectful mothers. Moreover, these discursive slippages reflect the more general trend for measures introduced in the name of modernisation and development to function to restrict women's mobility and to enforce more traditional definitions of women's roles (Gascoigne 1991; Patel 1992). In this case the elision of cultural definitions of proper mothering with the universal human need for water in this aid appeal indicates two more general issues: first, the impossibility of representing such needs outside cultural practices; second, when such abstraction is attempted, as in claims to unitary knowledge, in this case psychological, it reproduces the ideological assumptions of those who produce the representations. Leaving aside for the moment the questions of whether this is inevitable, or whether this process can be mitigated, these are the assumptions that the recourse to developmental psychology currently functions to maintain within international aid and development policy.

Marketing and quantifying human development

The resonance between human development and programmes to alleviate the poverty of the South becomes most disturbing in the UN Development Programme *Human Development Report*. This documents the comparative health and wealth of the North and South, the third version of which appeared in 1992. Here, the commodification of human development as a condition of economic development becomes complete: 'The concept of human development . . . is a form of investment, not just a means of distributing income. Healthy and educated people can, through productive employment, contribute more to economic growth' (UNDP 1992: 12). While in previous UNDP reports human development was defined in terms of enlarging people's choices, the 1992 report claims to have moved 'from a discussion of mere *means* (GNP growth) to a discussion of ultimate *ends*' (UNDP 1992: 2). Hence a notion of individual development is being championed that is more than economic growth:

> Human development is concerned both with developing human capabilities and with using them productively. The former requires investment in people, the latter that people contribute to GNP [Gross National Product] growth and employment.
>
> (UNDP 1992: 2)

The document thus appears to take welfare issues seriously, acknowledging: 'The free workings of markets often tend to increase the disparities between rich and poor' (UNDP 1992: 7). In order to measure these disparities it puts forward a Human Development Index (HDI) which 'combines life expectancy, educational attainment and income indicators to give a composite measure of human development' (UNDP 1992: 3). As 'social indicators' this takes life expectancy, adult literacy and mean years of schooling (p. 19). But even within its terms of reference, its success in reflecting real disparities between richer and poorer countries is circumscribed from early on. Esteva (1992: 17) describes how the 1990 UNDP Report revised its original measure of GNP *per capita in real dollar terms* in favour of the simple aggregate of GNP. Hence the real disparities within and between countries have been masked by failing to acknowledge: first, how the local economies that produce the GNP are governed by global finance fluctuations (in terms of access to and unequal exchange rates); and second, by compounding together the measure of national production as if its profits were distributed equally to all its citizens.

Before we get too dazzled by the acronyms and claims, it is worth reflecting on the starting assumptions. The HDI presumes that development can be quantified, with no reflection on what is being quantified. Post-structuralist critiques of the knowledge base of developmental psychology see the domain of 'individual development' as arising from technologies of classification and segregation rather than any clear definition of what development is or should be (Ingleby 1985; Rose 1985, 1990). In claiming to expose inequalities between countries of the North and South, ratings of abstracted economic units are being presented as if they were conditions of individuals. Further, these are cast in terms of Northern criteria which are then treated as universal measures. Hence the Human Development Index claims to function as the instrument to measure disparities between North and South, as represented through numerical 'distance':

> [The HDI] then takes the distance travelled by each country from the minimum towards the maximum (expressed as a percentage as the basis – the combination with other indicators). The breakthrough in the HDI methodology was to choose distance as the common denominator.
>
> (UNDP 1992: 19)

Development is thus defined unproblematically as the differential between the North and the South – confirming how neocolonial patronage lurks within even benign international initiatives. Moreover, there is no equivocation or apology over the presumed direction of development. The text continues: 'This choice also gives the index a dynamic quality – a measure of movement towards a desired objective' (p. 19). How is it that the differences between North and South can be reduced to a simple measure, that the complexity of a 'dynamic' becomes a unilinear arrow? In his critique of the discourse of 'standards of living', Latouche argues:

> The currently dominant accounting categories present a radical form of cultural imperialism. It is not only that happiness and the joy of living in countries of the Third World are reduced to the paltry level of GNP per head by this globally imposed statistical butchery, but the very reality of diverse other arts of living is flouted and misunderstood in their richness and potentialities.
>
> (Latouche 1992: 259)

In fact there are efforts to address structural patterns within and between countries in the HDI by providing composite measures in terms of gender, provincial–regional and rural–urban disparities. As the authors readily acknowledge, these dramatically alter the general HDI profiles for each country. Hence attention to specific factors that structure development comes to fracture and fragment the HDI general comparative instrument. Even within its own terms, then, the HDI as a general tool of comparison becomes incoherent, but this contradiction remains obscured by the mystifications produced by its statistical technology (Ingleby 1985; Rose 1985). Similar conceptual and political problems no doubt inform the proposed Human Freedom Index and Political Freedom Index.

Notwithstanding its claims that 'the concept of human development does not start with any predetermined model. It draws its inspiration from the longterm goals of a society. It weaves development around people, not people around development' (UNDP 1992: 2), the UNDP aided by its technology in the form of the Human Development Index is underscored by a uniform model of technological progress and industrialisation, with the added handicap for the South of now being accorded responsibility for ecological preservation. In addition, the inclusion of population control in the list of 'essential human goals' along with universal basic education, primary health care, safe water and elimination of serious malnutrition (UNDP 1992: 8) reflects how questions of the disparities in consumption between North and South have been conveniently transposed into a discourse of 'overpopulation', and ignores how multinational companies basing production in the South for cheap land and labour are responsible for much of the environmental damage within which Southern people have to live.

The quantification of development thus coincides with the expansion of global capitalism. In accordance with its exhortation to invest in individuals in order to capitalise on their capacities for production and consumption, the UNDP ultimately leaves this process to the vicissitudes of supply and demand with the slogan: 'Markets are the means. Human development is the end' (UNDP 1992: 1). As Latouche comments:

> The basis for evaluating both physiological and psychological need is utility. The triumph of utilitarianism is thus the condition that has to be met to make ambitions like maximization and equalization of living standards conceivable. The reduction of the multiple dimensions of life to what is quantifiable finds its purest mode of expression in money and its locus of realization in the market economy. The generalization of the market accelerates its motion, which in turn facilitates its extension.
>
> (Latouche 1992: 256)

Displacing and relocating development

Reviewing and revaluing the relationship between time and space has become the stock in trade of discussions of postmodernism and postmodernity (see Massey 1992 for a review). Postcolonial critiques demonstrate the centrality of the dynamic of 'otherness' to Northern human subjectivity, showing how colonialism and imperialism have produced racialised and gendered positionings, at 'home' as well as 'away' (Chaudhuri and Strobel 1992; Ware 1992). As a possession, as property and domain, space expresses both the history of colonialism and the inscription of cultural and sexual difference. As in the way of master–slave relations, the North gains its sense of presence from its masculine repudiation of its absent other (Said 1978), so that we can gain a clear image of the North through its psychological and economic projections and displacements on to the South.

But time too marks out relations of dominance and histories of domination. In this sense, time is also space, since culture informs our notions of development. The temporality of development holds within it a set of ambiguities that are not arbitrary. The resonance between the regulation of individual growth and change by developmental psychology and that of Southern countries by international organisations betrays their common origins in modern, Northern apparatuses of surveillance, and modern, Northern models of subjectivity. At a moment when the rational unitary subject of psychology, soldiering on towards a culturally Northern and male maturity, is fragmenting under the gaze of poststructuralism (Henriques *et al.* 1984), so also the assumptions that underlie discourses of 'Third World development' are attracting increasing criticism outside poststructuralist and postmodern writing, as prescribing a linear trajectory towards industrialisation and technologisation (Sachs 1992).

In its current forms, the spatiality of models of child development is simply a line, an index of its historical origins, a trace remaining from the effort to regulate, control, and ultimately efface, diversity. But impoverished as it is, this mere trajectory, this line, is a space – a space that demands interrogation of the cultural and colonial assumptions that inhabit it. The reduction of space to time, as in Piaget's (1941/1952) description of the shift from ordinal to cardinal numbering, transforms relations of difference into those of order – mapping on to the distribution of colonial privilege. I have been describing the resonances between representations of North–South relations and of individual development as structured within international aid policies and programmes.

The task for those of us involved in making or commenting upon models of development is to disrupt the homologies between the neocolonialism of international development policies and the tendencies towards cultural imperialism structured within universalised norms and stages in developmental psychology. This is not a call for the construction of some new, improved variety of developmental psychology, since this would merely reproduce the problem; in Foucault's words 'to imagine another system is to extend our participation in the present system' (Foucault 1977: 230). Rather, adopting this position demands that we scrutinise the multiple investments within general models of psychological development. Insofar as it is possible at this point to envisage the topology that alternative models of child development might take, this may not mean the end of the project of such models – and certainly does not make less relevant international policies and programmes for children. Indeed, these are precisely the issues being addressed in the development of indicators to monitor the UN Convention on the Rights of the Child (Boyden 1993; Ennew 1993). But it may well mean the end of the discipline of developmental psychology as it is currently organised.

Attention to the spatiality of development requires a redistribution of disciplinary boundaries (for example, from psychology to anthropology) marking the fragmentation of a unitary psychology into multiple psychologies. It also involves acknowledging and redistributing the cultural and economic resources that produce and maintain the psychological models. So, for example, Dawes and Donald (1994) question the appropriateness of norms and criteria used to evaluate the conditions of children in South Africa, whilst also drawing critically upon the international research picture. Similarly, the anthropological research of Nieuwenhuys (1994) and Kurtz (1992) questions cultural and gender assumptions about child labour, and about psychological and psychoanalytic development respectively. Work such as this undermines the dynamics of homogenisation and universalisation that form the conceptual and political continuities linking neocolonialism, models of economic development and child development.

9 The abnormal distribution of development

Policies for Southern women and children

The focus on economic policy continues in this chapter, this time drawing on feminist critiques of the relations between gender and development, explicitly juxtaposing the emerging debates about gender and development with discussions of children, especially girl children. The chapter foreshadows later emphases in sociological literature on how the discourse of vulnerability and victimhood is central to Northern discourses of childhood (Christensen 2000; Meyer 2007), but takes these further to draw attention to the practical consequences of this differentiation in terms of the intersection of gender and culture. It focuses on three sets of debates: how the anomalous treatment of the development category of 'the girlchild' expresses specific problems about prevailing conceptualisations of the relations between interventions for women and for children; second, how models of psychological and economic development recapitulate and retroactively legitimate each other; and third, how the allocation of particular gendered characteristics map on to other geographically distributed inequalities. In particular the opposition between 'development' (for the North), and 'survival' (for the South) is explored, while the agenda for changing these models of development is clarified.

As argued in Chapter 8, analyses of the 'psychological complex' suggest that the cultural resources that inform developmental psychological models are highly cultural and class specific (white, middle class, of the Northern hemisphere), giving rise to a globalisation of development that is reinscribed within international aid and development policies. In homogenising difference to its norms, this globalisation paradoxically reproduces the North–South opposition as an expression of cultural and political imperialism, such that while Northern children 'develop', dominant discourses of children of the South are preoccupied with 'survival'. By such means the cultural hegemony of a unitary model of psychological development remains intact. This chapter takes the arguments of the book further by discussing the 'abnormal distribution' of development, in particular drawing attention to the ways in which cultural and gender inequalities flow from the norms and generalised descriptions central to the current practice of developmental psychology and to urge that this is an important site of intervention for feminists addressing gender and development issues (Wingfield and Saddiqui 1995/6). It anticipates subsequent critiques of international development (e.g. Croll 2006) that call for a shift from the policy focus on the girlchild to one of girls' rights, to connect girls' and women's positions (UNIFEM 2003; UNDAW 2005; UNICEF 2007) as well as intersectional analyses of the race/gender relation (Yuval-Davis 2006).

In this chapter I want to pose a number of questions about the discourses of development that developmental psychology participates in within international aid and development programmes. My purpose in drawing attention to these issues is to highlight how the intersections between gender and development that feminists have identified in relation to economic models of development are also reproduced within, and bolstered by, psychological models. I will be tracing through the consequences of repressing the cultural resources that inform developmental psychological models in relation to their function within policies and programmes for children. This is of importance in relation to three areas of feminist debate and activity: first, the consequences for women of measures that claim to champion the interests of children; second, the conceptualisation of the relations between women's and children's rights; third, the anomalous suppression of gender and corresponding privileging of masculinity in developmental psychological models, which, when applied to children of the South, can be seen to turn into its 'other' with the policy focus on 'the girl child'. Thus I will be arguing that children's issues are gender issues in a variety of ways, and that feminists and other critics of models of economic development also need to attend to the cultural assumptions that inform psychological models of gender, childhood and development.

By means of this focus on developmental psychology I will argue that while economic and psychological models purport to be universal, the geographical distribution of *psychological* development maps on to *economic* inequalities between the Northern and Southern hemispheres as an extension of the models' suppression of gender and cultural differences within the North. However, this does not mean that developmental psychology only reflects these differences; in some respects it may actively contribute to them. I will be drawing in particular on United Nations (UN) documentation on women and children to urge that supporting the development of children in so-called developing countries poses a number of theoretical and political challenges, and to demand that we reflect on some of the initial premises and discourses of 'development'. The chapter concludes with an evaluation of rights rhetoric and legislation.

At the outset I should make clear that while discourse analysis and poststructuralist ideas within psychology and social theory generally have fuelled postcolonial critiques, these also are based on Northern models (Harasym 1990; Spivak 1993). Moreover, I am not suggesting that an adequate response to globalisation is the assertion of particularity or revaluation of locality. I shall be arguing that the task for critical theorists of development (psychological and otherwise) is to develop analyses that attend to cultural particularity without sliding into either cultural hierarchies or romanticised orientalism and its cognates, whilst also warding off the relativism incipient within the discursive celebrations of difference (where difference stands in for oppression).

All our children?

The rallying cry 'All Our Children' is persuasive and emotive. (*All Our Children* was a television series broadcast in Britain in 1990 to coincide with the passing of, and UK ratification of, the UN Convention on the Rights of the Child. It was concerned with raising issues of equal opportunity for all children in Britain, as in other countries.) It implies that all children share the same attributes and the same needs. As mobilised in children's rights literature and legislation, there is an appeal to universal aspects of the condition of childhood, which in much of the world are certainly in need of promotion and protection. Yet the significations set in play by the image of the child are multiple and contradictory. Children are typically abstracted from culture and nationality to connote such qualities as innocence and the quintessential goodness of humankind untainted by the cruel, harsh contaminating world. Thus the child often functions to reproach the rest of the adult world for its misdemeanours, with imagery of children connoting both the future and a moral voice of the 'good self', as on a Paris tourist postcard where the image of a blond, blue-eyed child carries the caption, 'Notre planète est unique il faut la protéger'. However, it should be noted that the opposition set up between 'innocence' and 'experience' is itself a product of a specific Western philosophical legacy, and one which works to pathologise those (especially Southern) children who cannot afford to be 'innocent' in their struggle for survival (Stainton Rogers and Stainton Rogers 1992; Burman 1994a, 1994b). The capacity for children to represent a generalised future has been mobilised within anti-nuclear campaigns and the peace movement (Williamson 1986). But if children are 'our' future, then it is interesting to see that the images of children who lay claim to the world are white European children.

The universalisation of Northern childhood thus mirrors the Northern colonial domination of the South. Where political-territorial affiliations are connected with images of children, these are treated as symmetrical relationships rather than relations of inequality, as in the (now outdated) image of Soviet–US relations from Benetton where identical twin girls sport different bags. Where cultural differences (coded through colour differences) appear, these have been linked with Christian symbolism associated with colour (elaborated again by Benetton in a now controversial image of the white-child-angel, black-child-devil). In these contexts we might also note that where black and white (children) are portrayed together, the white figure adopts a protective (as in the cover to the BBC booklet *All Our Children*, where the white girl has her arm around the black boy) and sometimes enveloping (another Benetton image shows a black baby surrounded by white teddies) stance towards the black, which, through the proverbial connection between children and animals, extends beyond the human to the portrayal of animals. As Pat Holland (1992) has noted, the representation of lone black children in aid appeals works frequently to pathologise their families and cultures, positioning these as failing to fulfil their duties. Colonial legacies blend into humanitarian concern, where in order to qualify for 'help' parents are either invisible or infantilised as incapable.

Just as the representation of childhood has been sentimentalised and abstracted from history and culture in ways that suppress cultural and gender inequalities, so developmental psychology has provided culturally based and culturally biased models that are taken as universally applicable, but are distributed across geographical and historical space in highly significant ways. Within contemporary aid and development literature, the representation of development is polarised so that developmental issues for children of the North concern early education and environmental enrichment, while in the South they focus on mere survival. Childhood has been fractured so that only children of the North develop, while children of the South are primarily portrayed as those whose childhoods have been stolen (cf. Vittachi 1989). While the discourse of freeing children of the South concerns abolishing child slavery and bonded labour, the package holiday company Airtours advertises 'Free children' to refer to one child travelling free on a package holiday when accompanied by two adults and a child (note the nuclear family ideology here).

It is significant that instead of this distribution making us examine the contents of what we understand by childhood, as a rejection of contemporary Northern and middle-class practices, the popular discourses of 'child-saving' measure the extent to which Southern children are deprived of the childhood to which they are entitled. And so these discourses reinstate Northern models. In part this is driven by the constraints of fund-raising and consciousness-raising in the North, where campaigns are premised on the assumption that such contrasts will be the most effective in eliciting a response, as in the 1992/93 ActionAid advertisements: 'Do you really need 50p more than she does?' and '£15 will intoxicate you for the night or innoculate her for life' (see Burman 1994b, and this volume Chapter 6). In terms of child (under) nutrition there are relatively clear measures such as the weight to height ratio, or middle arm circumference (although even these are not unambiguous, since they could arise from illness, particularly diarrhoeal infections, rather than absence of food). But criteria for child *development*, like the notion of childhood itself, are less easy to determine.

In terms of the role of psychology in child welfare promotion, from the late 1980s onwards international bodies such as the United Nations International Children's Emergency Fund (UNICEF) have come to recognise that psychological development can promote rather than simply succeed child survival (McGuire and Austin 1987; Myers 1992). Despite a rhetoric of cultural sensitivity and specificity, the developmental psychology that is entering UN policies still retains a commitment to prescriptions for child-care and development that are assumed to transcend cultural variation. It thereby globalises what are, in fact, middle-class, Northern models (Boyden 1990; Burman 1993, 2007b).

Are children's issues also gender issues?

Questions of gender intersect with those of culture in the globalisation of developmental psychology. While the girl signifies the charm, helplessness and vulnerability of Northern notions of childhood, the playful, active, discovering child of cognitive developmental models reflects culturally masculine qualities, portrayed in the toy advertisements' subscription to imagery of scientists, construction workers and astronauts (Burman 1995c). If the state of childhood is feminised (note the visibility of girl-gendered children in the aid appeals above), the developmental trajectory from childhood to maturity within models of cognitive (e.g. Piagetian) and emotional (e.g. Bowlbyan) development describes a transition from attachment to detachment, from dependence to autonomy, that is shot through with gendered assumptions (Broughton 1988; Walkerdine 1988).

Despite this implicit focus on gender, models of the developing child are portrayed as gender as well as culture free. Like culture, gender is a floating variable that somehow, somewhere along the purportedly unitary developmental pathway, becomes attached to 'the child'. Notwithstanding the generality of the psychological models and their reflection within international legislation, the gender specificity of the supposedly gender-neutral 'child' of international aid and development policies is reflected in the qualification of 'the girl child'. The need to address the situation of girls as a particular class within the group of children arises from documentation of how the key issues of survival, access to health care and access to education dramatically affect girls more than boys. Significantly, in Nigel Cantwell's (1992) 'Introduction' to the *Travaux Préparatoires* [Working Documents] of the 1989 UN Convention on the Rights of the Child, he identifies as one of its key achievements the inclusion within Article 24 (on access to health and education) of the states' requirements to 'work towards the abolition of traditional practices such as female circumcision and preferential treatment of male children'.

In this sense, and in contrast with their representation within psychological models (where gender is suppressed), children's issues are very much gender issues. In addition to the role of reproductive technologies in preselecting boy children and aborting girl baby foetuses, which is dramatically affecting the sex ratio in some areas of the world (Patel 1989; Sen 1990), mortality rates for girls are higher than those of boys (Hart 1992: 4), and of the 25 per cent of primary school children in the South not enrolled in schools, two-thirds are girls (Colclough with Lewin 1993).[1] Moreover, a study in India documents how children, especially girls, and women get less to eat (e.g. Batliwale 1984), while all over the world the overwhelming majority of children who are sexually abused or involved in prostitution are girls (Ennew 1986), although this is not to dismiss the sexual exploitation of boys. In terms of debates about child labour, one of the various factors put forward to account for the under-enrolment of girls in school is that girls work twice as many hours as boys, and their domestic responsibilities are continuous rather than time limited. They often take on adult responsibilities before the age of ten in order to relieve their mothers for paid work (UNICEF 1992b: 18). Other reasons reported for under-enrolment are poverty, low status of women, concerns about girls' moral safety, early marriage or pregnancy, inappropriate school facilities, limited job opportunities and uncertain economic returns (UNICEF 1992b: 17). Structural Adjustment Policies (SAP) have exacerbated the costs of food, education and health care provision, and the pressures on girls and women have correspondingly increased (Patel 1992). It was in response to such data that the decade from 1991 was declared the Decade of the Girl Child, and UNICEF produced specific policy documents for girls (e.g. UNICEF 1992b). A strategy UNICEF advocates to counter the low status of girls and women is to attempt to revalue women's and girls' contribution to production.[2] In line with the quantification of development (see below) this is cast in rather disturbingly economistic terms as in, for example, the document 'The Girl Child: An Investment in the Future' produced by UNICEF to promote national programmes of action.

Are women's issues also development issues?

By the same token, it could be argued that women's issues are very much development issues. That is, that the issues of poverty, health and education, of reducing exploitation, and promoting equality and opportunity that are central to development policies, are particularly associated with women's positions. Indeed, the emergence of the notion of the 'feminisation of poverty' in discussions of welfare and the labour market reflects an acknowledgement that the burden of poverty falls disproportionately on women. However, current moves towards 'integrating women in development' not only fail to recognise that women have always been central to development, but have also been criticised as functioning to colonise the informal sector (now that the formal sector is either exhausted or saturated) and thereby to extend the exploitation of women. As Peggy Antrobus argues:

> Far from not taking women into account these policies are actually grounded in a set of assumptions – a gender ideology – that assigns certain roles and characteristics to women. Indeed, it is clear to me that both components of structural adjustment policies – those aimed at *reducing consumption* (the austerity measures reflected in government expenditures in social services) as well as those aimed at *increasing export-oriented production* (the emphasis on the promotion of Export Processing Zones) are dependent on assumptions about the roles into which most women have been socialised.
>
> (Antrobus 1989: 3)

Similarly Vibhuti Patel (1992) argued that the slogan of 'Integrating Women in Development' was a euphemism for the exploitation of Southern women who are used as a cheap, flexible, 'docile and nimble-fingered' workforce for multinational companies seeking to reduce manufacturing costs by basing production in Southern countries and promoting home-working and the casualisation of labour. Her analysis has been prescient of the outsourcing culture within multinational corporations.

By this analysis, the process of development has not favoured women. Indeed the drive towards income-generating activities has undermined women's subsistence activities, and therefore worked to the detriment of both women's and children's welfare. The equation of income generation with making money has served the interests of international capital by orienting women's work towards export-oriented production, but eroded their resources. The process of internationally governed development has therefore impoverished women more and deprived them of the means to withstand the retractions of services caused by the compulsory implementation of structural adjustment policies (SAP).

Are women's issues also children's issues?

The question arises, then, of whether women's issues in development are children's issues. And there are certainly common sets of concerns around health, education and labour, given the increasing numbers of female-headed households and the necessary continuity between the positions of girls and women (since girls become women). Hence the 1992 UNICEF policy review called for the UN Convention on the Rights of the Child to be implemented in conjunction with the Committee on the Elimination of Discrimination Against Women (CEDAW).[3] However, tensions between the interests of women and those of children remain. In their evaluation of Save the Children funded projects, Gill Peace and David Hulme (1993) challenge the assumption underlying the promotion of income-generating schemes that overall increases in household income necessarily 'trickle down' to ameliorate the condition of children, although where the household is female headed this assumption is more likely to be merited. They also call for the need to explore the relationship of participation in income-generating activity with child education, since the increased value of child labour within a small enterprise, rather than poverty alone, could account for children missing school. Similarly, greater childcare responsibilities may fall on girls to permit their mothers to participate in the scheme.

Correlatively, interventions for children mean greater responsibilities for women. The GOBIFFF formula that currently dominates child survival and development policies (Growth monitoring, Oral rehydration to treat diarrhoea, a major cause of infant and child deaths, Breastfeeding, Immunisation, Feeding supplements, Female education, and Family spacing) places increased demands on women: to take their children to be immunised, to monitor their growth, to be available to breastfeed, and so on. While the documentation sometimes discusses 'parents' and 'childcare activities', this work usually, and usually correctly, is assumed to be done by women.

One area where psychological theories exacerbate the potential for women's oppression lies in the export of Northern prescriptions for child stimulation and development. At the same moment when critiques of the role of developmental psychology as regulating women as mothers are beginning to be heard in the North (Urwin 1985; Walkerdine and Lucey 1989; Marshall 1991), we have those models being promulgated as prescriptions for child survival and development in the South. Parent education, paraprofessional home visiting, injunctions to exploit any antenatal or infant health check to 'integrate' development with health advice (e.g. Myers 1992) all widen the scope for the evaluation and pathologising of poor, uneducated women. These are women who fail to conform to the latest brand of developmental psychological theory that has found its way in fairly unadulterated form into the texts and practices of health care professionals of the South. This is not to say that some of it might not be useful, but rather that despite the rhetoric of cultural specificity and sensitivity, many of the starting assumptions remain unexamined for their specificity of context of formulation, that is in the North (see Woodhead 1990; Burman 1993). If the discourses of sensitive mothering and autonomous children are rooted in the production of the self-regulating, self-governing citizen of the North (Walkerdine 1984; Rose 1985, 1990), then their globalisation within aid and development policies adds cultural stigmatisation to their existing class and gender chauvinisms. As Sathyamala *et al.* (1986) in their handbook for rural health workers in India point out, the requirement to provide a 'stimulating environment' is in danger of succeeding the attribution of lesser intelligence as a current means of pathologising poor, Southern women:[4]

> Here understanding of what is meant by a 'stimulating environment' should be questioned. Since most researchers come from economic and cultural backgrounds which are totally different from those of the poor people, their studies tend to perceive and measure poor people from

> their own standards. This perhaps could also explain the bias that the environment of poor people is non-stimulating.
>
> (Sathyamala *et al.* 1986: 142)

Teaching mothers to play with their children may be of less importance than providing mothers with the childcare and local schools to afford them the time necessary to raise the financial status of the family. While these are not mutually exclusive interventions, all too often in these days of SAP the extra burden for both economic and psychological development falls on mothers and families rather than on national or international aid and development organisations.

Women as mothers

Two other components of the GOBIFFF formula for the promotion of child survival call for scrutiny in terms of their implications for women's welfare and rights: family spacing and female education. Added to the regulation of women's adequacy as mothers is the extension of control over their bodies in the name of children's health. The rationale for and focus of health services for women in Southern countries is often principally oriented around their health needs as mothers. Yet maternal mortality is not the major cause of death for women in the South. As Sathyamala *et al.* (1986) comment on the Indian context:

> While it is true that the child's health is dependent upon the mother, this is no justification for concentrating on a woman's health only during motherhood . . . It therefore seems as if the medical profession is only interested in supervising women so they can perform their reproductive functions properly.
>
> (Sathyamala *et al.* 1986: 150)

The association between family size and child survival is used to justify the implementation of draconian population control policies, which serve purposes other than health promotion. Population control has become integral to aid and development programmes, so that international loans are linked to family planning programmes (Duden 1992). Patel (1992) notes that the only sector of funding for women which increased in the 1991–92 Indian budget was 'population control'. Although presented as a basic human right that empowers women, in practice this is far from the case. Poor women seeking employment in poverty alleviation schemes are forced to accept dangerous birth control drugs and devices. This also further colludes in the pathologising of the South by the North, in rendering Southern countries as responsible for 'overpopulation'. The issue is not overpopulation but distribution of resources:

> Massive sums have been provided by the USAID to push controversial contraceptives like Norplant/Net-O-En which are banned in most of the Western countries. Advocacy for 'population control' has been a crucial concern of NEP-SAP. Poor women are also blamed for causing environmental crisis by breeding like 'cats' and 'rats'. It is time to ask our policy makers, to what extent top-down population control programmes that violate basic human rights of Indian women be justified? Secondly, by victimising the victims of the patriarchal class society aren't we ignoring the major causes of environmental crisis such as industrial toxic wastes, chemical fertilizers, nuclear armaments, overconsumption of the affluent in both the first as well as the third world. Moreover, what about the first world where population growth has declined yet environmental conditions have deteriorated?'
>
> (Patel 1992: 12–13)

While all this may seem remote from the domain of psychology, dominant forms of psychology contribute to these problems by subscribing to a normative model of the family, through researching mothering and child development as though each woman only had one child, inaccurate even in the North (Munn 1991), and in reflecting the widespread medical and patriarchal assumption that mothering is the primary psychological issue for women.

Education for all?

Similar problems attend the emphasis on female education. It is widely documented that women's education correlates with both reduced fertility rates and increased child survival rates. More often the association between maternal education and fertility is simply stated rather than interpreted. When put forward explanations vary, ranging from raising women's status in the family and empowering her to be more assertive over birth control (Vittachi 1989), or in terms of child survival, that women's literacy correlates with class, or her ability to buy tinned baby food and thus reduce the risks of infection (Sathyamala *et al.* 1986). This link between education and aspects of reproduction has led to rationales for girls' education being formulated specifically on the grounds of its supposed impact on future children. 'Educate a girl and you educate a nation' reads the caption to a picture of girls and young women in school in Anadhura Vittachi's (1989) book *Stolen Childhood* (the book accompanying the television series publicising the UNCRC). Even more disturbingly girls' education is promoted on the grounds of population control. 'Education is the best contraceptive' was the slogan of the World Bank 'Poverty Report' in 1986. In Colclough with Lewin's (1993) UNICEF and Overseas Development Agency (ODA) funded research into the factors relevant for achieving primary education for all children, they report that support for this (principally from the

World Bank) 'was informed by the growing amount of evidence which demonstrated that primary schools were truly productive in a strictly economic sense, and that they affected people's behaviour in ways that supported a wide range of development goals' (p. 26).

It is apparent from the frequency with which fertility rates appear within the text that critical among the 'wide range of development goals' is population control:

> Data from the World Fertility Survey indicate the strength of a decline in fertility associated with education: a comparison of women with up to three years and those with seven or more years of schooling reveals a reduction in total fertility rates by between two and three children for each of the African, Asian and Latin American regions. The negative relationship between these variables appear to be stronger when schooling is widely spread amongst the population. The presence of these externalities obviously adds to the case for universalizing primary schooling.
>
> (Colclough with Lewin 1993: 30)

This is summarised thus:

> Again the importance of female education must be emphasised: creating schooled and literate women is critically important as a means of enhancing both present and future human capabilities.
>
> (Colclough with Lewin 1993: 32)

Hence the elision between woman as mother and girl as pupil means that a double move takes place: not only are women primarily considered in terms of reproductive activities, but childhood is so thoroughly gendered that 'the girl child' is regarded as an incipient woman, and thus a future mother. It is paradoxical that within dominant Northern developmental psychological models, the *invisibility* of gender and correspondingly implicit celebration of culturally masculine qualities works to pathologise girls' reasoning (Gilligan 1982) and educational achievements (Walkerdine 1990b). But in the Southern context, the *visibility* of gender functions to combine the oppressions of being a child and being a woman together for 'the girl child'.

What this discussion of educational access suggests is that, in contrast to the gender-free discourses of childhood and adolescence in the North, which offer some scope for manoeuvre for girls and young women (as Hudson's 1984 interviews with 'adolescent girls' suggest), it seems that 'girl children' of the South are scarcely children at all. They are girls. This is an issue that is either ignored by or only inconsistently addressed by the conceptions of 'rights' that underpin conventional views of development, and I return to this later. What should be noted at this stage are the ways North–South relations distribute salience of gender within psychological models of development, such that it is girls' gendered categorisation, rather than specifically their status as children or young people, that is made topical in the South. Clearly the problems of conceptual absences and salience that here are allocated as a function of their geographical distribution recall discussions about the limits of identities portrayed as static and additive (Bondi 1993). In the arena of international development policy and programming we see such conceptualisations being acted out in a particularly clear and problematic way.

The economisation of development

Let me emphasise that for some parties at least subscribing to arguments that make women's and girls' entitlements conditional upon supposed national or international benefits is no doubt an effective strategy to enlist support from organisations for whom women's welfare or rights are not priorities. Nevertheless, the trend towards marketing human rights in economic terms threatens to fuse state and religion to set up new forms of fundamentalisms governing women's bodies and minds. Humanitarian arguments for the promotion of child survival and child development are now taking something of a background role, and economic arguments are presented as the most persuasive. McGuire and Austin's (1987) UNICEF report *Beyond Survival* was subtitled *Children's Growth for National Development*, and the economic rationale (in terms of production and productivity, education and reduced demands on health care resources) is presented first and occupies the most space, with less than half a page on the 'humanitarian rationale', which ends with a warning about society squandering its potential (p. 22). Child growth promotion becomes something to 'sell' in the marketplace. They introduce their report with the following:

> Identifying growth failure as a pervasive injustice is not sufficient reason for a policy maker to allocate scarce resources in attacking the problem. In the real world of budget deficits and negative real growth in revenues, new endeavours must make their case in competition with other important or existing or new programmes, and the resource allocation often rests on economic efficiency and political expedience. Traditionally, advocacy efforts to promote growth in children have emphasised the humanitarian rationale. We will now set forth the economic case.
>
> (McGuire and Austin 1987: 6)

Similarly in a section on 'family planning' in its 1992 Annual Report, UNICEF talks in terms of 'returns':

> Experience confirms that when CSD [child survival and development] and family planning are undertaken together, the returns are greater than either could accomplish on its own.
>
> (UNICEF 1992a: 17)

However, the abstraction of the language of 'returns' and 'benefits' fails to specify who benefits. Colclough with Lewin (1993) say:

> Earlier in this book we reviewed evidence which shows (Chapter 1) that providing girls with primary (and secondary) education is critical to economic progress. It is, then, a profound irony that the benefits of primary schooling are especially high for girls, yet that under-enrolments are strongly concentrated among them.
>
> (Colclough with Lewin 1993: 264)

All this begs the question of whether the benefits are for girls, or for economies of countries which are pressured into placing population control above all other health and welfare interventions. The move in international agency programming from 'welfare' to 'workfare', that is from giving grants or subsidies to setting up schemes for self-employment, suggests that 'enterprise' can be the solution to poverty. Again economistic rationales prevail over those of genuine development, with participation within the design and running of income-generating projects increasingly being promoted on efficiency rather than democratic grounds (Kabeer 1992; Peace and Hulme 1993). Reviewing the discourses deployed by advocates of Women In Development, Kabeer (1992) notes that the rationale for women to be targeted for projects moved in the 1980s from welfare considerations to calling for women to be recognised as productive agents and an under-utilised resource. She criticises this move as setting up welfare and efficiency as competitive rather than complementary: welfare provision supports women's efficiency.[5] Moreover, in terms of the efficiency of health care provision, Sathyamala *et al.* (1986) report that the association of health care with coercive distribution of birth control devices leads to women in India being suspicious of and less likely to use health services. Thus such measures actively reduce women's (and children's) access to services.

Development for whom? Psychological challenges

I have been arguing that the current discourses of psychological development provide a polarised representation of who develops and where, which maps on to the North–South divide (and again the various norths and souths within the North and South). It also appears that the process of economic development all too often is at the expense of women's and girls' personal development, that is, that measures laying claim to women's and girls' interests may not function in those ways.

The slippage of unit of analysis from individual girl to the rhythms of economic planning reflects a project of homogenisation and abstraction common to both discourses of development; that of developmental psychology and of economic development. Both elaborate a developing subject that reinscribes rational individualism – itself a peculiarly Northern construction that owes its origins to strategies of population management and control. In developmental psychological models efficiency considerations are paramount, with the child portrayed as a resource to be cultivated, maximised towards the goal of (gender-allocated spheres of) production (Rose 1990). The rational unitary subject of psychology is an abstraction, a construction of tools of classification and measurement no less than is the manufacture of the monster of 'population' from peoples of the South (Duden 1992). In this sense international agencies like UNICEF have no need to cast their development goals in economistic terms, since these already structure the psychological models they draw upon.

Now at a time when feminist critiques are challenging the unity of the category 'woman', and black women are challenging the commonality of black and white feminist goals (Amos and Parmar 1984; Carby 1987), the challenge for psychology is, first, to recognise that unitary psychological models function as normative, regulatory apparatuses. This leads, second, to the recognition that the models reflect a Northern-based modern progressivism which maintains the opposition between North and South. This opposition reproduces the more general economic development discourse which positions the South as lacking, or as needing to catch up with the development of North. The discourse of development therefore legitimises the homogenisation of all cultures and globalisation to that of Euro-US (Sachs 1992). We need to reconceptualise our attachment to 'the child' within developmental psychological models as no longer the essential emergent or authentic self awaiting realisation, but as an ideological artefact which suppresses class, gender and cultural differences, and which reproduces inequalities between North and South. When psychology has dissolved into multiple, diverse and fragmented psycholog*ies* then the project of theorising children's, girls', boys', women's and men's practical developmental needs becomes more possible.

Rights and wrongs: women and children

It may seem as though the above proposals decry or diminish international child protection work that uses discourses of children's needs or children's rights. This is not my aim. However, the discourse of rights also needs to be scrutinised for its adequacy in promoting the interests of women and children, both together and separately. Historically, the notion of rights is linked to that of citizenship, in which women and, to an even greater extent children, are ambivalently positioned. Moreover, as feminist political theorists are now pointing out, the appeal to equal rights is predicated on a social contractual model of 'civil society' in which claims to equal status (through the concept of fraternity) are precisely exercised in relation to access to, and control of, women and children. The subject who exercises rights is thereby designated masculine. As Anne Phillips (1987) put it:

> Because the family is now completely out of the picture, liberalism can more plausibly pretend that we are indeed the private and isolated individuals on which its theories rest. In seemingly universal concern over the limits of the state and the freedoms of the individual, liberalism talks in effect of a world occupied by men.
>
> (Phillips 1987: 15)

Modern liberal democratic discourse, then, instead of invoking traditional patriarchal authority, justified its social arrangements by naturalising women's subordinate status (Pateman 1989). From this perspective, where the division between public and private – so central to the conditions endured by women and children – is the structuring principle of liberal measures such as UN humanitarian policies, the extent to which liberal rights measures can address the needs of women and children appears circumscribed:

> The fraternal social contract story shows that the categories and practices of civil society cannot simply be universalised to women. The social contract is a modern patriarchal pact that establishes men's sex rights over women, and the civil individual has been constructed in opposition to women and all that our bodies symbolize, so how can we become full members of civil society or parties to the fraternal contract?
>
> (Pateman 1989: 52)

While claims for women's rights have been made on the basis of extending to women the freedoms enjoyed by men, these have been appealed to by virtue of rights due to adults in general. Hence women's rights have been counterposed to children's. Notwithstanding the general tendency to assimilate women's interests with those of children in a manner repudiated by feminist analyses (but largely reflected within contemporary UN policies), there are additional complications in the intersecting politics of equal rights legislation which do much to explain the mutual suspicion of women's and children's rights movements. In her historical analysis of English custody and divorce legislation, Susan Maidment (1984) highlights how the 'welfare principle' as the paramount consideration within child custody cases emerged between 1886 and 1925 (and culminating in the Guardianship of Infants Act 1925) both in relation to, and as a device to counter, feminist demands for equality within family law. (Prior to this issues of child protection were more concerned with social stability and reduction of demands on state welfare, Eekelaar 1986). Hence reductions in the legal authority of men in families were justified in terms of their responsibilities as fathers (in relation to children) rather than as husbands (in relation to women), making the concessions to women's custody and divorce rights secondary to the interests of their children:

> Each time that women's organisations sought to achieve joint guardianship between wife and husband, Parliament extracted a compromise, in order to quieten them, which allowed women rights only incidentally to extending the principle of the child's welfare. The rise of the welfare principle did not come essentially out of concern for the interest of the child but out of the fight of women's groups for equality of legal rights.
> (Maidment 1984: 145–146)

Notwithstanding the multiple determinations of its emergence, however, the welfare or 'best interests' principle has become the cornerstone of national and international legislation about children. But the inescapably normative content of rights poses problems in equating children's interests and their rights, as children are not considered the best party to judge their 'best interests', and because the content of these interests is informed by legal practice which itself recycles familial ideology as either common-sense or professional expertise (Dingwall and Eekelaar 1986). Moreover, as Jo Boyden and Andy Hudson (1985) pointed out in their Minority Rights Group report on children, since children are not always considered able to exercise those claims on their own behalf, children's rights are determined in terms of duties and responsibilities towards children rather than the traditional understanding of rights as 'a relationship between two people, one asserting a claim and the other recognising it' (p. 4). John Eekelaar (1986) notes in relation to English law that this tends to mean that the 'basic' and 'developmental' interests of children take priority over those of 'autonomy' (and despite the rhetoric recent developments show little evidence of changing this; see Bell 1993b). While the 'three Ps' (Cantwell 1992) of the UN Convention on the Rights of the Child move from Protection and Provision to Participation, consulting children (or adults for that matter) in aid and development projects does not necessarily mean that the services or interventions will actually reflect the wishes of the so-called project partners, as UNICEF itself recognises (Drucker 1986; Hart 1992; Ogun and Houston Smith 1992).

The issue of child participation highlights problems not only within the notion of child rights, but within the concept of rights generally. Rights are by definition generalised and universalised principles, which like the psychological subject and political theory they reflect through the public–private opposition are abstracted and individualised. Available representations of psychological development, like the more general models of economic development, mask these key tensions of abstraction and individualism. These tensions also lie within child liberation discourses and child rights discourses in the conflict between evaluating children within their cultural context and treating them as equal subjects transcending cultural practice:

> The mundane facts of children's everyday experience have meant that liberatory aspirations are uneasily linked with the demand for rights.

> The one keeps children outside cultural constraints; the other insists that they enter on comparable terms to adults.
>
> (Holland 1992: 84)

Two points are relevant here with respect to the above discussion of rights discourse. First, as the earlier analysis of 'the girl child' also demonstrated, it is impossible to divide absolutely issues relevant to women from those of children. This is in contrast to the way discourse of rights sets up parties as distinct and competing rather than continuous or allied (Denise Riley 1987 also makes this point in relation to apparent contradictions within feminist campaigns for childcare provision in the North). Second, the rights discourse presumes an equality of positions that effectively denies the histories of class, gender and cultural inequalities that constitute what it means to be a child (or a mother) in any particular time and place. This homogenisation of subjectivity sets up a corresponding opposition between individual and society, which is reflected in tensions within aid images between the abstraction and locatedness of development. To quote Pat Holland again:

> The aim is for a recognition of differences that do not lead to conflict, but this is precisely where the image of childhood runs up against its limits. Childhood is sought as that space beyond conflict, before those rigid differences have taken hold, as a point where 'humanity' aspires to an impossible escape from 'society'. But children live out their lives structured by the imperatives of culture, gender and language. An effective demand for children's rights can take place only within these structures.
>
> (Holland 1992: 99)

In the case of rights legislation for women and children, it could be argued that equal positions are presumed precisely because this effaces those different histories, and thereby empowers by according equal rights to previously disadvantaged groups. Diane Elson (1992) follows Kabeer (1991) in arguing for the importance of distinguishing normative and material entitlements in recognising women's culturally structured economic vulnerability to inform international interventions to address women's poverty. International agencies are also beginning to recognise how policies for women and children cannot occur without structural changes.[6] The 'Further Actions' section of the UNICEF (1992c) policy review progress report, *Achievements Made in the Implementation of the UNICEF Policy on Women in Development, including the Situation of the Girl Child*, includes the following statement:

> While culture is a crucial bond in society, it can sometimes be used unquestioningly to perpetuate a system of inequality against girl children

> and women merely for being born female. Therefore, fundamental changes are needed in the socialisation and education of children, both girls and boys, as well as in the complex system of attitudes, power and privileges that determine the allocation of resources and entitlements between women and men within the family, community and nation.

Assuming the banner of the 'rights of the girl child' thus sets the discourse of human rights against that of respect for cultural practices in two ways: either (in the case of international aid and development bodies) it invites the charge of cultural imperialism in assuming the moral high ground to ride roughshod over religious and cultural traditions, or conversely (in the case of multiculturalists) it paralyses criticism for fear of being paternalistic and culturally chauvinistic (as seen, for example, in Yuval-Davis' 1992 analysis of how these debates have been played out in Britain, and the journal *Women Against Fundamentalism* for international analysis). While these are complex and urgent issues, critical psychologists are disabled from entering debates about the goals and contexts of development by the predominance of models of which the ideological overdeterminations either prescribe the answers or proscribe the questions. Failure to enter those discussions vacates a key arena of intervention in the struggle between the polarities of homogenisation and differentiation. It leaves the domain of psychological development open to the co-option of those liberals who can only accord equality by denying difference, or to the reactionaries who treat cultural differences as essential and inevitable.

To summarise: questions of the functions and limitations of a liberal rights framework, exemplified within developmental psychology through interpretations and applications of international development policies such as the 1989 UN Convention on the Rights of the Child, pose for feminist academics and policymakers the challenge of moving beyond the assumption of the neutrality of scientific and professional practices, to grappling with the questions of power, privilege and justice which they involve. For developmental psychologists this means moving beyond universal models to attend both to differences and to the power relations that suppress and/or construct those differences. This is not to suggest that there are no 'universals', nor that in some circumstances asserting universal needs or rights may not be strategically important (e.g. Kerr 1993). Rather, we should be attending to the impact of, and interventions made by, the attribution of either universals in, or differences of, demands or needs. In this sense, developmental psychologists have much to learn from critics of models of economic development, and feminists can gain from the articulation of both sets of issues in addressing the positions of women and children. For feminists committed to challenging the current organisation and distribution of psychological and economic development, we cannot afford to ignore how relations between gender and childhood inform, and are theorised within, international aid and development policies.

Part IV

Afterwords

What follows postdevelopment?

The final part of the book moves from critique to consideration of consequences of such critiques of development. Together they ask the questions: Are there alternatives to development? What lies after 'postdevelopment'? Can the unhelpful historical connections between models of individual, child, national and economic development be turned into generative resources to envisage other possible forms?

Rather than bringing closure, the three chapters comprising Part IV offer a dialogue on such questions. Chapter 10, 'Rhetorics of Psychological Development: From Complicity to Resistance' assumes a more accessible narrative tone in both reviewing and taking further the arguments and interpretive frameworks drawn upon earlier, now to reframe understanding of what the key problems are. It builds on and further explicates the cyborg metaphor and temporal and methodological juxtapositions of psychology and psychotherapy introduced in Chapters 1 and 2. The final two chapters of the book open up a set of perspectives on children's multiple positionings, thematised around the trope of 'between two deaths/debts'.

Chapter 11, 'Between Two Debts: Points of Suspension in Childhood and Economic Development', brings in some further theoretical perspectives to facilitate more systematic analyses of the multiple levels and diverse forms in which children and development are linked, and ends by outlining and evaluating the methodological strategies drawn upon in both the chapter and the book as a whole.

Chapter 12, 'Between Two Deaths: Reconfiguring Metaphorics and Ethics of Childhood', elaborates on the discussion of morality and ethics surrounding childhood drawing on literary and psychoanalytic resources. These are used to take further the critique of the motif of developmental time (and progress), and to consider their consequences for (the various) practitioners of development. These analyses are then applied to inform a final return to the key concerns of the book, in terms of the relations between 'child, 'image' and 'nation'.

10 Rhetorics of psychological development

From complicity to resistance

This first chapter to Part IV brings together the range of critical commentaries and resources mobilised so far in this book – from discussions of therapy, to imaginary models of subjectivity – to consider accounts of what post-development in practice might look like. Such an ambitious – if also urgent – project can only perhaps be approached by way of glimpses and the elaboration of some methodological-ethical principles, without risking reconstructing other orthodoxies. Indeed, part of the argument put forward here is that – given the power of the edifice of 'development' – such recuperations are always inevitable. But rather than failing to try, we can – as in the Irish playwright Samuel Beckett's injunction – 'fail better', and perhaps do more than merely reproduce the same exclusionary practices.

This chapter anticipates and resonates with more contemporary discussions within critical and feminist psychology (Squire 1991; Foster 2004; Strauble 2005), and builds in part on the conceptual analyses outlined in Part I, especially Chapter 2, while it reviews how the enabling and disabling consequences of postdevelopmental arguments continue to reverberate within the aid, development and rights-based programming literatures (cf. their treatment in Matthews 2004; Gready and Ensor 2005; Harriss 2005). While Chapters 11 and 12 tackle some of the more thorny conceptual questions posed by such efforts, and import some additional perspectives, this chapter aims to move the narrative tone of the book from analysis of the problems towards the formulation of some positive, if necessarily piecemeal, strategies and resources.

In this chapter I analyse developmental psychology as a radical resource inspiring and reflecting conceptual-political models of social and individual change. In the first part I discuss how developmental discourse has implicated psychology in politically unhelpful agendas, in particular through its subscription to, and definitions of, notions of nature and (descriptive or prescriptive) normality which then function in moral-political practices outside psychology. I offer as illustrations of these claims two urgent examples; first, in economic models of development, that is, how the convergence of terminology between economic and psychological notions of development gives rise to specific occlusions as well as collusions within international aid policies; and second, from psychotherapy, how at the very moment that developmental psychology is called upon to justify psychotherapeutic models it so fixes these to a normative, antitherapeutic account of causality and temporality.

The second part of the chapter moves from discussion of problems with developmental discourse to a consideration of how such claims might be necessary and desirable. Here I describe two other examples – cyberpsychological and postdevelopmental discourses – which simultaneously mobilise, but invite critiques of, the modern trappings of developmental models. I end the chapter with some reflections upon how these indicate ways in which we may be able to negotiate the paradoxical imperative both to benefit, but yet emancipate ourselves, from the coercions of development. Hence, even if we cannot dispense with development – inside and outside psychology – we may yet be able to offer informed commentaries that support critical interventions towards alternative (anti)developmental agendas.

Developmental psychology functions as a slippery but pervasive resource within models of social and individual change. I see it as 'slippery' in the sense that assumptions about the purposes, directions, structure and allocation of development figure implicitly – if not explicitly – within all conceptual frameworks and political programmes. They do this whether they are concerned with describing the human condition or rather aiming to intervene in current social arrangements. This has tended to mean that developmental psychological notions – through their pervasive character – have often functioned in unhelpful ways, whether through the banal invisibility of their circulation or as explicit 'expertise'. Political agendas of all persuasions subscribe to developmental norms whose claims to generality belie the dominant social hierarchies around gender, culture, class and heterosexual relations that drive them. Hence the first half of this chapter addresses two key arenas in which psychology participates, economic development and psychotherapy, to consider the political collusions it becomes embroiled in at the very moment it is called upon to offer its 'external' advice. For in the name of offering 'relevant', 'applied' and apparently 'objective' support to those different disciplinary practices, it legitimates the same developmental assumptions that underlie them too.

But in drawing attention to these problems I want to make clear at the outset that I do not want simply to catalogue here the evils of the (various disciplinary) developmental legacies to which we in psychology are heir. I do not intend this to be a 'feel-bad', guilt-tripping chapter that berates us all for complicities we perhaps know only too well. I want to emphasise that I am concerned with *effects* of developmental psychological *discourse* as they arise within material practices, and not with specific models or frameworks, nor with the intentions of its authors or practitioners. Hence my title topicalises 'rhetorics' of developmental psychology: for I believe that we need to watch our language – whether we see such 'rhetoric' as consciously persuasive, or as neutrally (scientifically?) descriptive. And when I say we need to watch our language, this is not only within the frame of a parental superego watching to catch us out for (personal-political) mistakes or slips we make. (This is where I would part ways with the 'political correctness' lobby, which always stays within an intentionalist and individualist framework.)

If we reflect for a moment, our parents may have told us that 'sticks and stones will break your bones but names will never hurt you', but the *effect* of them telling us this was almost always by way of comfort for the damage that names *had* indeed done to us. What can social constructionist and deconstructionist ideas offer those of us concerned with the apparently fundamentalist and essentialist realms of traditional psychology? If anything, such perspectives should surely help us look at what our words do as well as what we mean by them. Perhaps through such attention we might even document how the life of those names, categories and activities beyond our intentions (indeed our wildest imaginings) can take us beyond ourselves, the 'selves' we currently all too ideologically construct, inhabit and suffer (Parker 1992). Perhaps they can intimate other social, as well as linguistic, arrangements. It is in such a spirit that I devote the second part of the chapter to a consideration of cyberpsychological and postdevelopmental discourses.

Thus the starting point (as argued extensively in previous chapters) is not only that developmental discourses reflect and inform other regulatory structures that oppress by their powers of scrutiny and evaluation. Beyond this lies a much larger question. This question is whether we can dispense with development. Three other questions then follow. Would we want to dispense with development? And even if we do, are we able to do so? And if not, how do we negotiate a way around and beyond its categorical impositions upon us? These are the key concerns that drive my interrogation of the four areas I now move on to discuss.

Occlusions/collusions in the convergence between economic and psychological development

Let me make a – perhaps controversial – assertion about the links between economic development and psychology. Insofar as it has any, psychology's contribution to broader debates about development has, it could be argued, usually taken the form of adding more useless (at best ineffectual, at worst harmful) measures to the panoply of social indices that are used by international agencies such as the World Bank (as we have seen so far in earlier chapters). These measures – by their abstracted and globalised character – inadvertently work to scale down people's claims to health, educational and welfare needs and threaten to impose Northern modes of living and being upon those already struggling to retain and restore their own ways of life (Sachs 1992). Thus the history of development programmes is one of inappropriate response to humanitarian disasters, of erosion of local cultures, and of tying aid packages to regimes of structural adjustment that thwart genuine reconstruction and development; in short, of a cultural imperialism in the name of universalisation that extends the historical colonisation and appropriation of resources of poor, non-industrialised peoples. As Middleton and O'Keefe comment:

> Globalisation, frequently misunderstood, has meant three things: the first is the concentration of world trade into the hands of the TNCs [Transnational Corporations], the second is the monopolisation of world markets and the third is the increased ability to move production to countries with low-wage economies.
>
> (Middleton and O'Keefe 1998: 20)

How did this sad state of affairs come about? How did the term 'development' come to mean its converse? The following definition of 'development discourse' applies as well as to developmental psychology as it does to economic development. It will help get us into the discussions of discourse and power, alongside convergences of disciplinary alignments on development:

> To understand development as a discourse, one must look not at the elements themselves but at the system of relations established among them . . . These relations – established between institutions, socio-economic processes, forms of knowledge, technological factors and so on – define the conditions under which objects, concepts, theories and strategies can be incorporated into the discourse. In sum, the system of relations establishes a discursive practice that sets the rules of the game: *who can speak, from what points of view, with what authority, and according to what criteria of expertise; it sets the rules that must be followed for this or that problem, theory or object to emerge and be named, analysed and eventually transformed into a policy or plan.*
>
> (Escobar 1997: 87, my emphasis)

Who can speak, from what points of view, with what authority and according to what criteria of expertise – these are the workings of power within discourse that Foucault (1980a) describes. Thus concepts and tools of investigation produce their own objects and effects. Psychologists, like development practitioners, generate knowledges through their methods and practices. At its core the discipline of psychology offers no substantive topic or theory, but rather what the models actually provide is a technological apparatus of classification and testing (Rose 1985). That is, as a discipline psychology does precisely that; discipline subjects through its practices of normative evaluation.

Once we invoke the rhetoric of development, other discursive objects emerge: notions of phases and stages, of inferiority and superiority; and, alongside these, the creation of activities or attributes as indicators of these stages (whether of household income per capita or object permanence, Sex role inventories or self-esteem rating scores). But above all, the discursive objects produced by developmental discourse are its subjects; those who are so classified and regulated. Hence the phrase 'the psychological complex' has been coined to refer to the power and permeation of psychological discourses within institutional and cultural life (Ingleby 1985; Rose 1985). Such discourses link the injunction to talk on chat shows, with magazine quizzes that test you and your partner's compatibility, and range from taking your baby for her milestone checks to being assessed using the 'parental bonding instrument' (see Burman 2007a).

However, as discussed in earlier chapters, the resonance between the discourse of development in psychology and in world economic development gives us pause for thought about their common cultural resources and political trajectories. In particular the concept of progress with its corollaries of continuity and linearity betrays their common origins in the nineteenth-century colonial nation state. Thus (to summarise previous arguments outlined earlier) the space of development is laid out across the world map with the direction of power flowing from North to South, but its value-laden temporal trajectory or chronology has a specific origin within the nineteenth-century European state. Following from this, the spatial distribution of development (that prescribes, in the name of describing, who develops and where) becomes a matter of urgent political contestation, both within the model of psychological development and the broader practices of world social and economic development that it mirrors and participates in (see Chapter 9 this volume).

It is the notion of progress that ties development to the discourse and misdeeds of modernity, and that binds the psychology of development to the economic practices of modern development programmes. 'Progress' is typically understood as referring to change from a position of deficit or inferiority to one of advancement, improvement or maturity. As an abstract, apparently scientific term shot through with evolutionary nuances, it is easy to forget the profound values that structure what counts as progress, and even more, how it came to be conceived of as a line of transition from one state or place to another (that maps so easily on to South to North). As Teador Shanin comments:

> The idea of progress was the dramatic resolution of two great riddles by linking them. What produced diversity? The different stages of development in different societies. What was social change? The neces-

> sary advance through the different social forms that existed . . . Thus the idea of progress became a powerful ideology of disenfranchisement.
>
> (Shanin 1997: 67–68, 70–71)

Progress thus came into being as a means of regulating diversity and change. The answer was to classify and order. Is not this what we do in psychology? Can we offer any alternative ways of viewing difference except as more-or-less pathologised deviation from culturally dominant norms?

Notions of distributive (and perhaps even restorative) justice, for example, carry within them notions of development as possession and identity: those who 'have' and those who 'have-not' – goods, qualities, access to resources, and so on. Politically we have to acknowledge existing relations of privilege in order to challenge social hierarchies and their associated inequalities. But, even in this urgent and socially committed project, generalised norms are invoked that reiterate the power of the privileged to define what is considered acceptable, 'normal', 'adaptive'. Such norms or naturalised descriptions rely upon the stuff of developmental psychological theorising.

So far this is a familiar story. Yet perhaps we developmentalists with our panoply of tests, measures and models paradoxically suffer from a touch too much concrete thinking. It is hard, perhaps impossible, to move beyond what is currently the case to what could be the case. And the tools we use reinscribe the world they practise on within the same terms, disallowing alternatives except as deviation or deficiency. So before we have even reached the traditionally 'psychological' terrain of traits and abilities, or social categories of age, gender, sexuality or class (for example), it is clear we are all interpellated, that is, called into being as individual and political subjects, according to the sign of development.

Hence the knowledge generated by development cannot really deliver on what it claims to illuminate. The more it fails, the more it manufactures technical devices to cover up the emptiness, the key absence of conceptualisation at its core. People, culture, gender and subjectivity slip away even as the discourse proliferates, and in the name of the developmental presumption of the applicability of its technical interventions, Third World cultures are eroded and devalued. The straight, confident and economical lines of modernity turn out to be deluded in their pretensions to have erased complication and deprivation. In the end it all comes full circle and its trajectory has to be recognised as the gesture of repudiation it is:

> Development assumed a teleology to the extent that it proposes that the 'natives' will sooner or later be reformed; at the same time, however, it reproduces endlessly the separation between reformers and those to be reformed . . . Development relies on this perpetual recognition and disavowal of difference.
>
> (Escobar 1997: 93)

As with economic development, developmental psychology has no good – politically beneficial or theoretically well-formed – model of what development is, why it happens, or how culture figures in defining and modulating patterns of development. All is subordinated to concepts of progress and development *as if they had a content and purpose in themselves*. And indeed they do; for it is the content of the dominant culture that has the privilege to remain invisible and thus more covert in its exercise of power.

Therapeutic coercions/normalisings

For my second example of a prevalent (mis)use of developmental theorising I want now to move from the public (but often sanitised) world of the ravages of international capital to the private and intimate world of therapy. This shift heralds another arena for – and perhaps trajectory of – development. For alongside the omnipotent view of history as legitimation that drives development, there is another more compulsive or neurotic view. This is a version of history impelled by the desire to return, to identify the founding moment when things went wrong, and (within some models) to put right what went wrong: in other words it is a project organised around 'the backward searchings of the question why' (Swift 1992: 106). Therapy as a social practice offers a looking back that seems to run counter to developmentalism. Yet the story of loss and trauma is perhaps only an alternative version of modern triumphalism; its story of regret, and sometimes nostalgia, is perhaps the necessary corollary of the modernist history told from the vantage point of the winners (cf. Benjamin 1970a). Moreover, it arises from the same modern commitment to insight. Knowing oneself, the answer to the Oedipal puzzle, presumes the modern reflexive subject it simultaneously deconstructs by revealing it to be contradictory, fragile and above all subject to a constitutive structural impossibility of total self-awareness (Burman 1996/7).

There is a current drive within psychotherapy to seek scientific legitimation for its own theories from empirical developmental psychology. This perhaps arises from an impulse to make psychotherapy 'reasonable' in more conventional ways, even if via a bizarre form of 'triangulation' by evaluating it according to methodological assumptions alien to its own philosophy of clinical case-study-led theorising.

Most current psychoanalytically informed psychotherapy trainings regard theories of child development as key resources for their work (cf. Miller *et al.* 1989; Reid 1997). Many even require trainees to engage in 'child observation' placements (the main exception here being Lacanian trainings which – as explained in some detail in Chapter 12 – thankfully maintain a principled antidevelopmental stance).[1] Yet the precise connections claimed between what children do, and how they change, and what adults recall in therapy remain elusive. (A parallel case could also be made here for the role accorded developmental theorising in psychotherapeutic accounts of group development, thus illustrating a second level of systematic confusion between trajectories in therapy and children growing up.) There is a deference in the therapeutic recourse to empirical developmental psychology that indicates an insecurity with the instabilities of adult recollection, and betrays a longing for (the credibility of) the apparent certainties of ages, stages and maturational mechanisms of the presumed individual, embodied child. Even where such claims are backed up with accounts that carefully interrogate and limit the intersections between psychological and psychotherapeutic theorising (as in Stern 1985; Stern *et al.* 1998), they rarely maintain the distinctions elaborated there between the normative, prospective account put forward by developmental psychologists and the retrospective psychopathological analytic gaze.

The current move from psychotherapeutic to developmental narratives thus tries to substitute a retrospective account with a progressivist account. The retrospective account is always vulnerable to mediation – whether by nostalgia (a romanticisation of what was, that perhaps never was in that way anyway) or regret, or just the backward looking, but fundamentally currently organised, question 'why'; while the naturalist-progressivist account is radically at odds with the key psychoanalytic assumption of the situated, selective and motivated character of recollection. Moreover, if psychotherapists are turning to developmental psychology for answers to the big questions framed around 'why', they will be frustrated. For psychologists' answers are only in the form of generalisations of documented instances, of lots of 'hows' rather than 'whys'. But in psychology we package together these 'hows' in such a form as if to offer an explanation – or at least a normative prescription, rather than a mere generalisation based on the corpus of instances recorded. Not only do psychologists work with an understanding of history that conflicts with the psychotherapeutic project but they actually cannot deliver on any notion of causality beyond mere association – and by some strange circularity are often prone to look to therapists for more meaningful answers (Burman 1997a, 1998b).

There is some justification in a convergence of the two schemes, in that both share similar origins (in the child study movement, in the birth of the modern secular commitment to science and reason); but like the connections between psychology and economics these are precisely the kinds of patterns and re-enactments we should be attending to in order to avoid repeating them. Witness the 1990s tangle over the 'memory wars', that is, over whether memories of childhood abuse can be recovered, or are rather produced, through therapeutic practices. This not only highlighted how high the stakes can be (literally – given the litigation instigated by both therapy clients and their accused parents), but also indicates a logical fallacy that slips unnoticed because (as discussed in Part II of this book) of the power of the rhetoric of childhood, and in particular (as elaborated in Chapter 5) the power of the little girl as a dominant representation of inner self (Steedman 1995).

Here 'new age' resonances enter humanist and even some psychoanalytic psychotherapies via their cultural resonances, and psychotherapy becomes the victim of its own popular misrepresentations. But at the same time we see the real agenda come to the fore: why psychotherapies are now subscribing to empirical developmental theorising has something to do with the respect accorded scientific psychology, that wards off being lumped together with all the 'quacks', the malpracticers who offer guided memory work, hypnotherapy, and so on (Burman 1998b).

Somehow the child that the woman in therapy recalls becomes conflated with (in the sense of being attributed the memorial practices or cognitive processing capacities of) a child within a developmental psychology experiment. And the results from one corpus of (child) research are fairly glibly applied to the other (therapeutic) arena, on the slim pretext that both have something do with childhood. Here the assumed power of the child is at work both as the generalised universal subject, with the developmental psychologist as arbiter of – not only what this child in this situation might say (and of course we make claims to children's knowledge rather than only their accounts) but – all children or indeed people in childlike (e.g. therapeutically regressed) states. Put so baldly, the claims sound as ridiculous as they are. But what they rely upon is the power of the child to represent otherness – of time or place: 'The innocent, naive gaze of the other that fascinates us in nostalgia is in the last resort always the gaze of a child' (Žižek 1991a: 114).

A Foucauldian framework helps make sense of how this could happen, i.e. by attending to the conditions of possibility of such chains of argument. The contemporary crisis of childhood that exercises us all, and has put developmental psychology in the limelight, arises at a confluence of two key debates: firstly, an unprecedented attention to the prevalence of the sexual abuse of children; and, secondly, people (mainly women) in therapy claiming to have recovered memories of abuse. These in turn can be linked to three key contexts: firstly, the increasing professionalisation of talking and helping relationships within the condition of alienation in late modernity; secondly, the rampant proliferation of the privatised service sector; and thirdly, the profound backlash to the impact of second wave feminism within some legislative and occupational arenas (Haaken 1998).

From regulation to resistance

If we are bound to psychological reductionism even within our economic relations and intrapsychic phantasising, what escape is there from the discipline of psychology's imperialisms and collusions? That is, given the centrality of some features of developmental theories to conceptual tools we have available for thinking about individual and social change, is it possible to transcend these? Can we do the prefigurative work of imagining other possible worlds and subjectivities without subscribing to some of the very notions that currently reproduce us within the invidious dominant hierarchies and polarities between mind/body, nature/culture and their associated litany – man/woman, white/black, reason/passion? If so, where do we start? If not, what can we draw upon within existing anti, or critical, or post, developmental practices that can intimate other ways of being without subjecting us to the overdetermined limitations of existing developmental schemes?

To offer a coherent alternative may feel desirable, yet prove not only inaccessible but also as tainted with present limitations as our current arrangements (except by reversing them perhaps). How do we make the transition between the unhappy conditions we inhabit now to formulate inspirational possibilities? Moreover there is the second problem that any utopia we can imagine is built of psychic materials from the present, so we may be shackling ourselves to a system that, precisely by virtue of its radical pretensions, actually reproduces – albeit in some distorted way – the very arrangements it sought to escape. Rather than foreclose radical possibilities by substituting one closed system with another utopian but elusive one, I want to offer in the second part of the chapter some inspirational resources towards negotiating the paradoxes of developmental powers of seduction.

According to a Foucauldian analysis, regulation and resistance function in relation to each other. Without seeing the power of development as unassailable and monolithic in its effects, nor overstating its intransigence and grasp on our minds as well as our bodies, the question arises: how can we move from being subjects of development's collusions to becoming agents of its change? With this in mind we consider two possible interventions.

From deadly serious to creatively funny: cyberpsychological interventions

One critical resource informing current social theory turns modernity's love affair with technology on its head, and watches in wonder as a new era of information overdrive exposes the poverty of our academic, social and political thinking (and here we reconnect with theories introduced in Chapter 2). Cyborgs fill feminist and postmodernist texts with alarming alacrity as heralding a new model of postfoundationalist subjectivity (e.g. Haraway 1991a; Hamilton 1998). Why? And, more importantly, is there anything in it for psychologists, in particular developmental psychologists? My answer is, perhaps, yes, but as ever only in a cautious kind of way. (Let us beware the breathless enthusiasm that has swept through discussions of cyberspace as itself a symptom of another problem.)

The cyborg is the brainchild of psychology, in particular cognitive psychology (with biogenetics now taking the foreground at a terrifying pace). Its origins are scarcely politically progressive, for the cyborg was designed as a killing machine – the ultimate in remote-controlled war games (replete with all the euphemisms and euphoria of virtuality – of 'taking out' instead of 'killing'). But the cyborg, as an intelligent system, has – like its progenitur discipline, itself a hybrid of psychology and electronic engineering, artificial intelligence – shown the individualism of psychology to be the hollow mirror fantasy companion of bourgeois capitalism (Bower 1990). There is some mileage in taking the intelligent machine a little seriously. For as a material system it underscores how Cartesian rationalism is an asocial, cultural artefact of Enlightenment thinking.

But before we go overboard on cyborg worship, we should first distinguish between the current feats achieved by cyborgs, and the cultural-inspirational possibilities they mobilise. The first are pretty limited, and certainly not particularly politically progressive. But the cyborg has kindled the cultural imagination to multiple and ingenious effects. Alongside the many science fiction representations that blur the boundary between human and machine (and their escalating approach to actuality with prostheses and cloning), there are political analyses inspired in particular by Donna Haraway's (1991a) 'cyborg manifesto' (introduced in Chapter 2) that have particular resonances for radical interventions in psychology. As a literary, political motif, the cyborg transgresses the structural binaries – of nature/culture, male/female, black/white, (dis)abled/aided – that organise contemporary social life and power relations. More than this, it has no developmental history, being fully functioning from the moment of 'life'; having no period of vulnerability and helplessness – no childhood in our terms – it has (so it is said) no sense of loyalty, or obligation to existing moral codes; and since it is unfettered by bourgeois inhibitions it can be unfaithful enough to envisage new political conditions that the rest of us are too blinkered by our attachment to our pasts to imagine. More importantly, the cyborg has no stable identity, and does not organise with others on the basis of similarity. Rather, its communities are temporary strategic alliances or affiliations organised around specific goals.

Let us pause to recall that the cyborg is being explored here as a political metaphor. And analysts make clear that we can function as cyborgs, and indeed many of us already do.[2] This is not a matter of whether how many dental cavities we have had filled, or whether we wear contact lenses, but how we think of ourselves and our actions with others. Indeed as Sandóval (1995) points out, many peoples on the periphery of the world order negotiate their daily survival in just such ways – and perhaps we do wrong to romanticise suffering (in the same vein as the charges levelled at Deleuze and Guattari for their romanticisation of madness and forced nomadity), but I do not think it is only this. Clearly such ideas have much in common with the notion of subalternity formulated by Antonio Gramsci and discussed in relation to postcoloniality by Spivak (1993) and others.

There are clear difficulties in knowing how far to develop the cyborg metaphor. And at the outset we should ward off the temptation to turn it into a subject, an identity, for by such means we recuperate the cyborg back into individualist psychology. (The fact that we only hear of cyborgs in the singular – 'the' cyborg – bolsters this, as indeed do the many cultural representations that portray the cyborg as lonely, agonised and longing to be, or to be like, a human.) Where these ideas become relevant for my topic here is as a strategy to disturb psychological representations of subjectivity. For the cyborg aggressively resists the trappings of subjectivity and identification (Gordo López and Parker 1999).

As we have seen in earlier chapters, the contemporary subject of psychology is the child, again usually also portrayed as singular – a sad reflection not only of the individualism of psychology but also its cultural/class assumptions, ignoring how many children grow up in large families and indeed may be extensively cared for by older siblings. As discussed earlier, this model psychological subject is invested with all the modern humanist fantasies of longing (including its mirror, rage) of the adult theoriser's own history and biography. Through the rosy lenses of what we wished we had been and done (rather than who we probably were and what we did), we impose on current children all kinds of cultural baggage. Such fantasies might be of intrusive intervention in the name of protection – such as that children are regarded as incapable of looking after themselves, are not allowed go out on their own; or, conversely, projecting our own desires for freedom on to children in exonerating them from social mores because 'after all boys will be boys' or 'you're only young once' or turning a blind eye to misery and bullying because 'we all know' that schooldays are the best days of your life.

What would happen if we tried to think of children, or indeed psychological subjects of all kinds, as we do cyborgs? Would we come face to face with the limits of our identifications instead of covertly reproducing them by recognising 'others' only to the extent they meet with our projections? And if so, we perhaps encounter other sets of feelings that lie beyond narcissistic gratification, including fear and horror (Creed 1987; see also Chapter 6 this volume). For these are the feelings evoked by those, including those children, who do not 'fit', who do not fit our models or ideas of how we should live – including our work, sexual or recreational habits. Or, to paraphrase the psychoanalytic question posed by Jessica Benjamin (1998), is there a form of recognition of another that does not colonise? Notice we have moved registers from the domain of theory-critique to that of affect analysis. Such a shift is, I think, helpful in thwarting the tendency towards reification and fetishism structured within psychological theorising, privileging the text, test and the model and forgetting about the psychologiser who interprets and acts with them. Thus, continuing the psychodynamic interpretation, the cyborg metaphor could be said to offer a transitional cultural space in which to play out our fantasies, thereby to come to recognise the structures that produce such fantasies as a means to construct others (Burman 1999).

Wishful thinking or political necessity? Postdevelopmental practice

I have been impressed by the ways in which critiques of the economic practices of development have applied equally to those of psychology – hence the rationale for this book. The cyborg as an inscrutable, novel (if culturally loaded) concept may be a useful exploratory device. But is this all that is left for us? Either political practice as conceptual play, or collusive maintenance of oppressive developmentalism? If deconstruction dismisses calls for reconstruction, what should we be doing with developmental discourse? Are there ways of engaging the critiques of developmental rhetorics we have discussed in more visibly active and engaged ways? Clearly there are no definitive answers, but here are some thoughts.

If we do not claim development, we know who will. Within development economics, it is a paradox that international non-governmental organisations (such as Oxfam) have to claim to be non-political while the World Trade Organisation, the World Bank and the International Monetary Fund all clearly see development as highly political. This has its relevance for psychologists and other practitioners who feel that it is possible to be in the business of manufacturing value-free facts. To assert that children's rights, for example, are not political, is precisely to make a very political statement, often to negotiate on behalf of children caught in war zones (UNICEF 1992a).

It seems to me that the rhetoric of development is too important to imagine that we could wish it away. For better or worse, it holds a firm grasp on the minds of many people – whether informing our fantasies or policies. A complete refusal to subscribe to development discourse may be both impossible and too big a political tool to surrender.

Let me emphasise that this is far from an unprincipled or relativist stance. Rather the issue becomes one of working with claims to or about development as a rhetorical resource. Development workers have perhaps always done this, as have some child rights activists. Indeed, maybe it is only us psychologists who have been so pompous as to be unable to read our own work ironically.

Once we challenge the political neutrality of the (conceptual) domain that we apply ourselves to and intervene in, then perhaps other political possibilities can emerge. Once we knowingly engage with dominant discourses of development, we can decide when to deploy and when to refuse this powerful rhetorical resource, which might also include acknowledging as 'developments' many activities currently deemed insignificant or even reprehensible.[3] Clearly psychologists cannot perform such evaluations without making relevant consultations over the meaning of the actions they observe, and so the realm of participatory practice necessarily takes centre stage in the process of theory building.

The effect of this is to disrupt every categorisation central to developmental psychology in ways worthy of the cyborg. Practice becomes theory, method becomes practice and theory, subjects become actors and experts, and psychologists become – what? Hopefully we can learn from the many kinds of cyborgs to lose our identity as psychologists and draw on post-developmental initiatives to become antidevelopmentalists. Postdevelopmentalists resist the grand claims that sold the world on development, and instead attend to traditions and cultural knowledges not typically consulted to inform policy. Once again we might note the ease with which 'post' initiatives have moved into religion, but my worry about this does not preclude drawing upon other cultural systems in warding off the dehumanisation of dominant developmental schemes. We might consider some of the headings offered by Rahnema (1997) in his elaboration of postdevelopmental 'signposts, a new language and new paradigms'. He opens his final section with the comment:

> The end of development should not be seen as an end to the search for new possibilities of change, for a relational world of friendship, or for genuine processes of regeneration able to give birth to new forms of solidarity. It should only mean that the binary, the mechanistic, the reductionistic, the inhumane and the ultimately self-destructive approach to change is over.
>
> (Rahnema 1997: 391)

One of the key points he makes is the need for interrogation of the motivations of the Western developers who rush into rescue 'others' to deal with their own powerlessness – a relevant issue for all psychologists, especially those concerned with children. Others include reconsideration of the size and appropriateness of any intervention – this is especially important given the (man-made) disasters that have followed programmes of Progress and Development; the centrality of supporting community development that promotes the self-reliance of its most subjugated members; the subversive potential of making diverse and surprising alliances; and a call to foster a 'bottom-up aesthetic order' which already has many strengths and supports within it. Above all, such perspectives call for caution over intervention. Why do we feel the need to intervene? And should we not think again when such disasters have befallen even the most well-intentioned interventions?

I must admit that I avoid many opportunities for using my speaking position as a (anti)developmental rhetorician. I retain an unqualified suspicion of development expertise, alongside acknowledging its inevitability or necessity. But most of all I am not convinced that any antidevelopmental account I express cannot be reframed within a traditional developmental programme, given my little control over how my words will be used. Moreover, despite antidevelopmental pretensions, I am as subject as anyone else to asking a shopkeeper what age of child this toy might be for. After all, I am not a psychologist in every sphere of my life and sometimes the mask slips.

Further, as a psychotherapist, I hear myself tell developmental stories – to myself, my colleagues and my clients, as well as intervening in discussions to point out that these are the narratives we therapists use to comfort ourselves in dealing with difficult situations ('it is the early stages'; 'it is coming up to/after the break', etc.). What we have to face up to is the insubstantiality and partiality (in sense both of being incomplete and personally invested) of the interpretational frameworks mobilised. It is not possible to dispense with them, nor does it seem advisable to imagine that we could invent a new one; nor even is it possible not to take the existing frameworks and their effects seriously – to do so would be inethical, foolhardy and culturally ignorant. But so constrained, perhaps it might be possible to be sufficiently irreverential and disloyal not to take the model so seriously that it disallows or disenfranchises political engagement.

11 Between two debts

Points of suspension in childhood and economic development

This chapter begins by evaluating the relation between children and development in terms of the relationship 'between two debts', so drawing upon but transposing Lacan's (1959–60/1992) description of the position of the subject as being 'between two deaths'. This seems appropriate given the ways that the economic disparities between richer and poorer countries are expressed, and intensified, by relations of debt and debt repayments in part precisely through so-called 'development aid'. This dramatically affects the conditions of, and for, children's lives through Structural Adjustment Programmes (for example). This motif of 'between two debts' is used to evaluate current debates in development studies and children's lives in 'developing' countries to highlight key ethical challenges posed by the linking of children and economic development.

Practical, political and symbolic 'debts', contingencies and relationalities are explored, particularly through an attention to the conceptual burden carried by the 'between' of 'between two debts' – drawing upon narrative and literary resources for this which include returning to some of Benjamin's ideas discussed in Chapter 3. Reflecting on the origins of this trope, conceptual-political connections are explored between debt and death as they structure 'developments', through the consideration of current conceptual claims arising from the study of children's lives. Attention in particular is given to the conceptual analyses offered by Katz (2004) and empirical examples from Burr (2006). The chapter ends by systematising and reflecting upon the methodological strategies that flow from the analyses formulated in this book, as also reiterated by the analyses in this chapter.

This chapter advances the arguments put forward in this book in at least two significant directions. Conceptually, it attempts to assess and destabilise the resonances between children and international development whose consequences have so preoccupied this book. So, by precisely recognising the similarities and differences between 'debt' and 'death', the impact of sociopolitical conditions in constraining and producing children's lives can perhaps be better envisaged. Methodologically, the juxtaposition of 'factual' and 'fictional' (even mythic) texts works to prompt evaluation of both the mutual relevance and narrative/rhetorical functions of each. Thus, the chapter moves from explicit engagement in international economic development discourse and accounts of children's lives to philosophical analysis of the status of the conceptual and practical links asserted to hold between these. This analysis supports the more abstract discussion of metaphors and ethics of childhood taken up in the final chapter of the book.

Lacan discusses the fate of Antigone as being between two deaths: physical and symbolic. Daughter of Oedipus, Antigone witnesses the enmity and rivalry of her brothers, one of whom, Polyneices, incites rebellion against Creon, King of Thebes, and for this is killed by him. Creon decrees that Polyneices' body should be denied burial, as a final gesture extinguishing his symbolic as well as physical being (a second death). But Antigone defies Creon's law by performing burial rituals over her dead brother, and because of this she is condemned to being buried alive; confined to a living grave, isolated, banished from society. Her punishment reverses the usual relation between physical and symbolic death: for while typically our symbolic lives and their trace outlive our physical beings, in the case of Antigone she is symbolically erased although not physically dead – or at least that is what Creon intends. Among others, Butler (2000) has taken up Antigone's dilemma as a metaphor for political renewal and change. As daughter and sister (ambiguously but incestuously intermingled) within intergenerational struggles, Antigone is held by competing emotional ties of duty and loyalty (and love) to both her country and her brothers; that is, in both cases to patriarchal relations. The agony of betrayal attends whatever action she takes; there is no satisfactory outcome. The ethical choice she makes condemns her to exile and expulsion. She is alive but not living; physically existing but prevented from asserting her symbolic life; therefore neither alive nor dead, but (it is said) in a zone between two deaths.

Antigone's 'choice' has inspired much philosophical, political and psychoanalytic discussion, which we will return to in Chapter 12 as a forum in which to pose anew the ethical-political dilemmas of development. For now, it is the sense of being caught up in, or as discussed later 'suspended between', forces neither entirely of, nor not of, one's making, yet with fateful consequences, that I mobilise here in transposing 'debt' for 'death'. The condition of children in relation to forces of economic development, and the ways in which the latter structure the forms of life available to live and develop within, can be understood as between two debts. These debts are macroeconomic, national and familial, and with multi-directional effects, since children are positioned between the (financial and affective) debts to and of their parents, but also between national and international development because of their status as supposed investments for the future.

The 'debt' is, correspondingly, both physical and symbolic, and functioning (as does the political and representational economy of children and childhoods) at national and international as well as individual levels. It is this double sense of the mutual shaping and significance of individual actions within larger and apparently implacable forces that I wish to attend to here. I do so not to reduce one to the other (for that is what so typically happens, and what this book contests in manifold ways); rather, instead to trace unstable and uneasy connections amid the shifting, uncertain but intertwined trajectories of individual lives and social conditions.

The paradigmatics of 'between'

We need first to explicate the economic and political subtleties of the relations implied by 'between' (two debts), as well as how this structures *what* it is between, that is, work the multiplicities and instabilities of 'between' to disrupt their normalised assumptions and foreclosed political possibilities. This relation is best described in terms that are neither entirely experiential nor spatial, but perhaps resembles what Katz (2004) calls 'countertopological'.

Neither experiential . . .

The 'caught between' of cultural conflict and intergenerational tension popular in 1980s British social work discourse (McLaughlin 2006) tended to resolve political and structural issues into merely interpersonal and even intrapsychic problems. In the same way as *Supernanny* and *House of Tiny Tearaways* television parent re-education fests today focus only on family interaction, rather than schools or the structural conditions that give rise to the pressures on parents (especially mothers) and children, this analysis always led back to, and so ultimately 'blamed' or placed the responsibility with, the families and minority cultures that the model was invoked to explain. Which is not to say that they are not experiential – as they are, in the ways that David Harvey (1989) has attempted to link experiential and economic changes associated with postmodernity through the notion of time–space compression. But the problem here is that we cannot (and should not) presume that structural-economic forces have direct correlates within personal experience.

To do so would – especially in the case of children and childhoods – run the risk of precisely invoking the idealist trope of personification that has characterised modernist models (Steedman 1995). Why should we think that the subjects on whom social forces act have an accurate or complete grasp of the vectors of power that govern them? Is this not an exemplification of precisely the problems of humanism, and along with this the attribution or imposition of a generalised mode of subjectivity? Indeed Katz (2004) points out that, far from experiencing time–space *compression*, the generation of rural Sudanese children and their households whose trajectories she followed experienced an *expansion* of time and space in the structure of labour and maintenance of livelihood. A key impact of global capitalism for them was that they had to travel further, and work longer, to forage for fuel, and to farm and sell their labour power.

. . . *Nor spatial*

Nor is a spatial reading of 'between' sufficient, as the trope that links one space or place to another. This reading would take the form of a comparative approach across sites or fieldwork arenas; the approach of anthropology or of cross-cultural psychology. As the 'cross-cultural' approach makes clear, such comparisons always presume hierarchy; they cannot quite shed colonialist heritages to allow normative assumptions implicitly to structure research questions and instruments (see Burman 2007b). Moreover they threaten to overlook the temporal dimension, the processes of historical change that drive such processes to produce these diverse effects across different contexts. This is not to say that such comparisons are not useful, in order to highlight gross disparities and inequities across regions or countries (see e.g. Penn's 2005 useful analysis). But the pressures of specificity demand ever more fine-grained analysis that, in the end, can lead to solipsism.

We cannot read off individual lives from generalised social statistics, and the latter can even be misleading in key ways. From within developmental psychology it is now well accepted that siblings grow up in dissimilar environments in part precisely produced by virtue of the impact of differentially structured relationships with each other (e.g. Dunn and Plomin 1990; Conley 2004). Apparently arbitrary factors such as birth order can determine children's workload and access to education of the children. A ten-year-old girl with an older sister might have significantly fewer responsibilities than not only a boy of the same age but also a girl differently positioned within a family. Similarly, if we apply a deductive model from economic status to the consideration of children's work (for example, in the claim that 'poorer families make poorer children work more'), we are in danger of missing some key factors. Katz (2004) points out that both children of poorer and richer families are affected by changes in modes of production, but differentially so. While the children in poorer households:

> not only added to their household's income, but in providing the means of existence under conditions of increasing commodification, their work enabled their families to avoid cash expenditures. But the nature of the changes underway at Howa tended to increase the labor time of children from wealthier households as well, particularly those headed by tenant-merchants. These children often had broader work responsibilities than others because of their households' economic diversification, which

> required that work be doled out along particular lines of specialization. Wealthier families tended to groom certain children for particular tasks so that all arenas of the household's work and economic activity – present and future – would be covered 'in house'.
>
> (Katz 2004: 145)

In juxtaposing young people's lives in New York with those in the Sudanese village she calls Howa, Katz attempts to ward off both a comparative reading and one that limits its claims to a specific locale. Her analysis is less an ethnography of a particular place than a critical ethnography of political-economic restructuring, or what she calls a 'countertopographical' analysis, to afford 'a more productive and spatialized understanding of the problems and their co-existence' (p. xiii).

Between human and child development

Most significantly for our purposes, perhaps, is the range of conceptually produced 'betweens' that mobilise children and childhood but where nevertheless children still disappear in their lacunae. There are two key forms and their interrelations have formed a substantive focus of this book (see also Burman 2008). This analysis has traced the slippages between models of developmental psychology and human development, and how this conflation has then been transposed on to the story of child development. Further, this conflation confuses or at best presumes units of analysis (from an organ, or organism, or species to an individual) and ties development to a historical chronology of the body (from womb to tomb) that has rightly attracted criticism for its devaluation of positive learning and transformative processes in adulthood and especially ageing. This also therefore commits the evolutionist error of reading off the story of general-typical development from that of an individual embodied child, so foreclosing analysis of contingencies of time and place in favour of the rampant individualism and voluntarism that characterise modernity.

Not only does this pressure towards measuring (and so better governing) produce a fictional 'child' that is abstracted from gender, class, racialised and other social axes and divisions (Viruru 2006), but along with all this is the occlusion of the cultural and national frame of individual human development. The subscription to a prototypical subject avoids analysis of the evaluation of different childhoods in different circumstances and the ways the political boundaries of national belonging, or exclusion, delimit what kind of childhood is available to be lived.

Between child and national development

This is where the problem of relating models of child development to international development policy really bites. As illustrations I will take four current examples, one addressing the hidden privileging of national agendas, and the others focusing on the complex negotiations between national and international understandings, or national renderings of international models – or rather the problems generated by the failure to acknowledge such complexity.

First, let us take the problem of age, or rather the meanings accorded age. Not only does this matter legally – in terms of age thresholds determining access to, and prohibition from, for example, alcohol, sex or armed combat (to take some key issues) – but there is also considerable variation in national legislative definitions of these. Park's (2006) discussion of government attempts to reintegrate and rehabilitate child soldiers active in the Sierra Leone civil war is instructive; recognition of the dangers posed for and by radicalised and militarised young people is giving rise to attempts to meaningfully involve them in post-war reconstruction and political representation.

This account still leaves intact the criterion of age, a marker whose inadequacy is well known in manifold ways (as an indicator of mental, emotional, physical qualities, for example) – where, even outside discussions of so-called learning disability (itself a contested category whose 'age-correlates' themselves contribute to the very structure of normalisation they deviate from, Goodley and Lawthom 2004), the set of equivalences elaborated between age, maturity, responsibility and autonomy can be questioned. To turn to the second example, the assumption guiding current British policy discussions of strategies to counter 'forced' marriage is that raising the age threshold for state recognition of marriage will maximise young women's capacities to resist the pressure to comply and to assert their free will. Here we might note in passing the conceptual limits structured around notions of 'choice', alongside the cultural tendency to ignore how the typology of 'forced' with 'free choice' or 'love' marriages not only presumes prevailing discourses of compulsory heterosexuality but also conditions of economic and interpersonal constraint.

A further key issue illustrated by this example is the assumption that greater age produces some ineffable sense of empowerment, authority, agency or other kind of capacity to control or direct key features of one's life course. Indeed, it seems likely that in this case greater age may be a disadvantage; in the sense that an older woman is likely to be subject to greater pressure to marry and be perceived to be too old to be 'choosy' about whom she marries (Hester *et al.* 2007). But beyond this, and without disrupting the key human (and sometimes child) rights issues involved, we should note how this debate – as it is currently formulated – focuses on presumed minority ethnic cultural practices at the expense of majority practices, ignoring how many pregnant women could be described as pressured, if not 'forced' into marriage. Even more significant is how this apparently child-sensitive and even pro-feminist agenda is deployed to cover for national agendas on immigration. For what is at issue is not the proscribing of certain marriage practices but rather the introduction of differential state recognition of marriage for the purposes of sponsoring a spouse to enter the country.[1] Not only is age a gender-related matter, then, but age criteria are deemed to matter legally only arbitrarily and opportunistically.

This also opens up the question of national interests in the determination of chronological age, for legal purposes. A third significant example, in terms of legal interpretations of what constitutes childhood, is the question of parental obligation to support young people in higher education, as in Canada where (at the time of this) the current debate focuses on parental responsibilities to children which effectively define childhood as a state of (financial) dependency that has no temporal endpoint. Of course what is absent from this discourse – as Cradock (personal communication, May 2007) points out – is how this contest over definitions of child–parent rights overlooks the responsibilities of the state to resource higher education (see also Cradock 2006, 2007). So we see how, even within the same geographical and political context, discourses of the active, 'smart' child and future citizen-worker can coexist with those of protection and provision in the service of the neoliberal state (Ailwood 2007).

Every child may matter, according to British government policy (DfES 2003), but a fourth example illustrates how some children clearly matter more than others (see Williams 2004 for a critique of the British policy of this name, while Mayes-Elma 2007 notes that the US programme 'No Child Left Behind' might better be described as 'Every Child Left Behind'; see also Bloch *et al.* 2006). Since the definition of a child under international legislation is 18 years, then refugees under 18 years are entitled to specific (financial, health and social) provision as children. Interestingly, given the acknowledged limitations of physical indicators of age, and the fact that some young refugees do not know or are not willing to disclose their age, the British government has made recourse to psychological (rather than, say, medical) tests to determine age in order to structure eligibility to services, and social workers are obliged to conduct so-called 'Merton assessments' (named after the case determining legal precedent) for this purpose.

Clearly how these can be any more reliable than physical measures is a matter of debate, yet we should not miss the historical repetition – from the turn of the twentieth to the twenty-first century – of psychology once again rushing to fill in for the authority of medicine in claiming this testing expertise (cf. Rose 1985).[2] The arbitrariness and injustice of such measures gives rise to horrific and tragic responses, as in the case of a detained asylum seeker who committed suicide indicating in his final note he was doing this so as to ensure that at least his son, as now an unaccompanied minor, would not now be deported, and would be able to access the services he had so far been denied (Athmal 2006). It is a significant indicator of the political allegiances made by the dominant psychological institutions that the American Psychological Association has recently issued a statement effectively supporting President Bush's policy on torture (Burton and Kagan 2007; Levine 2007; see also http://www.ethicalapa/com).

Between international and national developments

It is now nearly two decades since discussions of globalised childhoods entered the social sciences. These discussions largely addressed concerns about the ways in which Northern models of psychological development were coming to structure both international development policy and national models of child development (cf. Boyden 1990; Woodhead 1990). At that point the purpose of the intervention was to highlight the limitations of the models in use, in terms of their inadequate representation of the range of childhoods lived in the countries from which the models were drawn, and their even greater inappropriateness or irrelevance to the lives of children and households in other countries. My earlier contributions to this debate distinguished between local, global and globalised models, where I addressed the homology between, or similarity of structure of, individual and economic models of development worked to warrant each a spurious but circular legitimacy (Burman 1996a). In particular the spectacular uptake and near universal (with the US a notable exception) international subscription to the UN Convention on the Rights of the Child marks 'child rights' as a privileged discourse around which international relations take place. Some of this concern around childhood has other effects, and possibly other motivations, as with the Harkin Bill put forward to abolish the import to the US of goods manufactured using child labour, which effectively works to bolster monopoly national market agendas and undermines Southern export programmes to the North. But, more than this, the discourse of child rights has come to mediate relations between international and national child-focused agencies such that it can also obscure recognition and evaluation of good as well as bad practice. Moreover, as Duffield (2001) has argued, national and international relations are now mediated by the increasing power wielded by international non-governmental (as well as governmental) agencies.

Burr's (2006) analysis of child programmes in Vietnam offers an important set of case studies that illustrate the contested and interactive character of national and international policy; while development studies analysts (e.g. Crewe and Harrison 1998; Laurie and Bondi 2005) emphasise the gaps between policy and practice, and the scope for local partners and stakeholders to transform a (perhaps inappropriately formulated) proposal into something more adapted for the context (or perhaps too adapted, in the sense of failing to generate the changes intended). Similarly, Burr shows how the complex relations between non-governmental organisations (NGOs) and international non-governmental organisations (INGOs), in a context of vigilant and rigid government surveillance, can undermine effective change: 'Different agencies remain unaware of each other's activities, so the children who are meant to be the ultimate beneficiaries of the aid programs are supported in a fragmented and often inappropriate manner that often ignores their real interests' (Burr 2006: 84). Burr is especially critical of

INGO workers, whose efforts to introduce and implement child rights become meaningless or even counterproductive because they are so far away from local customs and understandings. She gives the graphic example of an INGO visiting a reform school set up by the Vietnamese government and to which it has only grudgingly allowed involvement from a local non-government agency.

> The next day, when Jack and I arrived, we discovered boys in his classroom tearing pages from the UNCRC pamphlets and rolling cigarettes from them. We were surprised, and as we tried to work out how they had gotten hold of the UNCRC, boys crowded around Jack and chanted laughingly, 'Freedom, we want our freedom now!' followed by 'We have the right to freedom'. The more astute children in the class, such as Thang and Diep, asked, 'OK, Mr Jack you give us some money and then we will have our freedom.' In other words, they knew, as did we, that the only way they could be released early was if they bribed their way out of the school.
>
> (Burr 2006: 149)

This was not (only) a matter of awareness of the Convention, but rather of the lack of national political infrastructure and service provision to be able to meaningfully implement change.

Burr emphasises the neglect within INGO practice of Vietnam's own national law on children that specifies children's responsibilities as well as their rights, which was introduced to coincide with recognition of the Convention. While discourses of culture are often mobilised to account for resistance to change around women and children's status (see also Burman *et al.* 2004), this explanation fails to acknowledge the cultural form and content of the international instruments and their agencies. Once rendered invisible, culture blaming comes into play in the portrayal of obstacles to programming: 'International planners often attribute failures to the fact that cultural influences can lead people to reject programs, but the bureaucrats have their culture too. One that may obstruct their views of other cultures, resulting in programs that are destined to fail' (Justice 1989: 151).

Burr's analyses dramatically show how initiatives formulated with the intention of empowering children and improving their lives can be counterproductive if they fail to take account of the local context and cultures of their application. Further, they will be resisted as imperialist or colonialist initiatives on such grounds. In this sense international instruments such as the UNCRC can be regarded as an instrument potentially, and sometimes actually, imposing a globalised model of childhood, and that features as part and parcel of a neocolonial, neoliberal world scene and the new global governance (Duffield 2001; Droz 2006). Similarly, Bornstein's (2001) discussion of child sponsorship illustrates how international humanitarian agencies can have unintended effects, so that the transnational exchanges and relationships elaborated through aid can produce new kinds of felt deficits as well as riches.

Between past and present

There is also a temporal 'between'; the 'between' that lies across, that both bridges and separates 'before' and 'after', between then and now, past and present. Children are positioned in multiple senses in this; with their 'now time' taken to exemplify the existential challenge to live in the present. Once again, the child becomes the token of something else, of everyone else: she is not herself. The problem of developmentalism's focus on children as 'becoming adults', rather than focusing on the current lives lived by children, has been extensively addressed by the new sociology of childhood (e.g. James *et al.* 1998). Yet, as previous chapters have argued, incipient idealisms need to be warded off from both directions: the futurity privileged in dominant models of development (via the unproblematic status until recently accorded 'progress') should not be matched by an equivalent sentimentalisation of past.

Problems of cross-cultural comparison are matched by those of history. Along with descriptions of contemporaneous childhood and childrearing practices in different parts of the world, histories of childhood are mobilised to destabilise the presumptions of the present tense; to intimate that children and childhoods are, and have been, 'other' than the ways they are lived now. There are of course risks in juxtaposing historical examples of child labour under industrialisation with twentieth and twenty-first century accounts of advanced capitalism penetrating Southern contexts. This is not only to do with the problematic of 'underdevelopment' that, along with polarised subject positions between 'us' and 'them', invites a discourse of backwardness and inferiority in comparing 'their' current history with 'what we did back then'. For it also ignores how global capitalism has different effects both locally and globally, and in elaborating the relations between these, that mark it as a distinct economic form. Just as we have seen (especially in Chapter 9) how it is too simplistic to map power differentials as geographical distributions (as well as to fail to acknowledge these, and indeed both threaten to institutionalise certain normalising homogeneities), so too are naive 'radical' historical narratives in danger of normalising the very 'conservative' historical narratives they seek to put in question.

Foucault's (1980b) notion of the 'history of the present' changed all that, along with Benjamin's (1970a) challenge to triumphalist notions of progress. All claims to history are motivated by demands of the present; while what counts as history is often only the story of the winners, leaving subjugated stories and unrealised possibilities untold. Both such lenses transform traditional modes of viewing children and childhoods, just as constructionist approaches to memory have impacted on therapeutic practices. Instead of recovering unknown pasts, we generate accounts to answer the questions we pose, whose narrative form offers the only record of what we cannot know (see also Burman in press, c).

Hence the ambivalence that surrounds children – interpersonally, and especially within social policy. For it is an impossible task for children to personify both past and future, whether ours or theirs. As Elias (2000) shows, the task of shaping a future society has long been linked with practices of childrearing, while Foucault (2006) was long preoccupied with the role of state regulation of child–family relations as constitutive of specific modern disciplinary practices such as psychiatry.

'Between' as points of suspension

But there is already a reading of 'between' that is all and none of the above. In the Preface to his autobiographical volume, which bears the subtitle *The Memory of Childhood*, the French novelist Georges Perec (1989) wrote of 'the points of suspension' that link its two narratives. Far from offering secure claims to knowledge, backed by the authority of experience, his account is a painful exploration of the limits of memory, its selections, elaborations and suppressions. The reader is presented with fragments of childhood memory, supplemented by textual footnotes and documentary references that juxtapose and comment upon corroborating indicators of historical accuracy. In both the layering and unravelling of authorial construction, the remembering subject becomes elusive. But if memories cannot quite be trusted, their inaccuracies are informative. The recollection of the broken arm that turned out to be a memory attached to the 'wrong' event, the childhood injury of another boy misremembered as his own; these 'errors' render physical the psychic impact of history. They are remembered as material and personally visible tokens or communicative 'supports' intimating the psychic traumas of wrenched lives and lost connections – with the bandages and restraining/supporting straps from this displaced broken arm as significant embodied representation of how these 'points of suspension' made their mark on the body:

> These fantasy treatments, more like supports than straitjackets, these *marks of suspension* indicated pains that could be named; they cropped up on cue to justify an indulgence the actual case of which was mentioned only in an undertone.
>
> (Perec 1989: 80–81, emphasis in original)

So the answer to the puzzle of Perec's 'autobiography', the question of what lived history links the two apparently separate narratives alternating throughout the book, is that there can be no direct connection (with the 'can' here a matter of psychic limits to unbearable knowledge as much as logical or physical capacity). One narrative explicitly addresses the imperfections of childhood memories, made ever more poignant by the limited encounters of beloved family life allowed to a child whose closest family members were deported and exterminated under Nazism, and whose own survival was only at the cost of disguise and traumatic separation. The second is a seemingly fictional historical narrative, apparently conceived by the author as a young person that details an alternative society, a dystopia oriented around the maximisation and exploitation of physical prowess and endurance. While it emerges that this 'Olympia' is some kind of allegory or parable of Nazism, how this relates to Perec's own 'personal' narrative remains obscure. Instead of connection, he cites precisely the break or split, even the expectation of the connection, as their relation:

> In this break, in this split suspending the story on an unidentifiable expectation, can be found the point of departure for the whole of this book: the *points of suspension* on which the broken threads of childhood and the web of writing are caught.
>
> (Perec 1989: Preface, emphasis in original)

It is in this sense, and perhaps only in this sense, that I invoke a relation between 'death' and 'debt', to describe the relation between children and development. Yet while apparently a topological metaphor, 'points of suspension' offers neither historical support nor revelatory promise. According to one reading, the phrase suggests lines (as in the accumulation of points), and breadth (as in suspension bridges), or depth or height (ropes down wells or up mountains) that permit the linking or joining, even the scaling, of separate domains. But 'points' equally qualifies perspective (points of view), even opinion and argument; the juxtaposition with 'suspension' also shows the latter to be concerned less with weighted lines plummeting hidden depths than with narrative forms (of suspense). 'Points of suspension' offers no easy resolution; indeed this is what, chemically speaking, a suspension is: the temporary coexistence without fusion of different substances; so describing its composition as 'points' is clearly both an ambiguous and only temporary possibility – a provisional coalescence. Like an Escher drawing, the phrase offers only the illusion of a stability of structure (of memory, of argument) deriving from, and relying upon, the combination of proximal cues and narrative frames mobilised by the viewer's or reader's expectation.

Between 'debt' and 'death'

> Every day this Government has been in power, every day in Africa, children have lived who otherwise would have died because this country led the way in cancelling debt and global poverty.
>
> (Tony Blair, final address to Labour Party Conference, Manchester, Tuesday 26 September 2006)

Despite their over-narrativised forms, more than alliteration and typographical substitution connect 'death' and 'debt', as they articulate the complex relations between children and development. There are of course overdetermined connections between 'debt' and 'death' structured into the inequalities of relationship between richer and poorer countries under regimes imposed by the International Monetary Fund (IMF) for aid that increasingly has become redefined as debt. These policies, as also the prototypical form of global capitalism, increasingly pressurise and transform local economies and ecologies with their focus on cash crops and international export markets (Shiva 1997; Roy 2001), have destabilised fragile governments, and have produced the detrimental conditions, including famines, that have continued to claim so many children's lives (De Rivero 2001; Penn 2005). As Blair's claim illustrates, children also figure rhetorically as metaphors of economic dependence and as tokens of the impact of economic support. In this sense children are positioned between two debts.

In the context of rigid Structural Adjustment Policies imposed by the IMF, policies have been introduced that contravene the articles of the UNCRC by privatising education and health services in poor countries, and so illustrate how discretionary and dispensible the discourse of child rights really is. Hence it is clear that poor children and families bear a disproportionate burden of the national debt, and suffer accordingly. As Burr (2006), Nieuwenhuys (2001) and many others have pointed out, to stigmatise working children in such contexts is to blame poor people for their poverty. Indeed, Burr points out how, contrary to INGO expectations, many children working on the streets do have families with whom they retain contact and to whom they may even send money. In some cases they support siblings back home to pursue their education. She comments:

> Perhaps we want to think of street children as abandoned because to do otherwise potentially casts the blame for their difficulties outside their immediate world. If parents actually love and care for these children, why are they having to work?
>
> (Burr: 2006: 121)

Similarly, she notes how children in orphanages may have at least one living parent. This is especially the case for girls who, because of the 'two-child policy' in Vietnam, and because of the pressure on widowed or divorced mothers to have male children with new partners, are more likely to be placed there. Once again this question of gender preference and gender ratios can be seen to arise from a fateful conjunction of familial, cultural, national and international economic issues.

It is important to recall that UNICEF first focused on preventing child malnutrition and reducing rates of infant mortality. It was only comparatively recently that the organisation acknowledged the complex intersections between physical and psychological thriving and, along with a shift to also address older children, espoused the child rights agenda, including participatory rights. This shift posed in new form the question of how to promote and engage with children's agency alongside the even more vexing and contested issue of how to evaluate or arrive at a common view of *what* they are, or should be, participating *in*.

In this book I have attempted to explore the contested relations between symbolic debts both incurred by and demanded of children, in relation to societal (national and international) investments in them and distributed across different countries, to reassert the need to attend to the physical materiality of children's lives over their symbolic status. Rather than eliding models of child, national and international development, such analysis may help us to distinguish the rhetorical load, or symbolic debt, carried by children from the physical and material challenges they both face and pose.

I have drawn upon critics of economic development, postdevelopment theorists such as Sachs (1992), Escobar (1997), Rahnema with Bawtree (1997), Mehmet (1995), as well as counterhegemonic readings of the emergence of development studies (e.g. Kothari 2005b). But while these accounts describe the changing social conditions that set the contours and limits of children's lives, there is comparatively little literature that actually explores children's lives in these contexts. Canella and Viruru (2004) use postcolonial analysis to inform the position of children – as developmentally immature and therefore 'other', and Hevener Kaufman and Rizzini (2002) provide an international relations focus on children's changing lives through globalisation. Nevertheless, there are comparatively few analyses that address the mutual dynamic of children's development in the context of global economic changes, and those that there are typically focus on one site or country (e.g. Viruru 2001; Katz 2004; Burr 2006). Ansell's (2005) recent volume is one exception, while Penn (2005) offers several regional 'case studies'. Overall, there are methodological tensions and interpretive costs to each approach, issues I take up in the rest of this chapter.

But before doing so we can note how a final link between 'death' and 'debt' lies within the very formulation of the two forms of developmentalism – socioeconomic and individual – as their joint and combined conceptual-political impoverishment, and the limits of their mutual implication.

Methodological implications

One way forward is to identify conceptual and methodological strategies that arise from the range of critiques examined in this chapter, and throughout this book. These strategies work to address and transform some of the prevailing oppositions that structure debates about the multiple forms of development which have formed the topic of this book. At least seven such strategies can be discerned from critical debates across the conceptual terrain covered by 'developments'. These are: to go beyond local vs. global; beyond work vs. play; beyond women vs. children; beyond production vs. reproduction; beyond identity politics-driven programming; beyond colonialism vs. development and, finally, beyond fact vs. fiction.

Beyond local vs. global

While, as a feature of the organisation of advanced capitalism, globalisation clearly has exerted tremendous and deleterious effects, this does not mean that all forms of cross-national and international relationships should be dispensed with. Nor that the local should be celebrated as a necessarily radical or essential alternative. Attempts have been made to destabilise prevailing conceptual inequalities and hegemonies in the elaboration of implicit norms and presumptions in such terms as 'Provincializing Europe' (Chakrabarty 2000) and glocalisation (Mendis 2007). In this vein, Harriss (2005) argues that there has been too much focus on local and transient political agendas, and too little attention to international political economy:

> The challenge for development studies now, therefore, lies not so much in resisting the critiques that derive from postmodernism, in 'post-development' theorizing . . . in reviewing its relevance through improved historical understanding of development, and of the moral and practical requirements of global justice . . . This calls for a *critical* engagement on the part of development scholars within development policy-making rather than placing development studies at the service of the fads, such as 'social capital' and 'participation' of the policymakers.
>
> (Harriss 2005: 39, emphasis in original)

Rather than treating either global or local as hegemonic or indeed as mutually exclusive alternatives, Katz argues for topography as both topic and method; that is, as a lens through which to be able to document specific impacts of the global on the local:

> In working out these 'topographies' of global capitalism, I am hoping to develop a *nuanced account of how the encroachments of capitalism are engaged and responded to across disparate geographies*. . . . Drawing out the structural similarities between these two sites and examining how particular children are deskilled and marooned within them is a means of forging a different geographical imagination, one that might enable new forms of political identification.
>
> (Katz 2004: xiii, my emphasis)

Such 'countertopographical' approaches resist the normalising and colonial legacies of cross-cultural comparisons, but attend to the resonances and divergences of the structuring of children's lives within diverse contexts, albeit under global political conditions but which play out in locally specific ways.

Beyond work vs. play

A second key opposition structuring representations and practices around children and childhood concerns children's work. Child labour is typically taken as a key indicator of children's oppression, but it is now increasingly recognised that not all work is exploitative. Denying children the opportunity to work would be unrealistic and unattainable – and impossible to implement or regulate since much of poor children's labour is not only central to their family's survival but is also invisible as subsumed within household labour (see e.g. Schlemmer 2000). In Chapters 7 and 8 it was argued that, within dominant representations, work and play structure images of North–South relations – with childhood for children of the North comprising play, and that of the South associated with work (while the problems with such conceptualisations were also reviewed there; see also Burman 2008). Yet in Northern contexts, with the rise of child-centred pedagogies, play is now seen as children's work: children are understood to learn through play, and much of early education claims rest on play as a vital educational tool (see e.g. Singer 1992).

This gives rise to two further tensions within the conceptual separation of work and play. From her detailed examples of Howa children's farming and shopping games, Katz (2004) emphasises that play has long been understood as imitative, and a vital arena for the practice of 'serious' matters such as work; while, as Qvortup (2000) has argued, if indeed schoolwork is now children's work then it should be counted as such and children and families should be recompensed accordingly for the loss of income to promote school attendance. Many critics are now highlighting how the separation between work and play is indicative of processes of specialisation and increasing segregation – of children from adults, and of the widening spatial and conceptual differentiation associated between home and school (Moss and Petrie 2002). Katz's (2004) analysis illustrates the further significant point that this formalisation of school and academic knowledge occurs alongside the impact of rapid changes in the skills called for through the introduction of a market economy, so that the children's play can no longer offer an arena of the continuity between adult and children's lives.

Beyond women vs. children

Similar conceptual complexities attend the relations elaborated between women and children, which – as Chapters 5–7 in particular emphasised – cannot be understood as mutually exclusive categories (as mediated through the position of the girlchild). The convergent and divergent meanings of gendered categories of youth come to mind here (discussed especially in Chapters 4 and 5, and to be taken up later in Chapter 12), while it is clear that – contrary to some applications of 'rights' discourse – the two categories of women and children are neither equivalent nor separable. Nevertheless working with rather than attempting to resolve these tensions allows for the attention to some interesting paradoxes. Thus Katz notes how children's work in the fields contributes to enabling the Sudanese women in the community she studied to observe purdah, as indeed rules about women's and girls' public participation were mediated by seasonal labour demands (e.g. with the rules for girls in particular relaxed for the harvest). While there are relational contingencies, then, as changing policies on the resourcing of childcare provision highlight, there is also a wider (national and international) range of issues that inflects tensions and overlaps of interest between women and children. What attending to this tension does import, however, is the significance of gender as an interacting and intersecting axis for understanding the woman–child–state relationship.

Beyond production vs. reproduction

The foregoing points emphasise the role of work and women and children's combined roles within the maintenance of the household economy. While Katz's focus on children's rehearsal and preparations for their future working lives leads her to discuss this in terms of social reproduction, Nieuwenhuys' (2001) specific focus on the interrelations between and contributions of women's and children's work (via the study of families in Kerala working with coir and fishing) gives rise to an analysis in terms of the superexploitation of women and children's labour power as the last resource of poor families. Jacquemin (2006) builds on this to discuss the failure of rights discourse to address the exploitation of young domestic workers because of the privatised and unregulated character of both the work and its setting. Thus the household economy as the site of social reproduction not only highlights the interrelations between women and children but, as subject to further pressures by global capitalism, the accommodations and survival strategies they use highlight the necessary and complex interrelations between production and reproduction.

Beyond identity politics-driven programming

As we have seen, the symbolic load carried by children leads child-focused initiatives to be mobilised within a range of arenas and to serve multiple agendas. Further, like all aid and development programming, there are 'fashions' in policy focus. The increasing reliance of state-level provision on the NGO sector, and bilateral funding strategies, has had mixed effects. As has already been established, not only are NGOs and especially INGOs now participating in and exerting their own increasing influence on the national and international scene, but the funding of NGOs is increasingly tied to specific projects rather than to maintaining general infrastructure.

Various critics have pointed to the ways in which increasing state funding of the 'voluntary sector' has worked not only to institutionalise and bureaucratise but also to deradicalise NGOs (Larner and Craig 2005). This has happened in two ways: first, by privileging service delivery functions over campaigning; second, by setting NGOs in competition with each other for funding, so making alliances and sharing of good practice more difficult (Chantler *et al.* 2001). While these are general features of the NGO problematic, the ways that policy initiatives tie funding to specific projects at the expense of general and systemic provision have particular resonance in child-focused work (Kjorholt 2005), to intensify the prevailing discourses of individualisation and abstraction that already saturate international child policy.

In particular, Burr (2006) discusses the impact of (actual and perceived) funding 'fads' generated by international directives on agencies, as working to generate competition between agencies to offer services to 'the girlchild' or 'street children' or 'child sex workers', or whichever category of child forms the current focus of concern (and funding). Not only does this generate sites of privilege, and correspondingly exclusion, in terms of service provision for children; it also ushers in an unfortunate dynamic implying lack of commitment to children in general. What this – admittedly – very general state of play around project-focused funding highlights is the limitation of structuring resources around specific child identities or positions. While intended to target areas of exclusion and marginality, such (ascribed or assumed) identity-focused initiatives inevitably bring in their wake other occlusions. An intersectional and systemic analysis of needs and provision is surely needed.

Beyond colonialism vs. development

On this score, it is worth highlighting a further key false opposition that can unhelpfully creep into 'developments': this is that colonialism was bad, therefore development is good. Kothari's (2005b) study of the continuities in personnel between colonial administrations and development consultants gives the lie to any such clear distinction. Moreover, through analysis of specific case studies she also highlights how impossible it is to map such periodisation on to individual practitioner orientations. What is clear is that not only were some personnel under the latter days of colonial administrations more attuned to specific contexts and needs, and in some cases more anti-colonial than the development practitioners who succeeded them, but also that development has – arguably – instituted features of a more insidious neocolonial regime. Thus the moral highground accorded 'development' as – certainly at a semantic level – an unquestionable 'good', demands careful re-evaluation, and the precise ways in which it is regressive or reminiscent of (rather than a progression from, or even a specific 'development' from) colonialism demands critical interrogation.

Beyond fact vs. fiction

This chapter, and this book, has drawn on a range of disciplines and textual resources to inform its analyses. These span the social and human sciences from disciplines as diverse as economics, geography to philosophy and literature (as well as psychology); while the examples of children's rights, entitlements and the conditions in which these are exercised have been drawn from both North and South. In particular, this chapter has highlighted in its form, and methodological approach, close connections between forms of text that are often considered to be distinct. In particular, the analysis here has drawn upon fable, upon literary accounts of biography and autobiography, as well as empirical social science research. These, it has been argued, are not only all at play within conceptualisations of children and childhoods and their claims on developments (as is reflected also in Trawick's 1992 account), and include an attention to emotional responses to biographical events, but they can usefully be deployed alongside each other to inform and evaluate the claims of each. If, as it is said, 'truth is stranger than fiction', then attending to the constructed or fabricated character of developmental texts and acknowledging the interrelations of fantasy, history and current reality allows for a different kind of evaluation of 'factual' truth claims. For it is through narrative that we grasp who we are: 'truth has the structure of fiction' (Lacan 1969–70, in Dunker 2004). Ultimately, children are positioned 'between two debts' because of what their life situations owe to past and present conditions not of their making, but which, as both acted upon and as actors, they play a part in transforming.

Development's debts to children and childhood

As the continuing criticisms of the Human Development Index formulated for the United Nations Development Report highlight (Kamdar 2005; Ranis *et al.* 2006; see Chapter 8 this volume), the failures of economic development to deliver on its commitments to children are painfully stark. The context for children's development is globalisation and increasing impoverishment, with accelerating debts owed by poorer to richer countries that are themselves the outcome of rigged and unequal terms of investment and lending, as Burr's (2006) case study illuminates. Both Burr's (2006) and Katz's (2004) case studies graphically show how children suffer most immediately from structural adjustment programmes, preventing national governments from following through on policy commitments to implement child health and education programmes, and echoed by the Committee on the Elimination of Discrimination against Women (CEDAW; UNDAW 2005). The widespread policy discourse of 'catching them young', that is to instil new habits or norms of behaviour through early intervention and in particular through earlier education, suffers from a key limitation. As Penn

(2005) notes, countries of the South can only ever hope to implement very much scaled down versions of the expensive programmes formulated from within and implemented in the USA. They instead rely on home-based (rather than centre-based) interventions and with much fewer resources. Penn therefore questions the relevance and application of the few longitudinal studies carried out in the USA that claim the efficacy of early intervention for such contexts.

So, rather than asking how children and development are linked, perhaps the question should be: how can we uncouple the overdetermined ways in which they are currently linked? To answer this question we have to unpack the multiple meanings and interweavings of children and development; not to prise apart individual growing and maturing from socio-economic development (for that is impossible), but rather to allow into our analytical space some recognition of the scope for play and interplay within their relations.

Here I am referring to 'play' in a specifically mechanical sense, as where the workings of a machine acquire through use (or 'wear and tear') some irregularities or disfluencies in their functioning; the wheels or cogs do not run entirely 'true'; or rather, by practice in real time-space, other trajectories and interactions come into being. Doubtless this analysis could move to less modernist and more technologically sophisticated metaphorics, since clearly the internet has profoundly transformed the possibilities for mobilisation and relationship that the contemporary anticapitalist and antiglobalisation movements are fully embracing.

What we are left with is that children are development's fodder, both in the sense of economic policies and models of individual growth and change. The industrial development of the global North relied on children's and women's labour and now, despite protestations to the contrary, it is consuming that of the South (Nieuwenhuys 2001). The rapidly changing conditions of life under contemporary neoliberal capitalism are what promote the fantasising and fetishisation of the young as (among others) symbols of novelty, flexibility and adaptation. Children are 'our future', so the cliché goes, and children are instrumentalised within national vistas of future of progress. Chapter 12 takes up the question of how these metaphorics might be further suspended or reconfigured.

12 Between two deaths

Reconfiguring metaphorics and ethics of childhood

This final chapter returns to the ethical-political questions at stake in the configuration of child, image and nation that were posed at the beginning of the book. It does so by extending the motif introduced in Chapter 11 as formulated by the psychoanalyst Lacan – of the subject as positioned 'between two deaths' – to apply to the problematic of 'developments'. While Sophocles' play *Antigone* has been taken to pose the key question of the ethical relation between the individual and the state, the practical, legal and emotional constraints of her position as young woman, or girlchild, not only establish the antiquity of the motif of the child as prototypical subject but can also prompt some rather different reflections upon this. This chapter draws on the philosophical discussions of *Antigone* to discuss models of development and the relationship between reason, ethics and desire, ending by revisiting the three key terms – child, image, nation – of the subtitle of this book, as explicated anew via the ways these arise within psychoanalysis.

If (as Chapter 11 suggested) key methodological implications follow from critiques of the interlocking and intersecting forms of individual, child, national and international development, we can also investigate whether other models are available to challenge both utopian models of economic development and the romance of the child. Chapters 3 to 8 addressed the exclusionary and pathologising effects of the nostalgia associated with childhood. Chapter 3 argued that Walter Benjamin's model of the child was more allied with a materialist analysis and provided more fruitful conceptual-political resources than those of postmodern accounts such as that of Lyotard. Since the publication for the first time of the English translation of his (two versions of) *Berlin Childhood Around 1900* in 2006, some much clearer representations of Benjamin's 'model' of childhood can be identified. These considerations are taken further to link Benjamin with Lacan's antidevelopmental framework.

We move, then, from homogenised, universalised development, to plural developments (as even specific and specifically different/divergent). But even beyond this, the chapter attempts to take the further analytic step of exploring what might be involved in a conceptual-practical arena without development – both in 'imagining there's no development', by analogy with Copjec's (2004) extension of Lacan's 'the woman does not exist' and, through other theoretical critiques, to imagine other 'development-free' spaces. Far from finishing the book with a shift away from urgent practical developmental questions, and despite (or precisely through?) resuming the cultural frame of Northern theory, this chapter aims to illustrate how unlikely themes, and even iconographies of childhood, can be used to generate fruitful interpretive resources that can perhaps even (after Butler 1997) turn back on themselves to dismantle or at least unsettle their hegemony.

Commenting on both the form and content of Benjamin's *Berlin Childhood Around 1900*, Peter Szondi writes of how Benjamin's redemptive project was one of seeking 'hope in the past':

> The future is precisely what Benjamin seeks in the past . . . Unlike Proust, Benjamin does not want to free himself from temporality; he does not wish to see things in their ahistorical essence. He strives instead for historical experience and knowledge. Nevertheless, he is sent back into the past, a past, however, which is open, not completed, and which promises the future. Benjamin's tense is not the perfect, but the future perfect in the fullness of its paradox: being future and past at the same time.
>
> (Szondi 2006: 18–19)

That this ('future perfect') tense is also invoked to characterise the feminist project of 'women's time' (Kristeva 1981) should alert us to the imaginary associations between child and woman that will be taken up later in this chapter. For now, though, let us stay with Benjamin. He looks to the past, including his own, as a site for the configuration of alternative possibilities that the future no longer allows: 'Benjamin, on the contrary, can disregard later events and devote himself to the invocation of those moments of childhood in which a token of the future lies hidden' (Szondi 2006: 21). But, still, we need to interrogate in what sense children embody a 'token of the future'. This seems precisely to recapitulate, rather than avoid, the romance of the child – which also thereby places the burden of responsibility for the future on the child. Moreover such accounts are always subject to, that is, they cannot avoid the charge of failing to distinguish fantasy from wish fulfilment. The problematic of the child is never, or never only, self-defined: the work of culture is about how children make sense of themselves within pre-existing conditions.

Set alongside the studies of children's lives in the South discussed in Chapter 11, Benjamin's evocation of his bourgeois, upper-middle-class Berlin childhood seems to exemplify exactly the exclusionary and privileged model under criticism here. Yet this was also the problematic Benjamin was addressing, in attempting to retrieve revolutionary possibilities in the most unlikely of places. Similarly, taking a 'classical' Greek tragedy as a point of departure could be seen to recapitulate exclusionary Northern presumptions of cultural superiority. Such criticisms may perhaps be both warranted and unavoidable but, as will be seen, these analyses work to unravel, rather than reinforce, their authority precisely because of the structural limits of the imaginary project. One of various traces of argument that connect Benjamin with the discussions of previous chapters, and with Lacan's analyses as elaborated below, lie in his acknowledgement of the desire *of* the child, as well as *for* the child: for as both Szondi (2006) and Mehlman (1993) point out, the emergence of erotic curiosity that Benjamin recalls from his encounter with the streets of Berlin is linked to the stirring of a political questioning.

From Amélie to Antigone: revisiting child, image, nation

The story of Antigone was briefly outlined at the beginning of Chapter 11, in motivating for its analysis of the problematic of childhood as 'between two debts'. Antigone is condemned by Creon, King of Thebes, to being buried alive, sent to live the rest of her life imprisoned in a cave for performing the burial rites for her dead brother. Her punishment, then, is to remain physically alive but disallowed from a life of social and personal meaning. This is what Lacan calls 'between two deaths'. Here we return to this original formulation ('between two deaths'). For the question of what, if anything, lies beyond the identification with/of the child not only leads us back to a discussion of Antigone, but also to the intertextual relations with the account of Amélie (as both young, beautiful, desirable young women) discussed in Chapter 5. Here, though, rather different conceptual resources will be considered to interpret the meaning and attention accorded these characters – both of whom name (the English version of) their texts. Rather than, as in Chapter 5, invoking Freud's jokework, or even the abjection surrounding images of children noted in Chapter 6, here Lacanian discussions are drawn upon to analyse the paradigm of identification in rather different terms.

As with the relations between 'debt' and 'death' discussed in Chapter 11, more than assonance connects Amélie and Antigone; for both stand as key prototypes of Northern human subjectivity, in particular as explorations of the possibilities for, and limits of, ethical action. But while it was argued that Amélie's femininity and beauty lure us away from the more negative reading of her missionary zeal and manipulations, the same qualities in Antigone work instead to emphasise her transgression (in disobeying Creon, and betraying her country). In so doing (as we shall see), this reveals how she is bound by the same rules of the law and country whose limits her fateful choices reveal. The point here is that the girl/child/woman Antigone is not a transcendent subject, a model of the child who triumphs despite hardship and overcomes the limits and constraints of her conditions; but rather one whose implication in those conditions further reveals their limits.

What this offers to the arguments elaborated in this book is a move away from the reductionisms and overdeterminations between the child and various (individual, national and international) developments discussed in this book. It does so not by invoking a child abstracted or separable from her context; nor even as personifying a Benjaminian past whose 'weak messianic claim' on 'redemption' allows for the imagining of alternative future possibilities (see Chapter 3). Rather, it shows how the condition and position of the child participates in the very system it critiques. Yet, drawing on a Lacanian framework, it will be argued that this is less a capitulation than a recognition of the necessary condition of human life. Moreover this child is, not insignificantly, but neither essentially – given the contingency of heteropatriarchy – portrayed as a girlchild. So instead of imbuing the child with qualities and aspirations that lie beyond her, we can perhaps see how what she is, indeed her very 'beyondness', is both necessary and necessarily bound to – subject to – the very system that she repudiates. That is, the child both reveals and unravels the limits of the system that oppresses her.

Lacan: against development

At this point it is worth offering a rationale for drawing upon Lacanian ideas here. Lacan's work is not a typical resource drawn upon even in psychoanalytic treatments of child development (although there is a thriving current of Lacanian child analysis; Mannoni 1973); still less within mainstream developmental psychology. Although sometimes regarded as a 'minority' psychoanalytic resource in Anglo-US contexts, and treated with suspicion in many contexts because of 'unorthodox' technical practices and obscure theoretical formulations, Lacanian psychoanalysts are in fact numerically dominant globally – hence recapitulating the wider dynamic of majority/minority relations. However, Lacanian ideas are a noteworthy resource for critical discussion of 'developments', since Lacan was resolutely antidevelopmentalist, in the sense of explicitly resisting normalised models of stages of development for their homogenising and regulatory features.

Lacanian time as logical, not developmental

Lacan addresses the question of time and identity as linked, through a discussion of 'a logical problem' expressed by the scenario of a prison warden presenting three (male) prisoners with a rather strange task. He ties on to their foreheads (i.e. on to a part of their bodies that they cannot see) one of five disks, of which three are white and two black. Forbidding them to disclose to each other the colour of the disk that each can see the other bears, he promises to release any who can offer a logical rationale for how he knows which colour he himself bears. The 'perfect solution' is that, 'after having contemplated one another for *a certain time*, the three subjects take *a few steps* together, passing side by side through the doorway, each of them furnishing a similar response' (Lacan 2006: 162, original emphasis). The prisoners succeed by determining what (colour) they are from how the others act. That is, each of them deduces that they must (all) be 'white' because if he were 'black' then one of the others would have been able to see this and moved to the exit first.

This model includes three key features worthy of note for the analysis here. First, it set itself against an individualist approach to individual development, since the subject is constituted through the relation with others. Second, it stands against a progressivist, linear understanding of chronological time – since it is only via retrospective reflection on how others see her/him that the subject can arrive at recognition of what s/he is. Third, the subject's specificity is guaranteed precisely through its structurally common relationship with others: 'If in this race to the truth one is but alone, although not all may get to the truth, still no one can get there but by means of the others' (Lacan 2006: 173).

While we could make much of the racialised associations of the black and white disks (which Lacan fails to comment upon explicitly), the parable is used by Lacan to illustrate the role of vision/spectacle/image in the construction of individual identities, and their inevitably interpersonal character. The process of identifying oneself is simultaneous with, and dependent upon, being recognised by another/others. This is the closest that Lacan gets to a theory of groups (building on, but clearly departing from, Freud's own rather limited analysis; Freud 1921), it also – crucially – asserts that this is a logical process (of reciprocity or relatedness) rather than some naturalistic maturational model. The 'time' in the model refers to a logical sequence, two 'suspensive scansions' (bridging three temporal points) that each of the protagonists (prototypical subjects who are, not insignificantly, portrayed as prisoners) must follow in order to derive their own self-knowledge. There is the moment of hesitation (after 'a certain time') while the three prisoners wait because they do not know what they are, and then the moment of comprehension as they realise that the others are waiting for the same reason and so must also be 'white':

> This reference of the *'I'* to the common measure of the reciprocal subject, or otherwise stated, of others as such . . . is provided by a certain *time for comprehending*, which proves to be an essential function of the logical relationship of reciprocity. This reference of the *'I'* to others as such must, in each critical moment, be temporalized in order to dialectically reduce the *moment of concluding the time for comprehending* to last but the *instant of the glance*.
>
> (Lacan 2006: 173, original emphasis)

Individual and group identities are thus mutually constitutive, and self-knowledge mediated via the other or others.

Perhaps Lacan was anticipating postcolonial critiques in his 'colour coding' of the disks, and more particularly the imaginary/fantasy characteristics associated with blackness, as an absent but constitutive presence in his sophism, since – significantly – all of the prisoners were 'white' (see also Parker 2006). Whether Lacan understood this paradigm as relating only to the structure of Northern subjectivity, or as indicative generally, touches on the wider question of the universality or cultural specificity of psychoanalysis that recapitulates many of the equivalent debates to those addressed in this book (see Parker 2008).

Lacanian causality as retroactive

We have already seen how two features of Lacan's critique are relevant here; that his model draws upon an understanding of time that is logical rather than chronological; while, second, he demonstrates that individual identities – and so subjectivities – are always relationally constituted and mediated via fantasy. In terms of the themes of this book, we should note the role played by image and vision, and the inevitably interpersonally negotiated character of (self)knowledge.

This model of temporality disrupts the homogeneous time of 'progress' critiqued by Benjamin (1970a) as merely documenting (and so vindicating) the 'story of the winners'. Once again we encounter the motif of 'suspension' (introduced in Chapter 11) as a way of interrupting, and so re-evaluating models of, chronological time. But Lacan takes this further. He elaborates a model of causality that is retroactive, based on Freud's theory of deferred action or *'Nachträglichkeit'* (Laplanche and Pontalis 1973). According to this analysis, it 'takes two traumas to make a trauma'; i.e. the event which precipitates the traumatic response does so because it relies upon and so reanimates a previous trauma. Yet it makes no sense to see the first event as 'causing' the second, since the first only comes to light by virtue of the second event; so that the second thereby necessarily constitutes it as it invokes it. There are wider consequences of this approach in terms of the debates concerning the role of early experience, child study, cycles of abuse, and more.

This model therefore stands against the reading of features of children's development as precursors to adult qualities or action. It also stands against a restorative model – for there is no way back (with resonances here of Benjamin's angel as well as Hollywood time-travel movies); not even backwards to the future perhaps. In terms of economic development we can see resonances in the dangers of romanticising or reifying either tradition or the 'pre-colonial' moment (both of which are sometimes mobilised by postdevelopment critics). In terms of children, it moves away from a model of trauma that imposes a normalised childhood in terms of aiming to restore this (cf. Summerfield 2001; Rodriguez Mora 2003), and which in turn informs the model of the 'psychosocial within humanitarian interventions' (Pupavac 2002b, 2004); for the first trauma that is mobilised by the second cannot be repaired. Instead what this means is that there is no pure, whole or uncontaminated subject; we are all constitutively divided. Thus this account avoids the split between the relative value accorded Northern and Southern children's childhoods.

It is, of course, a moot point whether trauma should be taken as the paradigm of 'causes' or precipitants to development, but this account at least stands against the normalising and abstracted impetus of mainstream models of both developmental psychology and economic development. It also poses the question of how many specific instances of 'development' comprise 'developments'. This links with Lacan's analysis of ethics and ethical acts; as necessarily 'one at a time' (i.e. specific 'case by case'), also expressed within the suspicion accorded bodies of generalised knowledge and claims to universality. Similarly, as elaborated below, the focus on ethics works to reveal the limits of law, and how reason is always compromised by desire.

Antigone and the limits of the law

Traditional readings of Sophocles' play *Antigone* take it as the paradigm of the tragic triumph of the sovereign autonomous subject over the state. In particular, Antigone's defiance of Creon's order is taken as the key fable for discussions of ethics. For example, Hegel attributed far-reaching political impacts to the play:

> As Hegel construed it, Antigone does what she has to do as defender of the divine law of the household and Creon does what he has to do as defender of the civic state. The result is mutual destruction, and the result of such tragic reflection for the Greeks was the gradual undoing of their faith in their ethical harmony and 'beauty' and their becoming more reflective and 'philosophical', which resulted in turn in the gradual and necessary undermining of the beliefs necessary to sustain their way of life.
>
> (Pinkard 2000: 211)

Lacan too bases his discussion of ethics on an analysis of *Antigone* in Seminar VII (Lacan 1969–70). Admittedly manipulating Sophocles' text to serve his own argument (De Kesel, forthcoming), unlike other commentators who focus on the responses of pity and fear that Antigone's plight is said to elicit, Lacan instead draws attention to the textual emphasis on Antigone's beauty to formulate a different treatment. This focuses on desire, and links ethics with the erotic (and steers a complex way through a dangerous aestheticism).

Contrary to dominant interpretations, according to Lacan the conflict between Antigone and Creon is less one of individual ethical impulse vs. public duty than of showing how Antigone's apparent death wish (in declaring and acting on her commitment to bury Polyneices in the knowledge of the disastrous consequences for her this would precipitate) is truer to desire than the death-loving superegoic functions of the law, including (as Butler 2000 emphasises) the generational ambiguity (owing to her incestuous origins) of her relationship with her brother-father Polyneices. While (as discussed later in this chapter) Copjec (2004) develops from this an analysis in terms of the structure of sublimation, on this basis formulating a Lacanian-based theory of postfeminist ethics (see also Restruccia 2006), De Kesel (forthcoming) reads in Lacan's treatment a parable of the contradictions of human subjectivity, of life's link with death, as a relationship between meaning and its limits that is necessarily elaborated within a symbolic system:

> Antigone's tragic gesture breaks through this repression and confronts the law and the entire symbolic order with its groundless ground: with an unattainable otherness or, what amounts to the same thing, with a radical and unfulfillable desire.
>
> (De Kesel, forthcoming: 15)

What is important here is that the rationale Antigone offers for her action in burying her brother does not concern him directly, or even her feelings about him. It is, rather, motivated to defy Creon's determination to efface the traces of her brother's existence; to deny his symbolic life (which lives on after the demise of his material existence). (Butler 2000 makes much of the ambiguous generational and sexual dynamics mobilised by Polyneices and Antigone's incestuous origins, as siblings born of the incestuous marriage of Oedipus and Jocasta; see also Mitchell 2003.) Rather than any personal relationship to her, it is this attack on the fact of his symbolic existence that prompts her transgression. Lacan attempts to show how Antigone had no alternative but to make this choice: for Creon's brutal judgement is not only startlingly cruel, it is also impossible:

> Even after Polyneices' death, (hence, as a corpse), Creon wants him to face what Lacan, following Sade, calls the 'second death', that is, a death that destroys him as a signifier . . . But the entire tragedy shows that this 'second death', the murder of the signifier is a lethal impossibility. It is precisely the signifier that Creon, whose own power he owes to the signifier, *himself* cannot touch.
>
> (De Kesel, forthcoming: 12)

What this means is that the law, which Creon seeks to uphold, is itself secured by a relationship to the symbolic order that cannot be transcended or transgressed without destroying it. Indeed, it is the need to expose the impossibility of Creon's project that is said to motivate Antigone's action:

> Her autonomy is not that of a free subject in the voluntarist sense of the word, but that of a subject insofar as it is the 'bearer' of a desire, a desire, note, that is that of the (symbolic) Other. Neither the real, nor the fixed signified, but the *signifier* and (which amounts to the same thing) the 'desire of the Other' lay down the law to her.
>
> (De Kesel, forthcoming: 15)

Antigone's position opposes that of Creon who is blind to his own desire, fettered by his own belief (in the rule of law) to the limits on which his logos is built; for our purposes, it is important to note that this analysis of Creon's fateful misunderstanding is linked by commentators to Christianity and modern scientific culture; whereas Antigone reveals how the symbolic order is founded on its own impossible desire:[1]

> In contrast to the presuppositions of Christianity and science, the autonomy of the 'logos' corresponds radically with its finitude, with the irrecuperable impotence of realizing its aspirations with respect to the real. It remains imprisoned in the unreal material it is made of, namely, its signifiers. This doesn't prevent the desire 'driving' this 'logos' from remaining thoroughly aimed at the real beyond the signifier. Here desire shows its most dangerous aspect because, when it gives into it, it becomes a mere desire for death. A 'logos' that could realize its own infinite aspirations and reconcile the gap separating it from the real would without question destroy itself because it would no longer desire. For psychoanalysis, it is once more a question of detecting and paying attention to this limit of 'logos' and desire.
>
> (De Kesel, forthcoming: 22–23)

Thus Antigone's action is taken to express a critique of modern scientific rationality, a rationality that is blind both to the impossibility of its own project, and to how it is driven by the very desire it seeks to transcend. Moreover, Lacan's analysis of her dilemmas also achieves a decentring of the (rational, knowing) subject by showing the impossibility of being the bearer of the desire it sees.

Development as positioned between two deaths

The story of Antigone can be taken as the paradigm of an ethical claim that points to the (logical as well as historical) limit of the rule of law. In this sense we can perhaps see her position as our own; and explore the consequences of her ethical-political stance for an analysis of the remit of developments. Although, as Neill (2005) points out, Antigone should be seen less as an ethical example than an example of the problematic of the ethical. Drawing on Žižek's (2001) account, the ethical act redefines previous notions of the 'the good', and so disrupts the Symbolic. Here the motif of 'suspension' discussed in Chapter 11, and mobilised anew in Lacan's discussion of logical time, acquires further meaning:

> The act, for Žižek, describes the moment of suspension of the Symbolic, the recognition of the limits of the Symbolic. In such a moment of recognition it is not that the Other would somewhere be integrated into a subsequent schemata . . . Rather, in a Žižekian act, one would assume the very location of the lack which persists in the Other.
>
> (Neill 2005: 3)

But this is not an easy position to identify, let alone assume: for it lies at the very junction between language and meaning.[2] Clearly there must be ethical-political consequences of the critiques we have been identifying for discussions of development. As with Lacan's analysis of Antigone's position, our fate is that we are already dead (i.e. tied into a symbolic system that is irrevocably severed from the materiality of the real). Development is already over, but we have to develop. What this offers is not (as is sometimes interpreted) an assertion of radical individualism, nor of a gloomy fatalism; but rather an understanding of the necessary constraints of existence; of the interplay of duty and desire; of meaning that arises from the relationship between life and death. Equipped thus, we can move to reconsider the key terms of this book's subtitle: child, image, nation.

Child

It should be noted, that gender rather than age have formed the major focus for discussions of both *Amélie* and *Antigone*. Thus, while drawing heavily on a recent account, my argument here offers a differently nuanced reading. In Chapter 5, I pointed out how Amélie's actions can attract evaluation as charming (rather than imperialist) by virtue of the triviality or inconsequentiality they signify as performed by a young woman (rather than the ambition, perfidy or malice with which older women are characteristically attributed in popular culture). Similarly, the significance of Antigone as a *young* woman works both to intensify the sense of waste of life (and, as we shall see, of *beautiful* life) as well as to interrogate whether she can really consciously or willingly 'choose' to invoke the fatal consequences of the repudiation of Creon's orders. Various interpretations (including by Copjec and De Kesel) note how the Greek text describes her as a 'girl', but make little of this other than seeing the marking of her youth as an indicator of her primary status as subject to/of Creon (although De Kesel does acknowledge her fiancé as a privileged mourner – thus highlighting her status as erotically invested as a potential lover. He is also Creon's son, introducing a further set of intergenerational familial dynamics to inflect the relationship with 'law'.) Rather than invoking some essentialised gendered ethic of care, that this is as much a *child* rights issue, as well as the paradigm of the child's necessary rebellion against their family/past/convention, seems to have largely escaped comment. This is despite the fact that Wilson (2002) argues that Antigone should be thought of as being at most 15 years old, and more likely 12 or 13. Indeed that the key recent treatments of *Antigone* have been formulated from the philosophical paradigm of feminist ethics (cf. Butler 2000; Copjec 2004), privileging gender over her other structural positioning as child, works to underscore the polarisation noted elsewhere in this book between women and children in both feminist and antifeminist treatments.

Since Antigone figures within the play, then, as both child and young woman, it is significant that the theme of desire emerges in Lacan's analysis through the focus on beauty – a trope that not only links ethics with aesthetics (and the role of 'art') but also returns us to the theme (addressed in Parts I and II of this book) of the erotics surrounding children and childhoods. De Kesel's treatment opens his account by showing how Lacan emphasises the description in the play of Antigone's 'radiant beauty':

> Beauty unmasks the deception through which we realize ourselves as the (subjects of) desire. On a conscious level, it grants us a view of the 'thing' and in this way supports our unconscious fascination with it. At the same time, beauty supports the necessary distance in relation to that dangerous 'thing' that even our best intentions unconsciously aim for.
>
> (De Kesel, forthcoming: 3)

Like Amélie, and before her Mignon (Steedman 1995; Chapter 5 this volume), we see how desire makes an object more than they are, and in so doing thereby in some sense deprives them of their own existence. Antigone's is a conceptual rather than corporeal beauty.[3]

So for Lacan her beauty is less literal, than to do with meaning – much as we have discussed the metaphorics of child and childhood (as often very far from the attributed 'attractiveness' of specific children):

> What is important in the character of Antigone is how she functions in relation to desire. Not, that is, how Antigone functions in relation to her desire, but rather how Antigone, as beauty, functions in relation to the desire of the one who watches her. That is, in relation to the desire of the spectator.
>
> (Neill 2005: 22–23)

Where De Kesel notes that 'the beauty shimmering through her is the signifier' (p. 28), we learn that the weight of this 'beauty' is what separates the child from the real and imports her into symbolic existence, as a signifier that obscures or even destroys: The purely symbolic 'support' on which everything is 'borne' – the signifier that represents her – shimmers through her suffering (De Kesel, forthcoming: 28). Here we see the costs of dominant images *of* children *for* such children, at the same time as having to recognise that we cannot entirely know about them outside these signifying systems. Beauty is linked with a dynamic of seduction or misrepresentation that mediates the confrontation with the real. So the attractiveness attributed to children often works to distance others from the realities of their emotional and physical lives.

Before we move on to explicate further this link with representation (in the section on Image below), we can note an interesting piece of biographical intertextuality that indicates how even (or especially) Lacan was not immune to the dynamics (of seduction/indulgence surrounding childhood) he described. The work of the psychoanalyst Winnicott was discussed earlier in this book (Chapter 6) as highlighting the sadism of sentimentality surrounding the child as an indicator of a wish to avoid engagement with its subjectivity. Elizabeth Roudinesco, in her authoritative history of Lacanian psychoanalysis, draws attention to the biographical resonances of Lacan's treatment of *Antigone*, and corresponding link between the ethical act and femininity, with the imprisonment of his stepdaughter Laurance Bataille for her political activities in support of the Algerian Liberation Movement. She quotes the letter Lacan wrote to Winnicott:

> Lacan brought her the typescript of his seminar 'The Ethics of Psychoanalysis'. The text was very apt: it was a commentary on Antigone's rebellion against Creon. . . . In a letter to the English psychoanalyst and paediatrician Donald W. Winnicott, written in August 1960, Lacan talked of the pride he took in his stepdaughter's political commitment. 'She's given us a lot of anxiety (we're proud of it), having got herself arrested because of her political connections. She's free now, but we're still worried, as the matter isn't closed.'
>
> (Roudinesco 1999: 187)[4]

Vestin (1997) also notes that Freud often referred to his daughter Anna as 'my little Antigone'.

Image

While Winnicott problematises the motives that lie behind the (dis)-identification with the child, or children (as was discussed in Chapter 6), Lacan goes further to base his entire theory on the impossibility of identification; or, rather, how all identification is based on misrecognition. Rather than offering an easy parable of subjectivity, then, Antigone resists such facile assimilation.

> For Lacan, the play's catharsis must purify us both in our tendency to pity Antigone and in our fear of being like her. The complex feeling she awakes in us, the fascination in which she holds us, is designed to give us a proper picture of our desire, including its finite and transgressive dimension.
>
> (De Kesel, forthcoming: 30)

But beyond the familiar dynamic of 'pity' and 'fear' surrounding iconographies of childhood there is more for us here in our analysis of the dynamics of representation. According to Lacan, not only does the desiring gaze misconceive its object; it also destabilises the viewing subject. For not only is transgression at issue here, but the matter of limits. Instead of the grandiose, omniscient subject of modernity, we have a fractured and finite one. De Kesel argues that Lacan's reading of *Antigone* invokes the structure of anamorphosis which, in turn, traces the structure of the imaginary image. For, because infused with desire, the image's promise of transparency is deceptive; what we see is what we (do not know that we) want to see. As the counterpoint to the mirror, the anamorphotic image – the image that only makes sense when viewed from a specific position – is taken by Lacan as the paradigm of representation; that is, as revealing its limits.

So not only is (the object of) knowledge put into question, but so too is the (identity or position of the) knowledge bearer. The subject that seeks meaning, that makes meaning of a representation, is therefore destabilised; for it cannot view and make sense of the fact of its viewing at the same time:

> In fact, at the moment when the epiphany of the fiction [of the image] appears, it is, strictly speaking, already undone because what we see then is precisely an image reflected in the anamorphotic field. The viewer becomes aware that everything is all just fiction and signifier only at the moment he suddenly sees an image glittering amidst the colourful chaos of the mute, empty mirror.
>
> (De Kesel, forthcoming: 34)

This analysis of the relationship of viewing reverses the usual interpretations we have encountered so far – in terms of the abstraction and reification of that which is viewed – to put the subject status of the viewer into question instead. It highlights the imaginary or fictive character of identity. The self or subject is decentred: at the very moment the subject recognises itself, it is separated from it. In this sense Antigone's predicament is our own: 'the subject is, strictly speaking, always "buried alive"' (De Kesel, forthcoming: 8). Further, the ethical-political message of *Antigone* is complex; for it not only both draws upon and refuses identification, but it also resists the move from morality to moralising: It 'shows us not what I ought or ought not to do; it shows us *what we are and do*. All Antigone can do is give us an *image* of ourselves as ethical subjects. This is why she can never serve as an *example*'

(De Kesel, forthcoming: 35). In terms of its application to the preoccupations of this book, what follows from this analysis is, first, a resistance to allowing the child to be taken as identificatory point, by showing how the identifying subject is destabilised by and through its desire for identification; and second, by showing how the ethical imperative can never be prescribed. Reflecting on the history of models of economic development, Chambers examines the limits to self-recognition this betrays. He comments: 'One methodology we need is to know better how to analyse the links between our choices, our acts of commission and omission, and those who are meant to benefit, and so to learn to make better decisions about what to do' (Chambers 2005: 82).

Nation

The third term in this book's subtitle, 'nation', has figured as the context for policy, practice and application around initiatives for and about children. While 'image' has figured the affective relational dynamics surrounding children, 'nation' has framed the material-political conditions for such relations (and indeed much can be done by highlighting the contrasts in national policies; see e.g. Moss and Petrie 2002; Dahlberg and Moss 2005). Moreover, as we have seen, both national and international policies draw on such imaginaries. What this analysis offers is a way of conceptualising child and individual, not as separate from, or other to, the nation/social – but as produced by and therefore limited to it. In *Antigone*, nation figures as the law; as Creon's power, and as the rule or claim of the symbolic, as both necessary and limiting – but as we have seen – also limited by its own failure to recognise its own partiality and so to overstep its claims to power. This sets up ethics as linked to the law, but not subsumed by, and fundamentally in tension with it. As Neill (2005: 26) concludes: 'It is not specially that *Antigone* or Antigone's act cannot function as an ethical example. It is rather that the ethical cannot be exemplified without recuperating it to a law. Which is to say, precisely, without rendering it other than ethical.' What this leads to is not a radical claim of something totally outside or other to the law, but rather as its *limit*. Antigone also shows us not only the desire that comprises us, but also its impossibility:

> She makes clear how the entire order, with its power and law, is at one and the same time desire *and* lack. Under circumstances where the law appears omnipresent and all-powerful, she assumed precisely the place where the law comes up against its own limits, thereby revealing how it cannot give or realize what it promises.
>
> (De Kesel, forthcoming: 12–13)

Examples in the domain of national and international development of such 'over-reach' (of the kind conceptually identified within Lacan's analysis of the necessary limits of signification) are only too numerous. Suffice it also to note here that government, paradigmatically represented by Creon and his city Thebes, extends also to new forms of governmentality that transcend national boundaries; so that the critique put forward can also be taken to include the remit of 'rational' efforts to improve and progress, and beyond the officially constituted domains of political representation.

Where does this leave development or development*s*? Chapter 11 ended by proposing that the task of addressing developments in its plural sense, as discussed in this book, implied some key conceptual-methodological strategies, each of which concerned commenting upon and reworking prevailing oppositions that structure the configuration of the child, image, nation within 'developments'. Taking the spirit of the last strategy – 'beyond fact vs. fiction' – forward, this final section of the book will consider what might be involved in imagining there's no development.

Imagining there's no development

It is time to reconsider what positing developments, rather than development, might and might not mean. The Introduction to this book presented a rationale for shifting the analytic focus from a unitary notion of 'development' to 'developments'. It also cautioned against a relativist reading of the recourse to multiplicity advocated here. The analyses in this book are not simply concerned with dealing with differences in terms of 'celebrating the other' (as Sampson 1993 proposed), or even representing the other – whether politically, textually or even artistically (as discussed in Wilkinson and Kitzinger's 1996 collection). Rather, as exemplified by the earlier discussions, there is a necessary implication of the other (or others) within the constitution of 'self' (and the various 'selves' that form the 'centre' of developmental theorising). This, correspondingly, highlights the impossibility of formally distinguishing self and other as having separate origins (though this certainly does not mean we are all equally positioned – so 'flattening' out power inequalities (see Burman 1990a; Parker 1998)). This is one key message demonstrated by Lacan's parable of logical time, and time – or rather a particular conception of time as homogeneous, linear, unidirectional – has inscribed dominant understandings of development: development as 'progress'.

We have seen how the story of Antigone can be used not merely to counter the singular against the general, whether as personal interest against general good, kingship against law, and feminine ethic of care vs. patriarchal obedience. The analysis above suggests that, rather than exemplifying its alternative, Antigone's act shows the limits of the law. Now we can revisit the claims made in the Introduction in the light of the conceptual debates reviewed here in Chapter 12, and informed by critiques of 'progress' formulated in earlier chapters, to reconsider what notions of singularity and particularity offer to an understanding of the ethics and politics of development.

Being particular about particularity

Copjec (2004) takes the title of her book *Imagine There's No Woman* from Lacan's provocative injunction to 'imagine there's no Poland'. In doing this she is elaborating the implications of Lacan's claim that 'the woman does not exist' (expounded in Seminar XX, Lacan 1988) to consider the political possibilities of representational interventions – as the subtitle of her book (*Ethics and Sublimation*) implies. In this Lacan is, of course, not disputing the existence of women, but rather highlighting the ways imaginary representations of what women are/should be like always mediate and distort relationships. Copjec takes this as a paradigm for considering the contemporary political structure of relationships, and the possible role of the arts in this.[5]

Here I want to apply features of her analysis to 'imagine there's no development', in particular in relation to her conception of the woman – exemplified by Antigone whom she positions as the guardian of the 'not-all' (or other than universal) of being which enables an ethics of the act, linking the 'not-all' to an analysis of singularity. Making this substitution is not as strange as it may seem, since, as we shall see, both 'woman' and 'development' share the properties of being abstract ideals exercising constitutive rhetorical, ideological and affective powers under modernity. To unravel this, for Copjec as for other commentators, Antigone represents the particular while Creon champions universality (of the law); while Lacan's analysis of the singularity of Antigone's act concerns its form not its content – i.e. its formal property of refusal.

In a discussion that has wide political significance, Copjec points out that celebrating particularity in itself is insufficient. Rather, drawing on Russell's paradox – that there can be no set of sets that does not include itself as a member – she shows that the opposition between universal and particular is itself untenable.

> There is no whole of being, no 'all there is', there are only appearances in their particularity. . . Lacan does not argue that there are no universals, only particular things; rather, he maintains that *universals are real.* To limit one's observation only to appearances, to particular things, is to overlook the existence of the real, which is precisely what makes an all of being impossible.
>
> (Copjec 2004: 4)

By this account, Antigone's refusal to acquiesce to Creon's demand indicates that she takes the universal as real. While Antigone perseveres (and many accounts interrogate why she does this, analysing the fluctuations of her resolve), Creon however is fixated. She may be governed by the other in terms of her desire to bury her brother; but, in her singularity, she is not governed by what the other wants. The implications of this for our analysis here is a refusal of the antagonism between universal and particular as being necessary or inevitable. Nor does it presuppose the privileging of one at the other's expense.

I suggest that imagining a world without development opens up the problematic of development, usually seen as the inexorable regime of advancing capitalism and globalisation, to reveal its gaps, absences, limits and internal contradictions. I want to use this analysis to revisit the tension between notions of particularity and universality that underlie critiques of the notion of 'development', and reconsider the conceptual-political consequences of refusing a general notion of development.

Copjec's discussion (via Lacan) allows for a conception of development that is singular, but refuses prescribed specific developments whose particularity is suppressed in the service of claiming a spurious universality. Thus the problem of development lies in the specification of content, which has always worked in the service of capitalist-patriarchal exploitation. Does this mean that other specifications might be more beneficial? This is not so easy to determine. Indeed, this could imply a conventionally spatialised understanding of the relation between form and content that the previous analysis throws into question. Instead what we might look for are non-developmental or 'development-free spaces'. But before discussing these, there is more to consider from Copjec's treatment.

'Progress' as the deferred/failed claim on immortality

In the early part of the book, Copjec (2004) explores the relations between conceptualisations of and claims to immortality, eternity and posterity within modern structures of subjectivity. She notes that the notion of singularity 'figures with, rather than against, the social bond' (pp. 23–24). Significantly, the objectification of knowledge under modernity (as exemplified by scientific method) transforms the process of acquiring knowledge to one which is beyond the individual. While clearly functioning to ward off the sense of futility:

> [This] threatens to turn the curious into functionaries of the process of knowledge and to render the possession of knowledge irredeemably fleeting and incomplete. For these reasons, no individual, only a generational series of them, can become the subject of knowledge.
>
> (Copjec 2004: 21)

This returns us to a reconsideration of the notion of progress (as discussed in particular in Chapter 10), but now in terms of a more elaborated treatment of its affective functions. Progress requires some recourse to a notion of eternity, that itself is no longer accessible in a scientific-technological society, 'subjective finitude and failure are effaced by the promises of progress' (p. 150).[6]

This analysis also applies to the role of development under modernity, which – it seems – cannot be transcended: 'Lacan's definition of the real is precisely that which, in language or the symbolic, negates the possibility of any metadimension, any metalanguage' (Copjec 2004: 95). This reminder of how there is no metalanguage, that is, no position outside prevailing social symbolic coordinates from which to judge or intervene, can be set alongside the problem of the impossible subject/witness of or to progress. It offers some insights for the project of unravelling of the particular of development. Moreover, it shows development as always particular, and its generalisation therefore necessarily a fabrication that not only suppresses its contingency but also renders impossible the project of connecting it back to its own, or indeed any, specific material context.[7]

Development: doomed to repeat?

Copjec's critique of progress is useful because it exposes the epistemological and affective – as well as economic – interests that sustain it. This has further consequences in terms of indicating why progress has been implicated not only in colonial structures of domination, but in maintaining ideological structures of rationalisation for this in the form of racism. The Freudian understanding of the project of therapy as thwarting the repetition compulsion is relevant here.

Drawing on this, and basing her analysis on the reception and interpretation of the work of Kara Walker, an African-American woman artist, Copjec suggests that the notion of race has come into being as that which allows the modern subject to survive its own death, as linked to notions of eternity and immortality: 'Henceforth he is not only an individual, but also a member of a racial group. The phenomenon of race (and racism) that results is unlike anything that preceded it and not only because race has now to assume the role of heaven, eternity, in safeguarding the subject's immortality' (p. 105).

But, as she notes, this is a negative notion – fuelled via the superego; it is based on the awareness of the gap between our expectation and their realisation: 'The notion of progress to infinity anchors us to our mortality, to a temporality that ensures our failure from moment to moment, to an infinity of failures, therefore an infinity of punishments' (Copjec 2004: 51). It is this pleasure in identification which is also an avoidance of confronting the limits of one's mortality, she suggests, that fuels the violence underlying all racism.[8]

There is a surplus of fantasy carried by some concepts, which she suggests is structured into the 'progress':

> We have subscribed to the historical fantasy of infinite progress, which turns out in Kant's reading to be nothing but a fantasy of infinite deferral. While, on the one hand, experience has shown, it binds us to

> death by reducing life to the struggle against it. And although the fantasy seems to hold out a promise of infinite pleasure, it in fact requires us always to tithe our pleasure to this promise. In short, the . . . ethical vocation as the pursuit of happiness and the cherishing of well-being, or physical life, has brought us the most unimaginable horrors and an undeniable 'contempt for life'.
>
> (Copjec 2004: 151–152)

The time of development has typically been understood as logico-mathematical time; that is, time as linear succession. But psychoanalytic conceptions question this by showing how the compulsion to repeat structures all actions, while causality works backwards, as retroactively recognised and interpreted. What can such notions bring to an understanding of 'developments'? Not simply that development is uneven, discontinuous, and even goes in contrary directions (although this is certainly what some development economists would wish us to address; De Rivero 2001). Beyond this, we might even want to open up possible gaps and ruptures in development, and consider what 'suspending development' might enable us to do.

Non-developmental spaces

Beyond substituting one kind of development for another, which always threatens to reproduce itself as the same, what else can address the problems of development? While this chapter and this book have stayed fairly close to a limited set of interpretive resources, just to show that these are merely indicative I will finish by highlighting some other newly emerging possibilities that invite an attention to 'non-developmental spaces'.

De Rivero (2001) proposes dispensing with the 'myth of development' and replacing it instead with an analysis that focuses on non-viable economies. This, he suggests, at least ushers in some more realistic, direct and practical ways of engaging with the pressing problems facing those national economies whose 'developmental' prospects (in terms of competing in world markets) are rapidly dwindling in the context of the increasing global irrelevance of labour and natural resources in informatic-structured, transnational economies. It is thus a major political move to refuse development discourse, and its suspension prompts very different ways of configuring both the relations and responsibilities between North and South. Thus, non-developmental spaces are those which refuse to bear this content and so are disturbing to prevailing structures of power and order.

From a very different arena, Motzkau (2006a, 2006b, 2007) puts forward the notion of 'development free spaces'. Her analysis focuses on professional accounts of the difficulties in interpreting child witness testimony in the context of child sexual abuse investigations. She goes beyond attending to how the professionals' discourse contains ambiguities and contradictions, in terms of their references to developmental psychological studies alongside naturalised, common-sense descriptions of 'you know what children are like' that especially involve age norms (see the judge's comment: 'nine year olds can lie nine year olds can tell the truth', Motzkau 2006a: 375). Rather than simply pointing out these contradictions, or indeed offering any other, more informed 'expert' knowledge, she uses this to show how there are instabilities and moments of questioning about development embedded within these accounts that can provide the basis for cross-disciplinary and interagency discussion (see also Nightingale 2005). Crucially, this discussion cannot sustain a project of constructing a 'better' developmental knowledge, but rather takes the form of considering the consequences of the limits to knowledge that all parties can, at least at some moments, acknowledge.

Like Tarulli and Skott-Myhre (2006) and Skott-Myhre and Frijters (in press), Motzkau highlights moments of destabilisation of developmental precepts (of time, of both technical and received common-sense knowledge about children), as offering a site for reflecting and reworking those orthodoxies, dubbing these paradoxical moments 'pragmatic voids as passages for change'. Rather than only being complicit in reproducing prevailing limited conceptions of children, memory, memorial accountability and change, she calls for practitioners to become 'co-conspiritors for change'.

There are practical consequences here, not only in the (consultative, participatory) stance adopted by the researcher, but also in terms of tackling the structure of anxiety and the 'rush to protect' that underlie child abuse interventions. Indeed, unpacking the time of the legal process itself is instructive; for, far from being continuous (and quick) it was variable: qualitative as well as quantitative, and running backwards as well as forwards. As well as chronological time, there was the duration of certain procedures, the time experienced by the child, witnesses, officers, judges in courts. 'But also the time zones of veridicality and the time zones of recall pointing to specific time spans, or intervals in chronological time' (Motzkau 2006a: 407; see also Motzkau 2001, 2006b, 2007). Again (as was claimed in Chapter 1) this can work to empower rather than deskill practitioners; for once the uncertainties and limits to possible knowledge are acknowledged, then this can work to inform more, rather than less, confident and considered interventions and corresponding partnerships.

There is an ethical imperative to act, even if – as Lacan's analysis of *Antigone* suggests – this action is fated to be realised and even formulated only within the same political-symbolic order it seeks to transcend. Far from condemning us to inactivity, and far from action being futile, there remains scope for intervention. But now, crucially, what intervention means is now understood as a significant part of the domain of action – for its paradigm threatens an incipient recapitulation of prevailing power relations unless it is continuously critiqued and reconfigured. Intervention can no longer be thought of as a direct application or translation of a plan, model or blueprint on to a passive and pre-existing arena. Rather than only challenging existing practice, the analyses discussed in this chapter, and in this book, aim to support more informed, attuned and just practice around children and other marginalised and disadvantaged peoples. This recalls Butler's (2000) discussion of *Antigone* which she calls the 'tragedy of the child' (p. 71), where 'her punishment precedes her crime, and her crime becomes the occasion for its literalisation', in which her 'crime' is overdetermined by the mere accident of her birth. This may involve risking existing knowledge, in order to build better approaches. It means envisaging claims against, as well as for, development.

Chapters 11 and 12 have put forward a range of resources concerned with 'suspending' the limited prevailing modes of thinking around children and development, drawing on literary, philosophical, psychoanalytic perspectives as well as accounts of detailed fieldwork. These are only some of the many interpretive frameworks that critical practitioners of development are formulating to open up more radical, equitable possibilities, to which this book has aimed to offer some contribution. Keeping developments plural is surely a part of this.

Notes

1 Dis/placing development

1 These questions were the focus of an interdisciplinary seminar on 'Rethinking Childhood' convened in September 2005 at Berkeley, University of California in which I participated, composed of historians (including an art historian), sociologists, psychologists, anthropologists and educationalists. I draw on them here as they seem to exemplify the general set of questions mobilised by the themes of children and childhood. The remaining two sets of questions which I have not reproduced above concerned child rights and children's artistic and cultural productions. None of the questions specifically identified particular disciplinary knowledges. This chapter is in part composed of my comments presented there.

2 Outside academic and professional/practitioner arenas, despite institutional and disciplinary pressures to appear 'useful' – in terms of advising government on policy and informing public opinion, I try to avoid press coverage. This is because (as a precise recapitulation of the problem) everything I say seems to get distorted into something else. This experience was vindicated by recent research projects I co-directed around domestic violence services for minority ethnic women in Britain (in which children feature in significant but complex ways), where my reports were reframed by the media to focus on the very theme that the research aimed to problematise; namely, the widespread presumption that black and minority ethnic women stayed longer in violent relationships (when in fact to the extent that this is true it is because of financial pressures, lack of service access and immigration status, Burman *et al.* 2004; Burman and Chantler 2005; Chantler 2006).

2 The child, the woman and the cyborg: (im)possibilities of feminist developmental psychology

1 I would qualify this latter claim now by citing Miller and Kofsky Scholnick's (2000) important collection.

2 There is now an updated text for this training (Reid 1997) along the same lines and, as I write this, a new journal being launched on infant observation, while I elaborate these arguments further in Burman (2002b).

3 I have attempted to extend these arguments in Burman (in press, a).

3 Pedagogics of post/modernity: the address to the child as political object and subject

1 Scandalously, the thesis was finally rejected by Horkheimer, as revealed in Adorno's edited collection of Benjamin's correspondence. Benjamin's chequered

relationship with the Institute for Social Research – as both critic and protector – is documented in detail in Brodersen (1996).

2 As indicated in the Introduction, these are thought to draw on *A Berlin Childhood* which appeared in English in 2006 under the title *Berlin Childhood Around 1900* (Benjamin 2006).

3 It is worth noting that it is not Mehlman alone who seeks out these kinds of psychobiographical interpretations. Doderer (1996) offers a less psychoanalytic, and more humanist, reading of Benjamin's communicative intentions via the radio broadcasts. Either way, equally vehement claims are made:

> Benjamin used the medium of radio as a means of direct address. From the condition of the typescripts and the comparison of tapes and scripts we know that Benjamin himself spoke to his listeners. He began his lectures with 'Dear Invisible Listeners' (*Verehrte Unsichtbare*), he frequently deviated from his prepared script and improvised. This kind of liberation from the constraints of a script was an attempt on Benjamin's part to actually converse with his listeners. In this he saw a fascinating opportunity, a means of deriving, from the text written on paper, some reality of life in communication.
>
> (Doderer 1996: 171–172)

Interestingly, apparently like Benjamin himself, Brodersen (1996) in his biography considers the radio broadcasts worthy of scant attention.

5 Sexuality: contested relationships around the control of desire and action

1 For – among other reasons perhaps precisely because of their influence – feminist, lesbian and gay and queer theory are often overlooked.

2 In Britain, until recently the age of consent to heterosexual sex was 16 while for homosexual sex (men with men, for lesbian sexuality has always remained unlegislated against, with mixed effects) the age of consent was 21.

3 Gearon's protests were expressed within the discourse of children's natural, innocent sexuality: 'Until last week it never even entered my head that there could be something seedy about these photographs . . . The accusers have polluted my images . . . What I was trying to do here is to give people a taste of the innocence in life' (printed in *The Independent* 13 March 2001). Columnist Mark Lawson (*Guardian* 10 March 2001) extended the domain for moral evaluation to include the children's future discomfort/embarrassment, rather than contemporary damage, in his comments: 'There's no doubt that, given the contemporary hysteria over child abuse, anyone who sent a roll of Gearon-like images to Boots for processing would find a copper standing next to the sales assistant when they went to collect them . . . While, for Emilee and Michael, the shots for Untitled were doubtless innocent fun with mum, you wonder about their reaction as teenagers and adults to the realization that they have been displayed naked around the world. That isn't a police matter, but it's an important moral one' (both reprinted in the *Guardian Editor* 16 March 2001: 6).

4 Shades here of the song that ends the *Brass Eye* programme which is discussed later: Male presenter: 'If a child takes your fancy, please remember, please remember, leave it for a couple of years' / Female presenter: 'I did' / [moves into song]. Female presenter sings: 'One day I want to, but not today' / Male presenter sings: 'She can be kissed, but in an innocent way' / Female presenter sings: 'And her cherry will ripen, naturally, in the soul' / Chorus [sung by all girls]: 'One day . . .' [ending with] 'One day, but not today, not even tomorrow' / Female presenter: 'But maybe the day after tomorrow' (my transcription).

5 When, and if, children display 'precocious' indications of sexual knowledge, the cultural imperative seems either to exclude them from the juridical-political consequences of 'really' knowing (hence entering the position of victim), or alternatively from the category of childhood (cf. Kitzinger 1988; Chapter 4 this volume). The vilification of the young child murderers of two-year-old Jamie Bulger in 1993 indicated the mobility of the dynamic of pathologisation from individuals to families, and to (working-class) communities (and thence to whole regions, with Liverpool as the signifier of British urban deprivation and moral degeneration). Clearly this dynamic of pathologisation is echoed across the world in the scandalisation over the sexual and labour activities, including exploitation, of children. Important as it is to challenge such exploitation, current approaches threaten to reinstate Western bourgeois morality as the norm for evaluation, and thus also to occlude how the richer classes have assumed and maintain their economic and cultural privilege precisely through the promotion of those practices of the exploitation of women and children's labour and sexuality that their privilege and distance permits their to abhor (cf. Narveson 1989; Scheper-Hughes 1989; Levett 1994). Indeed, while Narveson (1989) claims that the organised sexual exploitation of children should be regarded within the general frame of poverty alleviation, this 'modern form of slavery' (p. 9) is associated with urbanisation and international tourism (Desai 2006).

6 Clearly implicit in what I am saying is that there is a need to attend to young people's own definitions and self-representations; and, as a group who have little access to technologies of representation and their distribution, there is indeed a role for advocates and activists to promote this. However, as our own histories as adults who were once children indicate, children are not necessarily any less subject to ideological constructions of childhood.

7 Michael Jackson's bill of rights for children, proposed at his talk at Oxford University Student Union on 6 March 2001, calling for children's inalienable rights to love, is in itself unobjectionable.

8 That this is also a self-consciously produced US representation is evidenced, for example, in the 1997 film *The Devil's Own*, where the (anti)hero's words, repeated as he is dying, are 'This is not an American story; it's an Irish one. Don't expect a happy ending' (Columbia, Laurance Gordon, Robert Coldberry).

9 So here the therapeutic discourse joins the developmental one. This is a paradoxical union if ever there was one, for as US psychoanalyst and developmental psychologist Daniel Stern has pointed out: 'Psychoanalysts are developmental theorists working backwards in time. Their primary aim was to aid in understanding the development of psychopathology' (Stern 1985: 19). So while developmental psychology (in its current primary forms) is concerned with observing infant and child behaviour, psychotherapy is concerned with arriving at a narrative of the client's biographical history. The psychoanalyst Stephen Mitchell (1988) has offered a more far-reaching critique of (what he calls) the 'developmental tilt' in psychoanalysis; while the longstanding infancy researcher Peter Wolff has persuasively argued against the current drift towards 'developmental psychoanalysis', arguing instead for 'the irrelevance of infant observations for psychoanalysis' (Wolff 1996). This shift in psychoanalytic thinking owes much to an equivalent drive towards claims to scientific credibility that I suggest itself indicates the impetus towards the closing of the ranks of the supposedly pukka professionals against the 'malpractitioners' and 'quacks' implicated in the false memory allegations (Brown and Burman 1997; Burman 1998b). This is also reflected in the current interest in connecting neurology and psychoanalysis (see e.g. Fonagy and Target 2004); a project that Freud abandoned, and later regarded as mistaken; and certainly one that until recently most psychoanalysts would have scorned. In particular the technological developments in functional magnetic

resonance imaging (fMRI) have been embraced as offering a way of linking neurology with psychology and psychoanalysis (and other disciplines too), and as a key route to 'prove' the efficacy of psychoanalysis under cultural conditions that not only demand 'evidence' for therapeutic efficacy but also fit with the biological/evolutionary paradigm.

10 This takes the form of Amélie's social isolation initiated by (putatively psychosomatically driven) childhood illness that warranted her parents' decision that she should be home-taught, the early death of her mother, and subsequent withdrawal of her father into his own model world.

11 Reminiscent of 'underneath it all you're loveable', the British lingerie ad slogan of some years ago, discussed by Scott and Payne (1984) as expressing the humanist dynamic of feminist counselling and therapeutic approaches, with their individualisation of women's problems shifting attention away from the conditions of their lives to their personal approaches to them.

12 For it is well documented that white refugees and asylum seekers are not subject to remotely the same treatment (Cheney 1996; Cohen 2001).

13 Although authorial intention cannot be at issue here, it is instructive to compare this film with the director's previous work. For although it shares some of the quirkiness and charm, *Amélie* lacks all of the much vaunted 'weirdness' and 'darkness' of his and his co-director Marc Caro's previous films, *Delicatessen* (1990) and *La Cité des Enfants Perdus/City of Lost Children* (1995). In the latter the key relationship (not unlike another French film *Léon*), which undoubtedly blurs protection and erotic connection, is between a little girl (named Miette) and a heroic (if rather simple) strongman. In this film, children are not only the prize, but also the bait and the agents. For their ingenuity and resistance is central to the successful outcome. But the children are disappearing/being kidnapped not only because of being wanted in themselves, but because of what they are wanted *for*. For their evil/pathetic captor imprisons children to try and steal their dreams because he has none of his own. This film, then, is a telling story of our uses of children. (The very name Miette signifies crumb, or dainty morsel, reflecting her positions as object of consumption as well as vulnerability.) Far from the 'sweetness' of *Amélie*, this is a disturbing film to watch, not only for the erotic investment in the little girl attributed to the viewer long before it glimmers for the strongman, but from its first moments in the protracted scenes of the screaming, howling, imprisoned infants terrified by the appearance of many tormenting Santa Clauses.

14 We might also note here the frequency with which filmic representations of lesbian relationships almost uniformly end in tragedy.

15 As Steedman (1995) notes, in the passage that explicitly addresses the rather opaque title of her (1995) book, *Strange Dislocations*: 'The child brought with it the story of its progress to that point: what its audience noted were its "fearful panting"; its painful concentration of effort, the strangeness of its postures. The heartwrenching seriousness of its efforts to please and all the slips it made. The child as acrobat could not conceal its art, and was a highly resonant figure for the idea of childhood shaped and forced by the adult hand. The strange dislocations were not simply those of the child's body but of the adult imagination too, in the uneasy understanding that what was being watched was not quite separate from the watcher' (p. 111).

16 Indeed the *Brass Eye* programme topicalised this preoccupation by opening with the question: 'Why is it that we cannot think of the British Isles without thinking of the word Paedophiles?' [with graphics which turned from 'British Isles' into 'Paedophiles'] (my transcription).

17 Although it should be noted that this was indeed both racialised and classed – for Far Right groups were identified as covert agitators; while the other violent

disturbances of the time were directed towards protesting against the settlement of refugees. The preceding public discontent concerned a European-wide mobilisation against high fuel prices that was also profoundly classed – being instigated by heavy goods vehicle drivers.

18 Previous *Brass Eye Specials* focused on other core areas of social concern, for example, the one on drugs was about a 'made-up' drug called 'cake' which was so convincing that questions were asked about it in parliament.

19 It was screened apparently a month after it was originally scheduled as it was then deemed 'incomplete' (*Guardian* 27 July 2001).

20 Calls to ban the programme were not quick enough to prevent it being repeated a day later, but in view of the response broadcasters cancelled its screening on the satellite channel E4.

21 These were both from supposed paedophiles and those who have been abused – thus both including 'balance' but also reflexively commenting on audience demand to see that which they repudiate and then castigate the informant for demonstrating: Voice-over: 'We asked Kelly to demonstrate North's perversions [shows a shadowy woman rubbing her breasts]. Anyone who'll do this on telly must be disturbed.'

22 One of the 'on the spot reports' showed reporter 'Ted Maul' outside 'Dredgemore Prison', describing the 'eruption of anger, the smell of burnt hair in the air', with the effort to sneak released sex-offender 'North' out in a '25-foot wicker phallus', giving rise to 'sheets of flame dancing to the beat of primitive animal justice; one man kebabed; a hundred forever scarred by a shared blood ritual; and yet an astonishing sense of community here now and a positive sense of a job well done, a shared sigh of relief, very much like the bizarre euphoria at the end of an hour's vomiting'. [Back to studio] Male presenter: 'And we're already getting emails; well done that crowd; even from hardened noncers'; Female presenter: 'Well it's been a great night Chris. Two million children now safe in the stadium'; Male presenter: 'A paedophile was attacked this evening in his car . . . Serves him right for being called Peter File' (my transcription).

23 Indeed the very naming of paedophilia as a (psychiatric) disease category works to distance it from everyday contexts of abuse and identities of abusers.

24 Including the ten 'Sordid Scenes that Caused the Outrage' noted (as a headline) by the *Daily Mail* (30 July 2001).

25 Some people might point to the ways HIV work has massively opened up discussion of sexuality and sex practices, but this is still within the frame of dangers and disease (see Shefer and Potgeiter 2006).

26 In terms of the lexicon of gastronomic consumption, it is perhaps noteworthy that the adjective 'sweet' was endlessly applied to *Amélie* (shades of Mignon here?), while *Brass Eye* was branded as being in 'bad taste'.

6 Appealing and appalling children

1 Such dynamics also enter into research and practice contexts addressing women and children in conditions of dire need and distress. I have attempted to analyse these in terms of notions of mirroring and parallel process in Burman (2004b) and Burman and Chantler (2004).

7 Beyond the baby and the bathwater: postdualist developmental psychologies for diverse childhoods

1 Now we might also add to this conception of spatially distributed households how (especially) women's migration for work gives rise to transnational relations of

caring (Hochschild 2000), as well as cross-generational mothering and 'other-mothering' (Hill Collins 1990).

2 Here I would now add De Rivero's (2001) alternative postdevelopment analysis of 'viable' vs. 'non-viable' economies, alongside Kothari's (2005a) review of alternative development studies discourses and Laurie and Bondi's (2005) attention to potential spaces for intervention even under neo-liberalism.

3 A key example of this, and one which informed my analysis here, can be seen in dominant discourses surrounding domestic violence provision for minoritised communities living in Northern contexts – where 'culture' is also reified, often elided with religion, and privileged over gender – see Burman *et al.* 2002, 2004; Burman 2005b.

4 I am aware that I am nodding to a wide array of frameworks here and moving very fast across a diverse range of conceptual resources. The general point I am making is that perspectives already exist in the social and human sciences, even in (culturally subordinated) histories of psychology, that would support such interventions. Although – or even precisely because – these resources are indeed radically different in form and focus, they offer some indication of the disciplines and culturally situated ideas that could be drawn upon. Perhaps their engagement and specificity have contributed to their marginalisation. That they have to be continuously reconstructed, recalled and returned to in order to apply to the domain of mainstream Anglo-Euro US psychology speaks powerfully to its regulatory pressures and its capacity to marginalise perspectives that do not fit its primary methodological and conceptual parameters (and Lubek 1993 has provided very illuminating analyses of the role of US textbooks in this process). The fact that this is achieved primarily inadvertently via methodological commitments to a positivist model of knowledge generation that culturally reflects US pragmatism and British empiricism (see Parker 2007) only underscores the point being made. For while ideas from the sociology of knowledge (Latour 1991; Knorr-Cetina 1997), social geography (Ingold 2000), and anti-capitalist (Roy 2001) and ecological perspectives (Shiva 1997) may arise within recognisably different disciplines, the works of Gibson, Vygotsky and Leontiev are in part psychological approaches that have originated with and been massively influential in non-Anglophone contexts (see e.g. Reed 1996 on Gibson; Stetsenko and Arievitch 2004 on Vygotsky; Langemeyer and Nissen 2005 on activity theory; Vianna and Stetsenko 2006; Pollard in press on Bakhtin). Significantly, along with renewed engagement with cultural historical ideas, developmental psychologists and philosophers of childhood are now appealing to the ideas of Deleuze to generate alternative models to privilege non-hierarchical connection over individual units of analysis (Tarulli and Skott-Myhre 2006; Skott-Myhre and Frijters in press). See also Chapter 12 for discussion of Motzkau's (2006a, 2006b, 2007) Deleuzian-informed notion of 'development-free spaces'.

5 This includes appropriation and surveillance of the designated others' space, knowledge and even claims to 'voice'. See also Alldred and Gillies (2002); Alldred and Burman (2005); Komulainen (2007).

8 Developing differences: gender, childhood and economic development

1 Hoyles (1989), Hendrick (1990, 2005), Christensen (2000), Cunningham (2002), Roberts (2006) and Meyer (2007) all make similar points. I draw on Holland in this chapter (and elsewhere in this book) as her account is particularly illuminating in exploring the relational associations and character of images of Northern and Southern children. Ansell (2005) offers a more recent practice-

focused account, while Canella and Viruru (2004) take up the implications of postcolonial theory for models of childhood.

2 Glauser (1990) and Burr (2006) writing from South American and South East Asian contexts respectively offer additional perspectives on the situation of 'street children', while Ansell (2005: 205) usefully tabulates the tensions between prevailing models of intervention. Discussing the situation of street children in Nairobi, Kenya, Droz (2006) highlights how the language of children's rights works to uphold the old colonial concerns about maintaining order in urban spaces and to reinstate traditional familial and business structures. Elsewhere I deal specifically with the methodological lessons that debates about gender and child labour bring to developmental psychological models (Burman 2006b).

3 This discussion remains unresolved, but there are useful analyses evaluating its conceptual and political consequences (Rao 1995; Phillips 2007).

4 Once again, these trends remain the same, despite creative interventions that attempt to support children's access to educational provision, including mobile and work-based schooling. Ansell (2005, Chapter 5) provides a useful overview of both the positive and critical arguments regarding the promotion of education and schooling within international development policy, together with some useful case studies drawn from different southern contexts.

5 A key example discussed in Burman (1996a) is the ideologically significant changes made to Bronfenbrenner's (1979) influential 'ecological model' of development. In this I trace how Bronfenbrenner's model of development of concentric, nested 'ecological niches' has undergone significant transformation from its original formulation to its inscription within international development policy documents. While Bronfenbrenner (1979) positions the mother–baby unit as the central 'nest', to reflect an indissolubly interpersonal and social model of development, this is changed in Myers' (1992) influential text, itself a key resource expressing and informing UNICEF policies, to place the baby alone at its centre. Thus, this returns a significant anti-individualist developmental psychological model to an individualist approach. In my discussion (Burman 1996c) I connect this textual transformation with the rise of abstracted parent training models within UNICEF, and the tension between indigenous culture and education that this initial split thereby engenders. In Burman (2008) I also note how the same error is made in some current developmental psychology textbook accounts that discuss Bronfenbrenner's model.

9 The abnormal distribution of development: policies for Southern women and children

1 As Ansell (2005: 135) notes, this trend remains the same, although 'there are 23 countries where more girls attend school than boys, there are 59 where boys' primary school attendance exceeds that of girls (UNICEF 2002c). Where the gender gap favours boys it is more often large and entrenched. There are 11 countries . . . where the gender gap in attendance is 10 percentage points or more (UNICEF 2002c)'.

2 This is a strategy that CEDAW and the section of the UN concerned with the Advancement of Women is also adopting: http://www.un.org/womenwatch/daw/egm/enabling-environment2005/index.html (see also Henshall Momsen 2004).

3 A conjoint perspective on the shared positioning of girls and women that both CEDAW and UNIFEM continue to maintain (see e.g. http://www.un.org/womenwatch/daw/egm/enabling-environment2005/index.html, UNIFEM 2003, 2007; Moser 2007.

4 Niewenhuys (2001) has amply documented how children's and especially girls' labour, together with women's, is the last resource available for (what she calls) 'superexploitation' from the world's poor (see also the reviews of this issue in Nieuwenhuys 2000; Henshall Momsen 2004; Ansell 2005).
5 Lister's (2005, 2006), Kabeer's (2005) and Henshall Momsen's (2005) analyses confirm that this trend has intensified in the twenty-first century, albeit in slightly different ways across the North and South.
6 CEDAW (2005) (http://www.un.org/womenwatch/daw/egm/enabling-environment2005/index.html) goes further to emphasise the inextricable links between education, health and employment issues, plus addressing how globalisation has intensified the oppression of women and girls.

10 Rhetorics of psychological development: from complicity to resistance

1 The trend towards structuring infant observation into psychotherapy trainings is, if anything, increasing – with some proposals even arguing that this would be relevant for other therapeutic modalities, such as group therapy.
2 Since the publication of this text, we have of course seen a massive development in the rise of virtual reality media, with the virtual interactive 'game' Second Life being a case in point. For an analysis that explicitly connects discussions of shifting forms of sexuality with technology, see also Gordo López and Cleminson (2004).
3 I am thinking here of activities that children engage in which are typically associated with 'deviant' childhoods – such as work and political engagement (including armed conflict).

11 Between two debts: points of suspension in childhood and economic development

1 Indeed the government agency commissioning this research (the British Home Office) pressed forward with measures to raise the age of a sponsored spouse to 21 years even before the delivery of the final research report. This example would seem to serve as a precise exemplification not only of political opportunism but also the discretionary relationship between research and policy – in this case even where the policymakers have commissioned the research.
2 Rose (1985) offers documentation indicating that early twentieth-century medicine became wedded to a social environmentalist perspective that was consistent with a focus on investments to improve public health, while the budding psychologists of this time focused on the classification and evaluation of individual differences, as linked to eugenic theories. While Richards (1997) offers a carefully framed historical assessment of the (limited and not exclusive) complicities of the discipline of psychology within scientific racism, Rose highlights the different perspectives adopted by the two disciplines of psychology and medicine, and also how the rivalry between them focused on which could come up with a testing apparatus first. A key claim of Rose's account is that psychology's increasing status relied upon the success of this claim to testing expertise, and it is because of this that psychology has become an administrative discipline focused on technologies of assessment rather than having any clearly formulated or tenable theoretical basis as its core. It is this rather circular relationship between psychological techniques and social policy, alongside the increasing circulation of psychological notions in culture, that gave rise to what both Rose (1985) and

Ingleby (1985) termed the 'psy complex' and contributes to subsequent discussions of governmentality (Rose 1990; Hultqvist and Dahlberg 2001).

12 Between two deaths: reconfiguring metaphorics and ethics of childhood

1 Joan Copjec ends her analysis of *Antigone* on a similar note: 'Creon's hounding of Polynices [sic] beyond the limit of death prefigures modern science's hounding of the subject beyond death, apparently without limit, into infinitely extendable states (in principle, at least) of *coma passé*. When she covers the exposed body of her brother, Antigone raises herself out of the conditions of naked existence to which Creon remains bound' (Copjec 2004: 47).
2 'Antigone takes her stand as it were in the "cut" between language and "meaning", in the fault line that ensures that no single signifier can pretend to ground "being". In the final analysis, meaning comes from nothing – "ex nihilo" – from the "cut" that language makes in the real' (De Kesel, forthcoming: 11).
3 As De Kesel puts it: 'Antigone's beauty was . . . to do with her locus of her appearance, the site "between two deaths". In this phantasmatic place, she can only function as a signifier and her beauty confirms the explicitly symbolic status of her person. Only in this capacity does she fully confront us with the desire we are, and purify us of all imaginary (self)images that miscognize this' (De Kesel, forthcoming: 31).
4 Laurence Bataille later became what Roudinesco describes as 'one of the best psychoanalysts of her generation, occupying a central place in the harem of the Lacanian movement' (Roudinesco 1999: 188).
5 Copjec's (2004) analysis deals extensively with (following a Lacanian diagnostic typology) what hysterical and perverse forms of visual representations can reveal about political and subjective conditions.
6 More specifically: 'Succession alone allows the individual enquirer to be taken up and included within the whole without limits of humanity, and it alone saves society from the pulverization of time. This solution also smoothes the structural insatisfaction, the unbearable gap, between the individual, whose share of progress is miniscule, and posterity, which "possesses in abundance" the happiness the individual seeks. Finally, this solution allows one to argue that the limits of human knowledge are merely temporal and thus capable of being gradually eliminated' (Copjec 2004: 24–25).
7 Here Butler (2000) adds a further challenge, exposing the particularity of the (representation of the) symbolic order: 'But why is the symbolic place singular and its inhabitants multiple . . . The structure is purely formal, its defenders say, but note how its very formalism secures the structure against critical challenge' (p. 71).
8 As she puts it: 'Focused on the finite, modern man can no longer reliably sustain the old idea of eternity, but he does manage to reconstitute an alternative from a scrap left behind by the old idea. This leftover or remainder is the superego, the libidinally cathected belief that there is – if not a heaven – at least something that escapes the ravages of historical contingency. The idea is a negative one, nothing more than the conviction that between our expectations and their realization there is always a shortfall, some compromise. Yet it is what survives of eternity in the modern world, and it lends to certain notion of race an element of ideality that is the source of its profound violence and its disdain for every historical obstacle, every contingency that opposes it' (Copjec 2004: 105–106).

References

Ahmed, S. (2004a) 'Declarations of whiteness: the nonperformativity of antiracism', *Borderlands e-journal* 4, 3. http://www.borderlandsejournal.adelaide.edu.au/vol3no2_2004/ahmed_declarations.htm (accessed 5 January 2007).

—— (2004b) *The Cultural Politics of Emotion*, Edinburgh: Edinburgh University Press.

Ailwood, J. (2007) 'Learning or earning in the "smart state": changing tactics for governing early childhood', *Childhood*, in press.

Aitken, G. and Burman, E. (1999) 'Keeping and crossing professional barriers: "race" and gender in psychotherapeutic research', *Psychology of Women Quarterly* 23, 2: 277–297.

Alderson, P. (2002) 'Young children's health care rights and consent', pp. 155–167 in B. Franklin (ed.) *The New Handbook of Children's Rights*, Abingdon: Routledge.

Alldred, P. (1995) '"Fit to parent"? Developmental psychology and non-traditional families', in E. Burman, P. Alldred, C. Bewley, B. Goldberg, C. Heenan, D. Marks, J. Marshall, K. Taylor, R. Ullah and S. Warner, *Challenging Women: Psychology's Exclusions, Feminist Possibilities*, Maidenhead: Open University Press.

—— (1996) 'Whose expertise? Conceptualising mothers' resistance to advice about childcare', in E. Burman, G. Aitken, P. Alldred, R. Allwood, T. Billington, B. Goldberg, A. Górdo Lopez, C. Heenan, D. Marks, S. Warner, *Psychology Discourse Practice: From Regulation to Resistance*, London: Taylor & Francis.

Alldred, P. and Burman, E. (2005) 'Hearing and interpreting children's voices: discourse analytic contributions', pp. 175–198 in S. Greene and D. Hogan (eds) *Researching Children's Experience: Approaches and Methods*, London: Sage.

Alldred, P. and Gillies, V. (2002) 'Eliciting research accounts: re/producing modern subjects?', pp. 146–165 in M. Mauthner, M. Birch and T. Miller (eds) *Ethics in Qualitative Research*, London: Sage.

Alston, P. (1994) 'The best interests principle: towards a reconciliation of culture and human rights', in P. Alston (ed.) *The Best Interests of the Child: Reconciling Culture and Human Rights*, Oxford and New York: Oxford University Press.

Amos, V. and Parmar, P. (1984) 'Challenging imperial feminism', *Feminist Review* 17: 3–20.

Ansell, N. (2005) *Children, Youth and Development*, Abingdon: Routledge.

Anthias, F. and Yuval-Davis, N. (1993) *Racialized Boundaries: Race, Nation, Gender, Colour and Class and the Anti-racist Struggle*, London: Routledge.

Antrobus, P. (1989) 'Women in development', paper presented at XVth Annual General Assembly of Development Non-Governmental Organisations, Brussels, 18–21 April.

Antze, P. and Lambek, M. (eds) (1996) *Tense Past: Cultural Essays in Trauma and Memory*, London: Routledge.

Archard, D. (1993) *Children: Rights and Childhood*, London: Routledge.

Ariès, P. (1962) *Centuries of Childhood*, London: Jonathan Cape.

Athmal, H. (2006) *Driven to Desperate Measures*, London: Institute of Race Relations.

Attar, D. (1988) 'Who's holding the bottle? The politics of breastfeeding', *Trouble and Strife* 13: 33–39.

—— (1992) 'The demand that time forgot', *Trouble and Strife* 23: 24–29.

Batliwale, S. (1984) 'Rural energy situation: consequences for women's health', *Socialist Health Review* 1, 2: 21.

Beinart, J. (1992) 'Darkly through a lens: changing perceptions of the African child in sickness and in health, 1900–1945', pp. 220–243 in R. Cooter (ed.) *In the Name of the Child*, London: Routledge.

Bell, V. (1993a) *Interrogating Incest*, London: Routledge.

—— (1993b) 'Governing childhood: neo-liberalism and the law', *Economy and Society* 22: 390–405.

—— (2003) 'The vigilant(e) parent and the paedophile: the *News of the World* campaign 2000 and the contemporary governmentality of child sexual abuse', pp. 108–128 in P. Reavey and S. Warner (eds) *New Feminist Stories of Child Sexual Abuse: Sexual Scripts and Dangerous Dialogues*, London: Routledge.

Benjamin, J. (1998) *The Shadow of the Other: Intersubjectivity and Gender in Psychoanalysis*, London: Routledge.

Benjamin, W. (1970a) 'Theses on the philosophy of history', in W. Benjamin *Illuminations*, trans. H. Zohn, London: Jonathan Cape.

—— (1970b) 'The task of the translator', in W. Benjamin *Illuminations*, trans. H. Zohn, London: Jonathan Cape.

—— (2006) *Berlin Childhood Around 1900*, trans. Howard Eiland, Cambridge, MA: Belnap Press.

Berman, L. (1993) *Beyond the Smile: The Therapeutic Use of the Photograph*, London: Routledge.

Bettelheim, B. (1983) *The Uses of Enchantment*, Harmondsworth: Penguin.

—— (1985) *Surviving the Holocaust*, London: Flamingo.

Billington, T. (2000) *Separating, Losing and Excluding Children*, London: Falmer.

—— (2006) *Working with Children: Assessment, Intervention and Representation*, London: Sage.

Billington, T. and Pomerantz, M. (eds) (2003) *Children at the Margins: Supporting Children, Supporting Schools*, Stoke on Trent: Trentham Books.

Birke, L. (1992) *Women, Feminism and Biology*, Lewes: Harvester.

Black, M. (1992) *A Cause for Our Times: Oxfam – the first 50 years*, Oxford: Oxfam.

Bloch, M., Kennedy, D., Lightfoot, T. and Weyenberg, D. (2006) *The Child in the World/The World in the Child: Education and the Configuration of a Universal, Modern and Globalized Childhood*, New York: Palgrave/Macmillan.

Blum, H. (1994) *Reconstruction in Psychoanalysis: Childhood Revisited and Recreated*, Madison, CT: International Universities Press.

Bollas, C. (1995) *Cracking Up*, London: Routledge.

Bondi, L. (1993) 'Locating identity politics', in M. Keith and J. Pale (eds) *Place and the Politics of Identity*, London: Routledge.

Bornstein, E. (2001) 'Child sponsorship, evangelism and belonging in the work of World Vision Zimbabwe', *American Ethnologist* 28, 3: 595–622.

Bourke, J. (2004) 'Gender, rape and modern war', paper presented at Gender and War dayschool, Centre for the Study of Women and Gender, Warwick University, May.

Bower, J. (1990) 'All hail the great abstraction: star wars and the politics of cognitive psychology', pp. 127–140 in I. Parker and J. Shotter (eds) *Deconstructing Social Psychology*, London: Routledge.

Boyden, J. (1990) 'Childhood and the policy makers: a comparative perspective on the globalization of childhood', pp. 184–215 in A. James and A. Prout (eds) *Constructing and Reconstructing Childhood: Contemporary Issues in the Sociological Study of Childhood*, Basingstoke: Falmer.

—— (1993) 'The development of indicators for the monitoring of the Convention on the Rights of the Child', Report for Rädda Barnen.

Boyden, J. and Hudson, A. (1985) *Children: Rights and Responsibilities*, London: Minority Rights Group.

Boyden, J. with Holden, P. (1991) *Children of the Cities*, London: Zed Books.

Bradley, B. (1989) *Visions of Infancy*, Oxford: Polity/Blackwell.

Brandon, S., Boakes, J., Glaser, D. and Green, R. (1998) 'Recovered memories of childhood abuse: implications for clinical practice', *British Journal of Psychiatry* 172: 297–307.

Bravo, J. (2005) 'In the interests of the child? Black women, staff and professional perspectives on issues affecting black children who have experienced domestic violence', unpublished MSc psychology thesis, Manchester Metropolitan University; also presented as paper at Critical Health Psychology Conference, Sheffield, April.

British Psychological Society (1995) *Recovered Memories*, Leicester: BPS.

Brodersen, M. (1996) *Walter Benjamin: A Biography*, London: Verso.

Bronfenbrenner, U. (1977) 'Towards an experimental ecology of human development', *American Psychologist* 32: 513–531.

—— (1979) *The Ecology of Human Development*, Cambridge, MA: Harvard University Press.

Broughton, J. (1981a) 'Piaget's structural developmental psychology I: Piaget and structuralism', *Human Development* 24: 78–109.

—— (1981b) 'Piaget's structural developmental psychology III: logic and psychology', *Human Development* 24: 195–224.

—— (ed.) (1987) *Critical Theories of Psychological Development*, New York: Plenum Press.

—— (1988) 'The masculine authority of the cognitive', in B. Inhelder (ed.) *Piaget Today*, New York: Academic Press.

Brown, L. and Burman, E. (1997) 'Feminist responses to the delayed memory debate: an editorial introduction', *Feminism & Psychology* 7, 1: 7–16.

Burgin, V., Donald, J. and Kaplan, C. (eds) (1986) *Formations of Fantasy*, London: Methuen.

Burman, E. (1990a) 'Differing with deconstruction: a feminist critique', pp. 208–220

in I. Parker and J. Shotter (eds) *Deconstructing Social Psychology*, London: Routledge.
—— (1990b) 'Time, language and power in modern developmental psychology', unpublished PhD thesis, University of Manchester.
—— (1991) 'Power, gender and developmental psychology', *Feminism & Psychology* 1, 1: 141–153.
—— (1992a) 'Feminism and discourse in developmental psychology: power, subjectivity and interpretation', *Feminism & Psychology* 2, 1: 45–60.
—— (1992b) 'Developmental psychology, and the postmodern child', in J. Doherty, E. Graham and M. Malek (eds) *Postmodernism and the Social Sciences*, London: Macmillan.
—— (1993) 'Towards a non-relativist discursive psychology: subjectivity and power in developmental research', pp. 433–442 in B. Caplan, W. Thorngate and H. Stam (eds) *Recent Developments in Theoretical Psychology*, New York: Springer Verlag.
—— (1994a) 'Poor children: charity appeals and ideologies of childhood', *Changes: International Journal of Psychology and Psychotherapy* 12, 1: 29–36.
—— (1994b) 'Innocents abroad: projecting western fantasies of childhood onto the iconography of emergencies', *Disasters: Journal of Disaster Studies and Management* 18, 3: 238–253.
—— (1994c) *Deconstructing Developmental Psychology*, London: Routledge.
—— (1994d) 'Developmental phallacies: psychology, gender and childhood', *Agenda: A Journal about Women and Gender* 22: 11–20.
—— (1995a) 'The spec(tac)ular economy of difference', *Feminism & Psychology* 5, 4: 543–546.
—— (1995b) 'The natural rights of the child', pp. 88–94 in I. Lubek, R. van Hezewijk, G. Pheterson and C. Tolman (eds) *Recent Developments in Theoretical Psychology*, New York: Springer Verlag.
—— (1995c) 'What is it? Masculinity and femininity in the cultural representation of childhood', pp. 47–67 in S. Wilkinson and C. Kitzinger (eds) *Feminism and Discourse*, London: Sage.
—— (1996/7) 'False memories, true hopes: revenge of the postmodern on therapy', *New Formations* 30: 122–134.
—— (1996a) 'Local, global or globalized: child development and international child rights legislation', *Childhood: A Global Journal of Child Research* 3, 1: 45–66.
—— (1996b) 'Continuities and discontinuities in interpretative and textual approaches to developmental psychology', *Human Development* 39: 330–349.
—— (1996c) 'Constructing and deconstructing childhood: images of children and charity appeals', pp. 170–184 in J. Haworth (ed.) *Psychological Research: Innovative Methods and Strategies*, London: Routledge.
—— (1997a) 'Telling stories: psychologists, children and the production of "false memories"', *Theory & Psychology* 7, 3: 291–309.
—— (1997b) 'Developmental psychology', pp. 134–149 in D. Fox and I. Pririlltensky (eds) *Critical Psychology: An Introduction*, London: Sage.
—— (1998a) 'Disciplinary apprentices: "qualitative methods" in student psychological research', *International Journal of Social Research Methodology, Theory and Practice* 1, 1: 25–46.
—— (1998b) 'Children, false memories and disciplinary alliances: tensions between

developmental psychology and psychoanalysis', *Psychoanalysis and Contemporary Thought* 21, 3: 307–333.
—— (ed.) (1998c) *Deconstructing Feminist Psychology*, London: Sage.
—— (1999) 'The child and the cyborg: metaphors of abjection and subjection', in A. Gordo López and I. Parker (eds) *Cyberpsychology*, London: Macmillan.
—— (2000) 'Method, measurement, and madness', pp. 49–78 in L. Holzman and J. Morss (eds) *Postmodern Psychologies, Societal Practices and Political Life*, London: Routledge.
—— (2001a) 'Engendering authority in the group', *Psychodynamic Counselling* 7, 3: 347–369.
—— (2001b) 'Fictioning authority', *Psychodynamic Counselling* 7, 2: 187–205.
—— (2002a) 'Therapy as memorywork: dilemmas of construction and reconstruction', *British Journal of Psychotherapy* 18, 4: 457–469.
—— (2002b) 'Madres cuidadosamente observadas', *Cuardenos de Psicología Social* 1: 207–218.
—— (2003a) 'Narratives of challenging research: stirring tales of politics and practice', *International Journal of Social Research Methodology* 6, 2: 101–119.
—— (2003b) 'Narratives of experience and pedagogical practices', *Narrative Inquiry* 13, 2: 269–286.
—— (2003c) 'Childhood and contemporary political subjectivities', pp. 34–51 in P. Reavey and S. Warner (eds) *New Feminist Stories of Child Sexual Abuse: Challenging the Tyranny of Truth*, London: Routledge.
—— (2004a) 'Taking women's voices: the psychological politics of feminisation', *Psychology of Women Section Review* 6, 1: 3–21.
—— (2004b) 'Boundary objects and group analysis: between psychoanalysis and social theory', *Group Analysis* 37, 3: 361–379.
—— (2004c) 'Organising for change? Group analytic perspectives on a feminist action research project', *Group Analysis* 37, 1: 93–110.
—— (2005a) 'Childhood, neoliberalism and the feminisation of childhood', *Gender and Education* 17, 4: 251–267.
—— (2005b) 'Engendering culture in psychology', *Theory & Psychology* 15, 4: 527–548.
—— (2005c) 'Kinder und Sexualität', *Das Argument* 260: 237–251.
—— (2006a) 'Emotions, reflexivity and feminised action research', *Educational Action Research* 14, 3: 315–332.
—— (2006b) 'Engendering development: some methodological perspectives on child labour', *Forum for Qualitative Social Research* 7, 1: http://www.qualitative-research/net/fqs -texte/1-06/06-1-1-e.pdf (accessed 5 January 2007).
—— (2007a) 'Developmental psychology', in W. Stainton Rogers and C. Willig (eds) *Handbook of Qualitative Methods in Psychology*, London: Sage.
—— (2007b) 'Between orientalism and normalisation: cross-cultural lessons from Japan for a critical history of psychology', *History of Psychology* 10, 2: 179–198.
—— (2008) *Deconstructing Developmental Psychology*, 2nd edn, London: Brunner-Routledge.
—— (in press, a) 'Beyond "women vs. children" or "womenandchildren": engendering childhood and reformulating motherhood', *International Journal of Children's Rights*.
—— (in press, b) 'Beyond emotional literacy in feminist research', *British Education Research Journal*.

—— (in press, c) 'Therapy and memorywork: political dilemmas of (re)construction', in J. Haaken and P. Reavey (eds) *Memory Matters: Contexts for Understanding Recollections of Sexual Abuse*, London: Routledge.

Burman, E. and Chantler, K. (2004) 'There's "no place" like home: researching, "race" and refuge provision', *Gender, Place and Culture* 11, 3: 375–397.

—— (2005) 'Domestic violence and minoritisation: legal and policy barriers facing minoritised women leaving violent relationships', *International Journal of Law and Psychiatry* 28, 1: 59–74.

Burman, E. and MacLure, M. (2005) 'Deconstruction as a method of research: stories from the field', pp. 284–292 in B. Somekh and C. Lewin (eds) *Research Methods in the Social Sciences*, London: Sage.

Burman, E. and Parker I. (eds) (1993) *Discourse Analytic Research: Repertoires and Readings of Texts in Action*, London: Routledge.

Burman, E., Gowrisunkur, J. and Sangha, K. (1998) 'Conceptualising cultural and gendered identities in psychological therapies: models and practices', *European Journal of Psychotherapy, Health and Counselling* 1, 2: 231–256.

Burman, E., Chantler, K. and Batsleer, J. (2002) 'Service responses to South Asian women who attempt suicide or self-harm', *Critical Social Policy* 22, 4: 641–669.

Burman, E., Smailes, S. and Chantler, K. (2004) '"Culture" as a barrier to domestic violence services for minoritised women', *Critical Social Policy* 24, 3: 358–384.

Burnell, P. (1991) *Charity, Politics and the Third World*, Hemel Hempstead: Harvester.

Burr, R. (2006) *Vietnam's Children in a Changing World*, New Brunswick, NJ: Rutgers University Press.

Burton, M. and Kagan, C. (2007) 'Psychologists and torture: more than a question of interrogation', *The Psychologist (Monthly Magazine of the British Psychological Society)* 20, 8: 484–487.

Butler, J. (1990) *Gender Trouble*, London: Routledge.

—— (1993) *Bodies That Matter*, London: Routledge.

—— (1997) *The Psychic Life of Power*, Stanford: Stanford University Press.

—— (2000) *Antigone's Claim*, New York: Columbia University Press.

Bywater, M. (2006) *Big Babies, Or: Why Can't We Just Grow Up?*, London: Granta.

Cairns, E. (1992) 'Society as abuse: Northern Ireland', pp. 119–128 in W. Stainton Rogers, D. Heavey, J. Roche and E. Ash (eds) *Child Abuse and Neglect: Facing the Challenge*, 2nd edn, Milton Keynes: Open University Press.

Cameron, J. (2005) 'Journeying in radical development studies: a reflection on thirty years of researching pro-poor development', pp. 138–156 in U. Kothari (ed.) *A Radical History of Development Studies*, London: Zed Books.

Canella, G. and Viruru, R. (2004) *Childhood and Postcolonization*, New York: RoutledgeFalmer.

Cantwell, N. (1992) 'The origins, development and significance of the United Nations Convention on the Rights of the Child', in S. Detrick (ed.) *The United Nations Convention On The Rights Of The Child: A Guide To The 'Travaux Préparatoires'*, Dordrecht: Martinus Nijhoff.

Carby, H. (1987) 'Black feminism and the boundaries of sisterhood', in M. Arnot and G. Weiner (eds) *Gender and the Politics of Schooling*, London: Hutchinson.

Carter, A. (1992) *Wise Children*, London: Faber.

Castoriadis, C. (1994) 'Radical imagination and the social instituting imaginary', pp.

136–154 in G. Robinson and J. Kendall (eds) *Rethinking Imagination: Culture and Creativity*, London: Routledge.

Chakrabarty, D. (2000) *Provincializing Europe: Postcolonial Thought and Historical Difference*, Princeton, NJ: Princeton University Press.

Chambers, R. (2005) 'Critical reflections of a development nomad', pp. 67–88 in U. Kothari (ed.) *A Radical History of Development Studies*, London: Zed Books.

Chantler, K. (2006) 'Independency and interdependence: struggles and resistances of minoritized women within and on leaving violent relationships', *Feminist Review* 82: 26–48.

Chantler, K., Burman, E., Batsleer, J. and Bashir, C. (2001) *Attempted Suicide and Self-Harm (South Asian Women)*, Manchester: Women's Studies Research Centre, Manchester Metropolitan University.

Chatterjee, S.K. (2005) 'Measurement of human development: an alternative approach', *Journal of Human Development* 6, 1: 31–44.

Chaudhuri, N. and Strobel, M. (eds) (1992) *Western Women and Imperialism*, Bloomington: Indiana University Press.

Cheney, D. (1996) 'Those whom the immigration law has kept apart – let no one join together: a view on immigration incantation', pp. 36–47 in D. Jarrett-Macauley (ed.) *Reconstructing Womanhood, Reconstructing Feminism: Writings on Black Women*, London: Routledge.

Chernaik, L. (1996) 'Spatial displacements: transnationalism and the new social movements', *Gender, Place and Culture* 3, 3: 251–277.

Cherry, F. (1995) *The Stubborn Particulars of Social Psychology*, London: Routledge.

Ching-Liang Low, G. (1989) 'White skins/black masks: the pleasures and politics of imperialism', *New Formations* 9, 24: 96.

Christensen, P. (2000) 'Childhood and the cultural construction of vulnerable bodies', pp. 38–59 in A. Prout (ed.) *The Body, Childhood and Society*, Basingstoke: Macmillan.

Clark, J. (2006) 'Discourses of transition in South Africa: a critical feminist analysis of Black women's life narratives within the cultural-political project of nation', unpublished doctoral thesis, Manchester Metropolitan University.

CLE (Continuing Legal Education, 2007, April), 'Definition of "child"'. http://mrc/Isuc.on.ca.jsp/pageFromCLE/loadPageCleMonth.do?id=32 (accessed 23 May 2007).

Cohen, S. (2001) *Immigration Controls, the Family and the Welfare State*, London: Jessica Kingsley Publishers.

Colclough, C. with Lewin, T. (1993) *Education for All: Strategies for Primary Schooling in the South*, Oxford: Clarendon Press.

Cole, M. and Cole, S. (1989) *The Development of Children*, New York: Scientific American Press.

Collins, C. (2003) '"Critical psychology" and contemporary struggles against neo-liberalism', *Annual Review of Critical Psychology* 3: 26–48.

Conley, D. (2004) *The Pecking Order: Which Siblings Succeed and Why*, New York: Vintage.

Cooke, B. (2001) 'The social psychological limits of participation', pp. 102–121 in B. Cooke and U. Kothari (eds) *Participation: The New Tyranny*, London: Zed Books.

Cooke, B. and Kothari, U. (eds) (2001) *Participation: The New Tyranny?*, London: Zed Books.

Copjec, J. (2004) *Imagine There's No Woman: Ethics and Sublimation*, Cambridge, MA: MIT Press.

Coulson, M. and Bhavnani, K. (1990) 'Making a difference: questioning women's studies', in E. Burman (ed.) *Feminists and Psychological Practice*, London: Sage. Full text available on www.discourseunit.com

Coulter, P. (1989) 'Pretty as a picture', *New Internationalist*, April: 10–12.

Cowen, M. and Shenton, R. (1996) *Doctrines of Development*, London: Routledge.

Cowie, C. and Lees, S. (1981) 'Slags or drags', *Feminist Review* 9: 17–31.

Cradock, G. (2006) 'Distributing children's rights and responsibilities: children and the neoliberal state', paper presented at the Child and Youth Rights Conference; Investment and Citizenship: Towards a Transdisciplinary Dialogue on Child and Youth Rights, Brock University, Canada, July.

—— (2007) 'The responsibility dance: learning or earning in the neoliberal state', *Childhood* 14, 2: 153–172.

Creed, B. (1987) 'Horror and the monstrous feminine: an imaginary abjection', *Screen* 28, 1: 44–70.

Crewe, E. and Harrison, E. (1998) *Whose Development? An Ethnography of Aid*, London: Zed Books.

Croll, E. (2006) 'From the girl child to girls' rights', *Third World Quarterly* 27, 7: 1285–1297.

Crush, J. (ed.) (1995) *Power of Development*, London: Routledge.

Cunningham, H. (2002) 'Ideals of childhood and the rights of the child: an historical perspective', paper presented at the Contested Childhoods in a Changing Global Order Series, University of Michigan.

Dahlberg, G. and Moss, P. (2005) *Ethics and Politics in Early Childhood Education*, London and New York: RoutledgeFalmer.

Dahlberg, G., Moss, P. and Pence, A. (1999) *Beyond Quality in Early Childhood Education and Care: Postmodern Perspectives*, London and New York: RoutledgeFalmer.

Daly, M. (1981) *GynlEcology*, London: Women's Press.

Danziger, K. (1997) 'The varieties of social constructionism', *Theory & Psychology* 7: 399–416.

David, M. (1988) 'Home–school relations', in A. Green and S. Ball (eds) *Progress and Inequality in Comprehensive Education*, Basingstoke: Macmillan.

David, M., Alldred, P. and Smith, P. (no date) 'Briefing paper for head teachers and PSHE co-ordinators: "Get Real About Sex": linking sex and relationship education to the achievement agenda – a report of the SRE Policy Action Research commissioned by Stoke-on-Trent LEA', Keele University.

Davies, B. and Gannon, S. (2005) 'Feminism/poststructuralism', pp. 318–326 in B. Somekh and C. Lewin (eds) *Research Methods in the Social Sciences*, London: Sage.

Dawes, A. and Donald, D. (eds) (1994) *Children and Adversity: Psychological Perspectives from South African Research*, Cape Town: David Philip.

De Kesel, M. (forthcoming) New York: SUNY Press.

Deleuze, G. and Guattari, F. (1977) *Anti-Oedipus: capitalism and schizophrenia*, London: Viking Press.

Department for Education and Skills (DfES, 2003) *Every Child Matters*, Green Paper, Cm. 5860, London: The Stationery Office.
De Rivero, O. (2001) *The Myth of Development: The Non-viable Economies of the 21st Century*, London: Zed Books.
Derrida, J. (1994) *Spectres of Marx*, London: Routledge.
Desai, M. (2006) 'Review of government of India's approach to child right to protection', paper presented at 'Investment and Citizenship: Towards a Trans-disciplinary Dialogue on Child and Youth Rights', Brock University, Canada, July.
Descombes, V. (1979) *Modern French Philosophy*, Cambridge: Cambridge University Press.
Despotis, D. (2005) 'A reassessment of the human development index via data envelopment analysis', *Journal of the Operational Research Society* 56: 969–980.
Dews, P. (1987) *Logics of Disintegration*, London: Verso.
De Zulueta, F. (2006) *From Pain to Violence: The Roots of Human Destructiveness*, 2nd edn, Chichester: Wiley.
Dingwall, R. and Eekelaar, J. (1986) 'Judgements of Solomon: developmental psychology and family law', in M. Richards and P. Light (eds) *Children Of Social Worlds*, Oxford: Polity Press.
Dinnerstein, D. (1978) *The Rocking of the Cradle and the Ruling of the World*, London: Souvenir Press.
Doderer, K. (1996) 'A "hermaphroditic position": Benjamin, postmodernism and the frenzy of gender', pp. 76–82 in G. Fischer (ed.) *'With the Sharpened Axe of Reason': Approaches to Walter Benjamin*, Oxford: Berg.
Downick, S. and Grundberg, S. (eds) (1980) *Why Children?*, London: Women's Press.
Droz, Y. (2006) 'Street children and the work ethic: new policy for an old moral, Nairobi (Kenya)', *Childhood* 13, 3: 349–363.
Drucker, D. (1986) 'Viewpoint on community participation: now you see it, now you don't', *Unicef News* 124: 2–3.
Duden, B. (1992) 'Population', in W. Sachs (ed.) *The Development Dictionary: A Guide to Knowledge as Power*, London: Zed Books.
Duffield, M. (2001) *Global Governance and the New Wars*, London: Zed Books.
Dunker, C. (2004) 'Truth structured like fiction: sexual theories of children viewed as narrative', *Journal for Lacanian Studies* 2, 2: 183–197.
Dunn, J. and Plomin, R. (1990) *Separate Lives: Why Siblings are so Different*, New York: Basic Books.
Eagleton, T. (1981) *Walter Benjamin: Or Towards a Revolutionary Criticism*, London: Verso.
—— (1985) 'Capitalism, modernism and post-modernism', *New Left Review* 152: 60–72.
Edelman, L. (2005) *No Future: Queer Theory and the Death Drive*, Durham and London: Duke University Press.
Edley, N. (2001) 'Unravelling social constructionism', *Theory & Psychology* 11, 3: 433–441.
Eekelaar, J. (1986) 'The emergence of child rights', *Oxford Journal of Legal Studies* 6: 161–182.
Elias, N. (2000) *The Civilising Process*, Oxford: Blackwell.
Ellenberger, H. (1970) *The Discovery of the Unconscious*, New York: Basic Books.

Elson, D. (1992) 'Public action, poverty and development: a gender aware analysis', paper presented at seminar on Women in Extreme Poverty: Integration of Women's Concerns in National Development Planning, Division for Advancement of Women, UN Office, Vienna, November.
Emerson, P. and Frosh, F. (2001) 'Young masculinities and sexual abuse: research connections', *Critical Psychology* 3: 72–93.
Ennew, J. (1986) *The Sexual Exploitation of Children*, Cambridge: Polity Press.
—— (1993) 'Monitoring the Convention on the Rights of the Child', report for Rädda Barnen.
Ennew, J. and Milne, B. (1989) *The Next Generation: Lives of Third World Children*, London: Zed Books.
Escobar, A. (1997) 'The making and unmaking of the third world through development', pp. 85–93 in M. Rahnema with V. Bawtree (eds) *The Post-Development Reader*, London: Zed Books.
Esteva, G. (1992) 'Development', in W. Sachs (ed.) *The Development Dictionary: A Guide to Knowledge as Power*, London: Zed Books.
Evans, M. (1990) 'The problem of gender for women's studies', *Women's Studies International Forum* 13, 5: 457–463.
Fischer, F. (1996) 'Benjamin's utopia of education as *Theatrum mundi et vitae* on the *Programme of a Proletarian Children's Theatre*', pp. 201–218 in G. Fischer (ed.) *'With the Sharpened Axe of Reason': Approaches to Walter Benjamin*, Oxford: Berg.
Fonagy, P. and Target, M. (2004) 'What can developmental psychopathology tell psychoanalysts about the mind?', pp. 307–342 in A. Casement (ed.) *Who Owns Psychoanalysis?*, London: Karnac.
Foress Bennett, J. (1997) '"This little girl who lives up a mountain": credibility, plausibility and the speech of the subject for autobiographical narratives of sexual assault', pp. 96–108 in A. Levett, A. Kottler, E. Burman and I. Parker (eds) *Culture, Power and Difference*, Cape Town and London: UCT Press and Zed Books.
Foster, D. (2004) 'Liberation psychology', pp. 559–603 in D. Hook, P. Kiguwe, N. Mkhize and A. Collins (eds) *Critical Psychology*, Cape Town: UCT Press.
Foster, J., Lopez-Calva, L., Szelcely, M. (2005) 'Measuring the distribution of human development: methodology and an application to Mexico', *Journal of Human Development* 6, 1: 5–25.
Foucault, M. (1977) 'Revolutionary action: "until now"', in M. Foucault *Language, Countermemory, Practice*, New York: Cornell University Press.
—— (1980a) 'Truth and power', in C. Gordon (ed.) *Michel Foucault: Power/Knowledge: Selected Interviews and Other Writings 1972–1977*, Brighton: Harvester.
—— (1980b) *Power/Knowledge: Selected Interviews and Other Writings*, Brighton: Harvester.
—— (1980c) *Herculine Barbin*, Brighton: Harvester.
—— (1981) *History of Sexuality, Vol. 1: An Introduction*, Harmondsworth: Penguin.
—— (2006) *Psychiatric Power*, London: Palgrave Macmillan.
Franklin, B. (2002a) 'Children's rights and media wrongs: changing representations of children and the developing rights agenda', pp. 15–42 in B. Franklin (ed.) *The New Handbook of Children's Rights*, Oxford: Routledge.
—— (ed.) (2002b) *The New Handbook of Children's Rights*, Oxford: Routledge.

Fraser, N. (1989) *Unruly Practices: Power, Discourse and Gender in Contemporary Social Theory*, London: Policy/Blackwell.
Freeman, M. (1993) 'Laws, conventions and rights', *Children & Society* 7, 1: 37–48.
—— (2000) 'The future of children's rights', *Children & Society* 14: 277–293.
—— (2002) 'Children's rights ten years after ratification', pp. 97–118 in B. Franklin (ed.) *The New Handbook of Children's Rights*, Oxford: Routledge.
Freeman, M. and Veerman, P. (eds) (1992) *The Ideologies of Children's Rights*, Dordrecht: Martinus Nijhoff.
Freud, S. (1905a) *Jokes and their Relations to the Unconscious*, Penguin Freud Library Vol. 6, Harmondsworth: Penguin.
—— (1905b) 'Three essays on the theory of sexuality', *Penguin Freud Library Vol. 7*, Harmondsworth: Penguin.
—— (1907) 'The sexual enlightenment of children (an open letter to Dr M. Furst)', *Penguin Freud Library, Vol. 7*, Harmondsworth: Penguin.
—— (1921) 'Group psychology and the analysis of the ego', *Pelican Freud Library, Vol. 12*, Harmondsworth: Penguin.
—— (1937) 'Constructions in analysis', pp. 255–269 in J. Strachey (ed.) *Standard Edition, Vol. 23*, London: Hogarth Press, 1966.
Frisby, D. (1996) 'Walter Benjamin's prehistory of modernity as anticipation of postmodernity? Some methodological reflections', pp. 15–32 in G. Fischer (ed.) *'With the Sharpened Axe of Reason': Approaches to Walter Benjamin*, Oxford: Berg.
Fulani, L. (1998) 'Beyond the ethic of care: the Kohlberg-Gilligan controversy revamped', pp. 140–158 in E. Burman (ed.) *Deconstructing Feminist Psychology*, London: Sage.
Gardner, F. (1996) 'Open to all possibilities', *British Journal of Psychotherapy* 12, 3: 343–349.
Gascoigne, L. (1991) 'Finding ways of working with women in patriarchal societies', in T. Wallace with C. March (eds) *Changing Perceptions: Writings on Gender and Development*, Oxford: Oxfam.
Gill, P. (1986) *A Year in the Death of Africa*, London: Paladin.
Gilligan, C. (1982) *In A Different Voice*, Boston, MA: Harvard University Press.
Gjerde, P. (2004) 'Culture, power and experience: towards a person-centred cultural psychology', *Human Development* 47: 138–157.
Glauser, B. (1990) 'Street children: deconstructing a construct', pp. 138–156 in A. James and A. Prout (eds) *Constructing and Reconstructing Childhood*, London: Falmer.
Glenn, E., Chang, G. and Forcey, L. (eds) (1995) *Mothering: Ideology, Experience, and Agency*, New York: Routledge.
Goodley, D. and Lawthom, R. (eds) (2004) *Psychology and Disability: Critical Introductions and Reflections*, London: Palgrave Macmillan.
Gordo López, A. and Burman, E. (2004) 'Emotional capital and information technologies in the changing rhetorics around children and childhoods', *New Directions in Child and Adolescent Development* 105: 63–80.
Gordo López, A. and Cleminson, R. (2004) *Techno-Sexual Landscapes: Changing Relations between Technology and Sexuality*, London: Free Association Books.
Gordo López, A. and Parker, I. (eds) (1999) *Cyberpsychology*, London: Macmillan.
Gordon, T. (1990) *Feminist Mothers*, London: Macmillan.

Graham, J. and Lynn, S. (1989) 'Mud huts and flints: children's images of the third world', *Education* 3–13 June: 29–32.
Gready, P. and Ensor, J. (2005) 'Introduction', pp. 1–46 in P. Gready and J. Ensor (eds) *Reinventing Development? Translating Rights-based Approaches from Theory into Practice*, London: Zed Books.
Gronemeyer, M. (1992) 'Helping', pp. 53–69 in W. Sachs (ed.) *The Development Dictionary: A Guide to Knowledge as Power*, London: Zed Books.
Gulrajni, M. (2000) 'Children's work and children's education: issues in development economics', discussion paper for International Conference on Rethinking Childhood: Working Children's Challenge to the Social Sciences, Bondy, Paris.
Haaken, J. (1998) *Pillar of Salt: Gender, Memory and the Perils of Looking Back*, London: Free Association Books.
—— (2002) 'Bitch and fem psychology: women, aggression and psychoanalytic social theory', *Journal for the Psychoanalysis of Culture and Society* 7, 2: 202–217.
—— (2003) 'Traumatic revisions: remembering abuse and the politics of forgiveness', pp. 77–93, in P. Reavey and S. Warner (eds) *New Feminist Stories of Child Sexual Abuse: Sexual Scripts and Dangerous Dialogues*, London: Routledge.
Hables Gray, C. with Figueroa-Sarriera, H.J. and Mentor, S. (eds) (1995) *The Cyborg Handbook*, London: Routledge.
Hacking, I. (1996) 'Memory sciences, memory politics', pp. 76–88 in P. Antze and M. Lambek (eds) *Tense Past: Cultural Essays in Trauma and Memory*, London: Routledge.
Hamilton, S. (1998) 'The cyborg, 11 years later: the not-so-surprising half-life of the Cyborg Manifesto', *Convergence* 3, 2: 104–120.
Hanmer, J. and Itzin, C. (eds) (2000) *Home Truths about Domestic Violence*, London: Routledge.
Haque, M.S. (2004) 'The myths of economic growth (GNP): implications for human development', pp. 1–24 in G. Muacumura and M.S. Haque (eds) *Handbook of Development Policy Studies*, New York: Marcel Dekker.
Harasym, S. (ed.) (1990) *The Postcolonial Critic, Gayatri Chakravorty Spivak, Interviews, Strategies, Dialogues*, London: Routledge.
Haraway, D. (1989) *Primate Visions: Gender, Race and Nature in the World of Modern Science*, London: Verso.
—— (1991a) 'A manifesto for cyborgs: science, technology and socialist feminism in the 1980s', in D. Haraway *Simians, Cyborgs and Women*, London: Verso.
—— (1991b) *Simians, Cyborgs and Women*, London: Verso.
Harding, S. (1993) 'Rethinking feminist standpoint epistemology: what is strong objectivity?', pp. 49–82 in L. Alcott and E. Potter (eds) *Feminist Epistemologies*, London: Routledge.
Harris, A. (1987) 'The rationalisation of infancy', in J. Broughton (ed.) *Critical Theories of Psychological Development*, New York: Plenum Press.
Harriss, J. (2005) 'Great promise, hubris and recovery: a participant's history of development studies', pp. 17–46 in U. Kothari (ed.) *A Radical History of Development Studies*, London: Zed Books.
Hart, A. (1989) 'Images of the third world', pp. 12–18 in M. Reeves and J. Hammond (eds) *Looking Beyond the Frame: Racism, Representation and Resistance*, Oxford: Third World First.
Hart, R. (1992) 'Climbing the participation ladder', *First Call for Children*, 2: 4.
Harvey, D. (1989) *The Condition of Postmodernity*, Oxford: Blackwell.

Hayter, T. (1971) *Aid as Imperialism*, Harmondsworth: Penguin.
—— (2005) 'Aid is still imperialism', in U. Kothari (ed.) *A Radical History of Development Studies: Individuals, Institutions and Ideologies*, Cape Town and London: David Philip and Zed Books.
Hekman, S. (1990) *Gender and Knowledge: Elements of a Postmodern Feminism*, London: Polity Press.
Hendrick, H. (1990) 'Constructions and reconstructions of British childhood: an interpretive survey 1800 to present day', pp. 35–59 in A. James and A. Prout (eds) *Constructing and Reconstructing Childhood*, London: Falmer.
—— (ed.) (2005) *Child Welfare and Social Policy*, Bristol: The Policy Press.
Henriques, J., Hollway, W., Urwin, C., Venn, C. and Walkerdine, V. (1984) *Changing the Subject: Psychology, Social Regulation and Subjectivity*, London: Methuen.
Henshall Momsen, J. (2004) *Gender and Development*, London: Routledge.
Hester, M., Chantler, K. and Gangoli, G. (2007) *Forced Marriage: The Risk Factors and the Effect of Raising the Minimum Age for a Sponsor, and of Leave to Enter the UK as a Spouse or Fiancé(e)*, London: The Home Office.
Hevener Kaufman, N. and Rizzini, I. (eds) (2002) *Globalization and Children: Exploring Potentials for Enhancing Opportunities in the Lives of Children and Youth*, New York: Kluwer Academic/Plenum.
Hill Collins, P. (1990) *Black Feminist Thought*, London: Routledge.
Hobart, M. (ed.) (1993) *An Anthropological Critique of Development: The Growth of Ignorance*, London: Routledge.
Hochschild, A.R. (2000) 'Global care chains and emotional surplus value', pp. 130–146 in W. Hutton and A. Giddens (eds) *On the Edge: Living with Global Capitalism*, London: Jonathan Cape.
Holland, P. (1992) *What is a Child? Popular Images of Childhood*, London: Virago.
Hollway, W. (1989) *Subjectivity and Method in Psychology*, London: Sage.
Hoyles, M. (1989) *The Politics of Childhood*, London: Journeyman.
Hrdy, S. (2003) 'The optimal number of fathers: evolution, demography and history in the shaping of female mate preferences', in D. LeCroy and P. Moller (eds) *Evolutionary Perspectives on Human Reproductive Behavior*, New York: Kluwer.
Hultqvist, K. and Dahlberg, G. (eds) (2001) *Governing the Child in the New Millennium*, New York and London: RoutledgeFalmer.
Imaging Famine (2005) http://www.imaging-famine.org/ (accessed 5 November 2006).
Ingleby, D. (1985) 'Professionals as socializers: the "psy complex"', *Research in Low, Deviance and Social Control* 7: 79–109.
Ingold, T. (2000) *The Perception of the Environment: Essays on Livelihood, Dwelling and Skill*, London: Routledge.
Irigaray, L. (1985) *Speculum of the Other Woman*, Ithaca, NY: Cornell University Press.
Jackson, S. (1992) 'The amazing deconstructing woman', *Trouble & Strife* 25: 25–31.
Jacquemin, M. (2006) 'Can the language of rights get hold of the complex realities of child domestic work? The case of young domestic workers in Abidjan, Ivory Coast', *Childhood* 13, 3: 389–406.
James, A. and Jenks, C. (1994) 'Public perceptions of childhood criminality', paper presented at the Childhood Studies Group day 'Childhood and Criminality', Keele University.

James, A. and Prout, A. (eds) (1990) *Constructing and Reconstructing Childhood*, London: Falmer.

James, A., Jenks, C. and Prout, A. (1998) *Theorizing Childhood*, Cambridge: Polity Press.

Jameson, F. (1984) 'Postmodernism, or the cultural logic of late capitalism', *New Left Review* 146: 53–93.

Jay, M. (1993) *Downcast Eyes: The Denigration of Vision in Twentieth-Century French Thought*, Berkeley: University of California Press.

Jenks, C. (1996) *Childhood*, London: Routledge.

Johnson, D. (1992) 'Cultural and regional pluralism in the drafting of the UN Convention on the Right of the Child', in M. Freeman and P. Veerman (eds) *The Ideologies of Children's Rights*, Dordrecht: Martinus Nijhoff.

Jordanova, L. (1989) 'Children in history: concepts of nature and society', in G. Scarre (ed.) *Children, Parents and Politics*, Cambridge: Cambridge University Press.

Josselson, J. (1987) *Finding Herself. Pathways to Identity Development in Women*, San Francisco and London: Jossey-Bass.

Jovchelovitch, S. (2004) *Knowledge in Context: Representations, Community and Culture*, London: Routledge.

Justice, J. (1989) *Policies, Plans and People*, London: Jessica Kingsley Publishers.

Kabeer, N. (1991) 'Gender dimensions of poverty. Analysis from Bangladesh', *Journal of Peasant Studies* 18: 241–262.

—— (1992) 'Feminist perspectives in development: a critical review', in H. Hinds, A. Phoenix and J. Stacey (eds) *Working Out: New Directions For Women's Studies*, Lewes: Falmer.

—— (ed.) (2005) *Inclusive Citizenship*, London: Zed Books.

Kamdar, S. (2005) 'Beyond the human development index: preliminary notes on deprivation and inequality', *Economic and Political Weekly* 40, 34: 3760–3761.

Kaplan, E.A. (1983) 'Is the gaze male?', pp. 321–338 in A. Snitow, C. Stansell and S. Thompson (eds) *Desire: The Politics of Sexuality*, London: Virago.

Kappeler, S. (1986) *The Pornography of Representation*, Oxford: Polity Press.

Katz, C. (1996) 'Towards minor theory', *Society & Space* 15: 487–499.

—— (2004) *Growing Up Global: Economic Restructuring and Children's Everyday Lives*, Minneapolis and London: University of Minnesota Press.

—— (2005) 'Partners in crime: neoliberalism and the production of new political subjectivities', pp. 227–236 in N. Laurie and L. Bondi (eds) *Working the Spaces of Neoliberalism: Activism, Professionalisation and Incorporation*, Oxford: Blackwell.

Kerr, D. (ed.) (1993) *Ours By Right: Women's Rights As Human Rights*, London: Zed Books.

Kessen, W. (1979) 'The American child and other cultural inventions', *American Psychologist* 34, 10: 815–820.

—— (1993) 'Avoiding the emptiness: the full child', *Theory & Psychology* 3, 4: 415–427.

Kincaid, J. (1992) *Child-Loving: The Erotic Child and Victorian Culture*, London: Routledge.

Kitzinger, C. and Wilkinson, S. (eds) (1992) *Heterosexuality*, London: Sage.

Kitzinger, J. (1988) 'Defending innocence: ideologies of childhood', *Feminist Review* 28: 77–87.

—— (1990) 'Who are you kidding? Children, power and the struggle against sexual abuse', pp. 157–183 in A. James and A. Prout (eds) *Constructing and Reconstructing Childhood*, London: Falmer.

Kjorholt, A.T. (2005) 'The competent child and the "right to be oneself": reflections on children as fellow citizens in an early childhood centre', pp. 151–175 in A. Clark, A. Kjorholt and P. Moss (eds) *Beyond Listening: Children's Perspectives on Early Children's Services*, Bristol: Policy Press.

Kleeberg-Niepage, A. (2005) 'Is there a childhood for children who work? Child labour and the western construction of childhood', paper presented at the International Society for Theoretical Psychology, University of the Western Cape, Cape Town.

Knorr-Cetina, K. (1997) 'What scientists do', pp. 260–272 in T. Ibáñez and L. Iñiguez (eds) *Critical Social Psychology*, London: Sage.

Kofsky Scholnick, E. (2000) 'Engendering development: metaphors of change', pp. 11–28 in P. Miller and E. Kofsky Scholnick (eds) *Towards a Feminist Developmental Psychology*, London: Routledge.

Komulainen, S. (2007) 'The ambiguity of the child's "voice" in social research', *Childhood* 14, 1: 11–28.

Kothari, U. (2005a) 'Introduction', in U. Kothari (ed.) *A Radical History of Development Studies: Individuals, Institutions and Ideologies*, Cape Town and London: David Philip and Zed Books.

—— (2005b) 'Authority and expertise: the professionalisation of international development and the ordering of dissent', pp. 32–53 in N. Laurie and L. Bondi (eds) *Working the Spaces of Neoliberalism: Activism, Professionalisation and Incorporation*, Oxford: Blackwell.

Kristeva, J. (1981) 'Women's time', *Signs: Journal of Women in Culture and Society* 7, 1: 13–35.

—— (1982) *Powers of Horror: An Essay on Abjection*, New York: Columbia University Press.

Kurtz, S. (1992) *All the Mothers Are One*, New York: Academic Press.

Lacan, J. (1959–60/1992) *The Ethics of Psychoanalysis. The Seminar of Jacques Lacan Book VII*, London: Routledge.

—— (1969–70) 'Seminar XVII: psychoanalysis upside down/The reverse side of psychoanalysis' (trans. C. Gallagher), unpublished.

—— (2006) 'Logical time and the assertion of anticipated certainty', pp. 161–175 in J. Lacan *Ecrits*, trans. B. Fink, New York and London: Norton.

Langemeyer, I. and Nissen, M. (2005) 'Activity theory', pp. 188–196 in B. Somekh and C. Lewin (eds) *Research Methods in the Social Sciences*, London: Sage.

Laplanche, J. and Pontalis, J.B. (1973) *The Language of Psychoanalysis*, London: Karnac Press/Institute of Psychoanalysis.

Larner, W. and Craig, D. (2005) 'After neoliberalism? Community activism and local partnerships in Aotearoa New Zealand', pp. 9–31 in N. Laurie and L. Bondi (eds) *Working the Spaces of Neoliberalism: Activism, Professionalisation and Incorporation*, Oxford: Blackwell.

Lather, P. (1991) *Getting Smart: Feminist Research and Pedagogy with/in the Postmodern*, London: Routledge.

Latouche, S. (1992) 'Standards of living', in W. Sachs (ed.) *The Development Dictionary: A Guide to Knowledge as Power*, London: Zed Books.

Latour, B. (1991) *Pandora's Hope: An Essay on the Reality of Science Studies*, Harvard: Harvard University Press.

Laurie, N. and Bondi, L. (eds) (2005) *Working the Spaces of Neoliberalism: Activism, Professionalisation and Incorporation*, Oxford: Blackwell.

Lavalette, M. (2000) 'Child employment in a capitalist labour market', pp. 214–230 in B. Schlemmer (ed.) *The Exploited Child*, London: Zed Books.

Leader, D. (2000) *Freud's Footnotes*, London: Faber.

Lehmann, H. (1996) 'An interrupted performance: on Walter Benjamin's ideas of children's theatre', pp. 179–200 in G. Fischer (ed.) *'With the Sharpened Axe of Reason': Approaches to Walter Benjamin*, Oxford: Berg.

Lesnik-Oberstein, K. (1998) 'Childhood and textuality', pp. 1–28 in K. Lesnik-Oberstein (ed.) *Children in Culture: Approaches to Childhood*, London: Macmillan.

—— (ed.) (2007) *The Last Taboo: Women and Body Hair*, Manchester: Manchester University Press.

Levett, A. (1994) 'Problems of cultural imperialism in the study of child sexual abuse', pp. 240–260 in A. Dawes and D. Donald (eds) *Childhood and Adversity: Psychological Perspectives from South African Research*, Cape Town: David Philip.

Levin, D. (1993) *Modernity and the Hegemony of Vision*, Berkeley: University of California Press.

Levine, A. (2007, January/February) 'Collective unconscionable: how psychologists, the most liberal of professionals, abetted Bush's torture policy', *Washington Monthly*, http://www.washingtonmonthly.com/features/2007/0701.levine.html (accessed 22 June 2007).

Lewis, D. (2005) 'Individuals, organization and public action: trajectories of the "non-governmental" in development studies', pp. 200–221 in U. Kothari (ed.) *A Radical History of Development Studies*, London: Zed Books.

Liebel, M. (2000) 'Social transformations by working children's organisations?', discussion paper for International Conference on Rethinking Childhood: Working Children's Challenge to the Social Sciences, Bondy, Paris, November.

Lieven, E. (1981) 'If it's natural we can't change it', in Cambridge Women's Studies Group, *Women in Society*, London: Virago.

Lister, R. (2005) 'Investing in the citizen workers of the future', pp. 449–462 in H. Hendrick (ed.) *Child Welfare and Social Policy*, Bristol: The Policy Press.

—— (2006) 'Children (but not women) first: New Labour, child welfare and gender', *Critical Social Policy* 26, 2: 315–335.

Littlewood, R. (1995) 'Psychopathology and personal agency: modernity, culture change and eating disorders in South Asian societies', *British Journal of Medical Psychology* 68: 45–63.

Löwy, M. (1985) 'Revolution against "progress": Walter Benjamin's romantic anarchism', *New Left Review* 152: 42–59.

Lubek, I. (1993) 'Social psychology textbooks: an historical and social psychological analysis of conceptual filtering, consensus formation, career gatekeeping and conservatism in science', pp. 359–378 in H. Stam, L. Mos, W. Thorngate and B. Kaplan (eds) *Recent Trends in Theoretical Psychology, Vol. III*, New York: Springer-Verlag.

Lucey, H. (2001) 'Social class, gender and schooling', pp. 177–188 in B. Francis and C. Skelton (eds) *Investigating Gender: Contemporary Perspectives in Education*, Maidenhead: Open University Press.

Lukes, S. (1973) *Individualism*, Oxford: Blackwell.

Lykke, N. and Braidotti, R. (eds) (1996) *Between Monsters, Goddesses and Cyborgs: Feminist Confrontations with Science, Medicine and Cyberspace*, London: Zed Books.

Lyotard, J.F. (1974) *Economic Libidinale*, Paris: Editions de Minuit.

—— (1983) 'Presentations', pp. 116–135 in A. Montifiore (ed.) *Philosophy in France Today*, Cambridge: Cambridge University Press.

—— (1984) *The Postmodern Condition: A Report on Knowledge*, Manchester: Manchester University Press.

—— (1992) *The Postmodern Explained to Children: Correspondence 1982–1985*, London: Turnaround.

Macaulay, R. and Gordo López, A.J. (1995) 'From cognitive psychologies to mythologies: advancing cyborg textualities for a narrative of resistance', in C.H. Gray, H. Figueroa-Sarriera and S. Mentor (eds) *The Cyborg Handbook*, London: Routledge.

McClintock, A. (1995) *Imperial Leather: 'Race', Gender and Sexuality in the Colonial Context*, London: Routledge.

McGuire, J. and Austin, J. (1987) *Beyond Survival: Children's Growth For National Development*, New York: UNICEF.

McLaughlin, K. (2005) 'From ridicule to institutionalisation: anti-oppression, the state and social work', *Critical Social Policy*, 25, 3: 283–305.

—— (2006) 'The subject of social work', unpublished PhD thesis, Manchester Metropolitan University.

Macleod, C. (2002a) 'Racialising teenage pregnancy: "culture" and "tradition" in the South African scientific literature', *Ethnic and Racial Studies* 25, 5: 778–801.

—— (2002b) 'Economic security and the social science literature on teenage pregnancy in South Africa', *Gender & Society* 16, 5: 647–664.

—— (2006) 'Early reproduction and gendered assumptions about adolescence and adolescent (hetero)sexuality', pp. 120–134 in T. Shefer, F. Boonzaier and P. Kiguwa (eds) *The Gender of Psychology*, Cape Town: UCT Press.

MacLure, M. (2006) 'The bone in the throat: some uncertain thoughts on baroque method', *International Journal of Qualitative Studies in Education* 19, 6: 729–745.

MacNaughton, G. (2005) *Doing Foucault in Early Childhood Studies: Applying Poststructural Ideas*, Abingdon: Routledge.

McNay, L. (1992) *Foucault and Feminism*, Oxford: Blackwell.

McNeil, M. (1992) 'Pedagogical practice and problems: reflections on teaching about gender relations', in H. Hinds, A. Phoenix and J. Stacey (eds) *Working Out: New Directions for Women's Studies*, London: Falmer Press.

McVey, C. (1994) 'Women in long term heterosexual relationships: a discourse analysis of a women's group', unpublished BSc, psychology undergraduate project, Manchester Metropolitan University.

Maidment, S. (1984) *Child Custody and Divorce*, London: Croom Helm.

Mannoni, M. (1973) *The Child, his 'Illness', and the Others*, Harmondsworth: Penguin.

Marks, D. (1996) 'Constructing a narrative: moral discourse and young people's experience of exclusion', pp. 114–130 in E. Burman, G. Aitken, P. Alldred, R. Allwood, T. Billington, B. Goldberg, A. Gordo López, C. Heenan, D. Marks and S. Warner, *Psychology, Discourse Practice: From Regulation to Resistance*, London: Taylor & Francis.

Marshall, H. (1991) 'The social construction of motherhood: an analysis of childcare and parenting manuals', in A. Phoenix, A. Woollett and E. Lloyd (eds) *Motherhood: Meanings, Practices and Ideologies*, London: Sage.

Marshall, H. and Woollett, A. (2000) 'Challenging youth: an exploration of visual and textual culture and identifications', pp. 118–132 in C. Squire (ed.) *Culture in Psychology*, London: Routledge.

Marshall, H., Woollett, A. and Dosanj, N. (1998) 'Researching marginalized standpoints: some tensions around plural standpoints and diverse "experiences"', pp. 115–134 in K. Henwood, C. Griffin and A. Phoenix (eds) *Standpoints and Differences: Essays in the Practice of Feminist Psychology*, London: Sage.

Massey, D. (1992) 'Politics and time/space', *New Left Review* 196: 65–84.

Masson, J. (1984) *The Assault on Truth*, Harmondsworth: Penguin.

Matthews, S. (2004) 'Post-development theory and the question of alternatives: a view from Africa', *Third World Quarterly* 25, 2: 373–384.

Mayall, B. (1996) 'Politics and practice in research with children', *Changes: An International Journal of Psychology and Psychotherapy* (special issue on 'qualitative research') 14, 3: 199–203.

Mayes-Elma, R. (2007) 'Judith Butler', pp. 62–67 in J. Kincheloe and R. Horn (eds) *The Praeger Handbook of Education and Psychology*, Westport, CT: Praeger.

Maynard, M. and Purvis, J. (eds) (1994) *Researching Women's Lives from a Feminist Perspective*, London: Taylor & Francis.

Mehlman, J. (1993) *Walter Benjamin: An Essay on his Radio Years*, Chicago: Chicago University Press.

Mehmet, O. (1995) *Westernizing the Third World*, London: Zed Books.

Mendis, P. (2007) 'Glocalization: the human side of globalization as if the Washington consensus mattered', http://www.lulu.com/content/590321 (accessed 5 January 2007).

Meyer, A. (2007) 'The moral rhetoric of childhood', *Childhood* 14, 1: 85–104.

Middleton, N. (1971) *When Family Failed: The Treatment of the Child in the Care of the Community in the First Half of the Twentieth Century*, London: Gollancz.

Middleton, N. and O'Keefe, P. (1998) *Disaster and Development: The Politics of Humanitarian Aid*, London: Pluto Press.

Miller, A. (1985) *For Your Own Good: The Roots of Violence in Child-rearing*, London: Virago.

Miller, L., Rustin, M. and Shuttleworth, J. (eds) (1989) *Closely Observed Infants*, London: Duckworth.

Miller, P. and Kofsky Scholnick, E. (eds) (2000) *Toward a Feminist Developmental Psychology*, London: Routledge.

Mitchell, J. (1974) *Psychoanalysis and Feminism*, Harmondsworth: Penguin.

—— (2003) *Siblings: Sex and Violence*, Oxford: Polity Press.

Mitchell, R. (2005) 'Postmodern reflections on the UNCRC: towards utilising Article 42 as an international compliance indicator', *International Journal of Children's Rights* 13: 315–331.

Mitchell, S. (1988) *Relational Concepts in Psychoanalysis*, Cambridge, MA: Harvard University Press.

Mitter, S. (1986) *Common Fate, Common Bond*, London: Pluto Press.

Mizen. P. and Pole, C. (2000) 'Why work at the edge? Motivations for working among school age workers in Britain', paper presented at International Conference on Rethinking Childhood; Working Children's Challenge to the Social

Sciences, Institute de Recherche pour le Developpement (IRD), Paris, France, November.

Mookherjee, M. (2006) 'Decolonizing the other's rights: feminism, multiculturalism and the right to mediation', paper presented at 'Beyond "Feminism vs. Multiculturalism": Revising the Relationship between Power, Beliefs, Identity and Values', AHRC Research Centre for Law, Gender and Sexuality, School of Law, King's College London and LSE Gender Institute Day Conference, London School of Economics, London.

Morokvasic, M. (2004) '"Settled in mobility": engendering post-wall migration in Europe', *Feminist Review* 77: 7–25.

Morrow, V. (1994) 'Responsible children? Aspects of children's work and employment outside school in contemporary UK', in B. Mayall (ed.) *Researching Childhoods*, Lewes: Falmer.

Morss, J. (1990) *The Biologising of Childhood*, Hillsdale, NJ: Lawrence Erlbaum Associates, Inc.

—— (1996) *Growing Critical: Alternatives to Developmental Psychology*, London: Routledge.

Moser, A. (2007) *Gender and Indicators: Overview Report*, New York: UNDP.

Moss, P. and Petrie, P. (2002) *From Children's Services to Children's Spaces*, London: RoutledgeFalmer.

Motzkau, J.F. (2001) 'Konzeptionen von Sprache und Kindheit in der Dekonstruktion der Entwicklungspsychologie', unpublished diploma manuscript, Insitut für Erziehungswissenschaften, Sportwissenschaften und Psychologie, Freie Universität, Berlin.

—— (2006a) 'Cross-examining suggestibility: memory, childhood, expertise', unpublished PhD thesis, Loughborough University.

—— (2006b) 'Speaking up against justice: children's rights, suspended testimonies and development free spaces', *International Journal of Critical Psychology*.

—— (2007) 'The semiotic of accusation: reconsidering the language of deconstruction in the case of developmental critique – taking a pragmatic step back towards critical impact', *Forum Qualitative Social Research* (online journal) (accessed 21 August 2007).

Muchawsky-Schnapper, E. (1989) 'Paul Klee's *Angelus Novus*, Walter Benjamin and Gershom Scholem', *Israel Museum Journal* 8: 47–52.

Mulvey, L. (1975) 'Visual pleasure and narrative cinema', *Screen* 16, 3: 6–18.

Munn, P. (1991) 'Mothering more than one child', in A. Phoenix, A. Woollett and E. Lloyd (eds) *Motherhood: Meanings, Practices and Ideologies*, London: Sage.

Myers, R. (1992) *The Twelve Who Survive: Strengthening Programmes of Early Childhood Development in the Third World*, New York and London: Routledge/UNESCO.

Narvesen, O. (1989) *The Sexual Exploitation of Children in Developing Countries*, Oslo: Rädda Barnen.

Neill, C. (2005) 'An idiotic act: on the non-example of Antigone', *The Letter* 34: 1–28.

New, C. and David, M. (1985) *For the Children's Sake: Making Childcare More than Women's Business*, Harmondsworth: Penguin.

Newman, F. and Holzman, L. (1995) *Lev Vygotsky: Revolutionary Scientist*, London: Routledge.

Newnes, C. and Radcliffe, N. (eds) (2005) *Making and Breaking Children's Lives*, Ross-on-Wye: PCCS.

Newson, J. and Shotter, J. (1974) 'How babies communicate', *New Society* 29: 324–357.

Nicholson, L. (1999) *The Play of Reason: From the Modern to the Postmodern*, Maidenhead: Open University Press.

Nicholson, L. and Seidman, S. (eds) (1995) *Social Postmodernism: Beyond Identity Politics*, Cambridge: Cambridge University Press.

Nieuwenhuys, O. (1994) *Children's Lifeworlds: Gender, Childhood and Labour in the Developing World*, London: Routledge.

—— (2000) 'The household economy and the commercial exploitation of children's work', pp. 278–290 in B. Schlemmer (ed.) *The Exploited Child*, London: Zed Books.

—— (2001) 'Who profits from child labour? Children, labour and reproduction', paper for Contested Childhood Seminar Series, Michigan University, 21 October.

Nightingale, A. (2005) '"The experts taught us all we know": professionalisation and knowledge in Nepalese community forestry', pp. 186–208 in N. Laurie and L. Bondi (eds) *Working the Spaces of Neoliberalism: Activism, Professionalisation and Incorporation*, Oxford: Blackwell.

Oakley, A. (1981) *From Here to Maternity: Becoming a Mother*, Harmondsworth: Penguin.

O'Dell, L. (1998) 'Damaged goods and victims', unpublished PhD thesis, Open University.

Ogun, R. and Houston Smith, K. (1992) *Innocenti Global Seminar On Participatory Development, Summary Report*, Florence, Italy, UNICEF International Child Development Centre, Spedale Delgi Innocenti.

O'Hagan, K. and Dillenberger, K. (1995) *The Abuse of Women within Childcare Work*, Maidenhead: Open University Press.

Omaar, R. and de Waal, A. (1993) 'Disaster pornography from Somalia', *Media and Values* Winter: 13–14.

Palmary, I. (2006a) '(M)Othering women: unpacking refugee women's trauma and trauma service delivery', *International Journal of Critical Psychology* 17: 119–139.

—— (2006b) 'Gender, nationalism and ethnic difference: feminist politics and political psychology', *Feminism & Psychology* 16, 1: 44–51.

Park, A. (2006) 'Children as risk or children at risk? International law, child soldiers and citizenship: the case of Sierra Leone', in S. Bittle and A. Doyle (eds) *Paradoxes of Risk: Inclusions and Exclusions*, Halifax: Fernwood.

Parker, I. (1989) *The Crisis in Social Psychology and How to End It*, London: Routledge (full text available on www.discourseunit.com).

—— (1992) *Discourse Dynamics*, London: Routledge (full text available on www.discourseunit.com).

—— (1997) *Psychoanalytic Culture*, London: Sage.

—— (ed.) (1998) *Social Constructionism, Discourse and Realism*, London: Sage.

—— (2002) *Critical Discursive Psychology*, London: Palgrave.

—— (2004) 'Psychoanalysis and critical psychology', in N. Mkhize, P. Kiguwe and A. Collins (eds) *Critical Psychology*, Cape Town: UCT Press.

—— (2005) *Qualitative Psychology: Introducing Radical Research*, Maidenhead: Open University Press.

—— (2006) 'Racing', *Psychodynamic Practice* 12, 4: 463–466.

—— (2007) *Revolution in Psychology: Alienation to Emancipation*, London: Pluto Press.
—— (2008) *Japan in Analysis: Cultures of the Unconscious*, London: Palgrave.
Parker, I., Georgaca, E., Harper, D., McLoughlin, T. and Stowell-Smith, M. (1995) *Deconstructing Psychopathology*, London: Sage.
Parker, I. and Shotter, J. (eds) (1990) *Deconstructing Social Psychology*, London: Routledge (full text available on www.discourseunit.com).
Parpart, J. (1995) 'Deconstructing the development "expert": gender, development and the "vulnerable groups"', pp. 221–243 in M. Marchand and J. Parpart (eds) *Feminism/Postmodernism/Development*, London: Routledge.
Patel, V. (1989) 'Sex determination and sex pre-selection tests in India: modern techniques for femicide', *Bulletin of Concerned Asian Scholars* 21: 1–11.
—— (1992) 'Women and structural adjustment in India', paper presented at the Development Studies Institute, London School of Economics, 27 November.
Pateman, C. (1989) *The Disorder of Women*, Oxford: Polity Press.
Peace, G. and Hulme, D. (1993) *Children and Income-Generating Programmes*, London: Save the Children Fund.
Pearson, R. (2005) 'The rise and rise of gender and development', pp. 157–179 in U. Kothari (ed.) *A Radical History of Development Studies: Individuals, Institutions and Ideologies*, Cape Town and London: David Philip and Zed Books.
Penley, C. (1989) *The Future of an Illusion: Film, Feminism and Psychoanalysis*, London: Routledge.
Penn, H. (2005) *Unequal Childhoods: Children's Lives in Poor Countries*, London: RoutledgeFalmer.
Perec, G. (1989) *W or The Memory of Childhood*, (trans. D. Bellos), London: Collins Harvill.
Peters, J. and Wolper, A. (eds) (1995) *Women's Rights, Human Rights: International Feminist Perspectives*, London: Routledge.
Pheterson, G. (1992) 'Street kids', opening address at Colloque International sur les Jeunes de la Rue et leur Avenir dans la Societe, 24–6 April, Montreal.
Phillips, A. [Adam] (1988) *Winnicott*, London: Fontana.
—— (1995) *Terrors and Experts*, London: Faber & Faber.
Phillips, A. [Anne] (1987) 'Introduction', in A. Phillips (ed.) *Feminism and Equality*, Oxford: Blackwell.
—— (2007) *Multiculturalism without Culture*, Princeton, NJ: Princeton University Press.
Phoenix, A. (1987) 'Theories of gender and black families', in G. Weiner and M. Arnot (eds) *Gender Under Scrutiny*, London: Hutchinson.
Phoenix, A. and Pattynama, P. (2006) 'Intersectionality', *European Journal of Women's Studies* 13: 187–192.
Piaget, J. (1919) 'La psychanalyse dans ses rapports avec la psychologie de l'enfant', *Bulletin Mensuel de la Société Alfred Binet* 1: 18–34, 41–58.
—— (1921) 'Une forme verbale de la comparaison chez l'enfant', *Archives de Psicologie* 17, 69–70: 141–172.
—— (1926) *The Language and Thought of the Child*, London: Routledge & Kegan Paul.
—— (1929) *The Child's Conception of the World*, London: Routledge & Kegan Paul.
—— (1932) *The Moral Judgement of the Child*, London: Routledge & Kegan Paul.

—— (1941/1952) *The Child's Conception of Number*, London: Routledge and Kegan Paul.
—— (1951) *Play, Dreams and Imitation in Childhood*, London: Routledge & Kegan Paul.
—— (1953) *The Origins of Intelligence in the Child*, London: Routledge & Kegan Paul.
—— (1957) 'The child and modern physics', *Scientific American* 197: 46–51.
—— (1969) *The Child's Conception of Time*, London: Routledge & Kegan Paul.
—— (1971) *Biology and Knowledge: An Essay on the Relations between Organic Regulations and Cognitive Processes*, Edinburgh: Edinburgh University Press.
—— (1972) *Psychology and Epistemology: Towards a Theory of Knowledge*, Harmondsworth: Pelican.
Piercy, M. (1992) *Body of Glass*, Harmondsworth: Penguin.
Pinkard, T. (2000) *Hegel: A Biography*, Cambridge: Cambridge University Press.
Pollard, R. (in press) *Dialogue and Desire: Bakhtin and the Linguistic Turn in Psychotherapy*, London: Karnac.
Pottier, J. (ed.) (1993) *Practising Development: Social Science Perspectives*, London: Routledge.
Pratt, G. (1992) 'Spatial metaphors and speaking positions', *Environment and Planning D: Society and Space* 10: 241–244.
Prout, A. (ed.) (2000) *The Body, Childhood and Society*, Basingstoke: Macmillan.
Pupavac, V. (1998) 'Children's rights and the infantilisation of citizenship', *Human Rights Law Review* March: 3–8.
—— (2001) 'Misanthropy without borders: the international child rights regime', *Disasters* 25, 2: 95–112.
—— (2002a) 'The international children's rights regime', pp. 57–75 in D. Chandler (ed.) *Re-thinking Human Rights: Critical Approaches to International Politics*, London: Palgrave.
—— (2002b) 'Pathologizing populations and colonizing minds: international psychosocial programs in Kosovo', *Alternatives* 27: 489–511.
—— (2004) 'Psychosocial intervention and the demoralization of humanitarianism', *Journal of Biosocial Science* 36: 491–504.
Qvortup, J. (2000) 'Does children's school work have a value? Colonisation of children through their school work', pp. 3–11 in Vol. 2 of papers for International Conference on Rethinking Childhood: Working Children's Challenge to the Social Sciences, Paris.
Rabinbach, A. (1985) 'Between enlightenment and apocalypse: Benjamin, Bloch and modern German Jewish Messianism', *New German Critique* 34: 78–124.
Radford, L., Sayer, S. and Amica, R. (1999) *Unreasonable Fears? Child Contact in the Context of Domestic Violence*, Bristol: WAFE.
Rahnema, M. (1997) 'Towards post-development: searching for signposts, a new language and new paradigms', pp. 377–404 in M. Rahnema with V. Bawtree (eds) *The Post-Development Reader*, London: Zed Books.
Rahnema, M. with Bawtree, V. (eds) (1997) *The Post-Development Reader*, London: Zed Books.
Ramirez, A. (1992) 'Honduras: the traffic in children', *Central America Report* 55: 5.
Ranis, G., Steward, F. and Samman, E. (2006) 'Human development: beyond the human development index', *Journal of Human Development* 7, 3: 323–358.
Rao, A. (1995) 'The politics of gender and culture in international human rights

discourse', in J. Peters and A. Wolper (eds) *Women's Rights, Human Rights: International Feminist Perspectives*, London: Routledge.
Raven, C. (2001) 'What makes satire work?', *Guardian, Friday Review* 31 July: 5.
Reagon, B. (1983) 'Coalition politics: turning the century', pp. 356–368 in B. Smith (ed.) *Home Girls: A Black Feminist Anthology*, New York: Kitchen Table Press.
Reavey, P. and Warner, S. (eds) (2003) *New Feminist Stories of Child Sexual Abuse: Sexual Scripts and Dangerous Dialogues*, London: Routledge.
Reed, E. (1996) 'The challenge of historical materialist epistemology', pp. 21–34 in I. Parker and R. Spears (eds) *Psychology and Society: Radical Theory and Practice*, London: Pluto Press.
Reeves, M. (1988) 'The politics of charity', in M. Reeves and J. Hammond (eds) *Looking Beyond the Frame: Racism, Representation and Resistance*, Oxford: Third World First.
Reid, S. (ed.) (1997) *Developments in Infant Observation: The Tavistock Model*, London: Routledge.
Restruccia, F. (2006) 'Review essay: a radical ethical imperative: sublimation love', *Journal for Lacanian Studies* 4, 1: 159–177.
Ribbens, J. (1994) *Mothers and their Children: A Feminist Sociology of Childbearing*, London: Sage.
Richards, G. (1997) *'Race', Racism and Psychology*, London: Routledge.
—— (2002) *Putting Psychology In Its Place*, 2nd edn, Hove, UK: Psychology Press.
Richardson, D. (ed.) (1996) *Theorising Heterosexuality*, Maidenhead: Open University Press.
Riley, D. (1983) *War in the Nursery: Theories of Mother and Child*, London: Virago.
—— (1987) '"The serious burdens of love?" Some questions on childcare, feminism and socialism', pp. 176–198 in A. Phillips (ed.) *Feminism and Equality*, Oxford: Blackwell.
Roberts, J. (1991) 'Walter Benjamin', p. 49 in T. Bottomore (ed.) *A Dictionary of Marxist Thought*, 2nd edn, Oxford: Blackwell.
Roberts, S. (2006) 'Minor concerns: representations of children and childhood in British museums', *Museum and Society* 4, 3: 152–165.
Rodriguez Mora, I. (2003) 'Psychosocial interventions in emergences: theoretical models and their ethical and political implications in the Venezuelan context', unpublished PhD thesis, University of Cambridge.
Rogoff, B. (2003) *The Cultural Nature of Human Development*, Cambridge, MA: Harvard University Press.
Rose, J. (1984) *The Case of Peter Pan: Or the Impossibility of Children's Fiction*, London: Macmillan.
—— (1986) *Sexuality in the Field of Vision*, London: Verso.
Rose, N. (1985) *The Psychological Complex: Psychology, Politics and Society in England 1869–1939*, London: Routledge.
—— (1990) *Governing the Soul*, London: Routledge.
Rose, P. (1991) *Never Say Goodbye*, New York: Doubleday.
Rotman, B. (1978) *Jean Piaget: Biologist of the Real*, New York: Academic Press.
Roudinesco, E. (1999) *Jacques Lacan*, Cambridge: Polity Press.
Roy, A. (2001) *Power Politics: The Reincarnation of Rumpelstiltskin*, Kottayam, Kerala: DC Books.
Rush, F. (1984) 'The Freudian cover-up', *Trouble & Strife* 4: 29–37.

Rustin, M. and Rustin, M. (1987) *Narratives of Love and Loss: Studies in Modern Children's Fiction*, London: Verso.

Rutkowska, J. (1993) *The Computational Infant: Looking for Developmental Cognitive Science*, London: Harvester.

Sachs, W. (ed.) (1992) *The Development Dictionary: A Guide to Knowledge as Power*, London: Zed Books.

—— (1999) *Planet Dialectics: Explorations in Environment & Development*, London: Zed Books.

Said, E. (1978) *Orientalism*, Harmondsworth: Penguin.

Sampson, E. (1993) *Celebrating the Other: A Dialogic Account of Human Nature*, Hemel Hempstead: Harvester.

Sandóval, C. (1995) 'New sciences: cyborg feminism and the methodology of the oppressed', pp. 407–422 in C. Hables Gray with H.J. Figueroa-Sarriera and S. Mentor (eds) *The Cyborg Handbook*, London: Routledge.

Sathyamala, C., Sundharam, N. and Bhanot, N. (1986) *Taking Sides: The Choices Before the Health Worker*, New Delhi: Asian Network for Innovative Training Trust.

Save the Children (1992) *Focus on Children*, London: Save the Children.

Scheper-Hughes, N. (1989) 'Culture, scarcity and maternal thinking: motherlove and child death in north east Brazil', in N. Scheper-Hughes (ed.) *Child Survival: Anthropological Perspectives on the Treatment and Maltreatment of Children*, Dordrecht: Reidel.

Schlemmer, B. (ed.) (2000) *The Exploited Child*, London: Zed Books.

Schlosser, E. (2001) *Fast Food Nation: What the All-American Meal is Doing to the World*, London: Allen Lane.

Scott, J. (1997) 'The infrapolitics of subordinate groups', pp. 311–329 in M. Rahnema with V. Bawtree (eds) *The Post-Development Reader*, London: Zed Books.

Scott, S. (1997) 'Feminists and false memories: a case of postmodern amnesia', *Feminism and Psychology* 7, 1: 33–38.

Scott, S. and Payne, T. (1984) 'Underneath we're all loveable: therapy and feminism', *Trouble & Strife* 3: 21–25.

Scourfield, J. (2006) 'The challenge of engaging fathers in the child protection process', *Critical Social Policy* 26, 2: 440–449.

Sen, A. (1990) More Than 100 Million Women Are Missing, *New York Review Of Books* 20 December: 61–68.

Shandon, M., Valsiner, J. and Gottlieb, G. (1997) 'Developmental concepts across disciplines', pp. 34–71 in J. Tudge, M. Shanahan and J. Valsiner (eds) *Comparisons in Human Development: Understanding Time and Context*, New York: Cambridge University Press.

Shanin, T. (1997) 'The idea of progress', pp. 65–72 in M. Rahnema with V. Bawtree (eds) *The Post-Development Reader*, London: Zed Books.

Sharp, R. and Green, R. (1975) *Education and Social Control*, London: Routledge and Kegan Paul.

Shefer, T. and Potgeiter, C. (2006) 'Sexualities', pp. 103–120 in T. Shefer, F. Boonzaier and P. Kiguwe (eds) *The Gender of Psychology*, Cape Town: UCT Press.

Shiva, V. (1997) 'Western science and the destruction of local knowledge', pp. 161–

167 in M. Rahnema with V. Bawtree (eds) *The Post-Development Reader*, London: Zed Books.

Shuler, D. (2006) 'The uses and misuses of the gender-related development index and gender empowerment measure: a review of the literature', *Journal of Human Development* 7, 2: 161–181.

Singer, E. (1992) *Child-Care and the Psychology of Development*, London: Routledge.

—— (2005) 'The liberation of the child: a recurrent theme in the history of education in western societies', *Early Child Development and Care* 165, 6: 611–620.

Skott-Myhre, H. and Frijters, J. (in press) 'Tramps and nomads: figures of youth in flight in Charlie Chaplin's *Modern Times*', *Young: Nordic Journal of Youth Research*.

Sohn-Rethel, A. (1977) *Intellectual and Manual Labour*, London: Macmillan.

Solberg, A. (1990) 'Negotiating childhood: changing constructions of age for Norwegian children', in A. James and A. Prout (eds) *Constructing and Reconstructing Childhood*, Lewes: Falmer.

Spandler, H., Burman, E., Goldberg, B., Margison, F. and Amos, T. (2000) '"A double-edged sword": understanding gifts in psychotherapy', *European Journal of Psychotherapy, Health and Counselling* 3, 1: 77–101.

Spence, D. (1982) *Narrative Truth and Historical Truth*, New York: Norton.

Spivak, G.C. (1990) *The Post-Colonial Critic*, London: Routledge.

—— (1993) 'Can the subaltern speak?', pp. 66–112 in P. Williams and L. Chrisman (eds) *Colonial Discourse and Post-Colonial Theory*, London: Harvester.

Squire, C. (1991) 'Science fictions', *Feminism & Psychology* 1, 2: 161–200.

—— (2001) 'The public life of emotions', *International Journal of Critical Psychology* 1: 16–24.

Stainton Rogers, R. and Stainton Rogers, W. (1992) *Stories of Childhood: Shifting Agendas of Child Concern*, Lewes, Harvester.

—— (1998) 'Word children', pp. 178–303 in K. Lesnik-Oberstein (ed.) *Children in Culture: Approaches to Childhood*, London/New York: Macmillan/St Martin's Press.

Stallabrass, J. (1995) 'Empowering technology: the exploration of cyberspace', *New Left Review* 211: 1–32.

Stanley, L. and Wise, S. (1983) *Breaking Out: Feminist Consciousness and Feminist Research*, London: Routledge and Kegan Paul.

Stanway, P. and Stanway, A. (1983) *Breast is Best: A Commonsense Approach to Breastfeeding*, London: Pan.

Star, S.L. and Griesmeyer, R. (1989) 'Institutional ecology, "translations" and boundary objects: amateurs and professionals in Berkeley's Museum of Vertebrate Zoology, 1907–39', *Social Studies in Science* 19: 387–420.

Steedman, C. (1983) *The Tidy House: Little Girls' Writing*, London: Virago.

—— (1995) *Strange Dislocations: Childhood and Sense of Human Interiority, 1780–1930*, London: Virago.

Stern, D. (1985) *The Interpersonal World of the Infant: A View of Psychoanalysis and Developmental Psychology*, New York: Basic Books.

Stern, D., Sander, L., Nahum, J., Harrison, A., Kyons-Ruth, K., Morgan, A., Bruschweiler-Stern, N. and Tronick, E. (1998) 'Non-interpretative mechanisms in psychoanalytic therapy', *International Journal of Psycho-Analysis* 79: 903–921.

Stetsenko, A. and Arievitch, I. (2004) 'Vygotskian collaborative project of social transformation: history, politics and practice in knowledge construction', *International Journal of Critical Psychology* 12: 58–80.

Strauble, I. (2005) 'Entangled in the Eurocentric order of knowledge: why psychology is difficult to decolonise', paper presented at the International Society for Theoretical Psychology, University of the Western Cape, Cape Town.

Stronach, I. Frankham, J. and Stark, S. (2007) 'Sex, science and educational research: the unholy trinity', *Journal of Educational Policy* 22, 2: 215–235.

Sudbury, J. (1998) *'Other Kinds of Dreams': Black Women's Organisations and the Politics of Transformation*, London: Routledge.

Summerfield, D. (2001) 'The invention of post-traumatic stress disorder and the social usefulness of a psychiatric category', *British Medical Journal* 322: 1105–1107.

Sunder, M. (2003) 'Piercing the veil', *Yale Law Journal* 112: 1399–1401.

Swift, G. (1992) *Waterland*, London: Picador.

Sylvester, C. (1998) 'Homeless in international relations: women's place in canonical texts and feminist re-imaginings', pp. 44–66 in A. Phillips (ed.) *Feminism & Politics*, Oxford: Oxford University Press.

Szondi, P. (2006) 'Hope in the past: on Walter Benjamin', pp. 1–36 in W. Benjamin *A Berlin Childhood around 1900*, trans. Howard Eiland, Cambridge, MA: Belnap Press.

Tarulli, D. and Scott-Myhre, H. (2006) 'The immanent rights of the multitude: an ontological framework for conceptualizing the issue of youth and child rights', *International Journal of Children's Rights* 14: 187–201.

Taylor, J. (1998) *Body Horror: Photojournalism, Catastrophe and War*, Manchester: Manchester University Press.

Thorne, B. (1987) 'Re-visioning women and social change: where are the children?', *Gender & Society* 1, 1: 85–109.

Timimi, S. (2005) *Naughty Boys: Antisocial Behaviour, ADHD and the Role of Culture*, London: Palgrave.

Trawick, M. (1992) *Notes on Love in a Tamil Family*, Berkeley: University of California Press.

Tuwihai Smith, L. (1999) *Decolonizing Methodologies: Research and Indigenous Peoples*, London and Dunedin: Zed Books and University of Otago Press.

United Kingdom Council for Psychotherapy (UKCP, 1997) *Notes for Practitioners: Recovered Memories of Abuse*, London: UKCP.

United Nations (1989) *Convention on the Rights of the Child*, New York: United Nations.

United Nations Development Fund for Women (UNIFEM, 2003) *Not a Minute More: Ending Violence Against Women*, New York: UNIFEM.

—— (UNIFEM, 2006–7) *Annual Report, 2006–7* (http://www.unifem.org/attachments/products/UAR07-Final.pdf, accessed 21 August 2007).

United Nations Development Programme (UNDP, 1992) *Human Development Report*, Oxford: Oxford University Press.

United Nations Division for the Advancement of Women (UNDAW, 2005) *Enhancing Women's Participation in Development through an Enabling Environment for Achieving Gender Equality and the Advancement of Women*, Report of the Expert Group Meeting, Bangkok, Thailand, 8–11 November (http://www.un.org/

womenwatch/daw/egm/enabling-environment2005/index.html, accessed 18 May 2007).

United Nations International Children's Emergency Fund (UNICEF, 1992a) *1992 UNICEF Annual Report*, New York: UNICEF.

—— (UNICEF, 1992b) *Negotiating Peace for Children, Survivors, 1: Rehabilitation of Children in Armed Conflict*, New York: UNICEF.

—— (UNICEF, 1992c) *Achievements Made in the Implementation of the UNICEF Policy on Women in Development, Including the Situation of the Girl Child: Policy Review*, New York: UNICEF.

—— (UNICEF, 2007) *Child Poverty in Perspective: An Overview of Child Well-Being in Rich Countries – A Comprehensive Assessment of the Lives and Well-being of Children and Adolescents in the Economically Advanced Nations*, Florence: UNICEF Innocenti Research Centre.

Urwin, C. (1985) 'Constructing motherhood: the persuasion of normal development', in C. Steedman, C. Urwin and V. Walkerdine (eds) *Language, Gender and Childhood*, London: Routledge and Kegan Paul.

Valsiner, J. (2004) 'Transformations and flexible forms: where qualitative psychology begins', keynote lecture at the Inaugural Conference of the Japanese Association of Qualitative Psychology, Kyoto, September.

—— (2006) 'Ambivalence under scrutiny: returning to the future', *Estudios de Psicologia* 27, 1: 117–130.

Vestin, U. (1997) 'Antigone – a soul murder', *Psychoanalytical Quarterly* 66: 82–92.

Vianna, E. and Stetsenko, A. (2006) 'Embracing history through transforming it: contrasting Piagetian versus Vygotskian (activity) theories of learning and development to expand constructivism within a dialectical view of history', *Theory & Psychology* 16, 1: 81–108.

Viruru, R. (2001) *Early Childhood Education: Postcolonial Perspectives from India*, New Delhi: Sage.

—— (2006) 'Postcolonial technologies of power. Standardised testing and representing diverse young children', *International Journal of Educational Policy, Research and Practice: Reconceptualising Childhood Studies* 7: 49–70.

Vittachi, A. (1989) *Stolen Childhood: In Search of the Rights of the Child*, Cambridge: Polity Press.

Vygotsky, L.S. (1978) *Mind in Society: The Development of Higher Psychological Processes*, Cambridge, MA: Harvard University Press.

Waites, M. (2005) *The Age of Consent: Young People, Sexuality and Citizenship*, London: Palgrave.

Walker, K., Burman, E. and Gowrisunkur, J. (2002) 'Counting black sheep: contextualising "race" and gender within therapeutic process', *Psychodynamic Practice* 7, 5: 55–73.

Walkerdine,V. (1984) 'Developmental psychology and the child-centred pedagogy: the insertion of Piaget into early education', pp. 153–202 in J. Henriques, W. Hollway, C. Urwin, C. Venn and V. Walkerdine, *Changing the Subject: Psychology, Social Regulation and Subjectivity*, London: Methuen.

—— (1985) 'On the regulation of speaking and silence: subjectivity, class and gender in contemporary schooling', in C. Steedman, C. Urwin and V. Walkerdine (eds) *Language, Gender and Childhood*, London: Routledge and Kegan Paul.

—— (1987) 'No laughing matter: girls' comics and the construction of femininity', in J. Broughton (ed.) *Critical Theories of Psychological Development*, New York: Plenum Press.

—— (1988) *The Mastery of Reason: Cognitive Development and the Production of Rationality*, London: Routledge.

—— (1990a) 'Sex, power and pedagogy', in V. Walkerdine *Schoolgirl Fictions*, London: Verso.

Walkerdine, V. and the Girls and Mathematics Unit (1990b) *Counting Girls Out*, London: Virago.

—— (1997) *Daddy's Girl: Young Girls and Popular Culture*, London: Macmillan.

Walkerdine, V. and Lucey, H. (1989) *Democracy in the Kitchen: Regulating Mothers and Socialising Daughters*, London: Virago.

Wallsgrove, R. (1985) 'Thicker than water?', *Trouble & Strife* 7: 26–28.

Ware, V. (1992) *Beyond the Pale: White Women, Racism and History*, London: Verso.

Warner, M. (1997) 'Introduction', in A. Carter (ed.) *The Second Virago Book of Fairytales*, London: Virago.

Warner, S. (1995) 'Constructing femininity: models of child sexual abuse and the production of "woman"', in E. Burman, G. Aitken, P. Alldred, B. Goldberg, C. Heenan, D. Marks, J. Marshall, K. Taylor, R. Ullah and S. Warner *Challenging Women: Psychology's Exclusions, Feminist Possibilities*, Maidenhead: Open University Press.

—— (2000) *Understanding Child Sexual Abuse: Making the Tactics Visible*, Gloucester: Handsell.

Weekes, J. (1996) *Sexuality*, London: Tavistock.

Wilkinson, S. (1988) 'The role of reflexivity in feminist psychology', *Women's Studies International Forum* 11, 5: 493–502.

Wilkinson, S. and Kitzinger, C. (eds) (1996) *Representing the Other: A Feminism & Psychology Reader*, London: Sage.

Williams, F. (2004) 'What matters is who works: why every child matters to New Labour, commentary on the DfES Green Paper Every Child Matters', *Critical Social Policy* 24, 3: 406–427.

Williamson, J. (1986) 'Nuclear Family, No Thanks!', in *Consuming Passions: The Dynamics of Popular Culture*, London: Marion Boyars.

Wilson, A. (2002) 'Antigone's age: notes and discussions of Sophocles' tragedy'. http://www.users.globalnet.co.uk/~loxias/antigone02.htm (accessed 26 January 2007).

—— (2006) *Dreams, Questions, Struggles: South Asian Women in Britain*, London: Pluto Press.

Wingfield, R. and Saddiqui, H. (1995/6) 'Fundamental questions: from Southall to Beijing', *Trouble & Strife* 32: 53–62.

Winnicott, D.W. (1958) 'Hate in the countertransference', in D.W. Winnicott *Collected Papers: From Paediatrics to Psychoanalysis*, London: Tavistock.

Wolf, N. (1990) *The Beauty Myth*, London: Vintage.

Wolff, P. (1996) 'The irrelevance of infant observations for psychoanalysis', *Journal of the American Psychoanalytic Association* 44, 2: 369–392.

Woodhead, M. (1990) 'Psychology and the cultural construction of children's needs', pp. 60–77 in A. James and A. Prout (eds) *Constructing and Reconstructing Childhood: Contemporary Issues in the Sociological Study of Childhood*, Basingstoke: Falmer.

—— (1996) *In Search of the Rainbow: Pathways to Quality in Large-Scale Programmes for Young Disadvantaged Children*, The Hague: Bernard van Leer Foundation.

Yuval Davis, N. (1992) 'Fundamentalism, multiculturalism and women in Britain', pp. 278–292 in J. Donald and A. Rattansi (eds) *'Race', Culture & Difference*, London: Sage.

—— (1997) *Gender and Nation*, London: Sage.

—— (2006) 'Intersectionality and feminist politics', *European Journal of Women's Studies* 13, 3: 193–209.

Yuval-Davis, N. and Anthias, F. (eds) (1989) *Woman-Nation-State*, London: Macmillan.

Žižek, S. (1989) *The Sublime Object of Ideology*, London: Verso.

—— (1991a) *Looking Awry: Lacan in Hollywood*, Cambridge, MA: MIT Duke Press.

—— (1991b) *For They Know Not What They Do: Enjoyment as a Political Factor*, London: Verso.

—— (2001) *Did Somebody Say Totalitarianism? Five Interpretations in the (Mis)Use of a Notion*, London: Verso.

Author index

Subject index

Northern Michigan University
3 1854 008 757 620